P9-DTP-155

2.1.99

50

Crisis and Creativity in the Sephardic World

Crisis and Creativity in the Sephardic World

1391–1648

Edited by Benjamin R. Gampel

Columbia University Press
New York

Columbia University Press
New York   Chichester, West Sussex
Publishers Since 1893
Copyright © 1997 Columbia University Press
All rights reserved

Library of Congress Cataloging-in-Publication Data

Crisis and creativity in the Sephardic world / edited by Benjamin R.
    Gampel.
        p.   cm.
    Papers presented at a conference held in November 1992.
    Includes bibliographical references and index.
    ISBN 0-231-10922-9 — ISBN 0-231-10923-7 (pbk.)
    1. Sephardim—History—Congresses.   2. Sephardim—Intellectual
life—Congresses.   I. Gampel, Benjamin R.
DS134.C75   1997
909'.04924—dc21   97-13685
                                                                CIP
                                                                r97

Casebound editions of Columbia University Press books are printed on permanent and durable
acid-free paper.

Printed in the United States of America

c 10 9 8 7 6 5 4 3 2 1
p 10 9 8 7 6 5 4 3 2 1

צי״לח
לזכר נשמת אבי מורי
ר׳ ראובן בן חיים מרדכי אשר וחיה מייטע ז״ל
שנפטר ביום כ׳ תמוז תשנ״ג
באמיתה של תורה חקר ודרש כל ימי חייו
תהי נשמתו צרורה בצרור החיים

Contents

Introduction

The year 1992 was filled with commemorations of an expansive moment in the unfolding drama of Western civilization—the "discovery" of the Americas by the much-heralded explorer Christopher Columbus. But 1992 also marked the passing of five hundred years since a dark episode in European history. On March 31, 1492, in the city of Granada, newly conquered from the Muslims, Queen Isabella and King Ferdinand signed an edict banishing all Jews from their kingdoms of Castile and Aragon. Iberian (Sephardic) Jews, having reached heights of political, economic, and social integration rarely even imagined by their medieval coreligionists, had to confront and adjust to their precipitous decline.

This traumatic expulsion of Iberian Jewry, though overshadowed by the momentous linkage of the New and Old Worlds, is an event of great significance in Jewish—and world—history. While Jewish communities had faced the impending and often sudden dissolution of their age-old settlements, it was the expulsion of Jews from Castile, Aragon, Portugal, and Navarre in the late Middle Ages that—prior to this century—served as the most repercussive instance of Jewish catastrophe. Iberian Jewry was uprooted and dispersed, Sephardic Jewish communities were transposed and reconstituted, and Sephardic Jewish culture was apparently transformed.

The story of the Sephardic diaspora, with its themes of communal crisis, demographic transposition, and cultural transformation, has drawn widespread attention during the past twenty years. Researchers in Europe, Israel, and America have illuminated significant aspects of the Iberian expulsion by uncovering new sources and advancing sophisticated interpretations of the event, its contexts, and its consequences. Three areas of research have been particularly noteworthy: (1) the reexamination of the decline of the much-vaunted Iberian *convivencia* (literally living together)—the profound symbiosis of Jewish, Muslim, and Christian cultures—and its effects on Sephardic Jewish culture, (2) the investigation of the mechanics of the expulsion and the coping strategies employed by the Jews in response, and (3) the interpretation of the impact of the expulsion on Jewish culture and communities in European and Mediterranean society in later centuries.

Given the confluence of the commemorative activities and the profusion of monographic studies, it was therefore timely in the fall of 1992 to bring together many of the scholars who pioneered these areas of inquiry and to have them offer learned papers and in so doing assess the state of current research. Because Sephardic studies encompasses a number of disciplines—among them history, philosophy, literature, comparative religion, linguistics, art history, and rabbinics—it was hoped that their meeting would encourage interdisciplinary discourse and exchange. It was also hoped that a conference might ultimately lead to the process of developing new integrating themes and conceptual frameworks.

To this end, in November 1992, the Jewish Theological Seminary of America (in conjunction with the Jewish Museum) and Columbia University's Center for Israel and Jewish Studies, all New York City institutions, convened an international symposium entitled "Crisis and Creativity in the Sephardic World: 1391–1648." The conference analyzed Jewish life prior to the expulsions, chronicled the expulsions, and surveyed their aftermath in Jewish, European, and Mediterranean cultures.

The essays in this volume address three main themes that have galvanized recent research on late medieval Iberian Jewry and the first century of the Sephardic diaspora. First, they assess the cultural vitality of the Sephardim in the waning years of their life in the peninsula. Second, they focus on the demographic transposition and response, as the dissolution of the Sephardic communities of Iberia confronted Jews with the critical decision—whether to convert or choose exile as Jews. They follow the Jews to their new places of residence and observe from a variety of vantage points how they struggled to establish their communities on foreign soil. Last, the essays treat the thorny issues of cultural survival and transformation—how the Sephardim grappled in their intellectual and literary lives with the impact of the expulsion—and then measure the effect of these traumatic events on the creativity of the diaspora communities.

A previous generation of scholars had argued that the last century of Jewish life in the Iberian Peninsula was intellectually impoverished. The decline in Sephardic cultural achievement was usually dated from 1391, the year when Castilian and Aragonese Jews were suddenly devastated by pogroms. For generations Iberian Jews, Muslims, and Christians had lived together in a variety of constellations with a remarkable degree of mutual tolerance. It was the abrupt rupture of this convivencia, scholars suggested, that augured poorly for the continued flourishing of the once-vibrant Sephardic civilization. More recent scholarship had demonstrated, to the contrary, that despite the seeming collapse of a pluralism (never satisfactorily defined) that had at times nourished Iberian Jews since the period of Muslim dominion in the eighth century, Jewish cultural and intellectual activity continued apace.

Acknowledging that the accomplishments of the fifteenth-century Iberian Jewish culture must be taken seriously, Raymond Scheindlin devotes his attention to the explosion of poetical creativity at the end of the fourteenth and the beginning of the fifteenth century. By examining the production of the Hebrew poets, Scheindlin is able to analyze the forms used by these writers and ask if their work can simply be termed epigonic. He offers us an understanding of the oeuvre and compares the quality of their poetry with verse written in contemporaneous Christian society. In so doing he grants us the possibility of appreciating their achievements anew. Seymour Feldman demonstrates that, contrary to older notions, Sephardic Jewish philosophers were active and flourishing in the fifteenth century. By comparing the work of Isaac Abravanel with that of his son Judah, who wrote in Italy after the expulsion, Feldman is able to identify the issues that engaged Sephardic philosophers while still living in the peninsula. He demonstrates how the expulsion opened these writers to encounters with unfamiliar

Kabbalah, to the traumatic effects of the expulsions. Scholem viewed these sixteenth-century mystical innovations as a belated mythic response to the trauma itself and to the enduring pain of exile. More recently, Yosef Hayim Yerushalmi has understood the sudden rise of historiography and historical interest among the Sephardic exiles in the sixteenth century as a deeply motivated attempt by Jewry to comprehend the processes that had caused this profound disruption in their lives.

But, as Moshe Idel asks so starkly, was the ocean of tears prompted by the trauma of the expulsion the matrix for the ocean of writing that poured forth from the pens of the exiled Sephardic authors? Idel realizes that, although he is inclined to answer the question negatively, changes in kabbalistic thought may have been indirectly affected as a result of the events of the late fifteenth century. The new environments in which the Jews lived confronted the exiles with another cultural landscape, and this encounter may have altered the emphases in their writings. In his essay Idel focuses on Italy, where he has determined that there were no essential transformations in the genres of literature studied by Italian Jews and that Sephardic mystical thought was subsumed by the Italians within their own kabbalistic categories. Idel argues that he is not attempting to divorce history from mentality but rather suggests that the first step in understanding alterations in intellectual structures is to understand these changes from within the writings themselves.

Hava Tirosh-Samuelson rises to meet the challenge posed by Idel. She examines the treatment of the ultimate end of human life in post-expulsion philosophical literature and argues that the emphasis on individual salvation—ultimately linked to national redemption—in the writings of kabbalists, philosophers, and halakhists was part of the message of consolation offered by writers who fervently wished to transcend history. This quest for transcendence to a time when evil would prove to be powerless, she argues, was a direct result of the expulsion trauma and ultimately directed Jews from the study of philosophy to that of Kabbalah. The study of philosophy, she notes, ironically moved to a wider audience but became the handmaiden of hermeneutics. Unlike Idel, Tirosh-Samuelson traces a palpable change in the course of Jewish intellectual history as a result of the crisis in Iberian society.

Menahem Schmelzer's essay demonstrates that the prolific production of the Jewish book in manuscript and in print in the Sephardic diaspora had its roots in the Iberian Peninsula. He chronicles the stories of some books that had been started by Sephardim in Iberia and were only completed in new places of residence. Dwayne Carpenter looks at the Hebrew introduction to *La Celestina*, originally written in Castilian by the converso Fernando de Rojas and then translated into many languages, including Hebrew. Again the connections between the culture of the peninsula and the postexpulsion Jew were many and unexpected. Vivian Mann, as well, introduces the theme of disjuncture and continuity in the manufacture of ceremonial art. She surveys the remaining items of the material culture of the preexpulsion Sephardim and shows how Sephardic aspects of these objects continued in the diaspora. Over time, as might be expected, the particularly Iberian character of this art gradually disappeared.

Finally, we turn to the lead essay of this volume, which broadens the perspective of these deliberations. Yosef Yerushalmi muses on the question of exile in Jewish history: since the Jews felt at home even while in the diaspora, he argues, they therefore experienced the pain of the expulsion as a double exile. For the exiles of Sepharad, with their exalted notions of their unique identity, the trauma of the expulsion may have been even more acute. The volume before you is dedicated to an examination of the results of this profound dislocation.

The plan for this book was first articulated in a memo I wrote in July 1986 to Professor Ismar Schorsch, chancellor of the Jewish Theological Seminary of America. It is now over a decade later and numerous people deserve to be thanked for their contribution to *Crisis and Creativity in the Sephardic World.* I would like to acknowledge my home institution, the Jewish Theological Seminary of America, and my colleagues and friends there as well as the associates at Columbia University's Center for Israel and Jewish Studies, directed by Yosef Hayim Yerushalmi. Most recently, my student and colleague David Wachtel has given unstintingly of his time to make this work as readable and internally consistent as such a volume has the right to be. Susan Pensak of Columbia University Press put the finishing touches on this work.

To all the authors who contributed to this volume I offer my thanks. I should note on their behalf that most of the essays were completed in 1992.

Finally, I dedicate this volume in honor of my mother Reema Gampel and to the memory of my father Reuben Gampel, who was with me while this volume was germinating but sadly passed away before he could witness the work's completion. May his memory be for a blessing.

Benjamin R. Gampel
23 Shevat 5757
January 30, 1997

PART I

Historical Overview

I

Exile and Expulsion in Jewish History

Yosef Hayim Yerushalmi

From the Cain of Augustine as figure or symbol of the Jewish people, to Ahasueros the Wandering Jew of the Middle Ages, to Leopold Bloom in Joyce's Dublin, the Jews have been and remain the archetype of exile in the Western imagination. And properly so. For exile—*galut*—has been a fundamental datum of Jewish history and Jewish consciousness for over two and a half millennia.

Though one might assume that any comprehensive history of the Jews is already intrinsically also a history of Jewish exile, it seems to me that a genuine historical anatomy of Jewish exile has yet to be written. The closest attempt we have, Yehezkel Kaufmann's magisterial *Golah ve-Nekhar* (1929–1930), still not fully appreciated, is replete with brilliant insights. Yitzhak Baer's little book *Galut*, a marvel of concision published in Nazi Berlin in 1936, is a valuable charting of certain focal points. Both remain mandatory reading. Each, in retrospect, is also transparently programmatic and inevitably bears the mark of the historical moment in which it was written. Another kind of history may be possible today.

You will obviously not expect such a history from me in the space of one essay. All I can offer here is an initial meditation on the subject of galut in which context, later on, I shall also raise the specific issue of expulsion (*gerush*) which is the focal point of this volume. I confess at the

The other dialectic, more subtle and often ignored, is central to my present purposes. I shall call it, provisionally and inadequately, Exile and Domicile, by which I mean the simultaneous awareness of being in exile, yet the profound sense of attachment to the land or place in which one lives, the sentiment *in exile* of feeling at home. Exile and Domicile, I shall argue, are only superficially contradictions. In reality they have often coexisted in a dialectical tension. This dialectic too is already implicit in the Bible. We have only to consider two well-known biblical texts directly linked to the Babylonian exile that, when juxtaposed, become almost paradigmatic.

Psalm 137:
By the rivers of Babylon there we sat and wept
as we remembered Zion. There upon the willows
we hung up our lyres, for our captors asked us
there for songs, our tormentors for amusement,
"Sing us one of the songs of Zion."

How can we sing a song of the Lord
on alien soil?
If I forget you, O Jerusalem,
let my right hand forget her cunning.

The other, equally familiar text, is Jeremiah's epistle (chap. 29) to the first exiles already in Babylon (a decade before the destruction of the First Temple and mass deportation of 586 *b.c.e.*), arguing against the prophets and soothsayers who were blithely forecasting an imminent return:

Thus says the Lord of hosts . . . unto all the captivity whom I have caused to be carried away captive from Jerusalem to Babylon.
Build houses and dwell in them, plant gardens and eat the fruit of them; take wives and beget sons and daughters . . . and multiply there and be not diminished. And seek the peace of the city to which I have caused you to be carried away captive, and pray unto the Lord for it; for in the peace thereof shall you have peace. . . . Let not the prophets that are in the midst of you, and your diviners, beguile you . . . for they prophesy falsely unto you in My name; I have not sent them.

Jeremiah's counsel apparently prevailed. And it would seem that Babylonia proved not at all an awful place to be. Its reality certainly did not correspond to the descriptions of exile as it had been anticipated.

Some fifty years later, when Cyrus of Persia conquered Babylonia and granted the Jews permission to return to their land, only a minority actually roused itself to do so.

Without placing value judgments on this development, let us merely note that the Jewish dispersion continued even after it became possible to return to the Land of Israel. The essential fact, then, is that the diaspora has been a permanent feature of Jewish history at least since the Babylonian exile and undoubtedly even earlier. Indeed, the ancient Jewish diaspora was more the result of natural migration than of forced banishment from the Land. Even in the latter case, however, Jews tried their best to turn exile into domicile. It was, in a sense, inevitable. The seventy years of exile that Jeremiah envisioned turned into centuries and millennia. Jews bought houses, and planted gardens, and procreated, and yes—without forgetting Jerusalem—they even sang on alien soil, perhaps nowhere so exquisitely as in Spain, but not in Spain alone.

II

Diaspora and exile are not synonymous. During the Hellenistic period, at least prior to the destruction of the Second Temple in the year 70 C.E., the communities of what was already a vast Jewish dispersion seem to have regarded themselves less as exiles than as colonies, branches of a living center. In Alexandria the Jews occupy two out of five residential quarters. Their status is far above that of the native, non-Hellenized Egyptians. They have extensive privileges. Certainly there is anti-Semitism, even a pogrom. But these Alexandrian Jews, who speak and write Greek, who translate the Bible into Greek, do not seem to feel themselves "in exile."

That, at least, is the impression we receive from Philo. The Jewish world, as Philo conceives it, extends from Rome to the Euphrates, from Macedonia to Libya. The Jews are everywhere, throughout the *oikoumené*—the habitable world. Philo does not attribute the diaspora to exile. He declares that

> so populous are the Jews that no one country can hold them, and therefore they settle in very many of the most prosperous countries in Europe and Asia both in the islands and on the mainland, and while they hold the Holy City where stands the sacred Temple of the most high God to be their *mother city*, yet those which are theirs by inheritance from their

fathers, grandfathers, and ancestors even farther back, are accounted in each case to be their fatherland in which they were born and reared, while to some they have come at the time of their foundation as immigrants to the satisfaction of the founders.

Jerusalem and the Temple play important roles in Philo's thought. But it is precisely with regard to them that he reveals a significant dichotomy between ideal and reality. For example, he knows very well the Deuteronomic demand that one be personally present at the Jerusalem Temple for the three annual pilgrimage festivals. Certainly some Alexandrian Jews made the pilgrimage, but for most it was difficult. Philo resolves the problem in his characteristic way, by allegorizing. The true Jerusalem, the true Temple, is at least in part a state of the soul: "What house shall be prepared for God the King of kings . . . ? Shall it be of stone or timber? One worthy house there is—the soul that is fitted to receive Him." And even more radically—"It often happens that people who are actually in unconsecrated spots are really in most sacred ones."

In the mentality of Hellenistic Judaism, diaspora does not yet carry all the heavy freight of the term *exile*, that is, so long as there exists the Temple cult in Jerusalem—and even if Jerusalem, like the entire Land of Israel, is already under Roman domination. The catastrophic dimension of exile really begins to unfold with the destruction of the Temple. Note, however, that unlike the Babylonians the Romans did not expel the entire Jewish population of Judaea. The disaster of the year 70 is initially more the loss of the Temple than the loss of the Land. It is this loss that is at the heart of the ensuing crisis and that begins to endow the diaspora with a genuine sense of galut.

III

Galut, exile, always had both theoretical and actual aspects.

Theoretically: From a religious perspective exile is the fundamental condition of Jewish existence from the destruction of the Second Temple until the ultimate arrival of the Messianic redemption. In multiple ways, Jewish thought elaborates a veritable metaphysics of exile that filters down to the humblest Jew. In theory exile is almost always tragic. From childhood on the consciousness of living in exile is inculcated in every Jew through liturgy and ritual, through three annual historical fast days, through the aggadah, and thus internalized. One prays always for redemption.

This awareness of being in exile is later reinforced by the polemical pressures of Christianity and Islam, for whom the exile of the Jews is a cardinal proof of God's rejection of the Jewish people. All three religions are in accord on one point—that the Jews are in exile because of their sins. They only disagree on the question of which "sin."

From the point of view of Jewish political theory Jewish exile is at its root lack of sovereignty and political independence—*shi'abud malkhuyot*—servitude among the nations. In another context and with other nuances the medieval Christian church and state will call it *servitus Judaeorum*. From whichever side it is conceived, exile as servitude carries with it a cluster of dismal connotations—alienation, spiritual and physical oppression.

On the theoretical plane virtually all Jews until modern times would probably have acknowledged that they were indeed in exile. But in their daily lives did Jews always feel exile as a curse? If living in exile had always been intolerable or almost so, why, then, did the majority of Jews not attempt to return en masse to the Land of Israel? Why, until Sabbatai Zevi in the seventeenth century, were active messianic movements always the work of minorities? Why did the Jewish dispersion always expand outward, to the far reaches of the Persian and Roman empires, to India and China, indeed to Spain, where Jews first settled in Roman times and which, after the Muslim conquest of the early eighth century, was the Islamic "Far West" and drew hordes of new immigrants?

Certainly there were periods when conditions in the Land of Israel were too difficult, at times impossible. But there were other times when such a return was quite feasible. In fact there were individual Jews and sometimes entire groups who installed themselves there and who, despite vicissitudes and adversities, maintained viable and sometimes important communities and institutions.

Judah Halevi, who not only yearned for Zion but actually left Spain to go there, was hardly representative of Spanish Jewry. Quite to the contrary, the anonymous friend who, in Halevi's poem *Devarekha bemor 'over rekuhim* tries to persuade him to stay put, undoubtedly reflected the majority opinion. The same is true of Abraham Ibn Daud, writing only a generation later, after the Almohad invasion of 1147 had put an end to Jewish life in Andalus and sent thousands of Jewish refugees flocking into the Christian territories. Typically, Ibn Daud does not counsel his fellow Jews to abandon the Iberian Peninsula. On the contrary, he seems full of optimism that Jewish life in the Christian North will be a repetition of the glories achieved earlier in the Muslim South. And even if the late Gerson Cohen was correct in arguing that Ibn Daud's *Sefer Ha-Qabbalah* contains an esoteric messianic message, the important point would remain that Ibn Daud's Hispanocentrism was such that he saw the messianic scenario as unfolding first in Spain itself.

I trust I will be taken at my word if I say that in asking why the Jewish diaspora always expanded rather than contracted, why its momentum was centrifugal rather than centripetal, I imply no criticism. Zionism, in its thoroughly different modern sense, is not at issue here. Conversely, if I now make an effort to understand certain inner forces that, through the ages, kept most Jews outside the Land of Israel, I do so not as a diaspora apologist. Sometimes, though we resist the notion, history is radically discontinuous. From what I have to say about the past nothing can or should be deduced concerning the current situation of world Jewry, which is, in these respects, literally unprecedented.

IV

It seems to me that among the factors that inhibited most Jews from taking an active initiative to return to their land of origin two were of primary importance.

The first, often discussed, was the powerful grip of Jewish messianic faith in the form in which it had developed. In brief, although originally the messianic "end of days" was conceived as something that would take place in a very near future, especially after the disastrous failure of three messianic revolts against Rome, the dominant tendency was to place the redemption in the hands of God alone, at His initiative, and in an indefinite future.

The second factor, worth dwelling upon, was the very success of Jewish life in dispersion and exile. Was galut, we have asked, intolerable or virtually so? Obviously at certain times and in certain places it was. But over the long haul, what the French more elegantly call *la longue durée*, it was far more than tolerable.

If, therefore, I concur with Salo Baron's lifelong rejection of what he termed the "lachrymose conception" of Jewish history (and especially of the Jewish Middle Ages as a constant vale of tears), it is not out of filial piety but because along with him I believe it to be a distortion of that history. Nor does it mean that I ignore the fact that this conception has very venerable pedigrees or that I do not recognize that there have been many occasions for tears in Jewish history. But all human history is full of tears, and Walter Benjamin's angel of history faces backward toward the past and sees only an ever-mounting heap of debris.

Nor are historical calamities themselves unique to exile and always attributable to it. Peoples who always remained in their lands have been periodically devastated by foreign invaders. Individuals and groups who were never exiled have been, and continue to be, unjustly persecuted and even slaughtered in their own sovereign countries. It will bear recalling that life for many Jews under some of the kings of ancient Judah and Israel, or some of the later Hasmoneans, was not always a bed of roses but rather an often oppressive, albeit native, *servitus Judaeorum*. Conversely, medieval Jews knew very well that the phrase did not mean that they were literally slaves or serfs. They were quite aware that their quality of life was generally far superior to that of the peasants who made up the bulk of the population and that in actuality their so-called servitude reflected a relatively high status, a direct relationship to the ruler that bypassed lower jurisdictions. *'Avadim 'anaḥnu li-melakhim*, wrote Baḥya ben Asher of Saragossa, *ve-lo 'avadim la-'avadim*—"We are servants of kings, and not servants of servants."

Without losing sight of any of its manifestly negative aspects, the fact is that on the whole Jews not only adapted to the conditions of exile but often flourished within it materially and spiritually, while managing to preserve a vivid sense of their distinctive national and religious identity. Except for times of active persecution it was quite possible to believe wholeheartedly in an ultimate messianic redemption, to pray for its speedy advent, but at the same time to wait comfortably for the arrival of the Messiah in God's own time without taking any deliberate initiative to hasten it. It is here, on the psychological plane, that what I have termed the dialectics of exile and domicile really begin to reveal themselves. What I propose is that it is simultaneously possible to be ideologically in exile and existentially at home.

V

We tend, of course, to focus on one side of the dialectic—that of exile as alienation. The other—that of what I have called "domicile," of *feeling at home within exile itself*—has received no comparable attention, would indeed be denied by many as a contradiction in terms. The lachrymose conception has perhaps contributed to this neglect. Certainly there is also a paucity of sources. Medieval Jews naturally tended to record their afflictions in the places of their exile rather than their attachments to them. The chronicles, such as they are, emphasize the sudden and dramatic catastrophe and ignore the longer but duller stretches of the quotidian. Nevertheless, out of occasional hints and fragments, sometimes indirectly and by deduction, we can at least recover sporadic echoes of a Jewish sense of rootedness and "at homeness" in the cities and lands of the dispersion that our conventional images of galut would not lead us to suspect. The point, it seems to me, is not without relevance to the theme of this volume. For only if we begin to realize the extent of the attachment of Jews to their places of residence can we also begin to savor with them the full bitterness of the experience of expulsion.

I shall not dwell upon the obvious—that even in adversity human beings become naturally bound by myriad ties to the place in which they were born, to the familiarity of its streets and the landscape of its countryside, to the house, however modest, that echoes with so many voices, so many memories. That Jews should have shared such universal feelings requires no elaboration. We should probe further.

That in both Christian and Muslim theology and law the Jews were, in effect, tolerated aliens is an objective historical fact. Given the irreducible difference and tension with the dominant religions, Jews were themselves inevitably conscious of the palpable differences that divided them from their non-Jewish neighbors. On this level one can safely state that Jews in galut were always aliens and felt themselves to be so.

One should come to realize, however, that in other dimensions Jews did not necessarily feel themselves to be strangers and that their sense of alienation varied widely in time and place. In daily life relations between Jews and Christians were often amicable, even intimate. It took a deliberate and protracted effort on the part of the Church, from the earliest councils to the Fourth Lateran Council of 1215, to demand increasingly rigid social barriers between them, and even so, as the repeated fulminations of popes and clerics reveal, the conciliar declarations were ignored with surprising frequency.

This is not to minimize the ultimately calamitous effects of the "teaching of contempt." It is merely to suggest that the barriers were never absolute and, moreover, that if Jews inevitably felt themselves to be aliens on certain levels, this did not prevent them from feeling themselves indigenous and at home in other respects. Virtually every European Jewry, not only Sephardic Jewry, had origin myths tracing its beginnings back to the destruction of the First or Second Temples or even earlier. While these traditions may have begun with an apologetic or polemical intent, they would not have been possible or believable without a deep sense of ancient and continuous rootedness in the land.

No Jewish community, and again I am not merely referring to Spain, was ever sealed off from its environment. In daily life Jews almost everywhere spoke the vernaculars of their surroundings. Linguistic assimilation was only one striking expression of a larger cultural assimilation that ranged from folklore to philosophy. World Jewry in exile, as Kaufmann correctly insisted, was religiously unified but culturally diverse. Because of the unique fusion of Jewish religion and peoplehood, Spanish, French, German, Italian, Yemenite, or Persian Jews all had a sense of belonging to one people, with a common heritage and a common destiny. At the same time each group displayed the markedly particular cultural characteristics of its milieu. Does this mean that these Jews felt themselves to belong to the nations among whom they lived? To be more specific, did Spanish Jews, as Kaufmann once asks, consider themselves "Spanish"? Such questions, prior to the rise of the modern nation-state, are almost meaningless. *Spain* is more a convenient and relatively modern rubric than the medieval reality of separate kingdoms and regions, each with its own political, cultural, even linguistic identity. Ironically, if there was any group in the different Spanish kingdoms that had a vivid sense of a unity that transcended these and other boundaries, it was the Jews, for whom the whole of Spain was *Sefarad*.

Yet *Sefarad*, *Zarfat*, or *Ashkenaz* were not merely fabricated Jewish equivalents for Spain, France, or Germany; they were Hebrew place names lifted out of their biblical contexts and superimposed over the map of contemporary Europe. But that was not all. In Castile the very topography of Toledo was assimilated to that of Jerusalem. Tradition had it that this and other cities in the region were named by the ancient exiles from Judaea and that their current names had Hebrew etymologies. Thus Toledo was really *Toledot*, or else *Toletula*, from the Hebrew *tiltul*—"migration" or "wandering." Escalona was derived from biblical Ashkelon, Maqueda from its biblical homonym (Joshua 10, 12, and 15), Yepes from the Hebrew *Yafo* (Jaffa). Samuel Ha-Nagid, the eleventh-century poet, scholar and vizier of Granada, moves through a biblical landscape. "I am David in my generation," he writes, identifying with King David, the poet-warrior. In his great battle poem *'Eloha 'oz*, his enemy Zuhair, king of Almeria, is called "Agag," and the latter's army is composed of " 'Amalek" (Slavs), " 'Edom" (Christian mercenaries), and "the sons of Qeturah" (Arabs). Nor is the phenomenon limited to Spain. Bohemia is "Canaan." The city of Nîmes in Provence is also *Kiryat Ye'arim*, literally "city of the forests," a town mentioned in Joshua and other books of the Bible and aptly applied here because Nîmes was generally thought to derive from the Latin *nemus*, "forest."

Such transpositions, I would urge, are more than mere wordplay. They reveal something about Jewish mentalities that deserves far more serious attention than it has received. They betray an intrinsic, oscillating duality. On the one hand, ongoing links to the ancient land of origin. On the other, the ability to somehow endow the place of exile with familiarity, to perceive it as "Jewish." And here, perhaps, we have a key to the larger phenomenon.

For ultimately what really made Jews feel "at home" in galut was *the Judaization of exile*. The outstanding success of Judaism in adapting itself to the absence of the Temple and the loss of the Land itself does not require extensive comment. While never forgotten, the loss of the Sanctuary and of political independence in the Land of Israel was counterbalanced (though never replaced) by surrogate institutions. For the Temple, the synagogue; for sovereignty, Jewish communal and sometimes supracommunal autonomy based on the rule of Jewish law; for the Land, the Jewish quarter or street—*judería, juiverie, Judengasse*—a Jewish territory in microcosm where, even in times of alienation from the gentile population, one could always feel Jewishly "at home." To say nothing of cities, towns, and villages where Jews constituted a majority of the population. A tenth-century Arabic historian called Granada "Granada of the Jews," while both a ninth-century Babylonian gaon and a twelfth-century Muslim historian referred to Lucena as a Jewish city (*madinat al-yahud*).

But a Jewish majority was hardly necessary. What was decisive in creating the Jewish map of exile and in making Jews feel "at home" was the portability of "Torah" in its largest sense, the ability to study and observe wherever Jews lived, the rise and movement of great centers of Jewish learning. Let us deliberately choose two examples beyond Spain and, for once, pay the closest attention to the language in which they are couched.

Describing the situation when Jewish life was at its heyday in Provence, and with obvious reference to the Mishnah Sanhedrin (chap. 11), which speaks of the three courts of law in ancient Jerusalem, one text states that in difficult decisions "one needs three courts: The one that sits on the Temple Mount, which is *Ha-Har* [literally "The Mountain," one of the medieval Hebrew names for Montpellier]; the second dwells at the gate of the Temple Courtyard—*be-fetaḥ ha-ʿazarah*—which is Lunel; and the third sits in the Chamber of Hewn Stone—*lishkat ha-gazit*—from which Torah goes forth to all its surroundings, and that is Nîmes."

Southern Italy was one of the earliest centers of Jewish learning in Europe. In what is surely one of the most famous verses in the prophet Isaiah we read: *Ki mi-Ẓion teze' Torah u-devar 'Adonai mi-Yerushalayim*—"For out of Zion shall go forth the Law and the word of the Lord from Jerusalem." In a twelfth-century text citing an earlier one, this becomes: *Ki mi-Bari teze' Torah u-devar 'Adonai mi-Otranto*—"For out of Bari shall go forth the Law and the word of the Lord from Otranto."

Montpellier, Lunel, Nîmes, Bari, Otranto (there are many other instances) can all be homologized to Jerusalem. (We will recall Philo's remark that people "who are actually in unconsecrated spots are really in most sacred ones"). These "new Jerusalems" are not in heaven but on earth, in the lands of exile, as in later centuries Amsterdam would be the "Dutch Jerusalem" and Vilna the "Jerusalem of Lithuania." Yes, of course these phrases are hyperboles, and the true Jerusalem is never forgotten—is yearned for, prayed for. But that Jerusalem is an eschatological Jerusalem, while these exist in the here and now, and within them one feels "at home."

Perhaps the point will become clearer if we turn momentarily to the great Hispano-Hebrew poet Moshe Ibn Ezra who was forced, sometime after the Almoravid capture of Granada in 1090, to flee to the Spanish Christian territories. Now, Ibn Ezra wrote a host of moving liturgical poems expressing longing for Zion and the Holy Land. Their utter sincerity need not be doubted. But he also wrote other poems suffused with aching nostalgia for the lost paradise of his beloved Granada and expressing his hope of yet returning there. The passion of these poems is at least as intense as those of Zion and, one senses, more personal and immediate.

One of them, virtually untranslatable, begins: "Till when in exile have my feet been sent forth and still have not found repose?" "Exile" here is not exile from Jerusalem but from Granada and Andalus. Toward the end, thinking of his Granadan friends, he writes: "*Tishkaḥ yemini*"—"let my right hand forget her cunning [a direct quote from Psalm 137, which we cited earlier] if I have forgotten them." And—if the Lord will return him to the splendor of Granada (*hadar Rimon*; *Rimon*, "pomegranate," was a Hebrew name for Granada), then he will drink from the waters of the river Genil and he will be in "the land in which my life was sweet and the cheeks of Time spread out before me." He ends by praying to God that He "call to freedom the captive of separation ['*asir ha-peredah*]." Separation from where? Not from Zion, but Granada.

This sense of what, for lack of a better word, I have called *domicile,* can be inferred from a close and alert reading of texts throughout the ages. I choose at random.

Estori Parhi, one of the victims of the French expulsion of 1306 (to which we shall yet return) actually made his way to the Land of Israel. He writes:

> From the schoolhouse they took me out, my shirt they stripped off and dressed me in exile's clothes, in the midst of my studies they expelled me from my father's house *and from my native land* [*me-'erez moladeti*]. . . . I found no repose until the King to whom peace belongs brought me . . . from captivity to the Land of the Hart—*'Erez Ha-zevi* [i.e., the Land of Israel].

But another French refugee cries out, *Hen gorashti me-'Erez Ha-zevi!*—"Behold, I have been expelled *from* the Land of the Hart!" thus applying the phrase *'Erez Ha-zevi*, which is always associated with the Land of Israel, to the Kingdom of France itself.

Moledet in its various declensions is not only "birthplace" but "homeland," and it is not used loosely. In his *Shevet Yehudah*, Shlomo Ibn Verga conjures up a dialogue between the Jews and the Almohad leader Ibn Tumart who has threatened them with conversion or death. They plead with him: "Let not our lord be angry, for you are our king and we are your people, and if we do not do your will, then expel us to another land. And where is there vengeance such as this, that we should leave our homeland [*'arzenu u-moladetenu*] and go to a people whom we have not known?"

Thus, on the scale of catastrophe exile is a lesser evil than forced conversion, but it is terrifying enough. It means to leave "our homeland" (literally—"our land and birthplace"). The Spanish exile Jacob Ibn Habib ponders, though only in retrospect, that it is sinful that "the lands of the gentiles were our homeland [*'erez moladetenu*] and our fathers and forefathers were buried there, and neither they nor we attempted by strength of hand to live in the Land of Israel." Similarly, among the retroactive consolations offered by Isaac Abravanel to his fellow exiles from Spain, we hear: "If leaving the land that is natural for you is difficult . . . do not regret this land of yours whose people curse you because you are far from their faith." The phrase that should catch our attention is the reference to Spain as "the land that is natural for you" (*ha-'arez ha-tiv'it lekha*). In 1526, in Siena, Italy, the banker Ishmael da Rieti, whose home is described as "a sanctuary for Torah and science," was visited by the messianic adventurer David Reuveni to whom he offered hospitality but no financial assistance for his project. Reuveni reports, "I said to him—'What do you want? Jerusalem, or to stay where you are?' And he replied—'I have no desire for Jerusalem, and neither will nor craving, except for Siena.'"

There is, for our purposes, a remarkably eloquent passage in the *Shevet Yehudah* concerning the recall of the Jews to France by Louis X. Ibn Verga attempts to describe the hesitations and inner conflicts of the French refugees:

Out of love for their country and homeland [*le-'ahavat 'arzam u-moladetam*] many returned to their cities . . . [while others said]: "But even though the king promises us security, if the masses rise how can we

be secure? . . . Therefore let us remain where we are and not bring the
anguish of expulsions upon ourselves, and let us never experience them
again!" But after a while they changed their minds and said: "Come, let
us return to the territories of our homeland [*le-'arẓot moladetenu*], for
she is our mother [*ki hi' 'imenu*].

At this point I think we can finally turn from the question of exile to
that of expulsion.

VI

Expulsion, gerush, is part of the negative history of exile, galut. It is, in
a real sense, a double exile, an exile within exile. If, as I have proposed,
Jews most often domesticated exile into domicile, then surely any expulsion of an entire Jewry or Jewish community was an expulsion from
home, a wrenching, traumatic ordeal. Expulsion, no less than massacre
or forced conversion, abruptly closes whatever gap there may have been
between exile as ideology and as lived experience, bringing the perception of galut to full consciousness, in its original, archetypal meaning.

Curiously, although the mass expulsion of entire populations was a
common phenomenon in the ancient Near East, in the Middle Ages
there were no such expulsions of Jews from Muslim lands. The policy
of expelling Jews appears only in Christendom, and even then, if we except the still obscure expulsion of Jews from the city of Alexandria by
the Bishop Cyril in 414, it surfaces relatively late—not until the end of
the thirteenth century (though there was an abortive precedent in
France under Philip Augustus in 1182). Why all this should have been
so may well be worthy of reexamination. But the question I want to
pose is of a different order.

I ask myself, given the history of Jewish expulsions, why is it that the
expulsion from Spain has assumed such primacy in Jewish collective
memory, overshadowing all others? After all, the Spanish expulsion was
hardly the first. The earlier expulsion from France in 1306 was no paltry
affair. Gersonides wrote of the number expelled as "twice those who left
Egypt," which, though an obvious exaggeration, still testifies to an
event of major proportions. Yet I am not aware that any conference was
held in 1906 on the six hundredth anniversary of the expulsion from
France nor, I suspect, will there be any on the seven hundredth.

Undoubtedly the antecedent glories of Spanish Jewry are a factor in the pride of place accorded this particular expulsion, as is the unusual articulateness of the Spanish exiles themselves. Compared to the richness of the texts in which they described their disaster and their reactions to it, firsthand Jewish accounts of other expulsions are sparse and, in some cases, nonexistent. To be sure, there may well have been texts that have not survived, but this can hardly be the entire explanation for the disparity. Sheer numbers may also be a factor (just how many Jews were expelled from Spain in 1492 can still turn otherwise serene scholars into matadors, but whatever the case the number must have exceeded those of any other single expulsion). Yet this too seems to me inadequate.

I would rather suggest that the profusion of personal and historical accounts emanating from the Spanish expulsion must somehow be related to the traditionally high, even inflated, degree of self-awareness on the part of Spanish Jews of their special identity and destiny as "the exile of Jerusalem that is in Spain" (*galut Yerushalayim 'asher bi-Sefarad*). "For the portion of God is His people," writes Isaac Abravanel,

> and that was the exile of Jerusalem in Spain while it dwelt in the land of its abode. . . . This is what the Holy One had in His world. . . . From where the sun rises to where it sets, from north to south, the likes of it never was before, a people treasured for praise, renown, and glory in its beauty and graciousness. And after it there will be no other like it.

To fall suddenly from such high estate—at least as it was perceived—into dire misfortune is the essence of tragedy, almost in an Aristotelian sense, and as such perhaps it demands and inspires at least a verbal catharsis.

Granted the plethora of sources, what else? The expulsion from Spain, I have stressed, was by no means the first. But perhaps this is itself the pivotal point. The importance of the Spanish expulsion is precisely that it was—not in a technical yet in a vital sense—*the last*, the culmination of a long series, of a chain of expulsions that had begun elsewhere in Europe several centuries earlier. Let us review them quickly.

In 1182 the Jews of the French kingdom were expelled by Philip Augustus, but the royal territory was still limited, the measure half-hearted, and the episode had relatively minor consequences; the Jews were back by 1198. The real chain of European expulsion began about a century later.

In 1290 the Jews were expelled from England. In 1306 they were expelled from the now much enlarged kingdom of France. Recalled in 1315, they were expelled again in 1322 and recalled once more in 1359. The final and definitive expulsion of the remnants of French Jewry took place in 1394.

In the course of the fourteenth and fifteenth centuries the Jews were expelled from most of the major cities of Central Europe.

Finally, in 1492 came the expulsion from Spain and, within a year, from its overseas possessions such as Sicily and Sardinia. The Low Countries being at that time under Spanish domination, no Jewish residence was permitted there to begin with.

But even the Spanish expulsion was not the end; there were epiphenomena. In 1492 many Spanish exiles crossed over into neighboring Portugal. They were accepted by John II upon the payment of considerable sums of money and on condition that their sojourn would only be temporary. The drama that subsequently unfolded in Portugal deserves to be recounted in detail, but let us turn directly to the decisive event. In 1497 John's successor, King Manuel, ordered the forced conversion of all the Jews within his borders, that is—both the native Portuguese Jews and those Spanish refugees who had not succeeded in leaving during the previous five years. In sum, though Manuel had issued a decree of expulsion in 1496, most of the Jews were not expelled. Rather, in 1497, through a mass forced conversion of singular brutality, Manuel rid Portugal not of the Jews but of any open manifestation of Judaism. And even this was not yet the end.

The Jews were expelled from the tiny but still independent Kingdom of Navarre in 1498. In 1501 they were expelled from Provence. In 1510 they were expelled from the Kingdom of Naples—in effect, from most of Southern Italy.

I would submit that the expulsion from Spain was—for the generation that experienced it and those that followed—more than the tragic uprooting of a once great Jewry. It was also emblematic, the quintessential symbol of a process through which, step by step, the Jewish presence was virtually eliminated from Western Europe and the global locus of Jewish life shifted from West to East.

Is this an artificial construct? I think not. On the perception of the Spanish expulsion as the climax of the larger process, let us take Abravanel as our primary witness:

Know that from the time that Judah was exiled and Israel scattered in their exile in the lands of the nations, there came upon them in the lands of Edom and Ishmael great persecutions, whether to destroy and slaughter, or whether to convert them by the sword. . . . But expulsion—that the kings of a land and its guardians should expel the Jews from their land, saying "Arise, go forth out of the midst of my people, you may not live in this land of ours"—this was unheard of.

The beginning was in France [i.e., the expulsion under Philip-Augustus], which was not all-inclusive, only from certain towns. But the first total expulsion from a kingdom was from the island that is called "end of the earth" which is *Inglaterra* [England]. . . . And after this in 5,066 [1306] was the first total expulsion from France during the reign of Philip [i.e., Philip IV], son of Philip, son of Louis. [Abravanel then describes the subsequent recalls and expulsions of French Jews until 1394, and continues]: And from thence there followed in our time the expulsions from Savoy and Provence and Milan and Ashkenaz and this last one itself, the expulsion of Jerusalem that was in Spain, and Sardinia and Sicily.

In his commentary on Deuteronomy 28:15, he writes:

And the meaning of "you shall perish among the nations . . . " [Leviticus 26] is that it refers to the afflictions and the slaughters that have passed over Israel in exile, that many died of hunger, plague, and the sword . . . and the expulsion of the Jews from England *and the other lands of the West,* and especially the expulsions from the whole of France . . . and even now in the expulsion of the exile of Jerusalem in Spain, which exceeded all the expulsions.

Abravanel is acutely conscious that the West has been emptied of Jews but, like others, he desperately tries to salvage some providential reason for this. On Isaiah 43: "We have seen with our eyes that the Lord roused the spirit of the kings of the lands of the West to expel all the Jews from their territory . . . in such a way that they emerged *from all sides of the West* and all of them passed toward the Land of Israel."

Perhaps the most succinct and telling expression of the larger significance of the Spanish expulsion is embedded in the remarks of the astronomer and halakhic chronicler Abraham Zacuto, who had gone from Spain to Portugal, then to North Africa, and finally to Jerusalem. He tells in his *Sefer Yuḥasin* how his great-grandfather had found refuge in Spain when he was expelled from France and notes the terrible contrast with his own time:

> And we, for our sins, have seen . . . the expulsion from Spain, Sicily, and Sardinia in 1492, and in the year 1497 after the expulsion from Portugal. For from France [in 1306] they came to Spain. But we [in Portugal] had the enemies on one side and the sea on the other [*Ve-lanu ha-'oyevim mi-ẓad 'eḥad ve-ha-yam mi-ẓad 'aḥer*]!

It can therefore hardly be accidental that not until the generation following the Spanish expulsion and Portuguese conversion do we for the first time hear a Jew, in this case the former Marrano Samuel Usque, indict not one particular country but cry out: "Europe, which swallowed me with its noxious mouth, now vomits me out." And again: "Now, Europe, O Europe, my hell on earth!" (*Póis Europa, Europa, mi inferno na terra!*)

With this my meditation, for it is hardly more than that, is at an end. We have traveled from exile as home to exile as hell. Both were realities.

PART II

Iberian Jewry: Culture and Society

2

⊡

Secular Hebrew Poetry in Fifteenth-Century Spain

Raymond P. Scheindlin

The Hebrew poets of Christian Spain, especially those of the four-teenth and fifteenth centuries, have received very little attention from students of Hebrew literature, and such notice as has been accorded their work has generally been disparaging. From Graetz, who labeled them "Dichterling," to Fleischer, whose word is "pathetic," the general opinion is that they were epigonic and decadent.[1] There are hardly any literary studies devoted to the poetry of the period. Even Pagis, who did so much to call attention to neglected areas of medieval Hebrew secular poetry, dealt with the period after the Hebrew Golden Age but sketchily. Yet even in the century of the breakdown of Iberian Jewish culture, poetry continued to be an important cultural institution as it had been in Spain before. If we want to understand the age, we have to devote some attention to its poetry and attempt to find more sophisti-cated ways to evaluate it. Although the age produced no Ibn Gabirols or Halevis, it did produce a corpus of poetry that literary history has to account for.

Unfortunately, the level of the discussion has been low. Some schol-ars say the poetry of the age is bad poetry, while others say it isn't so bad.[2] But no one has attempted to say specifically what it is like, to de-scribe it as a literary phenomenon or school recognizably distinct from the Hebrew poetry that preceded it. Judgment has preceded definition and description. We have been told how to relate to these poets before we have been told what they did. Since the poetry has not been described, the nature of the decline has not been clarified and could not be accounted for.

The purpose of this paper is not to exonerate the poets of fifteenth-century Spain of the charge of being epigones but to call attention to some of the distinctive aspects of their achievement in hope of starting discussion of the meaning of their work and its place in Hebrew literary history.

The latest significant corpus of Hebrew poetry from Spain derives from the circle of poets centered in Saragossa at the end of the fourteenth century and the beginning of the fifteenth century. The main figures in this circle were four poets: Solomon Da Piera (c. 1340–1420), Vidal de la Cavalleria (Joseph ben Lavi), Vidal Benvenist, and Solomon Bonafed. These poets exchanged poetry with each other and with many other friends and correspondents from about 1390 to 1420.[3] We do not know if this means that poetry really petered out after them or not, but this is the last extant poetry sufficient in quantity to afford an overall picture of poetry of the age and to justify generalizations. It is not a negligible body of literature. Even though part of the work remains unpublished, more is available than is generally realized.[4]

We shall proceed by examining the ode, or *qaṣīda*, the dominant poetic form in this period, using this form to exemplify both the dependence of the poets on the earlier models and their attempts to modify it for their own purposes. Then we shall reflect on the cultural situation that created the literary impasse of the age.

The Qaṣīda in Panegyric

The qaṣīda remained the dominant poetic form among the Saragossa poets, as it had been in the Golden Age. Strophic poetry continued to be written, but not nearly as much as in the earlier period,[5] and the strophic poetry that was written was not exclusively in *muwashshaḥ* form.[6] Short poems and epigrams remained an important part of the literary culture, especially verses with homonym rhymes of the type written compulsively by Todros Abulafia back in the thirteenth century. But the standard poem of the age was the long monorhymed poem in Arabic quantitative meter. As in the Golden Age, the qaṣīda was used for panegyric (*madīḥ*), lampoon (*hijā'*), and lament (*marthiya*); these three types of qaṣīda account for the bulk of the poetry of the age.

A well-known example of such a qaṣīda is Bonafed's "Shemesh yekar yareda tokh maʿaravenu."[7] The poem was addressed to Vidal de la Cavalleria (Joseph ben Lavi) during the Tortosa disputation. According to the heading, apparently written by Bonafed himself, Bonastruc Demaistre had presented a poem of greeting to this distinguished personage and de la Cavalleria had replied in a suitable manner. Bonafed then sent his poem, alluding to the words of de la Cavalleria's poem and lamenting the conversions.

Bonafed's poem adheres to both the prosodic conventions and the two-part structure of the qaṣīda.[8] The first part is a lament over the hardships of the times and the suffering caused by fate (called *zeman*, in accordance with Arabic convention accepted in the Golden Age). The second part is a panegyric on de la Cavalleria, acclaiming him as the champion who will lead the Jews to victory. Between these two parts is the typical *takhalluṣ*, or transition passage, reading: "Until now Time seemed wise in doing harm, and only today does our mind realize what a fool he is; / . . . / he hurriedly gathered the assembly of all who know the law and religion, and indeed among them is the master, who restores our souls." The master, of course, is de la Cavalleria himself, who clearly is still perceived as being in the Jewish camp.[9]

This poem conforms quite closely to the patterns established in the Golden Age, with one exception, namely, the repetition in the last hemistich of the words of the opening hemistich. This is a characteristic feature of the serious poetry of the period. I believe that it is not merely a technical detail, but that it points to a shift in the conception of the qaṣīda, perhaps to a shift in the esthetic principles behind the qaṣīda, a conjecture I have dealt with in more detail elsewhere.[10]

In a qaṣīda by Don Vidal Benvenist we can observe the contradictions that resulted from the survival of this Golden Age form into a later age.

Don Vidal Benvenist sent his friend Shneur a poem beginning "The earth adorns herself in her ornaments."[11] The poem opens with a description of the earth as a garden in spring. The reawakening earth is compared to a young woman who dresses in colorful clothing and sets up a pavilion among the myrtles, surrounded with fragrant roses, where she drinks wine and awaits her lover. The wine is also compared to a girl. After a transitional section, the poet goes on to speak of the poem's addressee, Shneur, praising him as a man of wisdom and steadfastness who enlightens the poets' eyes with his good counsel and support.

This poem, too, is a panegyric in classic two-part form. The first part is a *nasīb*, or erotic prelude, which is linked by a takhalluṣ to the body of the panegyric.

Not only does the poem resemble the qaṣīdas of the Golden Age in a general way, but it also makes clear references to a particular Golden Age poem on which it was modeled. This model was the magnificent panegyric addressed by Judah Halevi to Ibn al-Yatom beginning, "Like a girl-infant, the earth was sucking."[12] The allusion to this famous poem is made in a number of ways: Vidal's opening hemistich is similar to Halevi's opening hemistich, the two poems have the same meter and are similar in their rhyme,[13] and, above all, the description, following the poem's opening, of the colors of the earth's spring garments, spring's fragrances, and the presence of wine, covers the same objects in approximately the same sequence as does Halevi's poem. Vidal's poem is less varied, less colorful, and less acrobatic—in short, less skilled—than Halevi's masterpiece. But it can certainly be said to continue Halevi's tradition—an epigonic poem if there ever was one.

But beyond the difference in quality, there are differences in style and thematic treatment that repay closer definition. Having imitated Halevi's comparison of the earth in springtime to a girl, Vidal employs the takhalluṣ to turn the poem in a direction that would have been unthinkable to Halevi. After depicting the earth as a girl in her finery awaiting her lover, the speaker says that it is him she awaits, in order to seduce him with her wanton charms and lead him astray. But he knows that this beautiful girl is a harlot, that she is not faithful, that she is as changeable as the seasons or as the sea. He spurns her in favor of a different type of beauty, saying: "Therefore I spurn her, and I yearn not for her splendid beauty, her adornments, and her perfection. / My soul yearns to dwell alone with wisdom, and to listen to her lovely words. / She is the fawn that I adore; the manna and the produce of her mouth are what I long to eat. / So I went up to the presence of the noble Shneur."

Halevi of course was perfectly familiar with the theme of the world as harlot, for it was a commonplace of moralizing poetry such as was written by himself and by his mentor Moses Ibn Ezra.[14] But the juxtaposition of this theme with the theme of the garden in the context of a panegyric qaṣīda would not have occurred to him, for it would have been contrary to his whole way of looking at life. In Golden Age moralizing poetry (*zuhd*) one could describe the world as a painted woman who seduces young men only to destroy them; but in a nature poem the comparison to a beautiful woman is intended as a compliment, not as a moral indictment. Halevi expresses no reservations about the attractiveness and wholesomeness of the imaginary girl whose preening is an extended metaphor for the earth in spring, especially since the purpose of this metaphor is to prepare the reader to be positively disposed to Isaac Ibn al-Yatom. Halevi's takhalluṣ reads as follows: "My soul greets eagerly the breeze of dawn, for through it, it embraces the fragrance of my friend. / The breeze plays and sways the myrtle boughs, sending its fragrance far to distant friends. / The bough of myrtle rises high, then doubles over, and the palm tree branches clap their palms to the song of birds, / waving and bowing toward the face of Isaac, and the whole world smiles to hear his name."

In Halevi, typically for a Golden Age poet, the garden in spring was the locus of good feelings, the site of aristocratic pleasure, and the symbol of membership in the leading class. His elaborate and unequivocally positive depiction of the garden is capped by the explicit reference to Isaac. The key to Halevi's poem is that the patron is in harmony with the garden/girl. The key to Vidal's poem is that the patron is at odds with the garden/girl, who turns from bride to harlot in the course of the poem's nasīb. Vidal's patron is to be praised not for his love of sensual pleasures and fragrant gardens but only for his wisdom and steadfastness. Though the poem may look like a Golden Age panegyric, its system of values is reversed from those of the earlier period. Indeed, by openly imitating Halevi the poet calls attention to the contrast.[15]

How then are we to appraise Vidal's poem? It is surely epigonic, coming as it does at the end of a venerable tradition and attempting to repeat the successes of that tradition. But it is not devoid of an independent vision: Vidal does have something new to tell us, whether we find the message congenial or not. No longer is the life of pleasure, which had been celebrated by the master poets of the Arabic period, a part of the satisfied self-image of the Jewish aristocracy; it has been replaced by more sober values. But the fifteenth-century poets failed to find a form of their own for the new message. Although Vidal's imitation of Halevi is a clever adaptation of an earlier form to a new situation, it is also an example of the continued use of a form that is no longer relevant to the situation.

The Qaṣīda in Lampoon

Vidal imitated Halevi's poem in another connection for the purpose of lampoon, in his poem beginning "The bride who yesterday was like a woman in mourning."[16] It will give us yet another way to think of the epigonism of the Saragossan poets.

This poem also resembles Halevi's poem in meter, rhyme, and in its use of qaṣīda form. The opening nasīb describes the earth in spring as a girl awaiting her lover; via a transition passage the poem goes on to the praise of a patron. But unlike Halevi's poem, Vidal's qaṣīda ends with satire, the butt of which is Solomon Da Piera, a distinguished member of the de la Cavalleria household and the senior poet of the Saragossa circle, who may also have been Vidal's own teacher. There is also a difference in the nasīb. Unlike Halevi, Vidal devotes some verses to the unhappy state of the earth before the coming of spring, a theme hinted at in the poem's first words.[17] This dark theme, uncharacteristic for a garden-nasīb, was probably intended to prepare the reader for the lampoon with which the poem is to end.

The transitional section of this poem is in some ways closer to that of Halevi's poem. As in the model, its instrument is the breeze: "The budding vine gave out its fragrance to every passerby as if it were a spice merchant. / Its fragrance cures the sick at heart, and through it the sad soul can be seen to be laughing. / It kindles the fire of love in the hearts of lovers, and is like a burning fire in their spirits. / Then the spirit of friendship led my spirit, and it went down to the nut garden and there encamped. / Amid the lovely fields in the company of friends my soul takes pleasure and pride in them. / The company of the Lavi clan is the crown of all glory, for it is crowned with good works, / but ahead of all it called Joseph to ask of him the secrets of wisdom." The Lavi clan in whose company the poet delights are the famous de la Cavallerias of Saragossa; the Joseph named in the poem was Vidal de la Cavalleria (Joseph ben Lavi), Benvenist's close friend and associate.[18]

Up to this point, the poem's shape and its allusion to Halevi's poem create the expectation that it was intended as a panegyric and that its purpose was to praise this Joseph. But now a dark note enters the garden and a second transition appears: "While it (my soul) was still speaking, a poem was sent to me, a false, self-vaunting gift, / speaking pridefully and saying, 'In my power are all the oases of poetry, and I have created all its towers.' " The poet listens in disbelief to the claim of this false poem that its unnamed author is the master poet of his age, and he is on the point of composing a reply, setting the record straight and uphold the honor of poetry. But his friends, the de la Cavallerias, advise him to spare the author in view of his advanced age; he agrees to control his righteous anger, and on this patronizing note the poem ends--if this is in fact its original end.[19]

This poem is not built on the conflicting values of the garden and wisdom, as is the poem discussed earlier. The poet's patrons, the de la Cavallerias, are described as being perfectly in harmony with the garden. Like Shneur, the object of the panegyric, they are distinguished for their wisdom (especially for their knowledge of astronomy), but, unlike Shneur, their wisdom is not at odds with the theme of the garden. The conflict is between the garden, with its fresh, youthful beauties, and the object of the satire, an elderly, self-important braggart of a poet. The poem is actually quite satisfying in its symmetry: the dead earth of winter at the beginning corresponds to the superannuated poet at the end, while the verdant earth compared to the bride corresponds to the poet's patrons, with whom they are joined by the breeze of the transitional passage.

This poem too reuses Halevi's poem, borrowing the theme of the garden as a girl ready for her lover and turning it into a sunny background against which to throw the contrasting shadow of satire. It is not just an imitation or a hackneyed, uninspired repetition, but rather is a new creation built on the foundation of a revered model, a variation on a famous theme.

The Impasse of Hebrew Poetry

Despite the existence of many interesting poems and the undoubted energy that was invested in the composition of Hebrew poetry in our period, there is no question that Hebrew poetry in Spain during its last century was less innovative and less varied than that of either the Golden Age or of Italy in the same period. One need only compare the poems just described with the magnificent poem written by Moshe Ramos on the eve of his execution in Palermo about 1430; despite the emotional pressure under which it was written, Ramos's poem is innovative in both theme and form. Likewise, the grandiose attempt by Moshe Rieti in *Mikdash me'at*, written in 1412, to produce a monumental work in terza rima in the manner of Dante's *Divine Comedy* shows just how limited was the Saragossan's literary vision. Even more striking is the introduction of the sonnet into Hebrew by Immanuel of Rome in about 1300, right on the heels of its invention by Italian poets and before its adoption in any other language—and a full century before Rieti.[20]

Conversely, what is probably the greatest Hebrew poem to emerge from fifteenth-century Spain, Judah Abravanel's "Time with its sharpened arrow has smitten my heart,"[21] for all its warmth and expressiveness, remains completely in the formal mold of the long Arabic monorhymed poem; with its numerous references to the poems written by Samuel the Nagid to his son, it can very well be seen as harking back to the beginning of the Golden Age. Thus it would seem as if contact with the literature of Christian Spain, whether in Latin, Castilian, Catalan, or any of the other languages, had no significant impact on the Hebrew poets.

The great creative burst in the tenth century called the Hebrew Golden Age had been the result of the stimulation of Jewish culture by Arabic society and letters. The flourishing of Hebrew literature in sixteenth- and seventeenth-century Italy likewise resulted from the stimulation of the Italian renaissance. But Hebrew literature of fifteenth-century Iberia seems hardly to have been open at all to the stimulation of the literature of its environment.

This insularity cannot be explained by the poets' ignorance of Latin or of the vernaculars. Bonafed knew Latin; he tells us explicitly that he had studied logic in Latin when he was taking instruction from a Christian scholar and he praises the writings of Albertus Magnus from personal knowledge. He wrote a poem in the vernacular and boasted of knowing Spanish and Arabic.[22] Vidal/Joseph de la Cavalleria imitated a Latin poem in Hebrew and translated Cicero from Latin to Castilian. Incidentally, he also translated a medical book from Arabic into Hebrew.[23] Da Piera's "Give thanks to foreign-speakers in their foreign tongue," addressed to Astruc Rimokh, implies a whole discussion on the propriety of writing poetry in the vernacular. In this poem Da Piera praises those who use the vernaculars, and especially Rimokh, for managing them so well. But the poem ends with Da Piera protesting that he himself has no intention of writing vernacular poetry: "The Hebrew language is my friend; what do I need with the language of the Chaldeans or the speech of the Ashkenazim? I sanctify the Holy Tongue as my priest; what need do I have for foreign speakers with their foreign speech?" That Da Piera did sometimes write vernacular poetry is attested by Vidal Benvenist, who praises him with the words "Foreign speakers he turned to mockery with his speech, and the poetry of the Arabs is nothing to him." In his lament on the death of his patron, Benvenist de la Cavalleria, Da Piera exclaims, "How many books from a foreign language were translated into Hebrew through the correctness of his speech!" which means that Benvenist either translated himself or commissioned translations from unspecified other languages into Hebrew; we can conclude that translators were available and that the contents of these works were of interest to readers of Hebrew. Moshe Abbas receives a letter from a writer who explains that he is writing in the vernacular because he is afraid of making mistakes in Hebrew.[24]

So there is ample evidence that men of the social standing of the Saragossan poets were knowledgeable in these languages and in their literatures. Why did this knowledge not have the same stimulating effect on Hebrew literary culture in Iberia in the fifteenth century that it had had in the tenth and eleventh--or that it was already having in Italy?

The failure of the Saragossans to respond to the stimulus of the literary movements of their environment is the more surprising when viewed against the background of the preceding period. The century from the arrival of the Almohads to the reign of Alfonso X of Castile, from the middle of the eleventh century to near the end of the thirteenth, when the Jewish elite largely moved from the Muslim to the Christian cultural spheres, is sometimes called the Silver Age of Hebrew letters; it was a period of renewed creativity in Hebrew literature, thanks in part to the fructifying influence of Romance literature on Hebrew writers. Though the evidence for this renewal is abundant, it has never been given its due by writers of Hebrew literary history. This period saw the rise of Hebrew fiction, an event usually credited to the belated Arabic influence of the *maqāma*, but which I have tried elsewhere to show is at least partially related to contact with the romance.

Evidence is found in the new attitude toward love displayed by the maqāma by Ibn Ṣaqbel, in the stories of Jacob ben Eleazar of Toledo, in the works of the preeminent poet of the age, Todros Abulafia, and in the novelesque attributes of Ibn Zabara's *Book of Delight*.[25] All these features suggest that the period of the shift from the Arabic to the Christian sphere in the twelfth and thirteenth centuries was not, as is usually said, the beginning of an epigonic age but that it was actually a period of literary experimentation stimulated by new cultural circumstances. The Hebrew writers of the age make the impression of moving toward a new synthesis of Hebrew and the Romance culture, a synthesis destined never to be fully realized. As late as the mid-fourteenth century we encounter tantalizing harbingers of a Hebreo-Hispanic synthesis that was never to be. The chief example is the career of Shem Tov Ardutiel (Santob de Carrión), who wrote poetry in both Castilian and Hebrew. Shem Tov's Hebrew prose work, *The Battle of the Pen and the Scissors*, though not a weighty production, is important for Hebrew literary history because, though in rhymed prose, it shows significant independence from the maqāma tradition and from literary techniques appropriated from Arabic. Also noteworthy is the less famous Isaac al-Aḥdab, a Castilian Jew writing in Sicily at the end of the fourteenth and the beginning of the fifteenth centuries, who adopted the troubadour *tenso* in Hebrew.[26] But these are isolated cases, quantitatively insignificant next to the great outpouring of poetry in classical forms by the poets of Saragossa.

Thus, the contrast between the age of Todros Abulafia and that of Solomon Da Piera is palpable. Whereas, in the former, Hebrew literature seems to be looking outward, in the latter, it seems to turn in on itself, even as the poems produced by Da Piera and his contemporaries habitually revert, in their last lines, to their openings.

There is an easy explanation for the inwardness of the Saragossans: the persecutions, mass conversions, and general upheaval in the Jewish communities of Iberia after 1391 alienated the Jews from their environment; the unrest of the times was unkind to creativity. According to this explanation, cultured Jews responded to the hostility of the outside world by withdrawing from it and reliving the literary glories of the past, producing a literature that was merely an extended homage to that past.

But the withdrawal of Hebrew literature may require a more complex explanation, because, for all that the Jewish community was deteriorating, it still had vitality, a vitality that lasted for much of the fifteenth century. Between episodes of persecution and upheaval Jews continued to serve as financiers and courtiers, to study Latin and the Romance languages, to translate books from Hebrew and Arabic into these languages and from these languages into Hebrew, to write poetry, and to commission illuminated manuscripts. Neither cultural activity nor relations between Jews and Christians ceased. Persecution of itself is not an adequate explanation.

Since upper-class Jews do not seem to have been cut off from Spanish society and culture even in the fifteenth century, we have to consider some features of that culture in order to understand the position of literary Jews within it. At the end of the fourteenth century and the beginning of the fifteenth century, all the creative energy of literary Christians in Spain was going into vernacular literatures, mostly in Castilian and Catalan. Latin appears to have become insignificant as a language of new literary creativity. The vernacular literatures of Spain themselves were changing character, for this period saw the introduction into Spain of literary currents from Italy; Dante, Petrarch, and Boccaccio were becoming the models for Spanish writers and were to remain the models throughout the fifteenth century.[27] Popular vernacular literature, folk songs and stories, continued to be produced in Spain, but they no longer enjoyed esteem among the cultured.

The new vernacular literature of Spain was not a popular literature but a courtly literature, tending toward artificiality and mannerism. The Castilian poetry of the period has been described as "artificial and conventional poetry . . . based on subtlety and quickness of invention, plays of imagery, and every kind of rhetorical device in the service of affected amorous discretion, flattery, fawning, and works of circumstance."[28] These traits actually remind us of the Hebrew poetry of the age. They suggest that the limited thematic repertoire of Hebrew poetry in the fourteenth and fifteenth centuries may actually reflect the trend in the poetry of the courts.[29]

There is another aspect of the literary picture of Aragon that reminds us of the state of Hebrew poetry. Here, the fourteenth century saw a conscious effort to revive the traditions of troubadour poetry, especially beginning in 1388, when a Consistory of the Gaya Sciencia was established in Barcelona with the help of poets imported for this purpose from France. This conscious revival of a school of poetry from a prestigious era of past literary activity produced a literature "consisting of Catalan and Valencian imitations of the Provençal Troubadours."[30] The Catalan poetry that they produced does not at all resemble the Hebrew poetry of the period, but that is not so important. What is important is what these two groups have in common, namely, the massive effort to re-create the achievements of an earlier period and the deriva-tive character of the resulting poetry. Perhaps the aspirations and vision of our Hebrew epigones were not so different from those of their Catalan counterparts. If the Hebrew poets of Saragossa constituted a society or school, as suggested by Steinschneider, this society might even have been formed in imitation of the Consistory.[31]

Thus the limitations of fifteenth-century Hebrew literature and its affection for old models may actually reflect analogous trends in the larger Spanish society, no matter how alienated these two societies had become religiously.

There is one final consideration that we should bring to bear on our attempt to understand the peculiar character of Hebrew literature in its last century in Spain. Secular Hebrew poetry in Spain had come into being as a high literature in a learned language, in imitation of Arabic court poetry, which was also written in a classical learned language. Despite occasional attempts to change direction in the twelfth and thir-teenth centuries by imitating Romance verse forms, Hebrew poetry never shook off this learned tradition. As Arabic culture receded from Spain, secular Hebrew poetry remained as its last vestige in a land where Arabic had once provided the prestigious literary models. Cut off by the Reconquista from its roots in the Arabic courtly world, Hebrew poetry lost its vitality. Latin and its literature could not replace Arabic as a model for Jewish writers, not because it was the language of the church, but because it was no longer a vital force in Iberian literature itself. Thus, by the time of the Saragossan school the traditions of Hebrew were still deeply rooted in Arabic soil. It was too late to change. Jews who re-mained Jews and participated in upper-class Jewish culture knew only one variety of Hebrew and only one way to write Hebrew poetry.

Courtly literature in the vernacular offered a very particular literary experience in an age when Latin was still widely known among the ed-ucated. It had a flavor, much appreciated in Spain and elsewhere, that came from treating elevated subjects in the vernacular rather than in the traditional language of high culture. But the vernacular of courtly literature was not the vernacular spoken in the street; it was rather a stylized variant of that vernacular with pretensions to being a language of high culture. This complicated flavor could not be achieved in Hebrew, for Hebrew was thought of as a classical language, the Jewish equivalent of Latin. If there had been an impulse to imitate the new vernacular literature of Spain, there was still no Jewish vernacular to be molded into a language of high culture. On the popular level, the natural process of Judaizing the Spanish folk song laid the foundation for the Ladino romancero, and whatever energy the community had for producing vernacular literature was expended in this direction. On the level of high culture, Hebrew was stuck in its own traditions. We may ask why the Jewish elite did not produce a Jewish literature in Castilian or Catalan as they had earlier in Arabic, but it is not surprising that no renovation was possible for Hebrew. Jews who had a taste for high culture in the vernacular acquired this taste outside the Jewish community, and the acquisition of this taste must have been part of the process of acculturation that led eventually to the conversion of much of the Jewish upper classes to Christianity.

The situation in Italy was quite different. The new wave of Hebrew poetry that appeared in the sixteenth and seventeenth centuries was a product of the Italian Renaissance, just as the Hebrew poetry of the Golden Age had been a product of Andalusian Arabic poetry. The inspiration for the Jews of Italy was, however, not Latin but Italian, as may be seen from the works of Immanuel of Rome and Moses Rieti, who based their work, respectively, on Dante and the thirteenth-century Italian sonnet. When Immanuel introduced the sonnet into Hebrew, he was free to do so because he did not have to overturn a whole tradition of Hebrew poetry based on Latin. He could re-create Hebrew in the image of Italian, as Dunash ben Labrat had re-created Hebrew in the image of Arabic. As Dante and Petrarch laid the foundations for the vernacular poetry of the Italian Renaissance, Immanuel and Rieti laid the foundations for its Hebrew shadow. But this could not have happened in Spain, where the relationship between Hebrew poetry and the language of the surrounding milieu had been established on quite a different basis.

3

1492: A House Divided

Seymour Feldman

The period from 1391 to 1492 in Iberian Jewish history has rightly received the attention of historians, who have recorded and attempted to explain this tragic story. In doing so they have emphasized the political, socioeconomic, and religious factors that contributed to the demise of Spanish Jewry on its native soil. Less attention has been given to the cultural history of the Jews during this period, especially in that area in which the Sephardim were quite renowned: philosophy. Considering the constant attacks and pressures from both the church and the masses, one might think that philosophy among Spanish Jewry would be at best a luxury, at worst dead. After all, threatened with physical extermination and increasing pressure to convert, Jews would have had little time or energy for philosophy, which, Aristotle claims, requires leisure and tranquillity. Yet this expectation turns out to be erroneous. As one can see from the final chapter of Colette Sirat's history of medieval Jewish philosophy,[1] Spanish Jews were still active in philosophy throughout this critical, indeed, disastrous period. To illustrate some of this philosophical creativity I shall single out two figures who came at the end of our period: one represents the "old order" of Iberian Jewish social and cultural life; the other is a voice of the new era in Jewish social and intellectual history. Yet both were of the same family; indeed, one is the father, the other a son. They are Don Isaac Abravanel and his firstborn son, Judah. Both left Spain in 1492 and took refuge in Italy. There the father completed several books that he had begun in Iberia and composed new ones, and the son wrote a philosophical work that became a best-seller not only in Italy but also in his native country. The focal point of my essay concerns their attitudes toward philosophy.

I

As Sirat's sketch of Spanish Jewish philosophy shows, the last chapter of this story manifests considerable diversity, especially in its general attitude toward the value and role of philosophy. Even though Hasdai Crescas leveled a devastating critique against Aristotelian philosophy at the beginning of this period, Sephardic Jews continued to study Aristotle and to advance the Maimonidean adaptation of Aristotle into Judaism. Some replied to Crescas's criticisms and defended Maimonides; others turned to a "different" Aristotle—to his practical philosophy of the *Nicomachean Ethics*—and adapted it to Jewish purposes. Some, however, continued Crescas's critique and reached the conclusion that philosophy was alien to Judaism and had to be rejected, especially at a time when Jews could no longer trust the non-Jew. It has been plausibly argued that Isaac Abravanel belongs within this latter "anti-rationalist" camp.[2] There is no doubt much in his vast literary corpus to support this thesis, and I myself shall discuss in detail several of his more antiphilosophical or, better, anti-Aristotelian passages. But before I begin, it would be useful to distinguish his approach to philosophy from another negative approach with which it may be confused.

At least since Tertullian, and perhaps even among the rabbis of the Talmud, there has been the view that Jerusalem has nothing to do with Athens. In Tertullian this hostility toward philosophy assumed an extreme form, notoriously expressed in the formula "I believe because it is absurd."[3] Modern scholars have labeled this attitude "fideism." Indeed, fideism is still alive, to be found within the Wittgensteinian tradition.[4] It is my claim, however, that Isaac Abravanel is not a Tertullian fideist. To be sure, he is critical of philosophy; but even in his more critical moods he still works within a philosophical frame of reference and uses philosophical argument. Instead of abandoning reason or philosophy altogether, Abravanel uses it against itself in order to limit its claims and pretensions. His work exhibits a comprehensive understanding of the standard medieval philosophical literature and evidences considerable philosophical insight. Nevertheless, even though he never completely emancipated himself from his philosophical education and vocabulary, he does take an antiphilosophical position, as can be illustrated by examining several passages from his biblical commentaries.

The Bible describes the Sinaitic epiphany in vivid terms: in revealing the Ten Commandments to Israel, God manifests Himself not only verbally but also by altering nature. Both the heavens and the earth were affected. Abravanel detects eight distinct wondrous phenomena in Exodus 19, each one of which reveals something about the contrast between prophecy and philosophy.[5] First thunder was heard, then lightning was seen in the sky, along with thick clouds covering the mountain, producing a small amount of precipitation (Judges 5:4–5). Soon thereafter, there occurred four very different phenomena: a very loud and persistent blowing of the shofar, followed by God's voice speaking in a human manner, while the mountain was now covered with fiery smoke and trembled. According to Abravanel, these two "quartets" signify the basic differences between two types of cognition, philosophy and prophecy.

The philosophical mode of cognition, albeit valuable in certain respects, suffers from several defects, which are symbolized by the first four phenomena. The thunder, expressed by the plural *kolot*, "voices," refers to the many diverse and discordant views of the philosophers. The lightning, by virtue of its fleeting nature, indicates the ephemeral and limited nature of human insight and illumination. The heavy cloud, of course, connotes the obscurity that philosophers themselves often experience and that they produce in others. And finally the small amount of rain refers to the quite modest results of the philosophical enterprise.

In contrast, each of the second group of wonders signifies a special virtue of prophetic cognition. The loud and lasting voice of the shofar symbolizes the clear, unequivocal, and continuous character of prophetic knowledge. The fire on the top of the mountain refers to the divine presence, whereas the trembling of the foot of the mountain signifies divine punishment. Finally, God's speaking to the people in a language that is comprehensible to them exemplifies a special kind of prophecy, one not recognized by the preceding medieval Jewish philosophers, perceptual prophecy, a mode of prophetic experience that requires the perfection of neither the intellect nor the imagination.[6]

Hence, the whole people of Israel became prophets at Sinai. Whereas the first four events were all ordinary natural phenomena, the second four were not; for the earthquake producing the trembling of the mountain occurred *only there*. Prophecy then is a supernatural, miraculous phenomenon.

Abravanel expands and refines this rhetorically formulated distinction in his account of Solomon's wisdom, a theme that was of considerable importance ever since Hellenistic times. Assuming that Solomon's wisdom was qualitatively different, precisely because it exceeded that of all the wise men of the East, Abravanel argues that it was really a form of prophetic cognition.[7] He then develops in detail the defining feature of Solomon's wisdom by means of a philosophical distinction that was becoming increasingly popular, although its roots were struck by Aristotle.[8] Methodologists were now distinguishing between two different kinds of procedures within science, which is, as Aristotle had taught, the search for causes: either we start with the phenomena and analyze them looking for their cause; or we reverse the procedure and begin with the causes and derive from them their effects. The former is an inquiry, a posteriori, the latter is a priori. This well-known Aristotelian methodological principle is adopted by Abravanel to make a non-Aristotelian point; indeed, he uses it to draw the distinction between Aristotle's wisdom, or human wisdom in general, and Solomon's wisdom. Whereas philosophers and scientists follow the a posteriori method of analyzing the phenomena and tracing them back to their causes, Solomon, and prophets in general, begin with knowledge of causes and then infer or apply this a priori knowledge to their effects or to special cases. The a posteriori method is discursive, involving analysis, definition, and experimentation; the a priori method is intuitive, requiring nothing but the immediate insight into the nature of the phenomenon and its consequences, or effects. As one can see, this distinction is invidious: it is clearly better to know the causes of something *straightaway*. Aristotle himself had recognized the virtues of this kind of cognition in his *Posterior Analytics* but reserved it for the highest and most fundamental type of intellectual activity, *theorein*, or *noiein*, an intellectual insight into the basic principles, or axioms, of a subject matter.[9] Abravanel, however, transfers this mental achievement to a different domain altogether—to prophecy, of which Solomon's wisdom is a subspecies.

Abravanel treats this topic in detail. We, however, shall single out only several of the specific differences that differentiate prophetic cognition from philosophical-scientific knowledge. Since the a priori intuitive mode of cognition is the immediate knowledge of causes given through prophecy, it is infallible. By contrast, however solid scientific information may turn out to be, it suffers nevertheless from some uncertainty; indeed, as contemporary methodologists have insisted, the defining mark of a scientific theory is to be *disconfirmable*.[10] In addition to their continually self-corrective character, Abravanel claims scientific hypotheses also suffer quite literally from superficiality. Based as they are upon perceptual data, scientific hypotheses are restricted to and hampered by the defects and limitations of our senses, which can only receive the external qualities of the phenomena. Sense perception can never penetrate to the real essences, or nature, of the phenomena, that is, to the formal causes. Anticipating Locke, Abravanel registers the complaint that empirical, or a posteriori, cognition has no access to the substance of things and can only offer information about the accidental, or superficial, features. This is particularly common, according to Abravanel, in medicine, where one often knows *that* a particular herb or drug provides a cure or relief but not *why* it does so. In some cases this is the result of overdetermination: the cure or relief can be attributed to several causes.[11]

The situation is worse when we turn to metaphysics. Aristotelian metaphysics is almost by its very nature a posteriori, and for two reasons. First, as indicated before, the primary principles of any domain are acquired from sense perception. This is true for metaphysical truths: that is, the law of contradiction and the law of the excluded middle cannot be demonstrated a priori.[12] Second, in its medieval form Aristotelian metaphysics was closely linked to astronomy; indeed this is true for Aristotle himself, at least in *Metaphysics* 12:8. Medieval metaphysics is in many respects the doctrine of the separate intelligences, most of which are the movers of the heavenly spheres. Herein lies the Achilles' heel of metaphysics! Abravanel delights in pointing out the differences among the philosophers on these issues and the almost insuperable difficulties that infect this discipline. Not only is there no agreement on the exact number of such intellects, but their differences and functions are also matters of controversy. Consider, for example, the debate between Avicenna and Averroës over the question whether God is

Himself the mover of a specific heavenly sphere. Or take the question of the Agent Intellect: is it a wholly transcendent being? Or is it in some sense immanent in us? Or is it entirely in us? Since the doctrine of the Agent Intellect was so important to the medieval philosophers—playing a role in their theories of cognition, immortality, prophecy and sunlunar generation—the failure of the philosophers to reach some agreement on this central topic is a clear sign of the utter debility of the discipline.[13]

Keeping in mind these criticisms of medieval Aristotelian science and metaphysics, it should come as no surprise to find Abravanel's account of religious belief to be considerably different from that of his predecessors, especially from that of Maimonides, who, he admits in his last work, was nevertheless always (besides the Bible) his main intellectual interest.[14] In his *Guide of the Perplexed* (part 1, chap. 50), Maimonides gives a brief but clear definition of belief. His definition is intellectualist: belief comprises conceptualization and verification. This general definition of belief applies to religious belief as well. Blind faith has no place in Maimonides' program. Abravanel rejects this whole approach. First, the word that Maimonides uses to designate belief, *'emunah*, is for Abravanel a technical term whose proper domain is religious belief, or dogma. We can readily appreciate this point if we ask ourselves whether there can be "false dogmas." Abravanel would say not. By definition an *'emunah* is a belief *taken to be true* by its believer, who does not grant its falsifiability. This is what defines a religious belief, as distinct from a scientific, philosophical, or historical belief, which can in principle be false.

Second, religious beliefs are not acquired through or confirmed by reason; rather, they are accepted and acquired through tradition, which in turn is based upon prophecy. Because religious beliefs derive from God, they are literally a priori and hence possess all the virtues that philosophers have ascribed to this type of cognition: infallibility, immutability, and clarity. Whereas a major goal of medieval Jewish philosophy was to "rationalize" religious belief, to show that such beliefs were philosophically and scientifically grounded, Abravanel rejected this conception. This does not mean that for him religious beliefs were groundless, as some contemporary fideists have argued;[15] rather, he stressed their groundedness in prophetic traditions, which in some cases may be supported *post factum* or even proved by philosophical argument. In this sense Abravanel is not a fideist: some religious beliefs may be beyond reason, but they are not contrary to reason; some religious beliefs can even be philosophically proved or defended. Here Abravanel is closer to Christian theologians like Augustine, who believe in order to know,[16] than to his own coreligionists Maimonides or Gersonides, whose rationalism he regarded as not only excessive but also unwarranted and arrogant.

To flesh out this sketch of Abravanel's attitude toward philosophy, I would like to consider briefly his particular positions on two of the more controversial questions in medieval philosophy: immortality of the soul and creation of the universe. Since I have written elsewhere about the latter issue,[17] I shall give more attention here to the former. Although Abravanel did not write a separate treatise devoted to the subject of immortality, he does discuss it in several of his biblical commentaries, especially in the commentary on 1 Samuel 25. The context is Abigail's saying to David, "Your soul will be bound up in bundle of life [*zeror ha-ḥayyim*] with the Lord your God" (1 Samuel 25:29). Abravanel takes the opportunity not only to explain the unusual phrase "bound up in the bundle of life" but to develop a theory of immortality of the soul.

Concerning this general question the medievals were especially troubled by three specific issues. (1) *What* exactly is immortal? (2) In what does immortality *consist*? And (3) *how* is it attained? In this section of the commentary Abravanel posits seven fundamental principles pertaining to the general question, several of which address these specific issues. The first principle states that the *rational* soul is immortal. In spite of his antiphilosophical attitude, Abravanel is still faithful to the medieval Aristotelian psychology, wherein human beings are distinguished from other animals in having intellect, or the rational soul. Indeed, Abravanel gives a philosophical reason for his contention that the rational soul is immortal: even though the human soul is created, it is nevertheless everlasting, since it does not inherently possess the cause of destruction. Although this philosophical theme is a medieval commonplace, what is noteworthy is that Abravanel, the critic of philosophy, uses philosophy to make his theological point. Since the rational soul is for Abravanel an incorporeal substance, as it was for Avicenna and Aquinas, it, unlike the body, does not suffer contrariety or decomposition; it is therefore essentially immortal.[18]

Abravanel's divergence from the philosophical tradition is evident, however, when we turn to his second, third, and fourth principles. In the second he claims that immortality is individual, or personal. Here he rejects the whole Averroist conception of immortality, which may have been the view of Maimonides as well, wherein immortality involves the abolition or loss of individuality, since it consists in conjunction, or union, with the Agent Intellect.[19] But Abravanel rejects this latter idea in his fourth principle: immortality consists in a cognitive or ontological relation not with the Agent Intellect but with God. In his third principle Abravanel rejects the whole intellectualist conception, indeed, bias, of this philosophical theory, which infects even Gersonides, who himself rejected the theory of conjunction with the Agent Intellect.[20] According to Abravanel, immortality is *not* the consequence upon or reward for intellectual, that is, philosophical, perfection. Influenced by Crescas,[21] Abravanel insists that immortality is the reward given for the observance of God's commandments, not for the mastery of metaphysics and physics. When the rabbis say in *Berakhot* 17a that the righteous enjoy the illumination of the divine presence, they did not mean that the righteous are either engaged in uninterrupted metaphysical study or unified with the Agent Intellect, as Maimonides and others suggested. Rather, they are the recipients of everlasting divine illumination by virtue of their merits in mitzvot, not metaphysics. This is "the bundle of life" mentioned by Abigail, who was certainly not a metaphysician; nor, for that matter, was David.

On the topic of creation Abravanel wrote several treatises, among which is his most philosophical and longest nonexegetical work, *The Deeds of God* (*Mif 'alot 'Elohim*). According to Abravanel, the doctrine of creation ex nihilo is *the* dogma of Judaism, if Judaism has any dogmas.[22] Now, this whole question has a venerable history, of which Abravanel provides a substantial account. By this time the variety of cosmological doctrines was considerable, and it was important, he believed, to settle matters once and for all. This resulted in a systematic defense of the doctrine of ex nihilo creation and a detailed critique of its rival theories. What follows are a few significant features of his approach that are relevant to our general themes.

It is useful to begin where Abravanel himself usually begins, with Maimonides. To Abravanel the master of the *Moreh* left this topic in a perplexing state: whereas Maimonides ostensibly defended creation ex nihilo, in reality he provided only an argument in behalf of creation; moreover, it is an argument that he himself admitted was not a strict proof.[23] The legacy left by Maimonides was therefore a mixed blessing. Several issues were still sub judice: (1) *What kind* of creation theory did Maimonides really defend? Did he really believe in creation ex nihilo? His argument for creation really doesn't settle the difference between creation ex nihilo and creation from matter. (2) Why did Maimonides not believe the question of creation to be decidable? Did he believe merely that no vigorous proof was available? Or did he believe that no such proof could ever be found? If he thought that the latter was the case, did he provide a metaproof that creation ex nihilo was not provable, as did Aquinas?[24] These perplexities were aggravated and compounded by Gersonides' defense of eternal creation. What was a Jew to believe when virtually every theory of creation had its defenders?

Abravanel explicitly states that the authentic Torah view is creation ex nihilo. Although he begins and bases his defense of this dogma with an exegesis of Genesis, he develops and expands it by means of *philosophical* arguments and *philosophical* counterarguments against its rivals. Since this topic is a long story requiring a separate study, I cannot tell it here. But a few points are instructive. Like Saadia and Crescas, Abravanel argues philosophically against the theory of creation out of matter, whose main Jewish proponent was Gersonides. Here he borrows a great deal from Crescas's "new physics" against Gersonides. One of Gersonides' main arguments against creation ex nihilo is the vacuum argument: if God created the world ex nihilo, there would have been a vacuum before creation and a vacuum would have remained surrounding the universe after creation.[25] To rebut this argument, Abravanel cites Crescas's counterclaim that the arguments of Aristotle against a vacuum are invalid and a vacuum is therefore not impossible.[26] Having dissipated the force of Gersonides' critique of ex nihilo creation, Abravanel argues for this latter thesis, using material from John Philoponus to construct a proof that he believes is virtually sound.[27] Maimonides' ambiguities have then been removed and the issue resolved once and for all. But the resolution is not just exegetical; philosophical argument is present throughout. Abravanel may often have said many nasty things about philosophy, but he was never reluctant to use philosophical arguments when they suited his purpose.

II

While Isaac Abravanel was preparing and mounting his defense of traditional Judaism against philosophical criticisms and reformations of it, his son Judah was thinking different thoughts. The facts of Judah's Italian exile are not as plentiful or as well known as those of his father's, but several that are known are relevant to understanding his philosophical career in Italy.[28] First, he did not live with his father during most of the latter's Italian sojourn, which, after a brief initial period in Naples and Sicily, was localized in several Adriatic towns and finally in Venice, where he died.[29] Judah, however, ventured forth to Genoa and Rome, two Italian cities that Isaac never visited, and seems to have returned several times to Naples, where there was a flourishing intellectual community.[30] Second, although there is some question as to whether Judah ever visited Florence or had direct contact with any of that city's literary figures, most scholars have asserted that Judah had more than just a passing awareness of the philosophy of the Florentine circle of Platonists. Indeed, even one scholar who denies any direct contact between Judah and the Florentine academy admits that, "without assuming that Leone (Judah Abravanel) knew intimately the cultural ambience of Pico's circle, it becomes most difficult to comprehend the genesis of . . . [Judah's philosophical magnum opus], the *Dialoghi d'amore*."[31] We shall see that the main themes of Judah's "Philosophy of Love" were discussed and developed by several contemporary Italian philosophers, and the subsequent and immediate popularity of his *Dialoghi d'Amore* has to be explained in terms of a receptive audience already familiar with the notion of "erotic spirituality," to use T. Perry's felicitous phrase.[32] Whether Judah had any direct contact with the Florentine philosophers or came to know their philosophy via a Jewish intermediary, such as Yoḥanan Alemanno,[33] it is evident that this was a world whose ideas had become part of his own intellectual makeup.

Moreover, it was an audience that Judah sought. Unlike the books of Isaac Abravanel, who wrote only in Hebrew and had no interest whatsoever in having his writings translated, Judah's *Dialoghi* became a "best-seller" during the Renaissance, having been translated into

French, Spanish, and Latin. At this point the controversial but important question of the original language of the *Dialoghi* is relevant. This has been a contested question for some time, with four different languages having been proposed. Most scholars today have rejected an original Italian version, since the Tuscan Italian of the editio princeps is not something that Judah could have acquired after living about *eight* years in *Naples*. Even if the first draft had been in Hebrew, as several scholars now maintain, it probably became "Italianized" via a Latin translation, which Judah either did himself or supervised.[34] At any rate, it was ultimately the Italian version that became the standard text from which all subsequent translations were made. It was through this translation that Judah became known as "Leone Ebreo." Both he and his book became part of Western literature, whereas the books of Isaac Abravanel are restricted to readers of rabbinic and medieval Hebrew. The only other philosophical book attributed to Leone is a work entitled *De coeli harmonia,* a work in Latin presumably dedicated to or written for either Pico or his nephew, also named Pico. Although this book is not extant, the report that such a book was written in Latin for a non-Jew is indicative of Leone's weltanschauung. Although faithful to his father's religious outlook, he saw himself as a philosopher who could philosophize in the non-Jewish world. He, like Mendelssohn two and a half centuries later, was a philosopher for the gentiles. Arriving in Italy eight years after Ficino had published his complete Latin translation of Plato's *Dialogues* and in the very year in which Ficino published his Latin edition of Plotinus's *Enneads,* Leone's own philosophical dialogues exhibit the influence of these two products of Renaissance Humanism and belong to a specific genre of Renaissance literature, *la filosofia d'amore.*

Let us now turn to the literary format of the treatise, especially its title. Although there were a few medieval philosophical treatises written in the dialogue form, it was not the preferred exposition or argument. Moreover, when we compare Leone's dialogical style with Gabirol's *Fons Vitae,* one of the few important examples of philosophical dialogues in medieval Jewish philosophy, we see a vast difference: whereas the latter's use of this form is artificial, indeed, uninteresting, since the Master does most of the talking, Leone's dialogues are vivid and balanced. The two characters engage in a genuine mutual philosophical discussion as almost equal participants. By naming the two characters "Philo" and "Sophia," Leone suggests that this dialogue about love is essentially philosophical in nature. To be sure, there are biblical and Jewish references; but the style and the content of the treatise fall within the genre of a largely secularized philosophy.

Perhaps the most explicit manifestation of this secularization is expressed in the theme of the book: love. Medieval philosophers were not oblivious to love, and a few actually wrote or said something about it. But in general eros was not a major issue for medieval philosophy; when it was discussed, it was usually in a theological context, particularly man's love for God. The *Dialogues of Love*, by contrast, places us in a different intellectual milieu, one whose parameters have been defined by Plato's *Symposium*, not Solomon's Song of Songs, which had become in late medieval Jewish philosophy the counterpart to Plato's encomium to love.[35] Throughout Leone's treatise it is the problematic of the *Symposium*, its vocabulary and conceptual framework, that provides the philosophical setting for the discussion of human love, a theme that is virtually absent in Maimonides and Isaac Abravanel.[36]

Leone's secularization of philosophy shows itself in two other ways. First, perhaps for the first time we find a work written by a practicing Jew containing allusions to classical pagan mythology. The medieval Arabic and subsequent Hebrew translations of Greek literature were quite selective: few of the great classics of Greek poetry, drama, or narrative were translated. When Japhet was permitted to dwell in the tents of Shem, he was allowed to bring in only some of his luggage, which was carefully examined and screened to keep out unwanted or dangerous items. Leone, however, shows no reluctance to use classical literary tropes. Although these pagan motifs are "circumcised," to use Arthur Lesley's trenchant but apt term, they are nonetheless present and used liberally.[37]

Second, if the *Dialogues* is novel for the presence of classical myths, it is also noteworthy for the absence of a prominent medieval theme that almost dominates philosophy from Augustine through Isaac Abravanel: the relationship of philosophy to religion, or the conflict of reason and faith. This topic hardly surfaces in the *Dialogues*. Leone simply assumes the significance and value of philosophy: it is not a problem for him, as it was for his father. He takes it for granted that for some people, at least, philosophy will be the way to attain the ultimate good. Indeed, it

is the highest expression of our goal: the *intellectual* love of God. Leone
clearly rejects then one of the conclusions of his father, who gave primacy to the observance of the commandments and minimized the role
of philosophical perfection.

I now turn to illustrate Leone's attitude toward philosophy by looking
at two specific issues of philosophical controversy, the very same ones I
considered in connection with his father. But now I shall reverse the
order: I shall treat creation first and then turn to immortality. Despite
his filial affection and loyalty, Leone rejected his father's cosmology, especially its emphasis upon creation ex nihilo. Leone's language is not always unambiguous, and he is occasionally ambivalent, but the overall
thrust of his cosmology is Platonic. It is a Renaissance Platonic cosmology, however, not just a restatement of the medieval Platonic model.

The first thing to note in Leone's discussion of this old debate is that,
unlike any of his medieval Jewish predecessors, he is aware of an alternative reading of Plato's *Timaeus*. Whereas Maimonides, Gersonides,
and Isaac Abravanel all understood Plato as saying that the divine
craftsman created the physical world out of some eternal formless stuff
at a definite instant (the first instant of time), Leone asserts that there is
an alternative way to interpret the doctrine of creation in the *Timaeus*,
that the world is eternally produced by God. Leone explicitly attributes
this view to Plotinus, who, he adds, attempted to reconcile Plato with
Aristotle. Yet Leone prefers the literal reading of the *Timaeus* as the
standard interpretation.[38] Evidently Leone was aware of the ancient debate within the Platonic tradition on whether Plato considered creation
nontemporal (that is eternal) or temporal. He was also aware of the existence of Plotinus, who is not mentioned in any Jewish philosophical
work prior to the late fifteenth century.[39]

Although he clearly recognizes the difference between Plato and the
"faithful" who believe in ex nihilo creation, Leone develops the notion
of eternal formless matter, or chaos, in such a way that it is difficult to
avoid the impression that he believes in it. Indeed, toward the end of
this section in the Third Dialogue, Sofia tells Philo that she is happy
with his attempt to reconcile Plato with the view of Moses and the kabbalists.[40] But in what does this reconciliation consist? Turning his attention now to Genesis rather than to the *Timaeus*, Leone offers the following reading of Genesis 1:1–2: "Before God created and separated the

heaven and the earth . . . from chaos, the earth (i.e., chaos) was empty and void." According to this reading, the act of creation is a "cutting," or separation of the primordial chaos, or formless material, resulting in a formed celestial domain and a formed earth. Like Gersonides, Leone sees the creative act as a forming, or shaping, of shapeless matter.[41] When he turns to the verse "And the spirit of God hovered over the face of the waters," Leone goes on to say that the "spirit of God" is "the supreme Intellect full of Ideas," which communicates form to the dark chaos, or matter, and thus "illuminates" it.[42] Forms, or Ideas, are also present in the Soul of the World, which, as Plato suggested,[43] is created along with the generation of the world, albeit not with the pristine purity possessed by these Forms in the divine intellect. It is from this Soul of the World that all the forms in the terrestrial world derive.[44] What we have here is a reinterpretation of the *Timaeus*, since Plato distinguishes sharply between the Divine Craftsman and the Forms.[45] Following, perhaps unconsciously, in the footsteps of the Middle Platonists, such as Philo Judaeus, Leone locates the Forms in God's Intellect or identifies God with these Forms.[46]

Actually, Leone departs from the *Timaeus* in another respect. He modifies Plato's doctrine of matter to characterize it as eternally *created*,[47] whereas in the *Timaeus*, the receptacle, space, or matter is never said to be generated. In reply to Sophia's question, reminiscent of Augustine,[48] about how anything can be both eternal and created, Philo claims that eternal matter or chaos can be said to be created because of its very imperfection and formlessness. As such it is not on the same level of being as God. Indeed, Philo then goes on to tell Sophia that this "chaotic" matter is eternally produced by God "from Himself."[49] At this point the Plotinian idea of the emanation of matter from the One begins to insinuate itself into Leone's cosmology.[50] But before we say more about this topic, let us note one more feature of Leone's reading of this theme from *Timaeus*. He retains Plato's metaphor of the receptacle, or matter, as the feminine factor in creation: God is the Father; whereas chaos is the mother.[51]

A few pages later, however, a significantly different picture emerges. The initial virtual identity of God and the Forms is rejected. In its stead Leone puts forth the thesis that the intellectual pattern, or the world of the Forms, is subordinate to and distinct from God, who "precedes the Idea of the Universe."[52] He now attributes the identity thesis to

Aristotle, whereas this new theory is designated as Plato's.[53] Yet it is, in fact, not the Plato of the *Timaeus*. For, as he developed this theme, Leone claims that the pattern, or the "ideal world," emanates from God, who not only is "above" the First Intellect but also "is beyond being."[54] Indeed, Leone says that Plato called God, or the Supreme Good, "the absolute," that is, "It Itself," that which cannot be qualified or defined in any way such that its unity would be impaired. Thus God is "prior" to His Wisdom, or the First Intellect.[55] Leone has now dropped his former reading of the *Timaeus* and replaced it with a Plotinian interpretation that is aesthetically formulated as three levels of beauty: (1) the author of beauty, God, (2) beauty itself, or the Intelligible World, or the First Intellect, and (3) physical beauty, or the physical universe. Leone has thus reinterpreted both the *Timeaus* and the *Symposium* in terms of the *Enneads*.

Once Leone has constructed this new cosmological model out of Platonic and Plotinian themes, he then uses it to interpret Scriptures. He returns to the opening verse of the Bible and gives it a different reading. When Moses says, "In the beginning God created the heavens and earth," the phrase "In the beginning" is to be understood as referring to the primordial wisdom, the First Intellect, through and according to which God created the physical world. Leone proceeds to identify this wisdom, which is virtually identical with Plotinus's Nous, with the wisdom mentioned explicitly by Solomon in Proverbs 8:22, where it is said that wisdom is God's *first* creation, or "first emanation." With this verse, as well as other passages from Solomon's Song of Songs and Ecclesiastes, Leone constructs a cosmological model that combines strands from Moses, Solomon, and Plato, understood in Plotinian terms. The novelty of this model is explicitly indicated in Leone's reidentification of the feminine factor in creation: whereas in the first model it was chaos, or matter, now it is wisdom, or First Intellect, that is the mother of the physical world; the Father, of course, is God.[56]

This is actually an old theme: it appears in Philo,[57] who also made the intelligible world, or Logos, a creature, just as Plotinus made Nous subordinate to the One. Leone takes Plato's original metaphor of the feminine factor in creation and attributes it to God's subordinate intellectual partner in creation, not to the material matrix. Although Leone does not link this theme to the rabbis, the idea is reminiscent of the rabbinic idea that God created the Torah and then created the world by looking at the Torah.[58] In distinguishing and subordinating First Intellect, or Wisdom, to God and at the same time making it an essential and active element in the creation of the world, Leone not only provides a reading of Genesis but also rewrites Plato's *Timeaus* in the light of what he learned from Plotinus.[59] The traditional doctrine of creation ex nihilo has receded into the remote background where the "faithful" reside, the term *faithful* having the Maimonidean sense of those who unreflectingly accept tradition.[60] Leone's father as we have seen, also accepted ex nihilo creation, but not unreflectingly.

Now, a few words about immortality. As several scholars have pointed out, one of the dominant concerns of Renaissance Italian philosophers was human immortality, in particular, the provability of immortality of the soul.[61] With the new translation and publication of Plato's *Phaedo*, this desideratum appeared to be realized, although the Aristotelian philosopher Pietro Pomponazzi argued against the philosophical provability of the doctrine.[62] Leone's position on this issue is different both from his father's basically Avicennian view and from that of his older Florentine contemporary Marsilio Ficino. Indeed, his theory of immortality turns out to be a blend of both medieval Aristotelian and Plotinian ideas. Despite Isaac Abravanel's rejection of the medieval Aristotelian idea of immortality in terms of an intellectual conjunction with the Agent Intellect, Judah Abravanel accepts the general idea of the conjunction of the intellect. The Italian verb *copulare* is used in this context throughout the *Dialoghi*. This term derives from the Latin verb, which was used in scholastic literature as the equivalent of the Arabic and Hebrew terms *ittisal* and *devekut*. Immortality for Judah consists in some kind of intimate link between the individual and a supernal reality. But the crucial questions are, who is this supernal entity and how is this link to be attained?

In the First Dialogue Leone reports the various medieval accounts of the doctrine of conjunction and claims that in *his* view the Agent Intellect, with which on the medieval doctrine conjunction takes place, is really identical with *God*, not anything subordinate to Him.[63] Now, there was some precedent for this idea in late antiquity: Alexander of Aphrodisias identified the Agent Intellect with God.[64] By adopting this identification Leone was, perhaps unconsciously, approaching his father's view that immortality is a return to God, not union with something else, albeit angelic in nature. Yet unlike his father Judah stresses the cognitive aspects of this relationship with God: "Our happiness consists in the knowledge and vision of God."[65] This knowledge is clearly philosophical or theoretical and is identified with the study of metaphysics.[66] It is clear then that Leone has not given up the medieval intellectualism rejected by his father.

Yet Leone's quasi-Alexandrian account of conjunction manifests another feature that reflects his own philosophical milieu. Although attained through philosophical reflection, conjunction is for Leone an *erotic* experience. Here Plato's *Symposium* is not only the mise-en-scène for the dialogues but is also its directing force. The requisite knowledge for immortality is a cognition that leads to the love of its object. It is an *amor Die intellectualis*, which Leone describes in the Third Dialogue in Plato's language of the aesthetics of beauty. Ascending from the level of the perception of sensual beauty, we move upward to the apprehension of spiritual beauty, which is separated from matter and thus perfect. This level is the knowledge of the First Intellect, or "the highest beauty." But this is not all. From that perception we go even higher until we apprehend the "giver of all beauty," God, "the supremely beautiful." And this is achieved only "with all powers of our intellect."[67] Using the language of Plotinus we can say that for Leone immortality is first the reversion of our intellect to the First Intellect, or Nous, and then to God, or the One. In his return to God we "partake" of the divine beauty and enjoy a "sweet union with it."[68] Like any good Platonist, Leone concludes his treatise by disparaging sensual love, which contains ugliness and harm.[69]

III

I have argued that two Abravanels represent two different outlooks on philosophy. Nevertheless, the elder Abravanel was not entirely a man of the Middle Ages; he was aware of some of the newer trends and ideas of the Renaissance, as has been ably argued by a number of scholars.[70] It has also been claimed that Isaac's theological position reflects the influence of Platonism, in particular the "new Plato" of the Italian Renaissance, which influence is quite evident in Judah. Almost one hundred years ago Jakob Guttmann noted in Isaac about a half dozen references to Plato, one to Plotinus, and several to Porphyry. But in his judgment Isaac's assimilation of Plato is "not very important and doesn't give the impression that he had read Plato himself."[71] Moshe Idel, Avraham Melamed, and others think otherwise. According to Idel, both Abravanels shared a common point of view that took over the Renaissance theme of the *prisca theologia,* the "ancient theology," and Judaized it by identifying it with the Kabbalah, to which they linked Platonism both historically and philosophically. Using the ancient legend of Plato's studying with Jeremiah, the Abravanels were able to present Judaism as the true embodiment of this *prisca theologia*: it was literally "the tradition" (*kabbalah*) and incorporated whatever is true in the "divine Plato."[72]

Although Idel and others are right in maintaining that Isaac had a positive attitude toward Plato, kabbalistically interpreted, I am still sympathetic to Guttmann's claim. In arguing for the influence of one thinker upon another, we have to determine the scope and depth of this influence, as well as envisage possible alternative sources for the similar ideas. In the case of Platonism, we must remember that it was not discovered in the fifteenth century. There was a medieval Platonic tradition.[73] So it is important to delineate what is new in the Platonism of late medieval or Renaissance thinkers. I now want to indicate why I believe Isaac's Platonism to be superficial.

First, as far as I can tell, Isaac mentions by name only three of Plato's dialogues: the *Timaeus,* the *Phaedo,* and the *Republic,* all three of which existed in the medieval Platonic corpus in some form or another. Although it is possible that Isaac knew some of the more recent Latin translations of Plato by Leonardo Bruni and Marsilio Ficino, it is quite significant that he makes no mention of nor shows an interest in the *Symposium,* one of the favorite dialogues for the Renaissance, as we have seen in the case of Judah.

Second, his most detailed discussion of a Platonic theme-creation from matter- is highly critical, as we have shown. He doesn't even exhibit the tolerance expressed by Judah Halevi and Maimonides for this theory, both of whom adhere, at least on the surface, to the traditional dogma of creation ex nihilo yet allow that Plato's theory is compatible with most of the ideas of the Torah.[74]

Third, although he approvingly mentions Plato's doctrine of the soul, especially the theory of transmigration, which he claims is the view of the Torah and the Kabbalah, he is oblivious to a major difference between Plato's psychology and the Jewish idea of the soul. Whereas Isaac insists that the soul is created ex nihilo, and is thus not eternal, Plato maintains in the *Phaedrus* that the soul is "not born and does not die."[75]

Moreover, if we look at the passages where Isaac makes the analogy between Plato's theory of transmigration and the kabbalistic doctrine of the gilgul, we see an interesting difference between his own view and that of Plato. In discussing the punishment of King Nebuchadnezzar, Isaac refers to the doctrine, which he attributes to Albertus Magnus, that the Babylonian king was transformed into an ox. Now, according to Plato, evil souls will be reincarnated as wild animals. But Isaac considers this view to be nonsense: human souls are not relocated in animal bodies.[76] In this discussion he makes no mention of Plato. But he should have, if he really knew Plato's doctrine of transmigration!

Another curious feature of Abravanel's point of view of Plato is his complete faith in the ancient legend of Plato's encounter with Jeremiah, from whom the Greek philosopher apparently learned the doctrine of transmigration and other "traditional," i.e., kabbalistic ideas.[77] What is strange about Isaac's restatement of the story is that ten centuries earlier Augustine had disproved it on chronological grounds and that several Renaissance scholars, including Bruni, had agreed with him.[78] In another context Isaac cites Augustine's *City of God*,[79] the work where the Christian Father expresses his doubts about the legend. Did he read only part of Augustine's work? Did he read it at all?

Idel adduces another text where Isaac makes a different analogy between Plato and the Kabbalah. Here we are concerned with Plato's theory of Ideas, or Forms, and the kabbalistic doctrine of the sefirot.[80] Isaac maintains that the Ideas and the sefirot are intentional objects of thought in God's mind, where they serve as paradigms for the creation of the world. Probably having the *Timaeus* in mind, Isaac sees an affinity (Idel's term) between the Forms and the sefirot. But this alleged affinity is more applicable to middle and late Platonism than it is to Plato himself. In the *Timaeus* the Forms are ontologically independent of the divine creator; they are eternal and underived from anything. If Isaac had read the *Timaeus*, he should have appreciated this important point. I suspect that he was relying upon some secondhand account of Plato's doctrine, which itself had been permeated by later interpretations.[81]

When we turn to his references to the later Platonists, we should note the following curiosities. First, is he really referring to Plotinus in the passage cited by Guttmann? I'm not so sure. Isaac claims that a certain "Pilotino" was a disciple of the disciples of Aristotle and that he believed the planets to orbit the earth by themselves without being attached to and fixed within spheres.[82] Now, this piece of astronomy, a subject in which the real Plotinus did not have much interest, is certainly not one that a disciple of Aristotle's disciples would be very likely to hold, since it contradicts a basic theory of Aristotle's cosmology. For Aristotle the planets do not themselves move but are fixed within their spheres, which are the bodies in motion.[83] This astronomical doctrine that Isaac attributes to "Pilotino" was actually held by earlier Platonists, perhaps even by Plato himself, a point Isaac is totally unaware of.[84]

Isaac's information about Platonists after Plotinus is also sketchy. As Guttmann had already noted, his references to Porphyry are confused. In one place he considers him to have been a disciple of Aristotle; in another he believes him to be a Christian! He is, however, aware that Porphyry wrote a commentary on the book of Daniel that was critical of traditional Christian interpretations of that book.[85] But he does not know that in that commentary Porphyry was also critical of the Jewish Bible.

Finally, in his *The Deeds of God* Isaac refers to the theme of the soul's body.[86] According to this doctrine all the incorporeal substances derived from God have an attachment to a body that is "spiritual and very fine"; the soul is attached to this body forever. This body is the "carrier" (*noseh*) of the soul. Now, this last term is one that is especially associated with the late Neoplatonist Proclus, whom Isaac never mentions by name. Proclus used the term *ochema*, "chariot."[87] But, as Guttmann suggested,[88] it is quite likely that Isaac learned of this idea from the medieval version of Proclus, the *Liber de Causis*, either from the Hebrew or Latin translations or indirectly from Yoḥanan Alemanno. Yet there is an important difference here between Isaac and Proclus: although for the Neoplatonists the soul can be said to be generated from some higher principle, this generation is eternal. Moreover, both the soul and its "chariot" are eternal entities. Isaac would reject these claims.

In measuring the extent to which one thinker is indebted to another, it is crucial to distinguish the different ways in which this influence can be manifested. It is one thing to cite or refer to a particular author, text, or idea approvingly in order to support one's own views that were independently arrived at. It is another matter when a particular thinker has interiorized the ideas of another author to the point where the former can be considered a disciple of the latter. And here one must be careful to take an exact measure of this interiorization and to determine its overall consistency. I maintain that Isaac Abravanel's Platonism is of the former type: he occasionally sees Plato as a useful ally to argue against Aristotle or his Jewish-Muslim followers. Where appropriate, he draws analogies between Platonic philosophical themes and the Kabbalah, although his eagerness to "circumcise" Plato sometimes leads to a distortion or error. Even if or when he was aware of the new Plato of the Renaissance, his knowledge was limited, superficial, and most likely secondhand. Indeed, it is difficult to imagine an elderly exile with failing eyesight trying to find a peaceful place to complete books planned or started in Spain, or beginning to compose new works, undertaking to study Ficino's new translations of Plato and Plotinus. If he did, there is little evidence that he learned much that is new or significant. As Idel has noted, the "friendship" between Plato and the Kabbalah predates the Renaissance.[89] It is likely that during his Italian exile Isaac learned or at least heard of some of the newer ideas of Renaissance thought, particularly Renaissance Platonism. But this *nova theologica Platonica* fell upon ears that had already been turned off to philosophy. If Plato was acceptable to Isaac, it was only because he was a kabbalistic manqué. If Isaac had known firsthand the complete and pure Plato, he would have considered him to be unacceptable. He was, after all, a philosopher.

To read Judah's *Dialogues of Love*, however, is to enter into a different world, one in which Greek philosophy is welcome. Although occasionally critical of Aristotle, Judah is always respectful of him, whereas his father regarded him as a "poisonous snake" by whose venom many Jewish thinkers had been fatally infected.[90] For Isaac philosophy is, in a way, our "original sin," redemption from which is provided by the Torah. Although occasionally some Renaissance light penetrates Isaac's essentially medieval mind, his attitude toward philosophy was negative. Not so Judah: for him philosophy was a divine gift to mankind.

4

▨

On Converso and Marrano Ethnicity

Thomas F. Glick

In the vast anthropological and sociological literature on ethnic relations, there is no allusion to the many very well-documented historical
case studies that converso and marrano monographs represent. Nor in
this very rich historical literature is there more than perfunctory allusion to the theoretical literature of ethnicity. It is the purpose of this
essay to review the converso and marrano problems from the standpoint of the sociology of ethnic relations and thereby extract the theoretical richness embedded in these historical cases.

Converso Ethnicity: What Are We Looking For?

Historians studying a wide variety of converso topics and situations frequently reflect their personal religious or ideological orientations in
their work. They have, as a result, reached vastly different assessments
of converso culture. Some portray the conversos as a group totally assimilated into Spanish Christian society; others portray them as a
covertly, but strongly, Jewish religious group. Essentialist arguments
abound at both ends of the spectrum. Thus a Jewish scholar asserts that
the conversos, no matter how acculturated, were "Jews in mentality,"
yearning only to return to the fold.[1] And at the other end of the spectrum varieties of Spanish Catholic opinion reflect an older "racialist"

notion that culture is somehow inheritable—that cultural contact results in only the most superficial of changes and that the basic cultural
contours of any ethnic group are preordained, fixed, and not subject to
significant modification.[2] The present essay seeks an orientation that
frees the history of the conversos from these mythic elements, which
impede an analytical approach to the problem and which obscure the
processes of social and cultural change affecting conversos.

We want to ask not only how "Jewish" the New Christians were but
also how "Spanish" they were, that is, to locate conversos along the path
of acculturation. More specifically, we might ask what constituted, at
different times and in different situations, the degree of enclosure of the
conversos and what facts influenced the degree of enclosure. By *enclosure,* I mean all those factors that contribute to the separation of one
group from another or to the maintenance of boundaries between one
culture and another.[3] Although the enclosure of conversos has typically
been characterized in cultural terms (for example, in terms of elements
of Jewish religion and associated philosophical or ideological orientations), we hold that the factors affecting boundary maintenance are
largely *social* in nature, even though their effects may have cultural
repercussions. The general point is persuasively argued by Pierre van
den Berghe:

> The analysis of ethnic relations must not be focused exclusively or even
> primarily at the cultural level; ethnic relations cannot satisfactorily be ac-
> counted for simply in terms of cultural differences, culture contact, and
> acculturation between groups. It is important to distinguish analytically
> the structural elements of ethnic relations from the cultural ones. The dy-
> namics of group membership, solidarity, and conflict, and the network at
> structured relationships both within and between groups, are at least as es-
> sential to an understanding of ethnic relations as the cultural dynamics of
> group contact. . . . Cultural differences are frequently symptoms rather
> than determinations of intergroup behavior, even in systems where the
> distinguishing criteria of group membership are predominantly cultural.[4]

It is easily demonstrated that social distance may produce secondary
cultural features. The reverse, that cultural distinctiveness may produce
social responses, is also true. But my position here is that the former
process explains more about the conversos than the latter.

Spanish Jews and conversos both prior to and after the expulsion were
an example of ethnically stratified social system. Therefore, changes in

the system at large affected each participant group. For this reason, the converso problem must be studied systemically. The relations between Old Christians and moriscos, for example, provide important clues to the processes affecting relations between the former and conversos. Furthermore, questions involving intergroup relations inevitably lead to an exploration of the nature of the power relations between those groups. Here again we denote the salience of social and economic factors in determining the degree of enclosure of ethnic groups, involved as they must in competition with each other for resources, prestige, and power. We must then ask, to what extent were social and economic rewards attained or withheld on the basis of group membership, or to what extent did group membership serve as a justification for an unequal distribution of economic and political rewards?

A Case in Point: The Chuetas

To throw into clearer relief the distinction, crucial in my view, between social and cultural factors as they influenced the shape of converso life, consider the situation of the Chuetas of Mallorca in the nineteenth and twentieth centuries. The modern Chuetas have many of the characteristics typically associated with European Jewish enclaves. The question then becomes, to what extent are such characteristics owing to cultural continuity with the group's Jewish ancestors or to relatively recent purely social pressures.[5]

The Chuetas, descendants of Mallorcan Jews who accepted baptism in 1492, largely escaped the rigors of the Inquisition until the late seventeenth century, when the community suffered two autos de fe. Inquisition documents show that those who were processed manifested a high degree of crypto-Judaism. At this point, two factors intervene to lessen the probability of uniform cultural continuity between the original Mallorcan conversos and their descendants in modern time. First, it appears that those who were processed in the auto of 1691 were all residents of the ghetto, the *call menor*; some of them may simply not have been conversos to begin with. Second, only fifteen families were subsequently stigmatized by having *sanbenitos* (penitential robes) inscribed with their names placed on public view in the cathedral. There were other Mallorcan conversos who escaped stigmatization as Chuetas and, conversely, the Chueta group was swelled by the steady stigmatization of other Mallorcans bearing those fifteen surnames, whether conversos or not.[6] Whatever the ethnic composition of the original group, by the end of the eighteenth century the Chuetas appear to have been homogeneously Catholic and petitioned the king for redress of grievances on the grounds of unfair discrimination against them, in view of their proven orthodoxy.[7]

The Chuetas of the past two hundred years have constituted a closed caste, with very little in or out-marriage on the island. The group's effective segregation from the rest of Mallorcan society was manifest in a structure of parallel institutions, typical of ethnically stratified societies. The Chuetas had their own religious confraternities, burial societies, and education facilities. They have typically been businessmen and artisans, especially jewelers, concentrated in the city of Palma. They have also been an exceptionally creative group, producing large numbers of artists and writers, and a preponderance of violin and piano teachers in twentieth-century Palma were Chuetas. Until very recently endogamy was regarded as a virtue. Stereotypes ascribed to Chuetas will be familiar to the Jewish reader: they were said to be skilled in business, avaricious, large-nosed, and their women were reputed to be beautiful. Psychologically, self-hatred was a Chueta hallmark. They felt themselves inferior to non-Chuetas and feelings of insecurity provided self-justification for their exclusion from the mainstream of Mallorcan society.[8]

In spite of the fact that Chuetas have been archly Catholic Catholics, religious to the point of exhibitionism, their social ostracism was consistently justified on grounds of their Jewish descent. The fact that their culture had no Jewish content was insufficient to ward off the ascription of Jewishness, which was held to be hereditary. There is ample evidence that any assumption of cultural continuity between fifteenth-century Jews and twentieth-century Chuetas is absurd. The question now is, what mechanisms or conditions have produced a sociocultural configuration among the Chuetas identical in many respects to that of communities of urban European Jews? In the case of the Chuetas social ostracism has given rise to a constellation of reactive secondary cultural features (using creativity to achieve prestige, endogamy, and so forth) that served to reinforce the enclosure of the group, originally distinguished on ethnic and religious grounds alone.

Thus for the Chuetas, acculturation to the norms of Spanish society was not accompanied by social assimilation. Put in other terms, diminution of cultural distance was not accompanied by reduction in social distance, and the group's level of enclosure remained high until the present century. Moreover, continued enclosure had the effect of generating secondary cultural characteristics that reinforced social and institutional mechanisms of enclosure. In Mallorca the maintenance of social distance was explained and justified by both Chuetas and non-Chuetas by reference to cultural distinctiveness, when in fact the process was just the opposite: social segregation generated all the subcultural traits.

The immediate antecedents of present-day Chueta culture and society extend back no further than the eighteenth century. Because of their distinct surnames, historians can track the Chuetas through civil documentation much more systematically than is possible for any peninsular converso group. *Limpieza* statutes were belatedly applied: craft guilds with Chueta majorities split in two; Chueta priests had to profess in peninsular or foreign dioceses or to join religious orders, to segregate them from the general public, and so forth. Meanwhile *foreign* Jews converted to Catholicism were integrated into island society in the same period with no ostracism.[9]

A Systemic Model

R. A. Schermerhorn proposed an ideal-type model of ethnic relations; it is based on the structural relationship between dominant and subordinate groups but at the same time provides for cultural outcomes of social relationships. The model is based on paired concepts of centripetal and centrifugal trends in social life: centripetal trends refer to cultural attributes such as the sharing of values and lifestyle and social structural features, such as participation in a common set of institutions and associations; and centrifugal trends are those that encourage separation of the subordinate from the dominant group. In terms of cultural outcomes, centrifugal trends typically result in high degree of enclosure, such as the retention of a distinctive language, religion, or other cultural elements, reinforced socially by the practice of endogamy and various kinds of segregation or enforced social distance.[10]

Whether the subordinate group can be integrated in the society depends on whether its modal tendency, either centripetal or centrifugal, is satisfied by the dominant group's acceptance of it. The bottom boxes in figure 4.1 indicate the modal tendency of the subordinate, and the top boxes reflect the superordinate groups wishes in regard to the subordinates: do they wish to associate freely with the latter or do they wish to maintain some degree of social distance. Integration results when there is a congruence of views on centripetal or centrifugal aims. Integrative functions are presented by cells A and B. In type A, the subordinates wish to assimilate and the superordinates wish them to; in type B, the subordinates desire cultural autonomy and the superordinates acquiesce in this wish.

Cells C and D apply to situations where there is no congruence of aim; the result is then ethnic systems that generate conflict. In type C the subordinates wish to assimilate but are not permitted to do so, resulting in a situation of forced segregation. Cell D reflects the converse,

FIGURE 4.I.

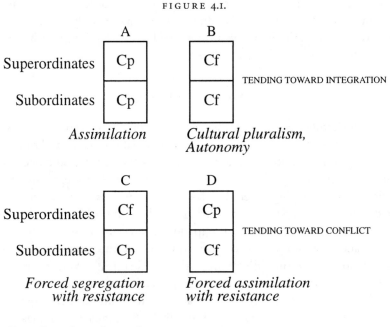

Cp = Centripetal trends
Cf = Centrifugal trends

where the subordinates wish cultural autonomy, but the superordinates insist upon assimilation.

Schermerhorn's model has three merits for the historian. First, it includes both cultural and structural features. Second, it insists on looking at superordinate and subordinate groups in reciprocal interaction. Third, it makes possible the comparison not only of different ethnic system characterized by the same or different cells but also of diachronic shifts from one cell/type to another. The case of Spanish Jews provides a superb illustration of the model, inasmuch as Jewish-Christian relations over the course of seven hundred or more years of interaction encompassed *all four* of the modal types envisioned by Schermerhorn (figure 4.2).

The pre-1492 situation is fairly straightforward: both Jews and conversos were, on the whole, well integrated into the society, the former on the basis of agreed-upon communal autonomy (cell B); the conversos, on the basis of assimilation, the terms of which were understood and accepted by both sides.[11] After 1492 there is a bimodal split in

FIGURE 4.2.

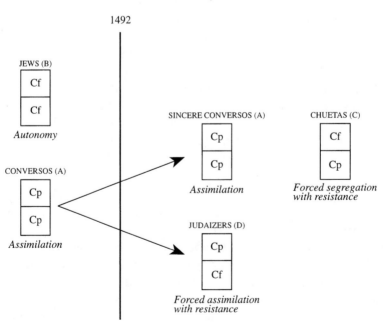

converso/Old Christian relations. Assuming that the dominant mode of the superordinates was, on the whole, favorable to assimilation, the sincere converts were in an assimilationist situation (cell A), whereas crypto-Jews are better described by cell D, implying forced assimilation with resistance. The matter is complicated, however, by the ambivalent attitudes of superordinates and their frequent unwillingness to validate the acculturation of sincere converts.[12] If the exclusionism informing *limpieza de sangre* is read as the modal type of Old Christians, then, instead of A and D, we would have a situation of C and B, respectively, for sincere converts and crypto-Jews.[13]

The pattern D to A, typically involving the assimilation of a minority group against its will, has never been effected in postnationalistic Europe, according to Schermerhorn.[14] He concludes tentatively that such a solution has frequently been blocked by factors of nationalism and wonders whether such a sequence of types was more common in prenationalist Europe. The case of families of Judaizers who finally assimilate corroborates the view that nationalism inhibits integration, inasmuch as the medieval idea embodied in cell B was no longer a possibility in imperial Spain. The progression D to A has higher probability in cases of voluntary migration, which is somewhat analogous to the situation of sincere converts. Schermerhorn's model suggests that in a system of intergroup relations in which the superordinate group is centripetal in orientation, the structural supports necessary for the subordinates to maintain a high degree of enclosure are absent, which makes their assimilation a foregone conclusion. Only in the case of a centrifugal mode on the part of superordinates will there be a mechanism for the creation of parallel institutions needed to perpetuate group boundaries over the long term, as happened in the case of the Chuetas.

Measuring Jewish Culture

We have noted in the case of the Chuetas that social isolation or discrimination can have the effect of producing secondary cultural features that serve to reinforce the boundaries of the subordinate group. Such secondary features may or may not coincide with the culture of original reference, although they may be so ascribed by superordinates. Such a consideration is particularly important in assessing the worth of studies that purport to see common converso values in religious, philosophical, and other writers of the late sixteenth century—values that are identified as "Jewish."

The discussion of crypto-Judaism has generally rested on the supposed survival of elements of Jewish religion and religious practice, pursued in secret by conversos.[15] The problem is that since in this context religious faith was the last redoubt of cultural distinctiveness, the last element to be dispensed with in the process of assimilation, it is entirely possible that conversos may have been generally centripetal, that is, assimilationist, in orientation while at the same time retaining one basic element of Jewish culture (for example, resolute monotheism, rejection of the Trinity). Declaration of Jewishness by a converso is, therefore, not in itself any indication of a high degree of enclosure.[16] Certain other elements of Jewish practice, related peripherally to faith, such as changing bedclothes on the Sabbath, may be regarded as simply habitual among some conversos and not evidence of enclosure at all.

The best cultural evidence for a high degree of enclosure are indications of elements that are identifiably Jewish but lack any direct religious significance. An example of such a trait would be the failure to learn the gentile calendar after 1492. In 1529 a Valencian artisan named Francisco Estella was asked by an inquisitor whether or not Ferdinand and Isabella had expelled the Jews in 1492. Estella replied that he knew the Jews had been expelled in the year 5252 of the Jewish calendar, but since he did not know the Christian calendar he was unable to say whether 1492 was the correct date.[17] The fact that Estella still had not learned the gentile calendar, thirty-seven years after the expulsion is pretty good prima facie evidence for a high degree of enclosure characterizing Valencian conversos. Such ignorance implies that in business dealings and social contacts Estella did not have to use the common calendar, because his circle of associates—mainly conversos—either did not require it or else also continued to use the Jewish calendar. Rejection of the Trinity, on the other hand, requires no social associations of any kind to persist in any individual. By the same token, evidence of a group of conversos attending a clandestine service on Yom Kippur says relatively more about enclosure than does the arrest of one individual for failure to work on that day.

We have, however, little notion of the non- or extrareligious dimensions of converso culture. Certain persons were referred to as *ajudiados,* that is, recognizably Jewish, perhaps on the basis of overt mannerisms or patterns of speech.[18] Unless more evidence is forthcoming on extrareligious elements of converso culture, a case for a high degree of enclosures among crypto-Jews cannot be made on cultural evidence alone, without corroborating evidence of extensive social linkages. The literature on converso participation in the *comunero* movement suggests that conversos took part as individuals and not as members of any articulated social group. But other evidence, also concerning sincere conversos, indicates the existence of rather extensive familial and patronage relationships. Such associations would be necessary to provide a sufficiently high degree of enclosure to perpetuate group identity after the first generation of converts. There has also been a marked tendency in discussions of crypto-Judaism to regard religion as coextensive with culture. The general passivity of crypto-Jews is indicative of their desire to achieve substantial acculturation to Old Christian values. Those who remained after 1492 and accepted baptism, even if secretly observant, had already made a very substantial decision to acculturate and assimilate.

How "Moorish" Were the Moriscos?

Put another way, were the moriscos more Moorish[19] than conversos were Jewish and, if so, why? Judging by the comparative outcomes, the moriscos were more successful than were the conversos at maintaining a high level of enclosure: they proved unassimilable and were finally expelled en masse in the early seventeenth century, whereas conversos were finally assimilated. What are the structural elements that were present to encourage the maintenance of morisco cultural boundaries and that were absent in the case of conversos?

The moriscos, preponderantly rural cultivators, with a sizable minority of urban artisans, were at first glance at the total mercy of Old Christian society. In a succession of measures undertaken throughout the sixteenth century, the state removed institutional support for group identity, including such measures as the prohibition of Arabic language, the annulment of contracts written in that language, and an absolute ban on all distinctively Muslim customs and attire. There was little status differentiation among moriscos, their elite having disappeared through emigration to North Africa. And there was scant intercaste mobility; the moriscos not only accommodated themselves to lower-caste status, but they were also effectively locked into it by the virtual enslavement of the rural sector to Christian landlords. Violent outbursts, such as the Alpujarras revolts, were repressed without compromise.

The moriscos bear out the prediction that the weakest group in a local cluster of ethnic groups should be the most ethnocentric.[20] The conversos, a more powerful group in terms of socioeconomic status, were less ethnocentric. A corollary to these propositions is that the strongest and most threatening out-group should be the target of most ethnocentric hostility from the in-group.[21] That conversos in fact drew more fire from Old Christians than moriscos did is indicative of their power. This also accounts for the patterning of intergroup conflict in sixteenth-century Spain: the Old Christians, through the Inquisition, initiated aggressive action against conversos, whereas, as befit their paternalistic stance toward Muslims, they took punitive action only in response to overt morisco uprisings.

There is also a correlation between group cohesion and degree of assimilation. The more highly assimilated the enclave group, the less social cohesion there is within the enclave. This point is also illustrated by a comparison of conversos and moriscos. The former, manifesting a high degree of congruence with Old Christian culture,[22] had a weakly articulated social network, as proven by the relative ease with which the Inquisition was able to monitor converso affairs. The moriscos were close-knit socially and much less far along the path of acculturation.[23] Put another way, a group as highly assimilated as the conversos could not possibly have had the social cohesion necessary to maintain the degree of enclosure that apologists for the crypto-Jews claim for them. Status differentiation also correlates with group cohesiveness. The enforced social leveling of moriscos by their lords enhanced group cohesion. In contrast, the emergence of a very powerful group of conversos in high places was a decisive factor in inhibiting cohesion within the group.

The key differences between conversos and moriscos concerning the maintenance of cultural boundaries may be summarized as follows:

1. The conversos were more powerful, politically and economically, and this attracted aggressive counteraction from the threatened Old Christians.
2. The moriscos' original culture of reference was less congruent with Old Christian culture than was that of the Jewish group, which, as a result, acculturated more rapidly.

3. The moriscos' ethnic boundaries were reinforced by the proximity of a homogeneously Muslim hinterland (North Africa) and by the military power of the Ottoman Empire.

4. The moriscos' religion appears to have been endowed with greater flexibility and resilience in times of adversity than was Judaism. The Jewish view of forced conversion was generally adverse, while Muslims were encouraged to bend with circumstances and await better days.

5. Strong social linkages were encouraged among moriscos by substantial spatial segregation. Conversos tended to be highly interspersed among the Old Christian population.[24]

6. The diminution of social distance between Old Christians and conversos lagged behind the diminution of cultural distance. That is, acculturation proceeded at a faster pace than did social integration.

7. If the moriscos were able to achieve what the crypto-Jew could not (continuous maintenance of their religious tradition), their cultural success was a measure of social failure. By the same token, the cultural failure of the crypto-Jews was a measure of their social success: they had won a place in Spanish society despite their impulses to the contrary.

The Ethnicity of Marranos

The above remarks were directed at the social and cultural status of Spanish conversos of the fifteenth and sixteenth centuries. By *marrano* I refer to the Portuguese conversos, many of whom returned to Spain in the late 1500s, either to stay or on their way to other countries. The marranos were more socially cohesive and enjoyed a higher degree of enclosure than their Spanish brethren did, no doubt because they had been allowed to settle in Portugal as an articulated community in 1492. The following remarks, however, speak not of Portuguese conversos in Spain but rather of marrano society elsewhere in Europe, especially Holland, England, and Italy. There, suddenly released from the terrible pressures applied by the Spanish church and state, the marranos were free to define, or redefine, their ethnic identities. Nevertheless, for this highly acculturated group, the process was frequently fraught with ambivalence.

The question of what is at stake in the matter of ethnic identities is perhaps clarified by the concept of cultural commuting. Coined by Pierre van den Berghe, this concept enables us to focus the issue of biculturalism on the behavior of individuals. Given a situation of cultural pluralism as described by van den Berghe in the case of Indians and Ladinos in Guatemala, "A" number of persons find it possible to move from one group to another, or to "commute" back and forth between two groups, or to be marginal to all groups.[25] The relevance to marranos will become obvious. A rural Indian can therefore easily master the skills necessary to pass for a Ladino in the city. In this construction, culture is used in the same way as language, such that an out-group person can habitually don the culture and use the language of in-group persons. The same is no doubt true of Berbers in Morocco, particularly, just as in Guatemala, when a mountaineer is a temporary immigrant in the city: he is a Berber in his village, an Arab in the city.[26] There are also well-documented cases of commuters adopting sharply different religious guises (such as animism and Christianity among the Karen peoples in Burma) and shifting back and forth between two religious modes. The Karen have attracted the attention of anthropologists interested in ethnic change because of the malleability and plasticity of their ethnic identity. They manage to adjust to the exigencies of their immediate cultural ambience without sacrificing their core identity; indeed, in this case, malleability of identity itself is part of that core.[27] Hence the relevance to a discussion of marranos.

But clearly we cannot directly compare marrano cultural commuting with that of tribal peoples whose base religious mode may not have been a "high" religion. Moreover while the anthropological literature of cultural commuting typically deals with short-range migration, the typical marrano commuter lived as a Christian in Spain and as a Jew in Holland or in different Italian city-states; that is, he crossed national borders. Second, the marrano variant of cultural commuting was highly constrained by its heavily ideologized social environment. Paradoxically, this sharply constrained situation may have actually encouraged cultural commuting, since it was everywhere unacceptable to be *nothing*.

The cultural commuter was a well-known social type in the Spanish world of the sixteenth and seventeenth centuries. Here I define a commuter as someone who changes in cultural guise, including religion, if not habitually then at least more than just once: he can switch back and forth. The quintessential cultural commuter in the Spanish tradition, however, was not a marrano, but a morisco. I refer to Cervantes's Ricote, a morisco who appears in part 2 of *Don Quixote*.[28] Ricote speaks from the vantage point of an ostensibly sincere convert to Catholicism, forced to leave Spain because of the iniquity of his insincere brethren. Exile was the worst possible punishment, for "Wherever we may be, it is for Spain that we weep; for, when all is said, we were born here and it is our native land." With his wife and daughter in Algiers, Ricote went to Augsburg where he felt more comfortable and then went annually to Spain on Catholic pilgrimages and also made some money on the side. He tells Sancho he is more a Christian than a morisco "and I pray God constantly to open the eyes of my understanding and reveal to me the way in which I may serve him. What surprises me," Ricote continues, "is that my wife and daughter should have gone to Barbary rather than to France, where they might have lived like Christians." Ricote, therefore, is part Muslim, part Christian and cannot sort out his ambivalence, but neither does he feel much anxiety about it. His family, like that of many marranos, was split, his wife and daughter (like the wives of many marrano "commuters") being more constant than he to their Semitic faith. Ricote's religious and familial dilemma and patriotic mien, it seems to me, are more consistent with the marrano gestalt than the morisco one. Cervantes no doubt knew this and perhaps was heightening the ironic effect of the Ricote episode by endowing a morisco with the instantly recognizable split personality and divided family of the marrano.

We can identify a number of cultural-commuting marranos. João Batista was born a Christian in Lisbon, circumcised in Flanders, and a Jew in Salonika; once baptized in Rome he returned to Portugal, then went to Safed where he was a Jew and briefly a Muslim, and finally ended his life as a Christian in Venice.[29] Enrique Nunes (known as Righetto Marrano) was another Portuguese New Christian who lived as a Christian in Florence and a Jew in Venice.[30] The novelist Antonio Enriquez Gomez was a Catholic in Madrid, identified with the Jewish community in Bordeaux and Rouen, and then returned to Seville where he lived as a Catholic under an assumed name and witnessed his own burning, in effigy.[31] The writer Miguel de Barrios was born in Montilla, circumcised in Livorno, and lived as a Jew in Amsterdam, with an interlude in Brussels, where he held a commission in the Spanish army and must have passed as a Catholic.[32] Captain Estevan de Ares de Fonseca, recounted in a declaration to the Inquisition in 1635 that he was born in Coimbra (a New Christian), was arrested by the

Inquisition to which he confessed his condition (to save his life, he said), went to Bordeaux and then to Amsterdam where he was circumcised, and then continued on to the East—Livorno, Venice, and Salonika where he displayed an openly Jewish identity. He subsequently went to Rouen and became a Catholic.[33]

In order to appreciate what such persons represent from a cultural or ethnic perspective, it is necessary to bracket the issue of faith, to take with a grain of salt self-serving declarations made by themselves or by others about them, and to look at their public persons and their behavior. It is clear that it was a widespread marrano mode to be ambivalent about ethnic identity. The type was recognized contemporaneously with pungent and very accurate descriptions: "halters between two opinions" (Isaac Aramah), or metaphorically as ships "with two rudders," or, as a priest described Gaspar Ribeiro as "neither Christian, nor Jew, nor Turk."[34] The mimetism of marranos, the ease with which they glided in and out of ethnic identities, was apparent to observers: "Portuguese of this type (marranos in Italy) are neither Christians nor Jews nor Moors . . . and when they go to the synagogue they carry a book of offices in the Christian style in the Portuguese language. They are hated by the other Jews because they bear nothing but the headgear of the Jews."[35]

Some historians have drawn conclusions about cultural commuting that accord well with what an anthropologist might say about it. Thus Pullan says of marranos in Italy,

> Some may well have regarded Christianity and Judaism, not as mutually exclusive faiths making total claims, but rather as equally valid systems of devotional practice, depending more upon ritual and upon dietary laws than upon inner conviction: as habits which one followed for the sake of profit, self-preservation or even pleasure.

Or Kaplan's observation that some marranos in seventeenth century London "preferred to persist in the habits which they had acquired as conversos and to preserve their Christian image, since, for them, Judaism was a matter solely of their inner identity."[36]

What I want to stress here is the normative nature of such behavior, which really just amounts to multiple role playing. It is so striking in both Christian and the Islamic worlds of the early modern period because it was anomalous (and very risky). But historians should recognize it for what it was. Essentialist definitions of ethnic identity are conducive ultimately to ideologized and misleading conceptions of true and false identities. Ethnicity is a collection of traits, traditions, values, and symbols that situate a group with respect to its ancestors and to other ethnic groups, and a single individual can easily partake of or draw upon more than one such collection. Thus F. K. Lehman concludes, with regard to the Karen:

> The whole business of insisting that there must be an objectively unique definition for a true ethnic category is vain. It is grounded in the romanticist tradition of associating a cultural inventory with something vaguely and mystically thought of as a unique historical experience, properly attached to racelike populations.[37]

The point is important because the notion of "true Jew"/"false Jew" turns up too often in the historiography of crypto-Jews. It is legitimate to specify the "core" identity of a carefully defined group but not to posit a "true" or "false" one. The identity of the cultural commuter is a real identity and we should validate it as such.

The marranos further illustrate a general point about the ambivalence of persons caught up in ethnic change. "In interethnic systems where, by mutual agreement as well as objectively, the parties are of unequal status and have very unequal access to mutually desired economic resources . . . ambivalence seems to be a function of the very fact of ethnic distinctiveness." You want what others have, but deny yourself getting it by stressing your identity.[38] This is the basis of the psychology of cultural commuters who are but extreme examples of normal social ambivalence. The commuter, by alternating between identities, satisfies in turn these two conflicting objectives. Commuting is a way of dealing with or acting out ambivalence.

A related aspect of the marranos' ethnicity is their tendency to constitute themselves as something approximating a closed caste within a general Jewish ethnic bloc. By closed caste, I mean an endogamous group for which both in-marriage and out-marriage are discouraged and highly controlled. Kaplan makes a case for the Spanish Catholic origin of this principle of self-segregation, which was given body in the course of the marranos' attempt to "redefine their identity."[39] (It is useful to recall that Américo Castro was excoriated for making a similar, but reverse case, that limpieza de sangre had Judaic roots. This is not as controversial an idea as it may first appear. Such ideas equating ethnicity with race were quite generalized: what is striking in both cases is their institutional forms.) The Amsterdam community (which Kaplan calls a "boundary-building" community) had precisely crafted rules regulating in-marriage (marry a nonmarrano and you and your children are barred from the congregation). The 'edot (culturally distinct subgroups within the Jewish community, for example Ashkenazim and Sephardim) had distinctive identities elsewhere, as in Italy, but the lines between them were not as sharply drawn, and considerable intercaste mobility was countenanced.[40]

With regard to language, I wish only to make a few brief observations. The first is that Cecil Roth's inventive comments on the sacralization of the Spanish language by marranos ought to be pursued. Roth observed that Portuguese marranos, even those who normally wrote in Portuguese, preferred Spanish as a liturgical language, "the semi-sacred tongue, the vernacular of the great mass of the Sephardi world, the language of its teachers and of its preachers." Thus the marrano diaspora was distinguished by the use of three communal languages: "Hebrew, the medium of prayer; Spanish, the medium of religious instruction and religious life; and Portuguese, the medium, one might say, of convenience."[41] Second, because of the deluge of studies of Ladino as a popular language (for example, the Ladino *romancero*), there has been virtually no investigation of the impact of Spanish high culture on the *Hebrew* culture of Sephardim. I mention only Dan Pagis's wonderful discovery of a line of a sonnet by Gongora translated and stuck into a Hebrew poem in seventeenth- (or perhaps eighteenth-) century Holland.[42] Finally I might cite the doubts recently expressed by Eleazar Gutwirth concerning the standard supposition of the virtual isolation of Ladino from normative Spanish.[43]

Coming to grips with marrano culture and society has produced a marvelous historical literature, the source of whose passion and dynamism is the social and psychological dilemma of the marranos themselves. The issue of the authenticity of the marranos' faith has undergone a serious reappraisal in the past decade, and the marrano dilemma, which seemed to have been a source of such anguish, if not embarrassment, for Jewish writers, has been cast in a different light. Yovel, I believe, has done as well as anyone in locating the existential dilemma of the marrano in his own society and in historical perspective. "He does not belong to any cultural context simply or naturally and feels both inside and outside any one of them."[44] This indeed is the psychological basis for the marrano variety of cultural commuting that I have been discussing. But, for Yovel, this is also the source of marrano creativity, because insofar as they could not accommodate to traditional cultural *or* ethnic structures marranos were harbingers and precursors of modernity. Indeed, that is an epitaph to celebrate in this quincentennial year.

PART III

Iberian Jewry: The Expulsions

5

▦

Order of the Expulsion from Spain: Antecedents, Causes, and Textual Analysis

Haim Beinart

The order of the expulsion of the Jews from Spain, signed on March 31, proclaimed on May 1, and carried out on July 31, 1492, ended a period of about fifteen hundred years of Jewish life in Spain. How did it come about that a millennia and a half of mutual interaction between Jews and non-Jews came to such an abrupt end? What were the reasons for the harsh treatment meted out to Spanish Jewry by the Catholic monarchs, Ferdinand and Isabella? From the Jewish perspective one wonders whether the Jews had any idea of the fate awaiting them! Once this fate became public knowledge, how did Spanish Jewry react? To answer these questions we must turn back the pages of history to the end of the fourteenth century.

In the year 1391 a great calamity befell Spanish Jewry. Anti-Jewish riots spread all over the country and reached most communities of both Castile and Aragon-Catalonia. Like a forest fire, the riots consumed and exterminated many communities. Soldiers, sailors, city dwellers, peasants, lower nobles and some of high status, officials and rabble alike went from place to place with the sole aim of destroying Jewry. The few communities that survived the riots were located primarily in those cities where the king, queen, infantes, and nobles were present to ward off the danger or where Jewish leaders like R. Hisdai Crescas managed to hire troops to protect the communities or where the Jews found refuge in a local castle, for example, in Perpignan. In summary, about a third of the Jewish population perished sanctifying God's name, another third survived as Jews, and the remaining third converted. Thus was created a new reality: Jews only yesterday became Christians overnight, severed from their Jewish past during a moment of weakness that they later came to regret.[1]

This was not, however, the only blow to Spanish Jewry. During the fifteenth century Jewish society confronted important renegades sent out to exterminate Judaism. In this context one should mention the former rabbi of Burgos, Shelomo Halevi, who, after his conversion shortly before the 1391 riots, became Pablo de Santa María. His conversion was perceived as a great victory over Judaism, and after studying in Paris he was appointed bishop of his hometown, Burgos. Another apostate was a physician from Alcañiz (a small town in Aragon) named Yehoshua Halorki who became a notorious persecutor of his brethren under the name Jerónimo de Santa Fe. They were greatly aided by the friar Vicente Ferrer, perhaps one of the greatest mendicant preachers of all time, who could move enormous crowds to tears or raise them to ecstasy.

On October 25, 1408, a law was passed in Castile forbidding Jews to act as tax farmers or to hold any other official positions that involved jurisdiction over Christians. This law based itself (especially regarding the jurisdiction) on the *Siete Partidas* (VII 24,3), which forbade Jews from having any authority over Christians on the grounds that this constituted a disservice (*deservicio*) to (Christ the) God. Religious grounds were often the basis for an internal anti-Jewish policy aimed at exerting social and economic pressure on the Jews. Considering that the tax farmers and tax collectors who ensured the constant flow of capital to the royal coffers were primarily Jewish, the law in effect obstructed good government. Perhaps it was felt that converso tax farmers and tax collectors would replace the Jewish ones, but such a solution was merely a palliative. Only at the end of the century, shortly before the expulsion, did the rulers of Spain try to find a solution to this problem. Matters did not stop here. During the minority of King Juan II, Pablo de Santa María rose to become the chancellor of Castile and the major force behind the 1412 Valladolid Laws, which were designed to exert economic and social pressure upon the Jewish population in the hope of creating another wave of conversions.

At the instigation of Vicente Ferrer, Jews in many towns were forced in 1412 to leave their living quarters. This friar was clearly concerned about Jewish influence on conversos and in addition hoped to apply added pressure on Jews to convert. Nevertheless, the 1412 laws could not be observed. Jewish physicians, for example, were prohibited from treating Christian patients or from selling medicines or foodstuff to them. Any Christian who valued his health had a private Jewish physician. Other proposed measures would have produced similar difficulties. Thus, the laws were repealed.

In Aragon another type of pressure was exerted, in the hope that its repercussions would reach Castile. A disputation was arranged between Jerónimo de Santa Fe, defending Christianity, and twelve famous rabbis of Aragon, representing Jewry. The person who stood behind this was the Antipope Benedict XIII. For about eighteen months in 1413 and 1414 these Jewish personalities occupied Tortosa as well as the small town of Peñiscola, far away from their homes, and were subjected to insult and abuse. This dispute dealt a severe blow to the Jewish population, and many Jews converted out of despair. With the help of his apostate henchman, Benedict hoped in this way to bring an end to Spanish Jewry and thus ingratiate himself with the Christian world. A ship in the port of Valencia stood ready to sail for Majorca in order to summon Vicente Ferrer and give him the honor of baptizing Spanish Jewry. It seemed as if the end had come. Fortunately, the Council of Cardinals in Konstanz deposed the Antipope Benedict and the plan never materialized. Spanish Jewry for its part mustered its own inner forces and successfully withstood these pressures.

Jewish leaders analyzed the situation to try to find the causes for the crises in Jewish society. If conversion was the result of momentary weakness, were not inner factors of religious, social, and intellectual disintegration really at fault? Rabbis and scholars pointed an accusing finger at the study of philosophy by people who lacked inner fortitude, while other Jews denounced the imitation of Christian customs and ways of life. All called for the return to a truly Jewish way of life. The desire for survival was great enough during the fifteenth century to allow the reconstruction of Jewish life in Spain, although clearly things were not the same as they had been before.

Two communities, both of Jewish origin, continued to live side by side: one remained faithful to the religion of its ancestors; the other was a Jewish community that had converted and then resented its deed as one of weakness. Church and government were aware of the situation and, in addition, many conversos whose families or relatives remained Jewish returned to Judaism. Already in the 1390s orders were given to separate Jews from Christians, the term *Christians* in this context referring to those recently converted. This order was not carried out, and it remained a problem that Catholic monarchs dealt with only in the 1480s. We shall return to this later on.

Jews and conversos not only shared common ground in living quarters,[2] they also held common messianic expectations and hopes for redemption. Conversos were accepted in synagogues for prayers; Jews would eat at converso tables and accept the meat they slaughtered. That Jews visited converso houses was thus proof that conversos were leading a Jewish life; in this manner the converso's esteem rose in the eyes of his brethren. Conversos contributed oil and money to Jewish synagogues and to the needy on Mondays and Fridays. Jews kept conversos informed of the dates of holidays and taught them the mitzvot. These examples illustrate only a few aspects of the meeting ground between Jews and their former brethren. All this was common knowledge, and it would later serve as the main reason for the expulsion of the Jews from Spain. This was not as yet publicly argued during the fifteenth century, however, and we may safely conclude that Jews and conversos were indeed one people, united in their way of life.

Turning to the efforts of the Jewish leadership to restore the Jewish communal organization to its full force and functions, we must bear in mind that Jewish life in the Kingdom of Aragon during the fifteenth century dwindled to small communities, and, except for Saragossa, more communities were in Valencia (a kingdom within the Crown of Aragon). The riots of 1391 put an end to the renowned community of Barcelona. When it was suggested that the community be renewed, the townspeople and municipality put up such strong resistance that the project was abandoned. In 1394 150 Portuguese Jewish families settled in Majorca after being guaranteed many privileges. However, this community, too, came under pressure, and in 1435 it ceased to exist, as its remaining members converted to Christianity.

The Jewish hegemony passed to Castile. In the 1430s the famous Rab de la Corte Abraham Bienveniste of Soria summoned to Valladolid the representatives of the Castilian Jewish communities to decide what measures should be taken to renew Jewish life. A unique document of ordinances has survived; written partly in Hebrew and partly in Spanish, it is probably one of the earliest Judeo-Spanish documents to be written in Hebrew letters.[3] But the Jewish communities were weak and could not restore Jewish life in its old form.

The Jewish population of Spain nourished great expectations with the coronation of Ferdinand and Isabella in Castile in 1474, an event that followed years of unrest, especially during the reign of Isabella's brother Enrique IV (1454–1471). Their ascent to the throne was fraught with problems, as nobles revolted against them and tried to arrange a marriage between the daughter of Enrique (Juana, known as "la Beltraneja") with Alfonso V of Portugal, in an attempt to unite Castile and Portugal. The uprising lasted well into 1475, and many conversos and Jews of La Mancha joined the rebels. Had this rebellion succeeded, history might have witnessed a reunification of Castile and Portugal over a century earlier than it actually occurred. When, in 1580, during the reign of Felipe II that reunification took place, it lasted until 1640. With the rebellion crushed, the Catholic monarchs settled down to consolidate their power.

When, in the process of Ferdinand and Isabella's gaining power and establishing their internal policy, one asks, was it decided to expel the Jews from Spain? The concept of total expulsion was certainly not new. It was raised back in the 1330s, when the Moroccans invaded Gibraltar seeking to recover the Iberian peninsula for Islam. Suspicions were voiced that the Jews would betray the country to the Muslim invaders, as they were said to have done in 711. Castilian Jewry, which in the thirteenth century had been settled as a colonizing element along the southern frontier as part of the reconquista of Castile and Aragon, was now regarded with distrust and deep suspicion. In any case, the Moroccans were defeated and the danger passed.

The idea of the total expulsion of the Jews was again raised by Alonso de Espina, a Franciscan monk of the Observantine faction in his treatise *Fortalitium Fidei* (Fortress of Faith). In addition to its local significance, this work became a handbook for anti-Jewish propaganda throughout Europe and was one of the books printed in Nuremberg in 1485, in Lyons later on, and so on. It was a book written against Jews, conversos, and Moors alike. Alonso de Espina suggested that the expulsion of all the Jews from England in 1290 should serve as a model for

Spain. By this he meant that if England had succeeded without Jews for close to two centuries, Spain could also live without them. In his opinion they were responsible for the alienation of the conversos from Spanish society as well as for all the other evils present in Spain. Tomás de Torquemada would later become the major executor of this idea, as we shall see.

In the meantime the Catholic monarchs, whose agreement to rule was based on the maxim *Tanto monta—monta tanto* (As much as one mounts [the throne], so does the other one), had more pressing matters to deal with: they had to subdue the rebellion against them. Had Alfonso of Portugal been victorious, it would have brought decided change to Iberian geopolitics. The Catholic monarchs managed to win over many nobles and towns that were organized into a brotherhood called Santa Hermandad, and, with the assistance of a strong group of clergymen, they carried the day.[4] Consolidation of power required the creation of a united monarchy in Castile and Aragon, and steps toward this goal were undertaken immediately. This meant, in fact, the establishment of a unified Christian state delineated by national borders and united internally. The policy of Ferdinand and Isabella could be characterized in the latter-day slogan of Carlos V: "Unum ovile et unus pastor," or "una grey y un pastor solo en suelo," in other words, "Un monarca, un Imperio y una espada"(One flock and one shepherd, one monarch, one empire, and one sword).

Several obstacles on the path to national and religious consolidation had thus to be removed, and the effort to do so accounts for the treatment of the conversos who were returning to Judaism, the war with Muslim Granada, and the expulsion of the Jews from Spain. The goal of national unification called for an elaborate plan of action. First, those circles that sympathized and collaborated with the crown had to be reinforced. These groups bore many grudges against the Jews and, at the Cortes (Parliament) convened in Madrigal in 1476, the Catholic monarchs made some initial concessions to them. Jewish communities in Castile were no longer allowed to try cases involving criminal offenses or to exact penalties of capital or certain corporal punishments. The first steps were then taken to force Jews to leave their residential areas. This was officially proclaimed on March 15, 1480, in the Cortes that met in Toledo. In addition, there was a renewal of the order that Jews wear a distinguishing red badge on the back and left shoulder of their outer garments. Strict orders were given, in many cases endangering Jewish travelers and exposing them to robbers and extortionists.[5]

Separation of residential areas carried with it the disordering of daily life. Two years were allowed for the Jewish population to leave its former neighborhoods. The Spanish municipalities had no choice but to take this order seriously, as its implementation required that new quarters be found for the Jews. To this end, special emissaries were appointed by the Council of the State and sent out to various towns to supervise the relocation. Documents depict the problems, litigation, and quarrels that persisted into the early 1490s. Indeed, real separation between Jews and Christians or, more correctly, between Jews and conversos was not effected until the expulsion of the entire community from Spain in 1492.[6]

The extant documents available on this separation reveal the full intent of this order. More than separation, the goal was to make life for the Jews intolerable. New quarters were located in the worst parts of town (in Segovia, for example, in the red-light district), far away from the town center, where the Jews usually had their stores and workshops. As they were forbidden to trade and work in the old location and were prohibited from preparing their meals or sleeping there, Jews found that they could not eke out a living. Houses had to be exchanged and were to be assessed by specially appointed officials. Thus, the value of a house vacated by a Jew was always less than the new one he was to enter. Of course, the Jew had to pay the difference. If he was incapable of doing so, the community had to provide the difference, with the result that the community became part owner of the house. The rulers did not think of creating conditions for new rent-lease arrangements. If the community lacked enough funds, the government permitted it to raise the existing tax on kosher meat and wine. Here another factor worked against the Jewish community: the rise in the cost of living. In many places new houses had to be constructed in small streets; quarters required the construction of items for purposes of defense, like walling and the opening of new gates, which according to rule and custom were closed at night. Not all the Jews grasped the significance of the decision to locate them in separate quarters. In some places they tried to reside outside the new quarters, in hopes that the government would not take any measures against them. But they were wrong. The local population, incited by anti-Jewish propaganda, complained to the Crown, which responded immediately.

What part was played by Tomás de Torquemada in this policy? He headed a group of extremists in the Spanish church that demanded strong measures against Jews and conversos alike.[7] Fanatically devoted to his objectives and endowed with extraordinary administrative talents, he became in 1482 the inquisitor-general of the Spanish national Inquisition. He was the person who pushed its establishment, having inherited the idea from Alonso de Espina, as noted above. In 1478 Pope Sixtus IV sanctioned its creation on the condition that Granada, the last stronghold of Islam in Europe, be conquered and Christian soil be purged of the infidel. The Inquisition began functioning in Seville on January 1, 1481, and thousands of Judaizing conversos were tried.

Another step against Spanish Jewry was initiated in 1483, an attempt to learn and accumulate experience for future action. The Inquisition ordered the expulsion of the Jews from all of Andalusia.[8] Although this order of expulsion is no longer extant, the edict of expulsion from Spain in 1492 testifies to its promulgation. The evidence regarding the order is more than sufficient. One month's time was given to the Jews of places like Seville, Córdoba, Jerez de la Frontera, and Ubeda to liquidate their business, sell their property, and leave; the order did not mention where the expelled were to go. Many joined relatives living in various places in Old and New Castile, others went to communities in Extremadura. The reason given for this regional expulsion was the bad influence Jews were exerting on conversos, thereby impeding their integration into established Christian society. The Jews had to leave in haste, with Dominican monks supervising and the mob hurrying the refugees on. Property values fell, as was to happen again during the 1492 expulsion. This time, however, Christian society itself was not yet ready for such a great change. Jews would continue to return to their original habitat for years, having been granted permission by the authorities to go back to their former dwelling places to oversee and liquidate what they left behind. This expulsion served as an incentive for the local authorities as well. In 1486 the town of Valmaseda in Vizcaya ordered the Jews living there to leave. Here the Jewish population, and especially Abraham Senior, appealed for help to the Crown and to the constable of Castile, Pedro Fernández de Velasco, the count of Haro, on whose land the town stood. Abraham Senior wrote personally to the constable, pleading that the Jews had nowhere else to go as did their brethren from Andalusia.[9] The Crown ordered their return, but the Jews who had left came to certain agreements with the local authorities with regard to their property. In the same year Torquemada personally ordered the expulsion of the Jews from Teruel, Saragossa, and neighboring Albarracin.[10] Ferdinand himself intervened in this instance, asking Torquemada to postpone the order for half a year. The inquisitor conceded, probably on some sort of quid pro quo basis. Local authorities took the law into their own hands vis-à-vis the Jews. Nevertheless, few Jewish leaders showed any premonition of the approaching danger. One of them, however, R. Yehudah Ibn Verga, expressed his foreboding with a symbolic act; he placed three pairs of doves on the windowsill and said:

> One plucked and slaughtered, and a note around their neck: These will be the last to leave (meaning those who will remain in Spain will be plucked of their property and slaughtered). The other pair plucked but not slaughtered, and they will be those of the middle (i.e., those who will not hurry to leave will only save their lives, but their property will be lost). The third pair alive and full in their feathers, their note said: they will be the first (to leave; they will save themselves and their property).[11]

Jewish historiography of that period expressed the view that it was Isabella who was influenced by Torquemada to take anti-Jewish measures, whereas Ferdinand was a moderate ruler who only yielded to his wife's demands.

The historian G. A. Bergenroth published the correspondence between Ferdinand and Isabella, which he discovered in the State Archive in Simancas.[12] This correspondence is of great significance, as it shows that Isabella was to act as a spokesperson on behalf of the Crown. In her opinion, the good of the kingdom and the good of Christianity were identical. Her zeal for her faith and state brought her to identify her own interests with those of Christ, whose name was never absent from her statements. We are inclined to conclude that her mode of thought and behavior was molded by the clerics who formed her inner circle of confidants, in particular, Tomás de Torquemada and Hernando de Talavera; they brought their influence to bear on the policies of the Crown. Their convictions became hers; their way, her way.

Isabella's beliefs were in full agreement with Ferdinand's regarding state and religion. Thus, plans and policy were mutually agreed on. The public roles played by the monarchs were determined by the tactics to be used in a given situation. Their ideas of unifying Spain were already crystallized well before either of them ascended to the throne; it would therefore be a historical error to see in their internal politics (which is what concerns us now) an improvisation or a reaction to changing circumstances. The Catholic monarchs knew exactly what conditions prevailed in their kingdoms and together they formulated plans for solving the problems they confronted, taking into consideration who would carry out their designs, the means that would be used, and the price the state would have to pay for their fulfillment. In this they were assisted by a loyal group of followers. They had to deal with the social and religious burden that had been passed on by the preceding monarchs.

The expulsion of the Jews was the historical outcome of this development. In the eyes of a contemporary observer this meant the uprooting of an entire population, one that had resided in Spain for as long as Christianity had been in existence. The Spanish Crown could not have attempted such a drastic action at the end of the fifteenth century unless it had laid out detailed plans in advance and had already assured itself of the support of the public. Initially, therefore, only limited measures were undertaken, on the grounds that the Jewish presence in Spain prevented the integration of conversos into Christian society. The argument had yet to gain wide acceptance: the responsibility for the failure of Spanish society to absorb the conversos was shifted onto the shoulders of Spanish Jewry. The Inquisition set out to establish this claim, and the edict of expulsion leaves no doubt as to the Inquisition's success in doing so.

Already at the beginning of their unified rule, and concomitantly with the formulation of their plans for the converso and Jewish communities, the Catholic monarchs started to prepare for the war against the Muslims of Granada. A special war tax that was increased annually was imposed on the Jewish communities. This, of course, should not be taken to mean that their expulsion was not premeditated. As long as Jews lived in Castile, they were expected to assume their share of the war costs. It was a very heavy burden on the Jewish population; it was imposed year after year until victory over the Muslims in Granada was final.[13]

In order to carry out the plans for the expulsion of the Jewish population, public antagonism against the Jews had to be fanned. Late in the 1480s many anti-Jewish pamphlets were circulated. In one pamphlet written by Ferdinand de Santo Domingo, one of Torquemada's henchmen, Torquemada was compared to Jeremiah the prophet whose mission was "to root out and pull down and destroy and to overthrow; to build and to plant" (Jeremiah 1:10). In another pamphlet, "Libro del Alboraique," named after the supernatural steed of Mohammed, the Jews were likened to that treacherous animal. This was not the end of it, however. In 1490 the Inquisition initiated proceedings against a group of Jews and itinerant conversos (as it clearly had no jurisdiction over Jews by themselves), charging that they had used black magic and the heart of a Christian child whose body was never found to plot the destruction of the Inquisition and all Christendom. The trial has become associated with the name of the supposed victim, El Santo Niño de la Guardia (the Holy Child from La Guardia, a village near Toledo). The proceedings were transferred from Segovia to Ávila, where Torquemada was at the time building the Dominican monastery (in which he would later be buried), so that he could personally supervise the trial.[14] It lasted well into 1491 and ended with the defendants condemned to the stake.

Torquemada was well aware that steps had to be taken to prepare the Crown and the populace for the expulsion of the Jews and for the loss of the services they had rendered to the Crown. In a memorandum to the queen dated not later than 1490 and entitled "Las cosas que por agora estan occurriendo que vuestra Altesa debe remediar por cartas," he proposed, in addition to other lesser measures, prohibiting the Jews from serving as tax farmers and tax collectors. We must bear in mind that the Jews were responsible for keeping up a constant flow of money to the treasury. Their sudden expulsion would mean financial ruin to the Crown. This advice was heeded, and, on December 10, 1491, while expecting their entry in Granada, the Crown responded with a detailed order forbidding most Jews to farm taxes in Christian localities; a small number of the greatest tax farmers were permitted to continue in that capacity: Abraham Senior and Yosef Abravanel (Don Isaac's son-in-law) in Plasencia. David Ibn Alfahar, however, was forbidden to continue farming taxes.

After eight years of siege, the battle for Granada was nearing its end. On January 6, 1492, the Catholic monarchs entered the city in a solemn procession: Europe was at last purged of Muslim rule. The next step in the program was soon to follow. On March 31, 1492, Ferdinand and Isabella signed the "Edict of the expulsion of the Jews from Spain, and all kingdoms, sovereignties and holdings." By May 1, a month after the signing of the edict, it had been proclaimed throughout Spain.[15] We do not know the reasons for this delay. Jewish historiography recollects that persons like Isaac Abrabanel and Abraham Senior most likely acted on behalf of the Jews, with Torquemada their primary adversary. Although we are not sure of those facts we do know for certain that Alfonso de la Caballería of Saragossa did intervene, but to no avail.[16] It is well known who prevailed. Legend has it that Torquemada overheard a meeting between the Jewish emissaries and King Ferdinand at which thirty thousand gold dinars were offered for the revocation of the edict. In great indignation, Torquemada entered and laid a crucifix on the table, declaring that once before Christ had been sold for thirty pieces. Though it is a legend, the story provides insight into the atmosphere that prevailed at the time and reflects Torquemada's power and involvement in the affairs of state.

In addition to the order of expulsion, detailed instructions were issued as to how the edict was to be promulgated in public and the expulsion carried out. The document, sent to Saragossa, orders that the contents of the order of expulsion were to be kept strictly secret and carried out to the letter after being read by the town's herald.[17] The Inquisition was ordered to supervise all stages of the expulsion in the Kingdom of Aragon. In Castile it was the task of corregidores and specially appointed emissaries. As to the order of expulsion itself, only a few copies have survived. For Castile we have those promulgated in Ávila, Burgos, and Toledo;[18] for Aragon, only the general order.[19]

Based on a comparison of the extant copies of the edict, it seems that the copy from Ávila is the original, the actual text that was read aloud and promulgated in that town. Those of Burgos and Toledo are approved copies. The three differ only slightly in some of the wording but not in terms of the context of the order itself. They are signed: "Yo el Rey"; "Yo la Reyna." The signature of the notary-secretary who prepared the order and is considered responsible for the document is found at the bottom of the document. The man, Juan de Coloma, was with the king and queen in Granada, where the order was signed.

A few prosopographical notes about the secretary may help clarify certain points about the chancellery of the Catholic monarchs.[20] Born in Borja (Aragon) of humble origins, he rose to become the trusted secretary of King Juan II of Aragon (Ferdinand's father), whom he

served for about eighteen years (1462–1479). With the fullest con-
fidence of his master and king, he signed all the documents during
the years Juan was totally blind. Appointed secretary by Ferdinand
after Juan's death, he was thrown out of office and imprisoned after
being denounced, probably unjustly. Restored to office in the spring of
1489, he was a confidential secretary of the king and thus responsible
for preparing many documents by order of royalty, countersigning
them with the formula: "Yo Johan de Coloma, secretario del Rey e
de la Reyna, nuestros señores la fize escreuir par su mandado"—
Rubrica.[21]

Juan de Coloma must have been the person who wrote and edited
the order of expulsion; that is, he is the one responsible for its contents,
while errors of letters or omissions of letters or words are to be attributed to the scribes or copyists of the chancellery.[22] He is also the person
responsible for the order of expulsion from the Kingdom of Aragon,
which differed in certain points from the order issued in Castile.
However, King Ferdinand is the only person named as signatory of the
order prepared for Aragon, with Juan de Coloma as countersignatory.[23]
A thorough analysis of the expulsion orders leaves one with the impression that the text extant for Aragon was perhaps one of the draft copies
prepared under the supervision of Torquemada himself, or of one of his
henchmen, Juan de Revenga, his faithful secretary. The length of the
edict may perhaps prove that such a document could not have been
published before it was read and reread and being finally approved for
publication.[24]

There is no doubt that when the order of expulsion was read by the
city criers all the titles of royalty were announced, so that the *Intitulatio*
is to be considered as the legal opening of this instrument. Added to this
are the names of those to whom the document was addressed, according
to the official hierarchy of the kingdom. To them were added all the Jews
and Jewesses of any standing, young and old. With this the protocol of
the instrument is concluded. The reasons for the expulsion are found in
a detailed description in the *Arenga*.[25] They affirm the measures taken by
Church, royalty, and society to cut off the conversos from their Jewish
brethren and the latters' influence upon them to get them to return to
the fold of their ancestors. The conclusion: the only way to save
Christian society from Jewish influence was to expel *all* Jews from the
kingdoms. Thus is the guilt of being expelled laid on the shoulders of

Spanish Jewry. It was a decision arrived at after deliberation and with the concurrence of church dignitaries, the upper and lower nobility, and persons of science and conscience.

How was the guilt of Spanish Jewry established? As early as 1484 Ferdinand had commanded the Jewish communities to order, under the threat of the ban, any Jew who knew of conversos keeping mitzvot to appear as a witness before the courts of the Inquisition. Although many disobeyed, we have found many inquisitional files in which Jews testified against conversos who prayed with them, gave them alms for the Jewish poor, were circumcised by them, and so on. The Inquisition was the source for information of this kind.[26] Thus, religious motives were the only reasons given, and there is no apparent economic basis for the expulsion. Indeed, the contrary is the case. The loss of the Jewish population resulted in grave economic repercussions for the towns and villages. Entire economic entities ceased functioning, and there was nobody to take over the social and economic functions that had been dominated by Jews for hundreds of years.

The edict dealt in detail with the orderly departure of the Jews from Spain. Perhaps those who initiated the order presumed that the Jews would convert and not leave after all. The Jews, however, perceived the order itself as a second exodus and as the beginning of the messianic redemption; they expected a repetition of the miracles of earlier days. For their part, the authorities tried to prevent the Jews from leaving: in many places monks and clergy went door to door trying to convince Jews to convert. Town mayors pleaded with Jews to stay behind, as otherwise their towns would perish. The population tried to profit from the order, however. Debtors stopped repaying their creditors, while Jews had to repay their debts. Jewish properties were seized, and the authorities had to intervene, appointing judges and arbiters to straighten out many demands. It was forbidden to take out gold, silver, or valuables. As the date of departure approached, real estate values dropped and a parcel of land or a house would be exchanged for a mule or any other means of transport. And smuggling of valuables, especially to Portugal, became common practice.

As for Jewish communal property—synagogues, hostels, schools, *mikva'ot* (ritual baths), and cemeteries were taken over by local authorities or sequestered by the Crown. As late as 1499 Ferdinand ordered the transfer of those properties to the Crown.

On July 31, 1492, the seventh of Av 5242 according to the Jewish calendar, the last Jews left Spanish soil. Because the date of the expulsion fell so close to the ninth of Av, Jewish tradition added it to the two great disasters of the Jewish people: the burning of the First and Second Temples. A chronicler of those days, Andrés Bernáldez, wrote with astonishment about the Jews on their way to their unknown destiny accompanied by tambourines and song.

Shortly after the expulsion chroniclers wondered how many had actually left Spain. If the answer was problematic in those days, it certainly remains so today. We have some information on the basis of which a rough estimate of the numbers can be made. The majority of Spanish Jewry was concentrated in Castile, with Castilian Jews (not conversos) thought to have numbered between 120,000 and 150,000 persons; Aragonese Jewry is estimated to have been about 50,000. Thus the total Spanish Jewish population was about 200,000 souls. We can reach this same number by calculating the numbers of Jewish communities in Castile and what they paid annually for about ten years in tribute for the war against Granada.[27] These numbers accord more or less with the population figures given at the time of the expulsion.

There is also data to be gleaned from the information available about Jews who crossed the border into Portugal. Portugal granted permission for a stay of about six months to each person who paid eight cruzeiros. Thus, most of the expelled—some 120,000 people—entered Portugal. They crossed the border towns: Badajoz in the south, Ciudad Rodrigo and Zamora in the north; and they settled temporarily not far from the Spanish border. Other smaller groups went to the Kingdom of Navarre, only to suffer expulsion again, in 1498.[28] What befell those who sought refuge in Portugal, were expelled from there in 1496, and then forcibly converted in 1497 forms a separate chapter in Jewish sufferings. A convoy of twenty-five ships, headed by Pedro Cabrón, left Cádiz for Oran in Algiers; their passengers were afraid to disembark, however, even though the Genovese corsair Fragon promised them safety, and they returned to Arcila in North Africa. Storms at sea forced the ships to seek refuge in Cartagena and Málaga, and when a plague broke out on the ships many died, while others, out of despair, converted. Those who reached Arcila stayed until 1493 and then went eastward to the Ottoman Empire, which opened its gates to these refugees. They were joined by Jews who left Portugal: about seven hundred families who

paid a high tribute and were permitted to settle in Morocco. It is estimated that fifty thousand persons set out toward North Africa and the
East. The odyssey of these unfortunate persons is an incomparable
tragedy in world history. Ships' captains extorted whatever could be
taken from them, leaving many of the refugees in deserted and abandoned localities without food and shelter. Little by little they made
their way to Italy and to the Balkans, the last having just been conquered by Turkey. The guaranteed safe passage by land and by sea was
often abused by those responsible for their safe conduct. Two persons of
Jewish ancestry, Luis de Santángel and Francisco Pinelo, intervened on
behalf of the expelled.[29] The Holy Land was also a major destination.
Sephardi communities were founded in time in Jerusalem and especially in Safed and Tiberias, where they came to play a very important role in subsequent centuries. Thus a diaspora was created: the
Sephardic Diaspora, or dispersion, which was later to settle in new areas
and reach considerable dimensions. Expelled Spanish Jewry opened
new pages in Jewish history.[30]

6

▦

Expulsion or Integration?
The Portuguese Jewish Problem

Maria José Pimenta Ferro Tavares

The Jewish question in Portugal toward the end of the fifteenth century cannot be separated from that of the rest of the Iberian peninsula, though the way the Portuguese authorities treated it would be different from the approach taken by the Spanish Catholic monarchs Ferdinand and Isabella. To begin with, unlike Spain, Portugal did not have the problem of forced conversions due to popular risings against the Jews, nor did it have to face the consequences of social and religious instability due to the presence of a large group of converts and their descendants.

This does not mean that in the medieval period no conversions had taken place in Portugal. Individuals had converted; some had joined religious orders, other were integrated through marriage into Christian families. Nevertheless, because the number of converts was so small we can conclude that these conversions were sincere and the integration of the converts and their descendants into Christian society was complete.

The problem began with the arrival in Portugal of Spanish conversos, first toward the end of the fourteenth century and later in the last two decades of the fifteenth. Many of these settlers took on Christian names, but they continued to maintain relations with Judaism and Jewish families. That was likely the situation with João Gonçalves, son of Abraham Lourebe, who lived in Silves; his is the only case I know of someone being condemned to death and having his property confiscated by the Crown for the heresy of Judaizing.[1] He was condemned by the ecclesiastical court presided over by the bishop, since there was as yet no Inquisition in Portugal.

Toward the end of the fifteenth century, however, the conjunction of social and religious factors changed. Beginning in the 1480s Spanish conversos, frightened by the establishment of the Spanish Inquisition, fled to Portugal, carrying with them the general stigma of being false Christians.

At first only suspicious of the conversos, the Portuguese Christians came to believe quite firmly that these were heretics, and there was agitation for popular uprisings against the Spanish conversos. King John II of Portugal forbade such demonstrations, however, and held the local authorities accountable for any such outbreaks, as occurred in Lisbon. Faced with a deteriorating situation, the king, with the permission of the pope, created a group of inquisitors for the entire kingdom; he also allowed conversos to leave Portugal as long as they went to live in other Christian lands.

The newly appointed inquisitors were charged with inquiring into the faith of the conversos who entered Portugal. If no charges could be proved against their Christian faith, they were allowed to remain or to leave. If they were found guilty, they were subject to penance or punishment.

It was under these circumstances that some conversos accused of Judaizing in Lisbon and Santarém were burned, and some Portuguese Jews suspected of proselytizing among them were imprisoned. João de Niebla, accused of celebrating the *Páscoa de Sabaoth* in the Arondim's house, was burned in Santarém. In his confession he denounced Arondim and Moses Mourisco for having lured him to the Mosaic Law.[2]

The mistrust surrounding the Castilian marranos finally fell upon the Portuguese Jews themselves, mainly on those in the large cities, where there existed religiously based social instability. The frequency of plague epidemics was perceived as a punishment for human sins, and one of these was the heresy of the marranos and society's acceptance of these heretics in its midst. Many believed that the health of the kingdom would be restored only if this heresy were wiped out.[3] John II condemned this superstitious notion.

There was, in addition, an increase in preaching against relations between Christians and Jews toward the end of the fifteenth century. Thus, there were such sermons as those of Master Paul of Braga or the appearance of a polemical manuscript, *Ajuda da fé* (The Help of the Faith), written by Master Antonio, physician to King John. Both were Portuguese conversos. If we know little about the former, the same cannot be said about the latter, who had been a rabbi from Tavira: he was baptized at court and his godfather was the sovereign himself.[4]

The hostility toward the Jewish minority grew with the arrival of the Spanish Jews, expelled in March of 1492. Their immigration was accompanied by yet another plague, which reinforced their rejection by both Portuguese Christians and some Jews. In addition, the number of newcomers and the large number of artisans among them aggravated the economic competition between the Portuguese Christian majority and the Jewish minority and threatened the security of the latter.

From the few known facts on the capitation payment for entry, we can state that the Jewish population in Portugal doubled, at the very least. From an original thirty thousand, the number of resident Jews in the kingdom now certainly exceeded sixty thousand, perhaps even one hundred thousand.

If some of the Jews entered Portugal legally, whether to settle permanently (the so-called six hundred houses or families) or to use the kingdom as a temporary passage en route to other countries, there were others who managed to enter clandestinely. When these individuals were caught, they were imprisoned and made slaves of the Crown.

From the latter, and from those who still owed a debt of eight cruzados for the capitation, the king ordered the removal of minors. They were baptized and given over to the care of Álvaro da Caminha. He took them to the island of São Tomé, there to raise them as Christians and make them producers of sugarcane and masters of sugar mills, as is recorded in the will of the captain of the island.[5]

The parents and the older children remained in the kingdom. In an effort to solve the problem of the Jews who were slaves of the king, John II issued a law on October 19, 1492, in which he guaranteed wide social and fiscal privileges to all Spanish Jews who converted.[6] Abjuration of Judaism was the condition of freedom for all those under servitude, and these were certainly the first to respond to the conversionist policy of the Portuguese king.

A similar measure was also taken by the king and queen of Spain, who, on November 10, published a letter of security to all Spanish Jewish refugees in Portugal who would like to return baptized to Spain or who wished to receive baptism in Ciudad Rodrigo or Zamora.[7] To those who returned as Christians, the sovereigns promised the repossession of their former properties and their integration into the majority society.

During 1493 and 1494 King John II of Portugal promoted the departure of Spanish Jews to other places. Royal documents, as well as both Christian and Jewish chronicles, are unanimous in relating the robberies and crimes committed by Christians and Muslims against the Jewish wanderers.

The German traveler Jerome Münzer wrote in his *Travels Through Portugal and Spain* that King John II had ordered the expulsion of all Spanish conversos by Christmas of 1494 and that they left for Naples. He wrote that the king also considered the expulsion of all the Jews of Portugal, by Christmas 1496, under pressure from Ferdinand and Isabella.[8] But the Portuguese chroniclers did not mention such a project, nor did King Manuel refer to it when, as we shall see, he issued his own edict of expulsion.

In spite of these developments, the Jews of Lisbon contributed money for the construction of sea vessels built in Porto, vessels that were probably included in the fleet of Vasco da Gama in 1497.[9]

King John died on October 25, 1496, with no direct heir, having been forced to appoint as his successor his brother-in-law Manuel, the duke of Beja. At the same time, the populace in Lisbon, Évora, and Porto moved against the Jews, while the widowed queen and the young new sovereign acted to restore order, holding the local authorities responsible for any disturbances.[10] Indeed, King Manuel began his reign with an act of toleration toward the Spanish Jews who were captives of the Crown, granting them freedom. The policy that followed would not lead anyone to think that expulsion was a possibility. And, until May 1496, Manuel confirmed and guaranteed the privileges of the Portuguese Jews.

The situation changed drastically when the king decided to marry the princess Isabella, eldest daughter of the Spanish monarchs and widow of Alfonso, son of John II. Such a marriage could eventually unify the entire Iberian peninsula under the crown of one king. The political consideration was followed by another—the growing certainty that the discovery of a route to India was near. In the growth of this knowledge there had been cooperation between Christians and Jews, among the latter, Joseph Vezinho, Rabbi Abraham of Beja, Joseph of Lamego, and Abraham Zacuto. To the king's wish for peninsular unification was joined the desire of the Christian bourgeoisie—which felt it had been pushed aside by Jews in the sugar trade of Madeira and the African monopolies—to keep the India trade for itself.

Based on these conjectures, we can understand the positions defended in the king's council (the date of its meeting is not known) and the decision taken by King Manuel. Two theses were presented: (1) allowing the Jews permanent residence, which was defended by the nobility and part of the clergy, who pointed to the potential loss of knowledge and wealth that an expulsion would entail, as well as to the fact that the pope permitted Jews in Rome and the Papal States, and (2) expelling the Jews, defended by the intellectuals and the Minor Orders.

Manuel's decision was entirely political, motivated by his goal of marriage to the daughter of the Spanish Catholic monarchs and heiress to their throne after the death of Prince John. In fact, the princess expressed reluctance about the new marriage. She, or Ferdinand and Isabella, required the fulfillment of a prior condition—the expulsion of all heretics from Portugal.

Who were these heretics? At first glance we might conclude that they were Castilian conversos who had found refuge in Portugal. However, the majority of these had already left for Naples, and those who remained in the kingdom were considered good Christians. The princess's refusal to cross the border into Portugal before the last Jews had left the country clearly indicates that they were included in the designation of heretics. We therefore understand that Manuel decided to expel the Jews in order to please his future wife. The royal edict making public the expulsion was dated December 5, 1496, and issued at Muge. The *Ordenações Manuelinas* complemented this with the expulsion of the Muslims.[11] Both would have to leave Portugal before October 1497.

Once the decree was promulgated, it was up to the king to execute it or to obstruct it, depending on his interests and those of the kingdom, since the consequences would be different for Portugal than they had been for Spain. In fact, the elimination of an active and enterprising minority such as the Jews represented, economically and culturally, an impoverishment of the kingdom, which was asserting itself for the first time as an important European power. Fully conscious of this, King Manuel played a double game, hiding his true intention, which was to have the Jews remain in Portugal. Unlike the Muslims, who in April 1497 received a safe-conduct from Ferdinand and Isabella and could leave Portugal with no restrictions, the Jews were limited, first in their ports of embarkation and then by a forced baptism of the majority, which occurred in several stages.

The descriptions of the forced baptism of Portuguese Jewry by the Jewish and Portuguese chroniclers do not make the process clear to us, nor do they reveal the complexity of what took place. The *Estaus* in Lisbon is the only place of baptism to which they refer, as if everyone was converted there. Nor is the timing of the baptism at all clear from the chronicles. It is as though the shock and chaos of the events wiped out the specific memories of time and place.

I believe that we can now supply the missing information about the conditions under which the forced baptism occurred. We know the terminal date for the departure of the last Jews from Portugal as the end of September 1497. Not all the Jews were baptized, as a Spanish Jew, himself baptized in Lisbon, related: "In the year in which the king of Portugal ordered that all the Jews of the kingdom should become Christians, this witness was in Lisbon and saw so many Jews . . . become Christians, and the Jews who did not want to become Christians could go away."[12]

But what happened in the meantime, when Manuel ordered the properties of the Jews to be sold, that is, at the time of the official liquidation of Judaism in Portugal? On a day we do not precisely know, but early in 1497, King Manuel ordered the law officers of the kingdom to take possession of the synagogues and all their contents, including books and ritual objects. This means that already at this time Judaism was on its way to becoming a secret practice: the cult could not be celebrated in the synagogues, open teaching disappeared, and Jewish schools and libraries were confiscated by the Crown. Jewish cemeteries, too were appropriated.

In March there were two instances of forced baptisms: that of children taken away from their parents on March 19, the Sunday before Easter, as an anonymous hand wrote in the *Foral* book of Torres Novas,[13] and then perhaps at Easter, at the baptism of the adolescents

and young Jews found in Lisbon, as related by Samuel Usque in his
Consolação.

The latter baptism is recounted by Jorge Manuel, a New Christian
from Tomar born in Castile. As he later told the inquisitors, he married
as a Jew and his first son was born in Portugal. But his child was taken
from him when he was seven or eight months old, by order of King
Manuel. Sometime later, Jorge Manuel came to Lisbon on business.
"And when he was in this city, the said lord (the king) ordered that the
Jews become Christians, and so they were put in the *Estaus*, from
whence he, Jorge Manuel, went out with other Jews and he was baptized at the Church of Santa Justa.[14]

From his testimony we can easily see that the Jews did not all go together to Lisbon, since he left his wife in Tomar and went there alone in
order to settle the goods his father had left him. As he related his own
baptism to the approximate time of his son's, we can also conclude that
the baptism in the *Estaus* occurred at Easter, unless there were others
left unmentioned in the documents or by the chroniclers. Easter 1497
was also the time mentioned by Damião de Góis, Usque, and others as
the time of baptism.

Despite the impression created by the chroniclers, I think that it is
incorrect to speak of a single collective baptism for Portuguese Jewry.
General baptisms occurred not only in Lisbon but also after the edict
on May 30, on many occasions and wherever the Jews lived, as the following attest.

Luis Álvares, formerly Solomon ben Haim, was baptized in Elvas in
August, 1497.[15] Justa Rodrigues, formerly Çinfana, born in Castile, was
baptized in St. Mary's Church in Setúbal as part of the general conver-
sion.[16] The same happened with Beatriz Rodrigues, formerly Lediça, in
Bragança, with Gabriel Serrão, baptized in Vinhais, with Margarida
Fernandes or Francisca de Valença in Miranda do Douro, with
Francisco Aires, baptized in Lousã, with Diogo de Leão and Francisco
Álvares, baptized in Évora.[17] All of them mentioned that they had been
baptized during the general conversion ordered by King Manuel.

On May 30 only some of the Jews received baptism, as Manuel issued a law guaranteeing substantial privileges to all who became
Christians. Calling for a voluntary conversion, he promised:

- that for twenty years he would not inquire into their religious behavior.

- that he would not accept any denunciation against New Christians made more than twenty days after the alleged heretical practice.
- that he would not confiscate their properties if the guilt of heresy were proved. In such cases the properties would still go to their Christian descendants.
- that he would permit physicians and surgeons the possession of Hebrew medical books if they did not know Latin.

The king concluded by guaranteeing a general pardon for all crimes committed by those Jews who converted by May 30. This pardon did not apply to Jews baptized after May 30.[18]

This document, endorsed first by King Manuel and subsequently by his heir, John III, at the beginning of his reign, should be considered the magna carta of the Portuguese New Christians. They used it in negotiations with the pope in Rome against the establishment of the Inquisition in Portugal later, during the reign of John III.

Damião de Góis reported this promise of Manuel in his *Crónica do felicissimo rei Dom Manuel* but he also wrote that the time limit for departure from the country had expired and that the promise not to inquire into religious behavior was a demand made by the Portuguese Jews to the king in exchange for baptism and the freedom and restitution of the children who had been taken from them. I believe that the chronicler is in error: the royal letter is dated May 30, while the last date permissible for departure was September 30. It is also very difficult to believe that the promises of rewards for all the voluntary converts could have been the response of the king to a people in captivity. This ordinance was more likely part of a conversionist royal policy, similar to that issued by King John II in October 1492 vis-à-vis the Spanish Jews. The intent of this policy was surely always the integration of the Jewish minority into Christian society. The law of May 30 proves that Manuel did *not* want his Jews to leave the country. On the contrary, the edict of expulsion of 1496 was merely an attempt to show Ferdinand, Isabella, their daughter (the future queen of Portugal), and the proponents of expulsion that there would be one religion—Christianity—in Portugal.

Indirectly, the reluctance of princess Isabella to enter Portugal in August 1497 confirms that the Jews (the "heretics") were still living on Portuguese territory. A small number of them refused to abandon Judaism, and they could leave. As for the rest, Manuel prevented their departure after their baptism and tried to promote their integration.

Symptomatic of *legal* integration were the disappearance of the special sections applying to Jews in the *Ordenações Manuelinas,* the adoption of Christian names and surnames, the end of the Jewish quarters, forced mixing by intermarriage, and admission to the nobility, the university, and the church.

In the end the integration so desired by King Manuel was a failure, perhaps with rare exceptions of which we are unaware. Most of the New Christians secretly affirmed their own history and religion, attending church but abhorring Christianity and regarding themselves as Jews. The insistence of the New Christians on maintaining their special identity had another face—the emergence of a renewed anti-Judaism on the part of the Old Christian majority, who did not forget that these were *Jews* and who called them by that name.

7

The Exiles of 1492 in the Kingdom of Navarre:
A Biographical Perspective

Benjamin R. Gampel

In the wake of the expulsion edict of March 31, 1492, the Jews of Castile and Aragon were confronted with two options: either to convert to Christianity and thereby remain in the cities, towns, and villages in which they lived or to go into exile. In the late spring and summer of that fateful year, many Castilian and Aragonese Jews who lived near the Navarrese border left their homes, crossed the frontier, and continued their lives as openly professing Jews. Until recently not much was known about those who took refuge within the Pyrenean kingdom; not their numbers, not where they hailed from, and not where they settled. Through the use of a wide variety of sources found in the Navarrese archives, I was able to trace the history of these Jewish immigrants after they had arrived in their new home. Still, it proved almost impossible to learn about their lives when they still resided within Castile and Aragon. Local Navarrese sources simply did not provide any information about their history prior to their emigration, with one exception: there are records in cases of refugees who sought to resolve legal difficulties with the family and business associates they left behind.[1]

Since the publication of my book, a number of monographs on the expulsion of the Jews have appeared, most significantly, the two-volume work by Miguel Ángel Motis Dolader on the expulsion of the Jews from the kingdom of Aragon.[2] The new data presented in these works have enabled us in this essay to write biographies of some of the émigrés and flesh out our general knowledge about the refugee population. We are now able to observe how individual Jews responded to the expulsion edict. Indeed, Ferdinand and Isabella's decree generated possibilities that would continue to influence the decisions of those who chose exile as Jews in Navarre for many years after 1492.

In their March 31 decree, Ferdinand and Isabella declared that by the end of July no Jews were to reside in the Kingdoms of Castile and Aragon. In the days and weeks following the publication of the edict, which in the various cities, towns, and villages of Castile and Aragon ranged from April 29 to May 1, Jews began to enter Navarre from both these Iberian kingdoms. Although municipal and other Navarrese authorities were unsure whether to receive them, the Jews continued to arrive, especially those coming from less than 150 kilometers away. Probably two thousand Jews crossed the border by land and by water, coming from frontier villages in both kingdoms and in larger numbers from the city of Saragossa.

It was very difficult for those who finally decided to leave Castile and Aragon to dispose of all their property prior to their departure. Some émigrés granted power of attorney to agents who could continue to dissolve their assets even after the refugees had already arrived in their new places of residence. Others personally divested themselves of their property after they arrived in their new homeland. So, for example, we know from Navarrese sources that on July 26, five days before the last Jew would be allowed to leave Castile and Aragon, Ezmel Abnarrabi, now residing in Tudela, sold all of the debts that were owed him in the kingdom of Aragon to a prominent Tudelan Christian, Pascual de Ayenssa, for ten thousand sueldos, a sum that Pascual paid immediately.[3]

Thanks to another document found in the notarial archives of Tudela, we know that Ezmel had lived in Aragon in Saragossa. He therefore was probably one of the many Jews who took advantage of the good road from Saragossa that ran along the Ebro into Navarre. But from the Navarrese documentation alone this is the sum total of our knowledge of Ezmel Abnarrabi's life prior to his arrival in the Pyrenean kingdom. We do not know when he traveled to Navarre or, more important, how he had amassed the considerable wealth that enabled him to sell his outstanding loans for ten thousand sueldos. Were there solely the information from the Navarrese archives, these questions would have remained subjects for conjecture.

But thanks to the labors of Miguel Ángel Motis Dolader we now know more. A document from the notarial archives in Saragossa informs us that Ezmel Abnarrabi was in the town of Cortes, the first town in Navarre on the Tudela-Saragossa road, one week before arriving in Tudela. He apparently had left his house in Saragossa on July 18 and the very next day, while in Cortes, granted his wife, Duenya Alazar, power of attorney to transfer some of his property to the Crown of Aragon to cover an outstanding debt to the royal coffers. His holdings, the document states, had already been frozen prior to this date.[4] Why did Ezmel wait until he crossed the border? Was his wife preparing to stay behind in Aragon or did she intend to join him later? And did the Aragonese Crown pursue him to ensure that he paid his debts to the royal coffers?

Motis has shown in detail how the property of individual Aragonese Jews, especially of rich members of the community, was confiscated so that the Crown could recover the outstanding debts of the Jewish communities. In the report on confiscated funds tendered to the royal authorities, we find the name of Ezmel Abnarrabi and learn that he was one of the wealthiest Jews in the kingdom. Indeed, on July 20 in Saragossa, two days after his arrival in Navarre, thirty-eight thousand sueldos were taken from him and his family and transferred to the Aragonese royal authorities. The royal officials were not empowered to take all that Ezmel owned; legally, he or any other emigrants were to be left with sufficient resources to enable them to depart the kingdom and establish themselves elsewhere.[5]

The document of July 20 indicates that Ezmel Abnarrabi had sold various credits, monetary and otherwise, to a representative of the Aragonese Crown for thirty-eight thousand sueldos. But this sale was just a formality. The reality had been spelled out in a document of July 14, which stated that no money was to change hands and that if the property listed in the "sale" did not amount to thirty-eight thousand sueldos, the outstanding sum was to be recovered from other property belonging to Ezmel. This source also recorded that credits worth twenty thousand sueldos had been transferred to royal officials. His wife, Duenya Alazar, as manager of his affairs, simply declared what was known to all parties: that the money was taken "by the *comisarios* of the expulsion of the city of Saragossa as part of the debts that the *aljama* of the Jews of the said city owed to the king.[6]

The thirty-eight thousand sueldos confiscated from Ezmel Abnarrabi was the second largest sum taken from any Jew in the kingdom of Aragon. The listing of properties that were "sold" for this large sum offers a glimpse of the vastness of his family's assets. Ezmel controlled outstanding credits in money, grains, and other items in localities that lined the Ebro River in the Aragonese kingdom. According to Motis's computations, 94 percent of his property was confiscated, aside from any of his belongings seized prior to this action.[7]

Once Ezmel arrived in Navarre, having brought with him, one supposes, all that he could to take up his new life, he appointed his wife, who had remained in Aragon, as his agent to effect the transfer of some of his assets to the royal authorities. The Crown of Aragon, concerned that Ezmel would leave without rendering to them what they thought was their due from the Jewish communities, made sure he signed this document, which was necessary for the legal transfer of the property, immediately upon his arrival in Navarre. He was even constrained to transfer additional sums of money the day following his arrival, sums that may not have been reflected in the previous accounting of his assets. Despite this, he possessed sufficient additional credits for which a prominent Tudelan Christian was willing to pay ten thousand sueldos up front.

Ezmel Abnarrabi may have left behind in Aragon a wife and thirty-eight thousand sueldos, but he was not impoverished. This was already clear from the known Navarrese sources. We know that on May 14, 1493, Ezmel Aunarrabi [*sic*], described here as being formerly of the city of Saragossa and now residing in the city of Tudela, released a Christian of the town of Juslibol in Aragon from all the debts that he owed him. This is quite surprising because included in the list of Abnarrabi's property confiscated by the Aragonese Crown—the list just discussed and that Motis brought to our attention—were all the credits that he possessed in Juslibol. The notary reported that to formalize the act of May 14, Ezmel "swore truly like a Jew."[8] Clearly, Ezmel was still involved in moneylending and speculative activities. Our Navarrese records tell us that a few months later, on October 25, Ezmel lent fifteen Navarrese florins to Pedro Escudero, of the Navarrese village of Corella, who offered houses he owned in his hometown as collateral. Ezmel was to be repaid in hemp, and, on February 12, 1494, Ezmel acknowledged having received the entire payment.[9]

Tudelan documentation continues to describe his activities. On April 29, 1494, Abnarrabi put up ten Navarrese florins so that a Christian, Martin Garcia, "presently residing" in the city of Tudela, could apprentice as a tailor with the local Juhan de Frias.[10] One can only speculate about why Ezmel offered the money to the younger Martin Garcia. Was Martin a relative who had recently converted to Christianity? We do know that when Ezmel Abnarrabi paid back a debt to a grandson, on June 6, 1494, Anton was very likely no longer of the Jewish faith.[11]

The year 1495, as the Navarrese sources attest, saw no diminution in Ezmel's financial activities. On March 13 he offered to be a guarantor on a debt of twenty-five florins owed by Simuel Almalcadi as a result of a legal proceeding involving the local bailiff.[12] And in May of the same year Ezmel was engaged in large-scale loans. Thus, on May 12 he lent one thousand Aragonese sueldos to the Tudelan merchant Pedro de Mongelos. Because such a large sum was involved, additional safeguards were placed in the contract to ensure repayment.[13]

The last reference to Ezmel Abnarrabi in Navarrese documents answers one of the questions posed earlier and serves as a fitting end to our story. We had lost track of Ezmel's wife, Duenya Alazar, after he appointed her as his agent on July 19, 1492. But on April 28, 1497, we read Ezmel's name in another loan contract. Again the debtor was Pedro de Mongelos, but this time the sum was fifty golden Navarrese ducats and the creditor was "Duennya [sic] Alazar, Jew, who was the wife of Ezmel Abnarrabi, Jew of Tudela." On November 29 of that year, Duenya acknowledged having been repaid.[14] It is not unreasonable to assume that Ezmel had died and that his wife, who, as we have seen, was his trusted associate, continued the family business. It is also likely that Duenya had stayed behind in Aragon for a few more days in July 1492 to settle their affairs and then crossed the border into Navarre to continue her life as a Jew.

Rabí Açac Çarça was another Jew who traveled to Navarre in 1492. He settled in the city of Sangüesa in the eastern sector of the kingdom. All that we know of him from the Navarrese sources is derived from his appearances in the minutes of the Navarrese royal chancellery, the *Libro del Registro del Sello,* during the years 1494 and 1495. We learn that on December 10, 1494, he, Salamon Anbron, and Jacó Ayeno were numbered among the "regidores de los judios foranos de Sanguessa," the councilors of the immigrant Jews of Sangüesa. They were summoned that day to appear personally in court at the behest of royal financial officials and the *jurados* of the *nativos*, the officials of the native Jewish community. It is likely that the point of contention between the two groups involved the apportionment of taxation responsibilities.[15]

That was not the only litigation in which Çarça was involved. Ten days later, on December 20, Johan Dezquiroz, the royal *portero*, was ordered to sequester the property of both Açac Çarça and Juçe Alfeda, Jews of Sangüesa, for having failed to respond to a suit pending against them in the royal court. On January 25, 1495, the *portero real* was instructed to lift the embargo on Çarça and Alfeda's property after sixty days. But on January 29 the sequestration was immediately lifted because Çarça and Alfeda had replied to the lawsuit brought by the Sangüesan merchant, Johan Frances. In yet another case recorded in the Libro de Registro del Sello, Çarça and Abraham, also a Sangüesan Jew, were ordered on December 22, 1494, to appear in the royal court three days later. No more details are forthcoming.[16]

This had been the sum total of our knowledge about Açac Çarça and his associates from the Navarrese sources. But a recently published document from the diocesan archive in Saragossa not only tells us much about Açac Çarça but also provides crucial information on the leaders of the Sangüesan *forano* community. On January 27, 1496, Alonso de Aragón, the archbishop of Saragossa, granted safe-conduct, effective until February 15, throughout the kingdom of Aragon to Rabí Açach Jana, alias Çarça, Jacó Fayeno [*sic*], and Jacó de Loarre, Jews who were inhabitants of the kingdom of Navarre and "formerly my vassals of the village of Biel."[17] There is no doubt that two of these three individuals are none other than Rabí Açac Çarça and Jacó Ayeno, *regidores* of the *judios foranos* of Sangüesa. If they simply wished to return to Biel, they would need to convert to Christianity. But, if so, why would they require a document of safe-conduct, unless they wished to convert not at the border but rather in their hometown? Or is it possible that their ultimate goal was to exit the peninsula, as had other Aragonese Jews in 1492, including their neighbors, from the hamlet of Biel? If that were so, however, safe passage only through the kingdom and not the Crown of Aragon, excluding therefore Catalonia and Valencia, would not help them get to any of the Mediterranean ports. In any event, they were to be guided within Aragon by Antón de Mur, the royal constable.

We do not know if Çarça, Ayeno, and de Loarre took up their erstwhile lord on his offer. But it appears from this Saragossan source that the leaders of the immigrant community in Sangüesa were seriously considering departing from Navarre. Whether for personal or communal reasons, and whether their goal was to leave the peninsula as Jews or to return to Biel as Christians, they may have determined that life was preferable outside the Pyrenean kingdom.

Jews from Biel, a hamlet approximately fifty-eight kilometers from the eastern border of Aragon with Navarre, had two options in 1492 if they wished to continue to live as Jews. Either they could take a short day trip to the city of Sangüesa or they could make the five-day trip by water or land or both to Tarragona, the nearest port of embarkation on the Mediterranean, approximately 271 kilometers away.[18] We now know from Aragonese sources that a large group of Biel Jews left on July 31, the last day allowed them, accompanied by a retinue engaged to protect them against marauders. A fierce storm forced them to overnight in Isuerre, a small town in the Val D'Onsella. The details of their travel were recalled four years later when the justicia of Biel, Johan Sánchez, was accused of financial improprieties relating to the Jews' departure.[19]

It appears from the documents surrounding the trial that many Jews who fled to Navarre returned to Biel as Christians. Whether Çarça, Ayeno, and de Loarre were among them is unknown. If, however, they had been part of the group that left for Sangüesa and were caught in the storm, it is possible that these leaders of the Sangüesan *forano* community may have been summoned to testify at the trial of Johan Sánchez and therefore granted safe-conduct. They may then have returned to Navarre afterward.

We know of other Jews who also decided in 1492 to seek shelter in Navarre rather than convert to Christianity but opted to leave the peninsula by a different route, through Aragon. According to Yosef ha-Kohen, the sixteenth-century Jewish chronicler, his family fled to Navarre in 1492 and was granted safe passage the following year by Ferdinand to travel down the Ebro River through Aragon to the Mediterranean, from where they set sail for Provence. I had suggested that Yosef's family were among the group of Jewish exiles allowed on

March 9, 1493, to sail down the Ebro River and exit the peninsula. Based on these new sources, we now see that permission for Jews to reenter the lands from which they were expelled—and possibly without converting—was not as rare as had been previously thought.[20]

Of course not all Jews wished or were able to obtain safe passage out of the peninsula. We know from a Hebrew text published in 1928 of a native Navarrese Jew, Shemtov ben Shmuel Gamil of Tudela, who probably left secretly sometime in 1498, after the Navarrese expulsion edict was already in effect, and eventually settled in North Africa. Because of the surreptitious nature of his journey he encountered severe difficulties leaving the peninsula before reaching his new homeland.[21] Other Jews were even less fortunate; they were unable as was Shem Tov Gamil to extricate themselves from imprisonment after being captured. An Aragonese source relates that on November 26, 1497, a decision was made in Alcalá de Henares about a group of Jews that had secretly left Navarre and who had been seized near the Navarrese-Aragonese border on the outskirts of Añon, near Tarazona. Since the captured Jews offered to be baptized, their death sentence was commuted and they were reduced to servitude instead.[22]

These new accounts do more than simply add material to a sketchy biography of Açac Çarça; rather they challenge our previous assertion of the relative stability of the post-1492 immigrant community in Navarre. There may have been more attempts than had been thought, both legal and otherwise, to leave the kingdom, whether to return to their hometowns as Christians or to live outside the peninsula as Jews. The story of Açac Çarça and his cohort may provide yet another example.[23]

While Ezmel Abnarrabi probably died a Jew in Navarre and Açac Çarça may have left the peninsula altogether, other immigrants to Navarre responded differently to the tumultuous events of the 1490s. With the recent publication of a variety of archival sources, some Navarrese Jews who had appeared in local sources but were not known to have been among the refugees can now be identified as having come to the kingdom in the wake of the 1492 expulsion. Among these is Simuel Çadoch, who lent sixteen Navarrese florins to Johan de Leyça on January 19, 1495, and was simply described by the Tudelan notary as a Jew living in the city of Tudela.[24] But in a recently published volume, again by Motis, on the Jews of Calatayud in the late fifteenth century, we learn much about both Simuel and his family and his emigration to Navarre. Calatayud contained the second largest Jewish community in the kingdom of Aragon after Saragossa and it possessed an active *al-jama* up through the days of the expulsion. In the first few months of 1492, before the promulgation of the Aragonese edict of expulsion, we find Simuel Çadoch as a resident of Calatayud engaged in business, especially the collection of debts, some of which are described as *comandas*, others as taxes. In one instance in January 1492, his brother Brahem purchased a comanda contract from him.[25]

Now that we can identify the Simuel Çadoch of Calatayud with the one who lived later in Tudela, we can employ two documents first brought to light in 1969 in the compilation of his biography. These sources show that in the wake of the publication of the 1492 edict Simuel Çadoch decided to leave Aragon. On July 2 he sold a comanda contract (in which two Muslims of the town of Morés, Mahoma Ferrando and his wife, Axala Ferrera, were obligated to him) to Nicholau Bernat and micer Johan Vives, the individuals who were deputized to oversee the dissolution of the local Jewish community. His action of two days later, absolving a Saragossan Christian of all the debts he owed him, may also have reflected his resolve to leave Calatayud.[26]

Although Simuel emigrated to Navarre presumably to continue to live as a Jew, our Navarrese sources inform us on August 11, 1494, that since Simuel Çadoque [*sic*] had converted, he had been able to obtain a moratorium on his repayment of a comanda contract, according to which he had owed four thousand Aragonese sueldos to Simuel Paçagon, the latter described as a "Jew, formerly of the city of Calatayud." Çadoch and Paçagon had negotiated this contract on November 5 of the previous year and it had been registered with the notary of the Tudelan *Judería,* Jaco de la Rabiça, "according to the counting of the Jews on the 25th of maresban of the year 5,254." Another source informs us that upon Çadoch's conversion he took the name Alonso Daybar, and yet another that on the same day, August 11, Alonso lent his uncle Miguel, described as a citizen of the village of Huesa in Aragon (and who had probably converted two years earlier), three thousand sueldos in a comanda contract to be repaid in five years time. The conversion of the Çadoch family did not serve to dampen their financial concerns.[27]

Without the new documentation Simuel Çadoch's conversion appeared as that of a native Navarrese Jew rather than what it actually had been—the belated adoption of Christianity by a Jewish immigrant from Aragon. Although Simuel had elected exile as a Jew in Navarre, a couple of years later, for reasons unknown, he changed his mind. On January 19, 1495, after Simuel had converted, the Tudelan notary Sancho Ezquerro still described Çadoch as a Jew of Tudela, but we should not be confused by this appellation. Even as late as January 4, 1497, when he lent Sancho de Legasa and Sancho de Mauleon twenty-six golden Aragonese florins and they promised to repay the debt within one month, he was still identified as Simuel Çadoch, Jew of Tudela. Another document dated January 4 makes clear not only that Sancho de Legasa was the guarantor of the debt contracted by Sancho del Mauleon but also that the lender was Alonso Deaynar [*sic*], merchant and citizen of Tudela, "who was called Simuel Çadoch before his conversion." So when on May 15, 1497, the notary Pedro Latorre registered that Simuel Çadoch, Jew, received sixty-seven golden florins from a Mastre Andreo and that a loan contracted on March 14 was therefore canceled, we can assume that the florins were borrowed from Alonso Daybar, even although the contract recorded his Jewish name.[28]

Çalema Paçagon traveled from Calatayud to Tudela, as had Simuel Çadoch, but Paçagon's Aragonese origins were already known from the Navarrese sources. On April 25, 1493, when Çalema Paçagon—who may have been related to Simuel Paçagon whom we have seen had business dealings with Çadoch—released Guillem Aznar of Aguilón from all debts owed him, Çalema was described by a Tudelan notary as a "Jew of Calatayut [*sic*] residing in Tudela." But, as with Simuel Çadoch, recently published sources from Calatayud enable us to learn more about Çalema; they show that prior to the expulsion the Paçagons were a large and distinguished family in this Aragonese city. And an item from a Saragossan notary reveals that on March 2, 1492, weeks before the expulsion edict was signed, let alone a matter of public knowledge, Çalema Paçagon as well as his brother Abram were described as "presently living in the Juderia of the castle of Tudela."[29]

These two members of the Paçagon family did leave Aragon as a result of the 1492 expulsion edict; but they were in Tudela only briefly and then returned to their hometown. Indeed, their fates were parallel to those of their families and friends who only arrived in Navarre later in the year. The Paçagon's itinerary—from Calatayud to Tudela and back and forth again—may reflect the fact that for some Aragonese

Jews crossing the frontier into Navarre may have been done frequently for business purposes. Calatayud sources indicate that on July 11, 1492, Çalema as *procurador* of his brother Brahem (to be identified with Abram), was back in this Aragonese city and sold various rentals, which they had received from their father, Mosse, to Nicholau Bernat and micer Joan Vives, who we may recall were the *comisarios* of the expulsion of the Jews in Aragon. A week later, Çalema was still in Calatayud when a local Jew sold a vineyard to two Christians. And on July 25, only six days before the Aragonese Jewish communities were to be dissolved, Çalema and two other Jews were deputized by officials of the Saragossan aljama to sell a rental that they possessed to the bailiff of the Jews and Muslims of the city.[30]

Brahem and Çalema's mother, Bona Dona Benardut, probably arrived in Navarre during the last days in which Jews were permitted to leave the Aragonese kingdom. Although the following activities all took place on Navarrese soil, they were all recently found in Aragonese notarial registers. On July 31 in Tudela she granted a Saragossan merchant power of attorney to sell the rights to some rental income that she possessed in the Aragonese kingdom. Her children also needed surrogates to resolve outstanding business interests to which they could no longer directly attend. On August 12 Brahem and Çalema appointed Juan de Taguenca, a resident of Aynçon in Aragon, to sell the rights to more than 891 sueldos that they collected annually from the aljama of Muslims of Alborge to the friars of the convent of Santa María de Rueda. On September 1 Juan sold these rights in Saragossa to the Muslim community itself.[31]

We already knew from Tudelan documentation that the Paçagon brothers continued to resolve their outstanding Aragonese business. For example, the local notary, Pedro de la Torre, recorded that on October 18, 1493, the nobleman Miguel Ferriz, who lived in Carinyena in Aragon and was presently staying in Tudela, reached an agreement with Brahem and Çalema Paçagon. On January 13 of the following year one of the chapters of the agreement—whereby certain properties and moneys of the brothers were to be exchanged for the sum of five thousand sueldos payable within four months by the Aragonese royal authorities—was canceled.[32]

By 1495 the entire business arrangement was radically altered. On April 13 Pedro de la Torre, the same Tudelan notary who had registered the contract and who had made the changes of the previous year, reported that Çalema Paçagon was now known as Charles de Berrozpe and had received a favor from the "king of Castile" releasing him from the obligations stipulated in the 1493 agreement. In light of this situation, Miguel Ferriz, "the molones," and Charles promised Brahem Paçagon, Charles's brother, who apparently remained a Jew, that he would receive the moneys still owed him despite these new developments.[33]

Although it is tempting to speculate about the motivation for Çalema's conversion to Christianity, we cannot be certain if his change of faith somehow afforded him the beneficent grace of Ferdinand of Aragon, here described as the king of Castile. The scope of this beneficence was more far-reaching reaching than is evident from the particulars of the agreement that Çalema, now Charles, had arranged with Miguel Ferriz in Tudela. A recently published royal document from the Aragonese chancellery makes the nature of this favor abundantly clear. Writing from Madrid on March 4, 1494, as the king of Castile, Aragon, and so on, Ferdinand acknowledged that Charles de Verrozpe [sic] of the city of Calatayud, newly converted to Christianity and formerly known as Çalema Paçagon, had petitioned to recover the houses of his father, Mosse Paçagon, located in the city, as they had been left at the time of the expulsion. Çalema also wished to recover the tax rolls he had collected, the *cartas de comanda*, and the debts that he had possessed, which had been confiscated as a result of the expulsion edict. Additionally, he asked that notwithstanding the agreement he and his brother Brahem had made, as Jews in Tudela, with Miguel Ferriz of Saragossa—testified to by the notary, Pedro de la Torre—various *censales*, cartas de comanda, debts, and other items should, as a favor, be returned to him.

Ferdinand wrote that he was mindful of the services Charles had graciously performed for him as well the other kindnesses proffered by Çalema's ancestors. Ferdinand mentioned as well that since Johan Cabrero, his chamberlain and adviser, had also intervened on Çalema's behalf, he would grant him his wish to recover all of these properties. The king indicated that he had consulted with all the relevant officials from don Alonso de Aragon, the archbishop of Saragossa and lieutenant general in Aragon, to the officials of Calatayud and the commissioners of the property of the expelled Aragonese Jews. He instructed all of them to take note of this order. While Ferdinand therefore declared that all Çalema's belongings, even if they had been transferred, would be returned to Charles, including the items pertaining to Miguel Ferriz, the king indicated that any property that had been taken to pay off Jewish communal debts and the like not be included.[34]

All Aragonese and Castilian Jews who emigrated to Navarre and wished to return to their homes were unable to enlist the support of the king of Aragon in their attempt to recover the property in their possession at the time of the expulsion. While it can be assumed that Simuel Çadoch, although he converted to Christianity, remained in the Pyrenean kingdom, it appears likely that his fellow Calatayud Navarrese immigrant, the former Çalema Paçagon, returned to Aragon.[35]

Brahem Paçagon remained a Jew in Navarre. In late 1497 or early 1498 the edict of expulsion of Navarrese Jews was published, giving the Jews until sometime in March 1498 to leave the kingdom. Most Navarrese Jews were not able to leave, however, because the lands that surrounded their kingdom did not permit Jews within their borders. As a result, nearly all of its Jews, including members of the Paçagon family, converted to Christianity. The Tudelan notary Juhan Martinez Cabero recorded on September 21, 1498, that one day in March, at the time of the expulsion, Ybraym Paçagon and his daughter were baptized by Pedro Murillo, the subvicar of Tudela's church of Santa Maria. Ybraym took the name Enrriq de Berrozpe. On December 13, 1498, in Tudela, Pedro de la Torre noted that Brahem Paçagon was now known as Johan de Berrozpe and that he released his brother Charles, whom we remember as the erstwhile Çalema, from the debt he owed him as a result of Ferdinand's having released Çalema from the agreement both brothers had struck with Miguel Ferriz. By the end of the fifteenth century, therefore, the Paçagon brothers were joined again not only in their religious faith but also in the possession of identical surnames.[36]

As more and more studies of Jewish communities on the eve of the expulsion are published, we will surely be able to identify other individuals who took refuge in Navarre in response to the edict of March 31. Thanks to these monographs, those who study the Sephardic exiles, whether in Portugal or in any of the settlements in the Mediterranean littoral, will also be able to connect the activities of some of these individuals with their history prior to their emigration in 1492. We will thus be able to explore the continuities and/or disjunctures in their lives before and after they left Castile and Aragon. The activities of some of the expelled in their new places of residence will be placed in their proper context. The publication of a relatively small number of documents from the kingdom of Aragon allows us to appreciate the wide range of behavior that was found in the immigrant community in Navarre: Ezmel Abnarrabi died a Jew in Navarre; Rabí Açac Çarça may have returned to his hometown or exited the peninsula; Simuel Paçagon returned in the mid-1490s as a Christian to his ancestral holdings and to Aragon, while his brother Brahem chose to remain a Jew but then converted in the wake of the Navarrese expulsion edict in 1498. It is all these individual stories taken together that will help us create a richer appreciation of the great expulsion of 1492.

PART IV

Continuity and Change in the Sephardic Diaspora:

Communal Life

8

🔲

The Self-Definition of the Sephardic Jews of Western Europe and Their Relation to the Alien and the Stranger

Yosef Kaplan

For they are very particular and do not mingle . . . with the Jews of other nations.

—Isaac de Pinto

"Senhores" Versus "Criados": The Origins of Dependent Relations

The Spanish and Portuguese Jews were the first to establish themselves in those places in Western Europe that were newly opened to Jewish immigration. This move began in the late sixteenth century but really took off in the seventeenth century. In fact, thanks to the special interest taken by their rulers, the gates of these cities and states were opened to Jewish settlers, welcoming them to take part in the financial activity of the members of the *Nação* (Spanish and Portuguese Jewish nation). In places such as Amsterdam and Hamburg their financial and social presence was already felt in the early seventeenth century. These Jews were an attractive economic factor during the Age of Mercantilism thanks to their experience in international trade, their ability to mobilize resources from a population dispersed around the world, and, no less, their connections with the Iberian Peninsula and their familiarity with the intricacies of its economy as well as their expert knowledge of the trade routes from Spain and Portugal to the New World.[1] The leaders of the Spanish and Portuguese community in Hamburg and Amsterdam and, later on, those in London, too, were international merchants with status and capital who contributed importantly to the prosperity of their new homes and thus acquired recognition for themselves and for their communities. This recognition was sometimes translated into extensive rights, unparalleled in other places in Europe where the Jews were settling at that time. In contrast to the impressive Sephardic financial, social, and cultural presence, the misery of the first German and Polish immigrants to reach those places in the wake of the settlement by the members of the Nação was conspicuous. Until the Thirty Years' War the number of Ashkenazic immigrants in Amsterdam was quite modest: they were individual Jews who gathered at the margins of the Spanish-Portuguese congregation in the city. Among them were beggars and peddlers who were employed by the Nação as meat sellers. But even a teacher of young children such as Rabbi Moses Uri Ha-Levi of Emden, who arrived in Amsterdam with one of the first groups of Portuguese conversos to settle there and who is even accorded the title of "Haham" (Rabbi) here and there in some early documents, was and remained one of the poor of the community (*pobres da sedaka*), dependent upon the mercies of the charity fund of the Beth Yaakov community. The first Ashkenazic settlers were later joined by refugees who fled from the turmoil of the Thirty Years' War. Until the mid-1630s they did not attempt to establish an independent congregation but were content to exist on the margins of the Sephardic community, which provided them with basic services.[2] They were not permitted to become members of the Spanish-Portuguese "Nation." The first three Sephardic congregations in Amsterdam did not accept Jews who did not belong to the Nação, and when they merged as a single community in 1639 they stated prominently and explicitly in the third clause of the unified bylaws

> that this congregation is established for Jews belonging to the Portuguese and Spanish nation who are now dwelling in this city and for those who will settle here; and the Jews belonging to any other nations who may come here can be accepted for prayer, if this seems fitting to the presiding *Mahamad.*[3]

This pattern is repeated in practice in other places in northwestern Europe as well. Though the fog clouding the origins of the Ashkenazic community in Hamburg is heavier than that obscuring the origins of the Ashkenazic community in Amsterdam, it is known to us that, beginning in the late 1620s, German Jews began to arrive there in great numbers, remaining dependent for a long time upon the Ashkenazic community in Altona. The juridical status of these Ashkenazic Jews was precarious from the first, and the Hamburg authorities expelled them in 1649. Most of the deportees moved to nearby Altona and Wandsbek, though a few found refuge in the homes of the Portuguese Jews of Hamburg. Some of the deportees returned to Hamburg a few years later, where they were joined by refugees from Poland and Lithuania who were fleeing the persecutions of the Cossacks and the Swedish invasion.[4] However, while extremely wealthy men such as Duarte Nunes da Costa (also known as Jacob Curiel) and Diego Teixeira de Sampayo, who took the Jewish name of Abraham Senior, were responsible for the affluent social image of the Sephardic community in the eyes of the surrounding society, most of the Ashkenazic Jews who frequented that city in the mid-seventeenth century were simple folk who managed to remain in the city as "servants of the nation" (*criados da naçao*). They were employed, that is, as servants in the homes of the Sephardic Jews. Men such as Joseph Ha-Cohen, Layzer (Eliezer) Meir, Copel, Moses Lulav, and Leib Ber who received the protection of the Naçāo, took it upon themselves in return "not to buy stolen goods and not to do anything immoral." The Ashkenazic servant women employed by members of the Naçāo were ordered on 19 Adar 5414 (March 3, 1654) not to marry within the boundaries of the city, and those who did not abide by that decision would be forced to leave.[5] Indeed, it is evident that the Ashkenazic immigrants were dependent upon their Spanish and Portuguese brethren, with whom they found refuge, and the members of the Naçāo displayed a paternalistic attitude toward the Ashkenazic settlers. This was also the case in London. When the *Sahar Asamaim* community was established, the bylaws of 18 Heshvan 5424 (November 18, 1663) also stipulated quite explicitly in wording identical to that of the bylaws of Amsterdam that the congregation was established for "Jews of the Portuguese and Spanish Nation" and that members of other nations would be accepted at prayers in the synagogue as long as the presiding Mahamad saw fit.[6] Indeed the leaders of the community there made a point of imposing numerous restrictions: in 1679 it was explicitly stated that the Ashkenazic Jews could not perform any function whatsoever in the synagogue, including being called to the Torah or honored with the performance of any ceremonial act. At the same time, they were exempted from the tax on their business earnings, and it was proclaimed that contributions would no longer be accepted from them; there were only three exceptions, including the janitor of the

Sephardic synagogue.[7] Four years later it was permitted to accept "voluntary contributions [from Ashkenazic Jews] and the *parnas* [syndic] on duty may call to the Torah any Ashkenazic Jew whom he finds worthy of such."[8] But on 23 Iyyar 5467 (May 25, 1707) they were barred completely, and the *parnasim* decided unanimously "that from this day the entry of any *tudesco* to this synagogue will not be permitted."[9]

Restrictions of this kind were also imposed in the congregations of the Nação in the New World, and even if it is true, as Wiznitzer claims, that the congregation of Zur Israel in Recife, in northeastern Brazil, which existed there during the time of the Dutch conquest, also accepted Ashkenazic Jews of any origin as *yehidim* [members], their numbers in the Jewish population were minuscule, and none of them ever occupied a position among the leadership.[10]

Particularism of this type need not surprise us, as it is not unprecedented in the Middle Ages and the early modern period. Jewish communities, like other characteristically corporate organizations, generally insisted upon maintaining their particularity and showed little desire to absorb strangers, even when the "stranger" happened to be close in culture and origin. In 1623, even before the heads of the Sephardic community in Amsterdam expressed their first reservations regarding the Ashkenazic refugees who had crowded in among them after fleeing from the horrors of the Thirty Years' War, the leaders of the Jewish community in Lithuania had already voiced severe complaints "about the beggars who rise up and wander throughout the land—and their path is an unpaved way, straying crookedly in the lanes of darkness." These beggars were none other than Jewish refugees from Germany, who sought refuge in Eastern Europe from the calamities that beset them during the bloody wars of religion. The heads of the Jewish community of Lithuania, who objected strenuously to their very presence, found them morally flawed and spoke abundantly against them in very negative terms.[11]

Nonetheless, the attitude of the Spanish and Portuguese Jews of Western Europe toward their Ashkenazic brethren, including the immigrants from Poland and Lithuania who settled in their communities during the seventeenth century, evinced signs of separatism decidedly different in essence from what had been common in the Jewish world until then. This variety of separatism took shape against the background of the concepts of segregation that the members of the Nação had internalized as "New Christians" in Iberia. They had suffered discrimination there as members of a minority of different origins within a society that imposed the majority religion upon them but was not prepared to absorb them as equals.

The "Honorable Name" of the Chosen People

One of the most pronounced identifying traits of the apologetics promulgated by the former New Christians was the emphasis upon the superiority of the Jews over other nations: they went out of their way to prove that the Hebrew nation was and remained the chosen people of God. Therein lay a clear and intentional, though generally implicit, reply to the ethnocentric arguments raised in Spanish political and social writings of the sixteenth and seventeenth centuries, writings that asserted that the Spanish nation was the true heir of the chosen people of biblical times.[12] These arguments, sustained by the victories and conquests of the Hispanic empire, did not disappear from Iberian literature even after the decline and crisis that struck Spain in the period of the last of the Habsburg monarchs.[13] The New Christians living as crypto-Jews had seen how their persecutors sought to deprive them of their status as the chosen people and tried to the best of their ability, after returning to the faith of their fathers, to reclaim its lost glory and restore chosenness to its original bearer. The apologists among them did not hesitate to make generous use of the Iberian terminology of the days of the Statutes of Purity of Blood (*limpieza de sangre*). In his polemical works Isaac Orobio distinguished between the Jews, who were of the seed of Abraham, and proselytes who had adopted the Jewish faith, whose origins were from the gentiles. The former belonged to the Nation, which was much more than a spiritual entity: only to them was given the "honorable name" (*honroso nombre*) of the "House of Israel." Converts, by contrast, never attained that high degree, even after many generations of intermingling with Jewry.[14] A sensitive ear cannot help noticing the use here of terms and concepts drawn from the basic elements of contemporary Hispanic social life. In fact, is there not in Orobio's words a kind of Jewish version of the Iberian principle of separatism, which distinguished between "Old Christians," who were also *puros* (pure) and *lindos* (beautiful), and the "New Christians," who derived from Jews or Muslims? Did Orobio not distinguish here between

"Old Jews" and "New Jews"? And is not the term *honorable name,* which he used in the context of this distinction, one of the characteristic signs of the social discourse that was consolidated in Spain at the time of the limpieza de sangre![15]

Proselytes, Indians, and Mulattoes

The literature of the members of the Nação contains no tendency to find fault with the religious faith of converts to Judaism. One seeks in vain in their works any hint at social discrimination against them. Nevertheless, one finds in the social life of the Western Sephardic diaspora, especially in Amsterdam, decided signs of a reserved and discriminatory attitude toward proselytes. Proselytes were not chosen to fill any post in the community, not even those "that have no authority but merely faithfulness." Some of them were occasionally even given tasks usually assigned to a *shabbes goy* (gentile servants who performed labor forbidden to Jews on the Sabbath).[16] In general it may be said that this community showed explicit reserve with respect to conversion. And among these converts it was the blacks, descended from slaves who had been owned by the Sephardic Jewish merchants in Amsterdam, who suffered the most discrimination. The regulation of 20 Sivan 5404 (June 24, 1644) forbade the calling to the Torah or the granting of any honor in the synagogue to circumcised black Jews, "for thus it befits the good name of the congregation and its proper government."[17] Black and mulatto women were permitted to sit in the women's section of the synagogue only in the eighth and backmost row of benches. Moreover, in the community cemetery in Ouderkerk a special section was established for "all the black and mulatto Jews"—even in death they were set apart from the other members of the Nação. It must be noted that blacks and mulattoes who were born of Jewish marriages and "those who had married white women in Jewish marriage" could be buried in the regular part of the cemetery. If this is so, then marriage to blacks and mulattoes was not forbidden in the mid-seventeenth century, even if explicit steps were taken to prevent the conversion of people with dark skin, whether black or mulatto.[18]

In the consciousness of the members of the Nação in Amsterdam the blacks and mulattoes were not the only perceived threat to the "good name of the community." Other outside presences were also capable of disturbing their equilibrium. Menasseh ben Israel was shocked by the identification in the literature of the time of the Amerindians with the Ten Lost Tribes. He said

> that the Jews (as was marvelously proven by the physician, Huarte de San Juan, in his book, *Examen de ingenios*, chapter 14) were the most attractive people and the handsomest, those with the best intelligence in the world; and how could the Indians be like that, in that they lack all those things: they are ugly in their bodies and rude in their intelligence.[19]

It must be pointed out that Menasseh ben Israel purposely distorted the words of Doctor Huarte de San Juan. That famous Spanish physician never spoke the words of praise here lavished generously upon the Jewish people in order to distinguish them from the inferior Indians. Although he did write respectfully of the wisdom of the Jews and of the sharpness of their wit, he never said a word in praise of their beauty, nor did he claim they were the wisest of all people. Actually chapter 12 of his work, which Menasseh ben Israel is purportedly citing, states that the *Greeks* "are the handsomest people in the world, with the highest understanding."[20] Thus, the rabbi from Amsterdam did not hesitate to distort the words of his source in the service of his point, the demonstration of "the superiority of the Hebrews" to the gentiles.

Although there are similarities, there are also essential differences between the separatist conception that struck root in the Western Sephardic diaspora and the ideology of purity of blood, which had spread within Iberian society and culture. The members of the Nação did not make a systematic effort to endow their separatism with a theological dimension, nor did they ever graft biological explanations onto their arguments. They did, however, internalize certain concepts that were part of the separatist discourse in Spain and Portugal, concepts that helped them to define their new identity. Yesterday's segregated and downtrodden, who had been deprived of their honor by the Old Christians in Spain and Portugal, now hailed their own ancestry as a symbol of their Jewish identity. These traits were meant first of all to accentuate their superiority to those descended from gentiles. Hence they took a reserved attitude toward proselytes, and hence they feared ethnic mixture that was liable, in their opinion, to blur the genealogical line of the "original" chosen people. The emphasis of separation from dark-skinned people reflects their fear that association with those regarded as inferior by the European community might decrease their own value.

In his appearance before Cromwell to present the advantages of the Jews so as to gain permission for them to settle in England again, that very Menasseh ben Israel, who rejected the inclusion of the Indians among the children of Israel, saw fit to recall, among the three things "that make a strange Nation well-beloved amongst the Natives of a land," "Nobleness and purity of their blood." But, whereas Menasseh ben Israel devoted detailed chapters to the two other benefits which he mentioned, "Profit" and "Fidelity," regarding the third, "Nobleness and purity of blood," he contented himself with mentioning very briefly that the "Nobleness" of the Jews "is enough known amongst all Christians."[21] Of course it is possible to regard this expression as an ironic response to the anti-Semitic arguments current in Iberian literature of those generations. Perhaps it would be more correct to see it as the expression of a line of thought typical among the victims of the limpieza de sangre. When seeking to redefine their identity after reaching "the lands of freedom," they drew from the Iberian repertory of concepts, particularly those that had been used against them by their oppressors. They sought to turn the tables and to use the very same concepts, or similar ones, to praise and extol their own ancestry and to highlight its virtues and superiority to all other nations. This is the background against which Isaac Cardoso's apologetic pronouncement is to be understood: "We wish to state very clearly that the Jews do not try to persuade the gentiles to accept their doctrine, for why should they do such a thing? Certainly not to gain nobility and splendor." This, according to Cardoso, is because there is no one among the gentiles who could compete in nobility and ancestry with the members of the Hebrew people.[22]

Assistance and Distance by Turns

We find that the members of the Nação used the concepts and strategies of Hispanic particularism not only to mark the boundaries of their identity with reference to proselytes and strangers from other nations but also to define boundaries between them and Jews of other origins, especially between themselves and the German and Polish Jews whom they encountered in their new dwelling places.

Despite this, however, the Spanish and Portuguese Jews never denied their affiliation with the rest of the Jewish people. As a community they acknowledged the unity of fate and shared existence of the Jewish people. The funds for ransoming prisoners that were maintained in every one of the Western Sephardic communities were offered generously to needy Jews of any origin, wherever they were. When disasters and persecutions afflicted Jewish communities during the seventeenth and eighteenth centuries, the Spanish and Portuguese Jews participated in the joint efforts to assist the victims. At the time of the pogroms of 1648–1649 and the persecutions of the Jews of Poland during the wars against Moscow and Sweden, the Sephardic community of Amsterdam collected considerable sums for the victims and to ransom captives. From the mid-seventeenth century the Talmud Torah congregation in Amsterdam had participated in the all-Jewish effort to ransom the Jews who had fallen prisoner to the Tatars and, after 1654, to the Muscovites as well. Even before the arrival in Amsterdam of David Carcassoni, the special emissary of the authorities responsible for the redemption of prisoners in Istanbul, the Talmud Torah congregation had sent two hundred florins to the community of Ostra, "for the ransoming of prisoners of that congregation and of the surrounding settlements." A similar sum was also sent that year to the community of Lvov. These two contributions, for Ostra and Lvov respectively, were sent via Hamburg and were intended to proceed to their destinations from there, together with contributions to be added by the local Sephardic community for the same purpose. David Carcassoni's mission in Amsterdam was very successful. The Talmud Torah congregation collected the considerable sum of more than 3,000 florins from its members to ransom the prisoners taken to Constantinople by the Tatars. These are but a few examples of the total monetary contributions which this community raised for the needs of "all Jewry" in times of distress.[23] In Hamburg the local Sephardic community decreed a fast day on 25 Adar 5430 (March 15, 1670), when they learned of the expulsion of the Jews from Vienna, and Isaac Senior, one of the pillars of the community, took it upon himself to write letters to both the queen of Sweden and to the pope begging them to intercede in rescinding the banishment. Monetary contributions to assist the communities of Eastern Europe were not lacking in the Hamburg community either, though they were more modest than those raised by the Sephardim in Amsterdam. From the 1670s onward the Hamburg community markedly reduced expenditures for help to communities and individuals outside of the Nação, because of its own financial distress. For this reason too, it also refrained, on 8 Teveth 5435 (January 5, 1675) from responding to the request for a loan made by the community of Lublin. A year later a request made by Cracow for assistance in ransoming prisoners was also refused, in the following terms: "We have more than enough to do in the assistance we must extend *to those who are our own*, and thus we will not [assist] Ashkenazic Jews."[24] Although expressions of that sort betray a tendency toward self-segregation, throughout the seventeenth century, that community maintained constant and close ties with the Ashkenazic communities of Altona and Wandsbek. Ties with Jewish communities beyond the boundaries of the Nação and the Sephardic diaspora in general, especially with Ashkenazic communities in Central and Eastern Europe, were also common in other Western Sephardic communities. The Jewish world became accustomed to seeing the centers of the Nação, especially the strong and wealthy community of Amsterdam, as an important source of support in times of trouble. They thus frequently turned to them with requests for economic assistance.

Particularly against the background of this willingness to share the fate of the entire Jewish diaspora, the tendency to self-segregation and separation from the Ashkenazic Jews living in their midst is all the more striking. Indeed, it grew more so as the numbers of Ashkenazic immigrants settling in their communities increased, especially during the Thirty Years' War and the wars in Eastern Europe during the 1650s. A bylaw formulated by the Mahamad of the Talmud Torah community in Amsterdam on 9 Shevat 5418 (January 13, 1658) exemplifies the expressions of self-segregation of the members of the Nação. It states that the Mahamad forbids the *robisim* (i.e., school teachers) to accept in their classes in the community "tudesco, Italian, and mulatto" boys.[25] The mention of German boys in the same breath with mulattoes emphasizes the low estimation in which the Spanish and Portuguese Jews held their Ashkenazic brethren who settled in the city: they accorded them rights equal to dark-skinned proselytes. Moreover, according to this regulation, it is only Ashkenazic boys who are liable to do harm to the good education of the Spanish and Portuguese members of the Nação! It does not speak of the Polish boys, whose number was growing at that time because of the mass emigration of refugees from Lithuania following the

Swedish invasion. Perhaps at that stage they still permitted them to study with the boys of the congregation. However, with the passage of time, especially after the Polish Jews had mingled with the Ashkenazic congregation, the *polacos* were probably included among those discriminated against. Furthermore, the regulation just cited does permit those Ashkenazic boys already enrolled for that year

> to continue with their studies in the aforementioned *midrashim*, but it goes without saying that their brothers will not be able to do so without a vote being taken in their cases, and from this day on no boy will be permitted to study in the Talmud Torah if he is a tudesco in origin from his father and mother, nor Italians or mulattoes, except for the sons of the yehidim of this holy congregation.[26]

At the same time, the leaders saw fit to state that even if only one of a boy's parents was Ashkenazic, he would not automatically be accepted for studies. Henceforth, the members of the Mahamad were to vote and decide who would be accepted for study in the community school. And if one of the robisim acted on his own initiative, without the prior permission of the Mahamad, to accept in his class a boy, one of whose parents was not a member of the Nação, he would have to pay a fine of twenty florins to the community charity fund. The Sephardic congregation of Hamburg followed in the footsteps of its sister in Amsterdam, and about a year and a half later, on 22 Av 5419 (August 11, 1659), its leaders adopted a similar decision, stating "that for the good of the pupils of our nation, it is fitting that no German boy should be accepted in the school." The decision of the Mahamad of Hamburg was even more extreme, for it also ordered the immediate expulsion from school of those already enrolled that year, that is, "all of those who are not of our nation, except four boys who are studying with the Senhor Haham Moses Israel and the *robi* David Israel."[27]

This categorical declaration regarding the harm that seven Ashkenazic boys could inflict on the good education of the "members of the Nação" implies apprehension lest the Ashkenazic children might, because of their moral flaws, infect the Sephardic children, who had no immunity against bad and harmful influences.

On the face of it, this is merely an expression of the deep social gap separating Sephardic and Ashkenazic Jews in Western Europe at that time. In contrast to the great respect accorded to the Spanish and

Portuguese Jews in official circles, and the legends current in the general community regarding their enormous wealth, the German and Polish Jews were viewed as miserable peddlers. The gap was particularly severe in places like Hamburg and London, where the Sephardic communities were smaller and socially more homogeneous and the number of Ashkenazic Jews who arrived there during the seventeenth century was quite limited. But in Amsterdam, where the Ashkenazic population equaled the Sephardic population by the 1670s (each of the two communities numbered about twenty-five hundred), the Sephardic Jews still retained their prestige as the principal established Jewish community with respect to economic and social importance.[28]

Beggars, Janitors, and Servant Women

Despite the absolute superiority of Sephardic Jews, there was there no lack of poor people within the Western Sephardic communities, and they experienced acute social problems. Nevertheless, the status of the community was determined by the weight of its wealthy members, with the poor among them simply ignored. By contrast, the status of the Ashkenazic Jews within that internal hierarchy was determined by the weight of their poor and indigent and not by the well-established Ashkenazic Jews.[29]

The Sephardic Jews in Western Europe generally regarded their Ashkenazic brethren as a community of paupers, an image that was reinforced with the waves of German refugees during the Thirty Years' War. From 1632 onward the regulations no longer speak of "poor tudescos" but rather of tudescos plain and simple, meaning in almost every case paupers and beggars.[30] The ordinance of the Beth Israel community of Hamburg dated 5 Heshvan 5414 (October 26, 1653) also uses the term *tudesco* as a synonym for "poor," ordering them "not to wander about at the gates." Words similar in spirit are found in the regulation of 6 Tishrei 5415 (November 27, 1654), which also discusses matters related to the "commandment to give charity to tudescos." Six months afterward a meeting of the Mahamad of Hamburg discussed the "scandal caused by the tudescos who wander about at the gates," and it was decided that

> after a warning has been given to the leaders [of the Ashkenazic congregation] in Altona and to those of the tudescos who dwell here, if they do

not better their ways, the Lords of the Nation, by means of a decree of the Senate of the City, will attempt to place two of them in the Rasphuis [the workhouse] so that others might learn a lesson from them."[31]

Although in London the number of Ashkenazic Jews was still minuscule, it was decided as early as 1679 that in the future nothing would be given to

> the tudesco foreigners who come to request more than the five shillings [which they received] from the charity fund, and from the day that the warden knows of their arrival [in the city], he will inform them that it was agreed to permit them to come to the synagogue only for four days, and afterwards they will be removed; and he will endeavor to send them to Rotterdam or to Amsterdam on the first ship to come along. And if any of them rebel and refuse to go away, the warden and witnesses will come, and they will go with him to the quarters where that tudesco is staying to serve notice that nothing should be sold to him on credit, and that the nation will return nothing to anyone who does so.[32]

Just as the term *tudescos* by itself generally is used as a synonym for paupers or beggars, so also the feminine form, *tudescas*, or the expression *moças tudescas* (Ashkenazic girls) usually refers to servant women. In a decision dated 13 Tishre 5415 (September 24, 1654), the Mahamad of Amsterdam forbade Ashkenazic women to enter the Spanish-Portuguese synagogue, and if one of them should violate that prohibition her mistress would have to pay a fine of two florins to the charity fund. The ruling seems to have been intended to prevent Ashkenazic women from taking places designated for Sephardic women. It is clear that the Ashkenazic women referred to here are servants, for the regulation states that the fine is to be paid by the mistress of the tudesca who violates it. The ordinance states explicitly that if the Ashkenazic woman who enters the women's section of the synagogue is free (*tudesca libre*), that is, not the servant of a member of the Sephardic congregation, and no one is responsible for her, she is only to be removed from the place with no further penalty.[33]

The situation in Hamburg was no different: the expression "tudescas que servem a os da nossa naçao" (Ashkenazic women who serve members of our nation) is very common in the registers of the Sephardic community. In the idiom of the Mahamad in Hamburg the word for "Ashkenazic woman" is used alternatively with the word for "servant woman," and the meaning of the two terms is identical. In that city the leadership of the Nação went out of its way to prevent tudescas from residing permanently in the city, and there is no lack of cases in which these women were expelled after their marriage to an Ashkenazic resident of the city.[34]

Tudescos were occasionally employed by Sephardic congregations as janitors, servants, and cleaners. In Amsterdam an Ashkenazic man by the name of Hertz served as the watchman at the entrance of the women's section of the Spanish and Portuguese synagogue from 1643 on. In 1669 the Mahamad appointed him as janitor, and he served in that capacity until 1681. For close to forty years that Ashkenazic Jew served the members of the Nação in Amsterdam, and after his death his sons, who had served together with him for a certain period, inherited his position.[35]

It is known that in Amsterdam the poor mentally ill members of the Nação were placed in the care of Ashkenazic Jews. In return for their efforts and for keeping the patients in their homes, so they would not have to be hospitalized in the Dolhuis, the municipal asylum, these Ashkenazic caretakers received a fixed salary from the community treasury. This situation lasted at least until the 1730s, when patients apparently began to be sent to the municipal institution. The documents of the Sephardic community of Amsterdam mention *o loco Carrilho* (Carrilho the madman), that is, Moses Carrilho, for whose keeping and care eight florins were paid every month to the Ashkenazic man who kept him in his home. This monthly fee, unchanged, was paid for thirty-four years, to "Carrilho's Ashkenazic man" (*o tudesco do Carrilho*), as his guardian was called. Undoubtedly it was not the same "Ashkenazic man" for all those years! In 1663, for about two months, five and a half florins were paid every week to an Ashkenazic man for keeping "Abraham Solomon Pinto the madman" in his home. Some months afterward various sums were disbursed to an Ashkenazic man for attending to that patient and escorting him to Ferrara, Italy. One gains the impression that the escort also remained with *o loco Pinto* in his new dwelling place for a number of years. For four months in 1686 Johanan Cohen and Samuel Polack, both Ashkenazic Jews of Amsterdam, alternately received various sums for keeping "the madman from Bayonne," apparently a poor patient belonging to the Nação in southern France who had made his way to Amsterdam. These are surely not the only such cases, and this was the way the Sephardic community of

Amsterdam looked after its poor mentally ill during the seventeenth century. The expenses for caring for wealthy patients were paid by their relatives, and it is quite likely that they too preferred to place their mentally ill with private caretakers rather than imprison them in the municipal asylum.

This custom of the Amsterdam Sephardic Jews has clear symbolic significance: at a time when the mentally ill in Christian Europe were increasingly viewed as deviant and threatening, and society took care to isolate them from the public and to imprison them in special institutions established for that purpose, the leaders of the Nação in Amsterdam saw fit to place their "fools" in the custody of needy and poverty-stricken Ashkenazic Jews, who could be hired to take care of the insane. Here, too, the mentally unbalanced are removed from the community, but in this case the Ashkenazic home becomes the "place of banishment," and thus it takes on some of the symbolic, repugnant, and threatening associations of the infamous "madhouse."[36]

"Vices and Customs Alien to Morality and to the Ways of Judaism"

There emerges from the foregoing a picture of the deep social gap separating Spanish and Portuguese Jews from German and Polish Jews. The dependence of the latter upon the goodwill of the former is a phenomenon repeated in one fashion or another in most of the Western centers in which the two groups met during the seventeenth century. The Ashkenazic Jews borrowed their first two Torah scrolls from the Sephardic Jews of Amsterdam when they established the first prayer group of their own, and it is typical that the man making the request was the donor's personal servant. Whether it be finding a place to pray or a place for burial or obtaining resources to care for the poor, the dependence of the Ashkenazic Jews upon their affluent Sephardic brethren is notable in every area.

However, the social reserve of the members of the Nação regarding the Ashkenazic Jews carried overtones that are not exhausted by the economic and social differences between them. One of the first ordinances of the Talmud Torah congregation in Amsterdam, passed in 1639, immediately after it was established through the unification of its constituent congregations, bears the title "Regulation about the tudescos." This ordinance, dating from the end of Tammuz 5399 (early

August 1639), protests against "the annoyance and discomfort caused by the tudescos who are in the habit of coming to this country." These words, written at the peak of the emigration of refugees from the Thirty Years' War, express reservations about the new Ashkenazic arrivals, "who loiter and beg for charity in the gates on Fridays and the Sabbath[!] . . . Because people give them donations, they stay and live in this country, and thus today there is such a large number of tudescos, and if no solution is found, perhaps many more will come in the future." But the crime of these beggars was not limited to the fact that begging had become a way of life for them, in addition, "many of them have vices and customs alien to morality and to the ways of Judaism." Hence the members of the Mahamad ordered that no alms at all be given at the gates of the synagogue and that if one of the Ashkenazic poor was arrested, "none of our men shall go and intercede for his release." Explicit mention is made here of the moral shallowness of the Ashkenazic beggars, which causes them to violate the Torah and the commandments.[37] Doubtless the mass immigration of Polish and Lithuanian Jews between 1648 and 1650 further exacerbated the problem of beggary among the Ashkenazic Jews and the friction between them and the Sephardic community, which resulted in harsher policies toward them. The leadership of the Nação in Amsterdam also had harsh words for the immigrants from Poland: "They are dangerous people, who have found that a life of beggary is good for them." However, something is responsible for the contemptible behavior of the refugees fleeing persecution in Eastern Europe: "Here they have absorbed the idle habits of the aforementioned tudescos"! The wording of this regulation indicates that the insidious ways of the German Jews had distanced the Polish refugees from the *bom judesmo* and induced them to violate the Torah. With their low standards of conduct, the tudescos had supposedly "infected" the Polish refugees, who learned to live a life of idleness, with all its accompanying vices. As at the peak of the Thirty Years' War, when waves of German refugees flooded Amsterdam, now too, at the end of the 1650s, the Sephardic community mobilized its resources to transport the immigrants from Eastern Europe out of Holland. If they remained in the city, it was feared they would become a social nuisance. Hence a regulation of 1658 forbids offering any assistance to these Jews beyond that officially given them by the Sephardic community.[38]

Apparently, the presence of masses of refugees created moral panic among the community of Spanish and Portuguese Jews. To emphasize the gravity of the situation and to warn all the members of the congregation not to violate the ordinance, it appended to it that "all the Senhores-yehidim of this holy congregation wish to discuss the benefit derived from this ordinance in their homes, and therefore it must be maintained as *one of the most severe and important ordinances instituted in this community* [emphasis added]." At that time the congregations of the Germans and Poles decided to take a similar position toward the waves of poor immigrants, apparently at the instigation of the Mahamad of the Sephardic community.[39]

Similar arguments in similar wording appear in the register of the Beth Israel congregation of Hamburg. Here, too, the Ashkenazic leaders joined in the chorus of detractors from the Nação who decried "the many Ashkenazic poor who come all the time and cause a nuisance in all the houses." According to the Mahamad of the Beth Israel congregation, it was actually the Ashkenazic leaders who raised the argument that it was the mercy shown by the Sephardic Jews to these poor people "that is the reason why so many of them come [here]." On 16 Iyyar 5424 (May 11, 1664) it was agreed among the leadership of both the Sephardic and Ashkenazic congregations of Hamburg that, "under penalty of excommunication, no Polish or Ashkenazic Jew shall come here to settle without prior acceptance by our Mahamad and theirs."[40] But arguments against the Germans who wandered about the gates of the houses continued to be raised before the Mahamad of Hamburg in subsequent years, and on 3 Tishrei 5442 (September 15, 1681) a complaint was registered against "the scandal caused by the arrival of poor tudescos who beg for alms at our gates." In Hamburg too, in 1681, the members of the Nação expressed apprehension regarding the plague spread by "the many tudescos who went to the fair in Leipzig [the place where the terrible plague lurked], and it is possible that because they were carried away by their greed they brought with them some infected article." The same regulations condemn the Ashkenazim who made a commotion in the streets, bought stolen goods, or were themselves suspected of theft, and who led an immoral life (*mãa vida*). They also refer to *tudescos vagabundos*, who disturbed the peace. They were ordered to leave the city, and all commerce with them was forbidden.[41]

From the foregoing it emerges that in the view of the members of the Nação in Western Europe, especially in the places where they encountered their brethren from Germany and Eastern Europe, a stereotypical image of the tudescos and polacos had developed. This negative image was indeed nourished by the economic gap between the two communities. More important, however, from the perspective of the members of the Nação, the poverty and slender means of the German and Polish Jews assumed moral implications that far exceeded actual social differences. Former New Christians who had only recently returned to the world of Judaism did not hesitate to condemn that which they saw as the degraded way of life typifying their German and Polish brethren and distancing them from bom judesmo. The poverty of the tudescos and polacos appeared to these Sephardic Jews not only as an expression of a social situation but also as a cultural trait indelibly stamped upon them, causing their depravation and distancing them from the ways of Judaism.

The Reformation of the Ashkenazic Jews and Their Education in Moral Conduct and Good Judaism

We have already mentioned that poverty in itself was not unknown among the members of the Nação; many of the Spanish and Portuguese Jews in Western Europe lived in conditions of severe economic distress. These poor members also caused the Nação more than a few difficulties in its daily struggles with them. The leaders of the community tried in several ways to direct various segments of the poor population to other countries and to distance them as much as possible from the centers of settlement of the Sephardic diaspora in Western Europe.[42] Although some of these poor Spanish and Portuguese Jews bore upon their brows the stigma of moral turpitude, this community of poor people in general could not be so characterized. The attitude toward them as a *collective* was quite different from that displayed toward the poor Germans and Poles, and this difference was expressed fascinatingly in Amsterdam with the establishment of the Avodat Hesed Society in 1642. At that time the height of the Ashkenazic migration from Germany, the Talmud Torah congregation of Spanish and Portuguese Jews decided to establish a special society to deal with the problem of poverty and beggary among the tudescos. The bylaws of this society explicitly state that the members of the Mahamad had sought a remedy for the many troubles afflicting the poor members of the Hebrew nation, "and especially the Ashkenazic Jews who were exiled from Germany because of the wars, the famine, the persecutions, and other evils, and to prevent the great damage caused us here by the indignity to His holy Name, the violation of His Torah, and the humiliation of His people." As this was caused by the beggary of the poor Ashkenazic Jews, the heads of the congregation decided that in the future these people should earn their bread by labor, and for that purpose the aforesaid society was established. It was meant to teach the poor tudescos a trade, so that through their study and labor they could support themselves with honor. The regulations stipulate explicitly that the supervisors of the society must be faithful in observing the commandments; they must see to it that everyone "prays in a quorum with clean hands, and similarly at meals, and they must guide them as much as possible in virtuous conduct." The society was thus intended not only to teach the Ashkenazic poor a useful trade but also to lead them to bom judesmo! These two goals are interrelated; the purpose of the society, that is, was to educate these poor people, whose morals had been corrupted by persecution and tribulation, to a high standard of moral behavior. Thus paragraph 7 of the bylaws prohibits "smoking and any gaming and also immoral behavior" within the walls of the institution. Paragraph 8 speaks explicitly of poor Jews who were arrested and imprisoned in the Amsterdam Rasphuis, where they were forced to violate the Sabbath, to eat forbidden foods, and to remove their hats during prayers. The Avodat Hesed Society was established to rectify that situation. Interestingly, the leaders of the Nação in Amsterdam saw fit to invest effort and resources in teaching the Ashkenazic beggars a productive trade; they were not concerned about their own Spanish and Portuguese poor whom they considered to be immune to moral corruption by virtue of their belonging to the Nação. It is not surprising, then, that when members of the Mahamad decided in 1670 to change the purpose of the Avodat Hesed Society and to cease caring for Ashkenazic Jews— and instead to devote the revenues of the society to the support of poor Spanish and Portuguese Jews—its character also changed. It became, henceforth, a welfare and assistance society, with no further connection to educational goals or the teaching of a trade. These purposes were not relevant to the poor members of the Nação, since they, after all, were not in need of reform.[43]

"Not by Marriage, nor by Covenant, nor in Any Other Way"

In 1762 the Portuguese Jewish philosopher and economist Isaac de Pinto composed a critical response to the blunt remarks written against the Jews by Voltaire in his *Dictionnaire philosophique* article "Juifs," which had been published six years earlier. Among other things, Pinto expressed himself in the following words:

> If at that time Monsieur de Voltaire had consulted the common sense in which he took such pride, he would have first distinguished the Portuguese and Spanish Jews from the rest, for they never mingled or joined with the masses of the other sons of Jacob . . . for they are scrupulous not to intermingle, not by marriage, nor by covenant, nor by any other means, with the Jews of other nations. . . . The distance between them and their brethren is so great that if a Portuguese Jew dwelling in Holland or England were to marry an Ashkenazic Jewish woman, he would immediately lose all his special privileges: he would no longer be considered a member of their synagogue, he would have no part in all sorts of ecclesiastical and lay offices, and he would be completely removed from the Nation. . . . They are of the opinion that they are derived from the Tribe of Judah, whose honorable families were exiled to the land of Spain at the time of the Babylonian Exile, and this opinion leads them to separatism and develops feelings of superiority within them, for everyone has regard for them, and even their brethren among the other nations seem to recognize them.

Pinto offered his own explanations for the social misery and moral degradation of the Jews of Germany and Poland:

> Is it at all surprising that they, who have been deprived of all benefit from society, who are fruitful and multiply according to the laws of nature together with those of the Torah, and whom every one holds in contempt and humiliates, and who are frequently persecuted and always reviled: is it at all surprising that their humiliated and oppressed nature seems as if it attends only to its needs?. . . . The contempt in which they are held destroys within them any root of the feeling of honor and virtue. . . . In Amsterdam and London there are a large number of extremely honest Ashkenazic Jews who deal with great integrity in commerce. They are not responsible for the behavior of the masses of Poles and Germans whom distress has driven from their countries, and their brethren in their mercy bring them into their homes. In the courts of Germany there were very honorable Jews. Anyone who opposes the

innocent paves the way to crime. . . . Distress, persecutions, and in-
dignities are what make them like members of another religion, for the
circumstances of their lives are similar.[44]

These remarks expressed a prevalent view among the members of the
Nação regarding their German and Polish brethren, a view reinforced
by decades of social contact in the lands of Western Europe. Cloaked in
the garment of contemporary enlightenment discourse, the Sephardic
Jewish intellectual presented here an approach that had already taken
shape among the members of his community in the seventeenth century. Pinto's phrases are devoid of emotional overtones, as though he
were trying to express an objective sociological truth that explained the
low cultural and moral situation of the Jews of Germany and Poland:
humiliation and oppression by Christian European society had marred
the Jews' moral fiber and distorted their humanity. The guilt lies not
with them but with their oppressors.

If they are treated honorably, the results are different, and this is the
proof: "In the courts of Germany there were very honorable Jews"!
Were those Jews not denied free access to the courts of their rulers, were
they not persecuted and reviled by the nations, they too would be capable of being "honest" and of supporting themselves "with great in-
tegrity." With that same "objective" tone, Pinto formulated his remarks
on the Spanish and Portuguese Jews, about whom he also spoke in the
third person: "They never mingled or joined with the masses of the
other sons of Jacob." Self-segregation and feelings of superiority are an
integral part of their sociological image, and those traits too are anchored in a different historical reality, which was their heritage and
placed its seal upon their conduct and way of life.

Pinto's remarks about the loss of community rights incurred by anyone who married an Ashkenazic woman were not his invention but
rather reflected the actual state of affairs in the Western Sephardic diaspora. The Spanish and Portuguese community in Amsterdam was especially strict in this regard: on 24 Kislev 5432 (November 26, 1671) it
decided that Ashkenazic Jews who married Portuguese or Spanish
women, "daughters of the Naçao," should not in the future be considered as yehidim in the congregation—"not them, nor their descendants, and after their death they cannot be buried in our cemetery." An
explicit clause was added at the end of the ordinance: "This regulation
is declared to include the Poles as well." It was evidently added at a later

date, probably after the Polish community was finally swallowed up by the Ashkenazic congregation.[45] Twenty-five years later, on the new moon of Elul 5457 (August 18, 1697), it was decided to expand the third paragraph of the bylaws of the unification of the congregations dating from 1639, with respect to the Spanish and Portuguese character of the Amsterdam community and the definition of the right of Jews "who are members of other nations" to pray in the synagogue of the Talmud Torah congregation. The members of the Mahamad warned that this third paragraph was not observed with proper diligence, "and the damage will increase in the future if no barrier is erected in that matter," for

> many Jews of other nations . . . come to this city without any reason other than the rumor that here they will receive support from our congregation; and all of this causes great damage and decline in the support which can be offered with generosity to the poor of our Portuguese and Spanish nation.

Hence it was decided:

> In the future the members of other nations will not be accepted as yehidim in this holy congregation, *and this also applies to those men of other nations who have married a Portuguese or Spanish woman, or regarding any Portuguese or Spanish Jew who marries a woman from another Jewish nation, and for this reason they will be removed.*[46]

From then on it was not only Ashkenazic Jews married to Spanish or Portuguese women who were deprived of membership rights in the congregation but also men of Portuguese or Spanish extraction married to women from other Jewish ethnic groups, principally Ashkenazic women. This subject was still a matter of concern to the syndics of the Sephardic community in the early eighteenth century.

On 8 Iyyar 5469 (April 17, 1709) the members of the Mahamad and the elders of the Nation decided to institute stricter procedures for accepting new members into the congregation. In the future, they ruled, the Portuguese or Spanish extraction of the candidate must be clear beyond any doubt, "and if the slightest doubt should arise" on the matter, two witnesses from among the members of the Nação were to be brought,

> well known and fit men, worthy of trust, and it will be incumbent upon them to declare under oath as a commandment of our holy Torah, that the candidate or candidates are members of the Portuguese or Spanish

nation, and that all the other conditions are fulfilled in them which have been stipulated in the ordinances of the Nation.

Further on the ordinance states explicitly, "Those who marry women who do not belong to the foregoing nations (that is, the Spanish or Portuguese) will be deprived of their rights as *yahid* . . . they and their descendants from that marriage."[47]

These strict laws of segregation lasted a long time, even beyond the days of Isaac de Pinto. In 1811 the Talmud Torah congregation of Amsterdam refused burial in the cemetery at Ouderkerk to a member of the congregation who had married an Ashkenazic woman; his body was ultimately buried in the Ashkenazic cemetery! And fourteen years after that the Sephardic congregation refused to bury an Ashkenazic woman next to her deceased Portuguese husband, not taking into consideration that they had been married for almost forty years.[48]

This strict policy is expressed fascinatingly in the attitude of the members of the Nação toward some of the rare Ashkenazic Jews who succeeded, thanks to extraordinary circumstances, in assimilating among them. The members of the family of Moses Uri Ha-Levi of Emden, who had arrived in Amsterdam with the first group of crypto-Jews from Portugal and had openly rejoined the Jewish people in Holland, insisted on retaining their rights as members of the Spanish and Portuguese community. For a certain time the members of the Mahamad recognized the rights of the aforementioned Moses Uri Ha-Levi and his son Aaron. As they said, "They had introduced the existence of Judaism into Amsterdam," and therefore were permitted to live among the Beth Yaakov and Neve Shalom communities. After 1639 the united Talmud Torah congregation continued to observe that tradition. Thus the well-known Ashkenazic printer Uri Ha-Levi and other members of his family enjoyed the rights of a yahid. In 1700, however, a man by the name of Uri Ephraim, also a scion of that family, addressed the community and asked to be accepted as a yahid. His request led to a new discussion of the entire question of the special rights accorded to the descendants of Uri Ha-Levi of Emden and a search was made in the community registers so that some principled decision could be reached on the matter. This search purportedly proved that the congregation had never obligated itself to grant the members of that family the "imaginary right," as they termed it, to become members of the community, and this shows that "the officials of that time did not see fit that these people should continue to live with us, and they knew that they were not suitable to the customs of our people." Therefore the Mahamad decided on 24 Elul 5460 (September 8, 1700) that "the aforesaid Uri Ephraim and others, who have already been accepted as yehidim in the past, shall continue within the congregation, but henceforth no one [of that family will be accepted for membership in the congregation] under any pretext in the world."[49]

With this strict supervision of the purity of the Nação the separatist strategy of the Western Sephardic diaspora shows itself in its fullest, most extreme form. Any reader of these regulations, who observes the manner in which they inquired into the pure "Portuguese or Spanish extraction" of candidates for membership in the congregation, cannot but recall the intense attention given by Iberian institutions and organizations at the time of the expansion of the Statutes of limpieza de sangre to verifying the pure origins—on all sides, *de cuatro costados*—of anyone who wished to join them.[50] When the New Jews came to consolidate their new collective identity, they found that the borderline separating them from Jews of other extractions was no less decisive than that separating them from those *membros da nação* who had merged with Christianity. To a great degree, sharpening the separation between themselves and the New Christians who chose to assimilate helped them consolidate the contents of their Judaism. Similarly, emphasizing the difference between them and "other Jews" contributed to maintaining the myth of their noble extraction from the Tribe of Judah and to the preservation of their connection with the world of Iberian culture. The deficiencies members of the Nação attributed to the Jews of Germany and Eastern Europe were intended to emphasize the virtues of a particular group within all Jewry: the "humiliated and oppressed" nature of the German and Polish Jews with whom they came into contact strengthened their self-awareness as members of the aristocracy of the Jewish people. The "lack of a feeling of honor" among the tudesco peddlers and beggars heightened the feeling of *honra* and *hidalguía* of those who had suffered humiliation in the Iberian world because they were regarded as lacking "an honorable extraction." What the Sephardic Jews termed the "vices and customs alien to morality and to the ways of Judaism" of the Ashkenazic refugees served to give legitimacy to the bom judesmo of the refugees from the Inquisition. But diligent care in keeping "a distance between them and their brethren" (a "great" distance, according to Pinto) also had another function: by means of that distance, they sought to exempt the members of the Nação from the grave accusations leveled by Voltaire against all the Jews. By emphasizing the uniqueness of the Spanish and Portuguese Jews, in contrast to "the masses of the other sons of Jacob," so too the leaders of the Nation sought to protect their social status in their new centers.

9

Prototypes of Leadership in a Sephardic Community:
Smyrna in the Seventeenth Century

Jacob Barnai

To get a good look at the internal world of the Jewish communities in the Ottoman Empire about a hundred years after the expulsion from Spain, one could do worse than to study the history of the Smyrna community in the seventeenth century. This community was unique among the large and famous Jewish communities of the Ottoman Empire, not to mention the smaller ones, in that it had been founded only a hundred years after the expulsion from Spain. It was established by Jewish immigrants from all parts of the Ottoman Empire, mainly third- and fourth-generation descendants of the Jews who had been expelled from Spain. They were joined by Romaniote Jews from the Balkan countries and, in the seventeenth century, by a large number of Portuguese marranos.[1] The Jewish community in Smyrna in the seventeenth century is thus the historical product of about a century of life in the shadow of the Ottoman society and regime, with all its implications. In addition, one must consider the societies of Portuguese marranos, as these, it turns out, were more important than had previously been thought.[2] This new community had a twofold nature—at once continuing its immigrant history but also creating something new. Moreover, it is also impossible to ignore the issue of Sabbateanism in Smyrna, as was the case with other Jewish communities as well. We will briefly examine this issue from the viewpoint of the central figures in the leadership of the community where Sabbatai Zevi was born, grew up, and acted as a messiah.

This essay will introduce the reader to the leadership of the Smyrna community in the seventeenth century by drawing portraits of some of its central figures. These biographies reflect both the continuity of the Smyrna community with the other Jewish communities and its novelty and uniqueness.

From the time that the Smyrna community began to develop, at the end of the sixteenth century, many sages, businessmen, and wealthy people immigrated there. Dozens of these are known to us by name from various sources, including books that they wrote and published. From these sources one can collect a sample of figures representing a cross-section of leadership types, as follows: (1) the rabbi-public worker, (2) the anti-Sabbatean kabbalist, (3) the pro-Sabbatean preacher, (4) the organizing rabbi, and (5) the halakhic authority and leader. Portraits of each one of these leader types will be broadly sketched, but in order not to make the sketches too broad we will briefly describe the first three types and then describe the last two at greater lengths, as they stamped a stronger impression on the history of the community.

The Rabbi-Public Worker: Rabbi Solomon ben Ezra

Any sort of community will have its behind-the-scenes figures, the operator whose activities are not always exposed to public scrutiny. One such figure is Rabbi Solomon ben Ezra of seventeenth-century Smyrna. A native of Ankara, he was apparently a student of Rabbi Moses de Boton.[3] It is not known exactly when he came to Smyrna, but we know that at least from the 1650s he was active in all the community's spheres of leadership and society and that he held an important place among the sages and supporters of the community. He was very active in getting manuscripts by the Smyrna sages published by Abraham Gabbai. He wrote introductions to several of these books and even prepared indexes for them.[4] In his and his sons' collections there remained a number of these manuscripts by Rabbi Jacob Berav, the sage who reintroduced the semikha (an attempt to renew the ancient Sanhedrin) in Safed, and a book by Joseph Escapa, "Rosh Yosef" Responsa, which was later taken to Germany and printed there.[5]

During the 1660s R. ben Ezra was considered one of the most important rabbis in the community. For one thing, he served in the key position of the community *kahya*, that is, its representative to the Ottoman authorities in the city.[6] During the 1650s and 1660s he was one of the heads of Pinto Congregation and one of the founders of a new congregation called Senora, which was established in 1660.[7] In the famous 1669 letter of the Sabbatean Abraham Michael Cardoso to the Smyrna judges, he was listed third among the five important rabbis in the city.[8] In my opinion he held a key position in the city at the time of Sabbatai Zevi's appearance as a messiah in 1665, and he was the author of the "anonymous responsum" concerning Sabbatai Zevi that serves as an important source for the Sabbatean affair in the city.[9] This responsum was published at the end of the nineteenth century by the rabbi of Smyrna at that time, Abraham Palagi. The responsum, written in 1666, contains authentic evidence about the state of mind in the community at the time of Sabbatai Zevi and about the leadership's influence on the community's belief in him. It also contains echoes of the power struggles in the city rabbinate, which went along with Sabbatai Zevi's takeover of the community. The author of the responsum beats his breast in repentance for his sin of leading the general public astray by encouraging them to believe in Sabbatai Zevi, but he claims that he did this out of the innocent faith that the Messiah had indeed arrived.

R. ben Ezra's status in the community continued to be very important in the 1670s and 1680s as well—occasionally more so than that of the rabbis chosen by the community. As is clear from the extensive contemporary rabbinic literature, he was close to all the important rabbis in the city and maintained a good relationship with the various sides at the time of the quarrels within the rabbinate. He was a coauthor of various halakhic decisions, and he left a number of responsa, some of which were published in books of his contemporaries or of later rabbis, while others remain in manuscript.[10] Most of his published responsa on topics of halakha and society are included in the book *Batei Knesiyot* (Synagogues) published by his grandson, R. Abraham ben Ezra, who was the chief rabbi of Smyrna in the mid-eighteenth century.[11]

R. Solomon ben Ezra died in 1688.[12] His two sons served as interpreters for the French consul in Smyrna in the late seventeenth century, thus continuing his tradition of public service.[13] His descendants continued to hold key positions in the community in the eighteenth and nineteenth centuries as well.[14]

The Anti-Sabbatean Kabbalist: Rabbi Solomon Algazi

R. Solomon Algazi was born in Bursa in central Turkey about 1610. He studied in yeshivot in Istanbul, and then lived in a number of other communities before settling in Smyrna prior to 1650.[15]

Although R. Algazi published books in many areas of rabbinic interest (halakha, midrash, aggada, and Kabbalah),[16] he was known principally for his kabbalistic work *Me'ulefet Sapirim*, which was published in Istanbul in 1660.[17] He thus represents the "kabbalistic sage," a type that, in contrast to what was believed until recently, had not been very prevalent in Jewish communities in general and in the Ottoman Empire in particular before the outbreak of Sabbateanism.[18] This holds for Smyrna, too; indeed, of all the extant works of the Smyrna sages written before the advent of Sabbateanism, only the above-mentioned book by R. Algazi deals with the Kabbalah. Moreover, it is a kabbalistic work based on the *Zohar* rather than on Lurianic Kabbalah, thus supporting the thesis that has been advocated by Moshe Idel in recent years. *Me'ulefet Sapirim* contains Hebrew translations of passages from the *Zohar*, which are "divided according to topic into thirty chapters so that they may be studied a chapter a day for all thirty days of the month."[19]

R. Algazi differed from the other Smyrna sages in more than his study of Kabbalah; when Sabbatai Zevi arrived in Smyrna as the Messiah in the fall of 1665 and took over the community, R. Algazi was one of the few people among all the sages and residents of the city who vigorously opposed him. Together with Rabbi Aaron Lapapa, he had to hide and fled to a nearby city.[20] As we shall see, it was precisely this kabbalist (although admittedly not a Lurianic kabbalist) who sharply and publicly opposed Sabbateanism, while the community's outstanding halakhic scholar, Rabbi Haim Benveniste, supported Sabbatai Zevi after some initial hesitation.

After the crisis of the Sabbatean conversion, R. Algazi made two pilgrimages to Erez Israel during the 1670s—something he had already wanted to do in 1662 (the year that Sabbatai Zevi went to Erez Israel from Smyrna).[21] He died in Jerusalem in the 1680s,[22] leaving a legacy of books that were widely distributed and also reprinted many times by European publishers during the seventeenth, eighteenth, and nineteenth centuries.[23]

The Sabbatean Preacher: Rabbi Elijah Hacohen Ha-Itamari

R. Elijah Hacohen Ha-Itamari differs from the other sages under discussion here in that he represents the post-Sabbatean period yet remained a Sabbatean. Born in Smyrna in the 1640s, he was already able to study within the city, with its sages of the mid-seventeenth century. His father, R. Abraham Hacohen (d. 1659), was a rabbi in Smyrna. R. Elijah was a student of R. Benjamin Melamed, a Smyrna sage, who opposed Sabbateanism.[24] Although R. Elijah left a large and variegated literary heritage in various areas, he was known mainly for his books on homiletics and ethics. Some of his published works were widely disseminated and are still in use at the present time. They were distributed not only throughout the Sephardic diaspora but also in the Ashkenazic communities of Europe, especially in Eastern Europe. His most noteworthy books are *Midrash 'Eliyahu*, *Midrash Talpiot*, and *Shevet Musar*.[25]

Although R. Elijah Hacohen was still quite young at the time that Sabbatai Zevi was active in Smyrna, after the latter's conversion he, like many Jewish sages in the Ottoman Empire at the time, began to introduce Sabbatean theology and clear Sabbatean motifs into his works.[26] He was well acquainted with the works of Nathan of Gaza and had a personal relationship with several famous Sabbateans in Smyrna, including Abraham Michael Cardozo and Daniel Bonafus. He lived to be quite old and died in Smyrna in 1729. Some of his students were among the most important rabbis in Smyrna in the first half of the eighteenth century, including members of the group of editors and publishers of the popular plagiaristic book with Sabbatean tendencies, *Hemdat Yamim*.[27] They even wove sections of R. Elijah's *Shevet Musar* into their own book without indicating the source, as was their wont.[28]

R. Elijah's books portray the social tensions in Smyrna during his time and display his own great sensitivity toward the poor.[29] It may have been these social topics, and perhaps also the type of homiletics, that made his books so popular for generations in all the Jewish communities. R. Elijah seems to represent many of the sages in the

Ottoman Empire in the generation after Sabbatai Ẓevi, with all this implies: intense messianic longing and preaching for repentance and an ethical and religious life, in an attempt to accomplish what Sabbatai Ẓevi had not succeeded in doing. His Sabbateanism, which is easily discerned by the modern scholar even though R. Elijah and his contemporaries attempted to mask it in their works (not so successfully, as it was suspected in their own generation as well), reflects the response of the sages of the Ottoman Empire to the crisis engendered by the failure of Sabbateanism.

The Organizing Rabbi: Rabbi Joseph Escapa

R. Joseph Escapa, born in Salonika around 1560,[30] was educated in its study houses, which were among the most important founded by the Spanish exiles in the Ottoman Empire. He left Salonika at the end of the sixteenth or the beginning of the seventeenth century with one of the great waves of emigration from the city in the wake of its severe economic crisis.[31] He stayed for a short while in Istanbul, where he came into contact with R. Joseph Trani (the Mahariat), the capital's chief rabbi. In Istanbul he also met the young R. Haim Benveniste, who was later to be his friend, his rival in halakhic matters, and his successor in the Smyrna rabbinate. R. Escapa arrived in Smyrna between 1625 and 1631.[32] As I see it, his Salonika upbringing and his short stay in Istanbul influenced his later career as rabbi of the Smyrna community and as the organizing founder of the community for many generations. He drew upon the customs of both these communities—the two most important Jewish communities in the Ottoman Empire—although they did not always see eye to eye on various matters. R. Escapa produced very little Torah literature: three small books of responsa, the first two of which were published during his lifetime, and the third posthumously, in Germany at the beginning of the eighteenth century.[33] Other responsa of his are scattered among the published books of other rabbis of his generation and among his various manuscripts.

R. Escapa left his stamp mainly on the regulations of the Smyrna community. Established by him and his colleagues in the community leadership, Smyrna, whose Jewish community had just been founded, was a "new city" from the halakhic viewpoint, and R. Escapa's regulations actually set the pattern of the community's organization for many generations. These regulations served as the basis for the leadership and for social and economic life of the city. In the late eighteenth century one of the rabbis of Smyrna, Raphael Joseph Hazan, wrote about him, "Our great rabbi and teacher . . . R. Joseph Escapa of blessed memory, whose waters we are drinking in the entire life of the city."[34] And, when the community regulations were published in the mid-nineteenth century, the editor wrote: "Going round and round about all the approvals and regulations that were written and established by our rabbi and teacher, who enlightened the world and its inhabitants, the holy man of the remnants of Great Assembly, the great and holy man be a blessing for us."[35]

R. Escapa arrived in Smyrna during the 1620s, when the city was in the midst of enormous economic development. The Levant companies in England, Holland, and France, which had established a foothold there, engaged in a flourishing trade between Europe and Smyrna. As a result the city attracted thousands of immigrants: Muslims, Christians, and Jews. Until the arrival of R. Escapa, however, there was no established organization or leadership among the groups of Jewish immigrants, and matters within the immigrant groups were dealt with separately.

R. Escapa's regulations were mainly in the areas of marital relationships, real estate, and taxes. These regulations have come down to us in the book *'Avodat Masa'*, published in Salonika in the mid-nineteenth century by an official of the Smyrna community.[36] The book is organized and laid out like the Talmud: in the center of each page the original regulations, Ladino or Hebrew—mostly from the seventeenth century, but some from the eighteenth and nineteenth centuries—are printed in large Hebrew letters. These are surrounded by the editor's own commentaries on the regulations, including discussions of the regulations, signaling changes that had occurred in them over time, and providing precedents illustrating these changes. The precedents are taken from the community account books and contemporary tax assessments; unfortunately all the sources used by the editor have been lost. This book is therefore almost the only source of information about the internal life of this community.[37]

The editor of *'Avodat Masa'* drew a clear distinction between the tax assessments on the one hand and the real estate deeds and *ketubbot* (marriage documents) on the other. Although the two types of documents were copied separately by two sages and were kept in separate places, they nevertheless have something in common—all deal with matters relating to the entire community. In a divided community like Smyrna there were undoubtedly many issues that were dealt with by the individual congregations, but these issues were not included among the documents pertaining to the community as a whole.

Three main blocks of regulations concerning issues of central importance to the community may be distinguished as well as some other regulations on additional issues. These key groups of regulations, established when the community was consolidated in the seventeenth century follow in chronological order: (1) marriage and divorce, (2) real estate, (3) taxation. The additional regulations concerned the leadership and the economy.

The first regulations on issues of marriage and divorce and on real estate matters were established in the 1630s, while the first tax regulations that we know about were established in the 1650s. The stages are not random. Since the city was a center of immigration, the community's first concerns were in the area of marriage and divorce, in order to avoid doubts about illegitimacy and similar problems. Afterwards the growing Jewish community needed to solve problems related to housing and the buying of stores and plots of land. As the taxes to be paid to the authorities were not particularly oppressive at first, only later were regulations in that area needed—after a number of years, when the authorities listed all the new immigrants and demanded that they pay taxes. Taxation by the community for its own purposes became an issue only after the community was consolidated; the central leadership and other institutions that were set up required funding. The individual congregations had apparently taken care of their own taxation as needed; but by mid-century, a central framework for taxation and regulations in other areas of life was established.

During this process of communal consolidation and the concomitant establishment of the regulations, one figure stands out—that of R. Joseph Escapa, who may be called the founder of a community organization that would last for generations.

Community life and leadership were dynamic, as is attested by the renewal of the legislation every few years on different issues. This is reflected well in the book 'Avodat Masa'. The regulations were changed by "the appointees under the authority of our rabbi and teacher, may God protect him, the chief rabbi or chief rabbis, with the assistance of an advisory council [*Ma'amad*][38]—as one of the regulations (rather freely translated). In the seventeenth century the organizers of the Smyrna community were already able to model their community along the lines of the most important and influential Jewish communities in the Ottoman Empire—Istanbul and Salonika. Many of the Smyrna rabbis came from these communities, bringing along a tradition of regulations and agreements. In 1600 the book *Masa' Melekh* was published in Salonika, collecting regulations and agreements on matters of taxation and other matters.[39] The Smyrna sages knew about these regulations, and it is clear that the regulations of the Istanbul and Salonika communities influenced them in their formulation of the regulations for their own community.[40]

R. Joseph Escapa had a difficult job in organizing the community. He had first to deal with the various immigrant groups, with their conflicting interests, traditions, and halakhic customs. He also had to contend with rivals for the leadership from among the rabbis of the city. His cochief rabbi in the community (from the late 1620s to the mid-1640s) was R. Azaria Joshua Ashkenazi, another immigrant from Salonika. They divided the rabbinate in such a way that each stood at the head of three congregations, and they also constituted an umbrella leadership for matters common to the community as a whole.[41] This system of a rabbi for each congregation and an umbrella rabbinate consisting of several chief rabbis for the community as a whole was not unique to Smyrna; it had developed in the large Jewish communities of the Ottoman Empire during the sixteenth and seventeenth centuries.[42] What was novel in Smyrna, however, was the division of the rabbinate between the two chief rabbis (where each one was responsible for half the congregations). This was done because no single candidate was found to be acceptable to all the congregations and groups. This joint leadership in Smyrna, with R. Escapa and R. Ashkenazi as chief rabbis, was filled with tensions and struggles, a function of social differences in the various groups of immigrants and of the halakhic and personal differences between the two rabbis themselves.

There were various controversies between the two chief rabbis of Smyrna, but the greatest publicity was accorded the controversy over *nefihah* (inflating the lungs of the slaughtered animal in order to conduct an examination for defects that could render the animal unkosher). The custom in Salonika was to be lenient in this matter and to permit eating the flesh of such an animal, while in the other Turkish communities, led by Istanbul, it was forbidden.[43] The various customs had developed in the sixteenth century, as Salonika continued the custom that had prevailed in Spain while Istanbul was influenced by the Romaniote and Ashkenazic custom that forbade it. But even though both of the chief rabbis of Smyrna were natives of Salonika, R. Escapa accepted the more stringent view and R. Ashkenazi continued the custom of Salonika. It is likely that R. Escapa had probably been influenced by the practice of the Istanbul rabbis during his stay there on his way to Smyrna. This controversy shook the leadership and divided the society in Smyrna, leading to the intervention of rabbis from Salonika and Istanbul in the community's internal affairs. This after all was not a theoretical controversy but one that concerned the daily life of every Jew in this traditional society. It could lead, for example, to social and personal separation between families if one member followed the rabbi who permitted this meat and the other followed the one who forbade it. Indeed, this is what happened in Smyrna. Moreover, the control over *sheḥita* (ritual slaughter) and kashrut in any Jewish community provided a very good income for those who did the work.

But this was not the only issue on which R. Escapa and R. Ashkenazi differed. There were many others, with R. Ashkenazi generally more lenient in his decision and R. Escapa more stringent.[44] This, it seems, reflected allegiance to the two halakhic schools of thought that had developed during the sixteenth century, where the Salonika school generally tended to be more lenient and the Istanbul school more stringent. Hacker has researched the rivalry for authority on the part of these two important communities during the generations immediately following the expulsion from Spain.[45] I believe it can be explained—at least as far as matters of kashrut are concerned—by the fact that when the Spanish exiles arrived in Salonika they found practically no Jews in the city, as the Romaniotes who had been there previously had emigrated to Istanbul, leaving behind only some Ashkenazic Jews.[46] In Istanbul, by contrast, the exiles from the Iberian Peninsula found a large well-established Romaniote community, and the conflict between them in all areas continued throughout the sixteenth century.[47] The Sephardic immigrants were unable to force their customs and halakhic decisions upon the Romaniotes in every area, and they were forced to swallow their pride and make compromises. The changes in halakha and custom that had developed in the Ottoman communities in the sixteenth century thus found their expression in seventeenth-century Smyrna. It is also possible that the various customs concerning kashrut have their source in Spain before the expulsion, as there were differences between the communities in Aragon, Castile, and Catalonia. This point requires investigation.

In the 1640s R. Ashkenazi became weak and ill, and R. Escapa tried to remove him from his post, take over his position in all the congregations, and become the sole chief rabbi. These attempts were met with fierce opposition both in Smyrna and from rabbis outside the city. But, from the time of R. Ashkenazi's death in 1648 until his own in 1661, R. Escapa remained the sole chief rabbi for the community.[48] And, indeed, it was during those years that he established the community's tax regulations, which continued to exert a great influence on the community's patterns of organization for generations.

Although he died several years before Sabbatai Zevi's appearance as a messiah in Smyrna, it was R. Escapa who twice exiled him from the city, in the 1650s and the 1660s, when he began his strange actions and declared himself the Messiah.[49] R. Escapa lived to be nearly one hundred, although in his last years he did not function well and a struggle for his position began even before he died.[50]

The Halakhic Authority and Leader: R. Haim Benveniste

R. Haim Benveniste was one of the greatest halakhic authorities and rabbis in the history of Ottoman Jewry. He was a many-faceted figure who lived in several communities and was directly involved in many of the halakhic, social, and religious problems that concerned Ottoman Jewry in the seventeenth century. He was born in Istanbul in 1603 to a noble and respected family of Portuguese origin.[51] His grandfather, R. Moses Benveniste, was the grand vizier's physician in the court of the Sublime Porte in the last quarter of the sixteenth century. R. Moses was convicted of spying for foreign countries (Spain and France) and was punished by exile at forced labor in Rhodes.[52] R. Haim's main teacher in Istanbul was R. Joseph Terani (the Maharit), son of R. Moses Terani (the Mabit), one of the greatest Safed sages in the sixteenth century. R. Haim's brother, R. Joshua Benveniste, and his nephew, R. Moses Benveniste, were also important rabbis in the capital during the seventeenth century.

At the beginning of R. Haim Benveniste's career as a rabbi he was appointed to be in charge of halakhic issues about family matters in Istanbul. In 1643 he moved to the city of Tire near Smyrna and was appointed rabbi of the city. In 1658 he moved to Smyrna, but there is no evidence that he was given any official rabbinic position. It seems to me that he made his move on the advice of some wealthy friends who were members of the Smyrna community in order to join the competition to succeed R. Joseph Escapa as chief rabbi: the latter was nearly a hundred years old at this time and was in decline. Even during the 1640s and 1650s, when he was still rabbi of Tire, he was very active in Smyrna's affairs. This struggle for the Smyrna rabbinate soon became very bitter. It began around 1660 and continued for quite a number of years, including the years of the Sabbatai Zevi affair. Its echoes died down only after Sabbatai Zevi's conversion and the death of R. Aaron Lapapa, one of the protagonists of the affair, in 1667.

There were many participants in the struggle for the leadership of Smyrna, including rabbis, from both the city itself and the outside (some of whom are discussed here), some wealthy supporters of the community and some rich merchants. As far as it is possible to follow this extended quarrel, it constitutes a reflection in miniature of the social and cultural composition of the community. The struggles took place among the various waves of immigrants and leaders, with their various halakhic schools of thought, and among various groups with different economic interests, each of which had its own candidate for chief rabbi. A number of rules were violated during the struggle: rival factions resorted to physical violence (such as throwing stones at the home of one of the candidates, R. Haim Benveniste) and approaches were made to the non-Jewish authorities and courts.[53]

During R. Escapa's final years, when an approved successor as sole chief rabbi could not be found, it was decided that the chief rabbinate should be redivided between two rabbis. This time each rabbi would be responsible for a particular halakhic area: one for financial rulings (*dinei memonot*) and the other for issues of life style (*'orah hayyim*), marriage, and divorce. The only candidate for the second area of responsibility was R. Haim Benveniste—but apparently not everyone was willing to accept him as the sole rabbi of the city or an authority on financial matters, which were very important in a trade city like Smyrna. When R. Escapa died at the end of 1661, the search began for a rabbi to handle financial matters. Rabbis in different areas of the empire were approached, but none could be persuaded to come and share the rabbinate with R. Benveniste.[54] Their refusal rested on various factors: unwillingness to shoulder the responsibility, their knowledge of how difficult things would be in such a divided city, and their recognition of R. Benveniste's strong personality and vast Torah knowledge. It seems, too, that R. Benveniste used his influence and connections to prevent the other candidates from coming to Smyrna. We actually possess enough evidence (mainly from R. Benveniste's own responsa) to demonstrate that all the people involved in this affair, both in Smyrna and in other communities, had known one another for many years before the quarrel began and had had many opportunities to debate halakhic and social issues, sometimes very sharply.

A compromise was finally reached, however: one of the Smyrna rabbis, R. Isaac de Alba, was appointed temporary judge in financial matters until a permanent rabbi could be found for the position. This "temporary" appointment lasted about four years, during which time R. Benveniste encroached on his colleague's area more than once and quarreled with him. In the spring of 1665 R. Aaron Lapapa, the rabbi of the neighboring town of Manissa, from which many Jews had moved to Smyrna, agreed to come to Smyrna in the position of chief rabbi for financial affairs.

R. Lapapa, a native of Manissa, was educated in the yeshivot of Salonika and Istanbul, studying under the same rabbis who had taught the other Smyrna sages so he got to know them there as well. The above-mentioned R. Solomon Algazi was his father-in-law. The many sources that have come down to us indicate that there was a very complicated relationship between R. Lapapa, R. Escapa, and R. Benveniste.

The relationship between R. Benveniste and R. Lapapa had generally been a good one, when they were rabbis of different suburbs of the city, that is, before they came to Smyrna. Once they became cochief rabbis of the same city they differed with each other on many issues, and the relationship deteriorated. Their joint appointment had lasted less than a year when Sabbatai Zevi appeared in the city as the Messiah and changed everything. He deposed R. Lapapa from his position and appointed R. Benveniste as the sole chief rabbi. Thus R. Benveniste achieved his goal, but at a heavy price: belief in Sabbatai Zevi! This demonstrates a serious opportunistic streak in the man.[55] Sabbatai

Ẓevi's conversion in Istanbul and the subsequent crisis among the Jewish communities led R. Lapapa's supporters to try to get him back into power, but it seems that they did not succeed. He died a few months later, in 1667.[56]

In this long complicated affair, which is only summarized here, social and political struggles were interwoven with halakhic controversies and with Sabbatai Ẓevi's appearance and Sabbateanism in Smyrna. R. Benveniste continued to serve as the city's chief rabbi until his death in 1673, but the echoes of the affair still resounded, although not quite so loudly. There are hints that he no longer wanted to be in charge of financial rulings and that he tried to atone for what had happened to R. Lapapa and for his own belief in Sabbatai Ẓevi.[57] It is possible that yet other rabbis were appointed to be cochief rabbis together with R. Benveniste—the accounts are not sufficiently clear. The degree to which Smyrna society was divided by the leadership controversy is attested by the fact that after R. Benveniste's death in 1673 the strife between the rival factions erupted once again. His son R. Israel Benveniste, who sought to succeed his father as chief rabbi and as rabbi of the Portuguese congregation, was rejected by some of the city's elite. In the end a compromise was reached and a cochief rabbi was appointed together with him—R. Solomon Halevi (ironically, also a Sabbatean).[58]

The episode of R. Benveniste's success at taking over the Smyrna rabbinate reflects not only the relationships among the rabbis of the city—and outside it—but also the social conflicts within the community. R. Benveniste's ambivalent attitude to Sabbatai Ẓevi and Sabbateanism also constitutes a reflection of the terrible dilemma in which the leaders of the Ottoman communities were caught, both at the time of the Sabbatai Ẓevi's appearance as the messiah and after his subsequent conversion. At first R. Benveniste opposed Sabbatai Ẓevi's messianism and later even cursed him in the synagogue on the Sabbath. But within a few days he changed his tune and became a supporter of the Messiah, who appointed him sole chief rabbi of the community while deposing his cochief, R. Lapapa. This rapid turnabout is difficult to explain as a change in ideology; it looks like sheer political opportunism. Moreover, R. Benveniste did not stop with the attainment of his goal of sole control of the Smyrna rabbinate. He also acted as a Sabbatean in all respects and, according to his own evidence, did not

fast on Tisha B'av in 1666, for which he repented bitterly after Sabbatai
Zevi's conversion.[59]

Having drawn some lines for a portrait of R. Haim Benveniste as a
leader and Sabbatean, let us now turn to another aspect of his personality: the halakhic authority. He was the central figure among the rabbis
of seventeenth-century Smyrna and the author of many books of halakha, including *Knesset ha-Gedolah* and *Ba'ei Ḥayyai*. While still a
young man he was the most outstanding student of R. Joseph Terani,
his principal teacher. He attempted to write a commentary on *Sefer
Mitzvot Gadol* (The Big Book of Commandments), but, according to
his own evidence, he did not have enough strength and dropped the
project after a short time.[60] Then he began writing his book *Knesset ha-
Gedolah*, a collection of discussions of halakhic issues in the order established by the *'Arba'ah Turim*. R. Benveniste attempted in this book
to collect various issues and decide them according to the *Shulḥan
'Arukh* as well as later authorities. He made use of many responsa in
print and in manuscript, in addition to books, some already published,
by halakhic authorities who came after the *Shulḥan 'Arukh*. He also
made considerable use of books by Ashkenazic authorities of the
sixteenth and early seventeenth centuries, such as R. Moses Isserles,
R. Solomon of Lublin, and R. Solomon Luria. In order to write the
eight-volume *Knesset ha-Gedolah,* he collected hundreds of responsa in
manuscript, many of which have come down to us in bound form.[61]
The first volume of this work, published in Livorno in 1658, was apparently the last book printed by the Gabbai printing house of that city.[62]
Later that year the printing house moved away from Livorno, and
R. Haim Benveniste also moved, from Tire to Smyrna. He published
some of the other volumes later, with the remaining volumes appearing
posthumously.

In his introduction to the volume on *'Oraḥ Ḥayyim* R. Benveniste
explains his system in the entire work and his purpose in writing it. He
describes the development of the halakhic literature up to his own day
with clarity and in great detail, concentrating on R. Joseph Karo and
his works. He then describes the commentaries on the *Shulḥan 'Arukh,*
especially that of R. Moses Isserles (*ha-Mapah,* "the tablecloth"): "And
if anyone should ask a question of a sage and rabbinic authority . . .
which will require him to search in the *Bet Yosef* and then to search very
hard and with great effort in the books of the halakhic authorities and

responsa that were written a long time afterward . . . the person asking the question will become weary."[63] This is the reason he decided to collect all the halakhot on all issues that were added after the work of R. Joseph Karo and publish them in his book *Knesset ha-Gedolah*.

R. Benveniste's four-volume work, *Ba'ei Ḥayyai*, is a collection of his responsa to three of the four sections (*turim*) of the *'Arba'ah Turim*,[64] with the addition of a small book of responsa to the fourth section, *'Oraḥ Ḥayyim*[65]—a total of 702 responsa, all of which were published after his death. These books demonstrate his literary productivity and his surpassing greatness in Torah learning. A survey of the responsa shows that dozens of Jewish communities, mainly in the Ottoman Empire, sent him halakhic questions, thus involving him in the affairs of many different communities. It seems that he overshadowed all his contemporaries among the halakhic authorities in his knowledge of halakhic sources in print and in manuscript from nearly every country. His decisions make use of sources from the sages of Turkey, Palestine, Egypt, Eastern and Central Europe, and Italy. He also carried on an extensive correspondence with hundreds of contemporary sages in the Ottoman Empire.

While R. Benveniste's deepest knowledge was in the area of halakha, his attitude toward Kabbalah is an interesting one. As far as I know he did not leave any writings on Kabbalah, either in print or in manuscript. It is nevertheless plausible to assume that, at a time when so many people were studying the Kabbalah, the man who was appointed by Sabbatai Ẓevi to be chief rabbi of Smyrna would be included among them. And indeed, when I examined his halakhic writings carefully, I found a number of references to the Kabbalah, although they appear only in the volume of *Knesset ha-Gedolah* relating to *'Oraḥ Ḥayyim* and the additional volume called *Sheyyarei Knesset ha-Gedolah*. The reason for the appearance of these references in only these two volumes is obvious—these are the volumes containing discussions of prayers and other laws that the Kabbalah is much concerned with. In these references R. Benveniste mentions the *Zohar* and R. Luria several times, and it is clear that he had some knowledge of the *Zohar* and the kabbalists' customs.[66] His knowledge seems to have been quite extensive, since he quotes the Zohar on a number of very different issues. It should nevertheless be noted that his citations of the *Zohar* and other kabbalistic writings are very few in number and do not appear at all in most of his other books.

Although it is clear from his writings that R. Benveniste was well acquainted with the kabbalists' customs, he did not always follow them. In two cases where there was a difference between them, he followed the halakha rather than the kabbalistic teachings. His use of the *Zohar* and other kabbalistic writings, it seems, was actually very limited in comparison with his use of other works, especially halakhic ones. I am of the opinion that he did not study the Kabbalah intensively and that his citations do not imply a deep knowledge of it. His use of the *Zohar* is entirely marginal.

Just as R. Joseph Escapa symbolized the founding of the community organization for subsequent generations, so R. Haim Benveniste became a symbol of the halakhic authority for his own and subsequent generations. His book *Knesset ha-Gedolah,* in particular, as well as his responsa—most of which were published only at the end of the eighteenth century but known to Smyrna rabbis in manuscript form—constituted the basis for the leadership of the community from the halakhic standpoint. At the time of the quarrel over the rabbinate after R. Benveniste's death, R. Solomon ben Ezra had already mentioned his books, some of which were still in manuscript form, as a basis for halakhic decisions that could be used by his heirs, especially his son R. Yisrael, who was R. ben Ezra's candidate for R. Haim Benveniste's position.[67] R. Haim Palagi, the most important rabbi of nineteenth-century Smyrna, held that R. Haim Benveniste's halakhic decisions are binding: "And also as the rabbi [wrote] we have accepted his teachings and we have acted accordingly."[68] In another place R. Palagi wrote: "And in particular if we have accepted the instructions of our rabbi and teacher the perfect sage R. Haim Benveniste of blessed memory to decide the halakha according to him. . . . We live almost entirely according to his word here in our city of Smyrna."[69] In sum, in the area of halakha R. Benveniste became the most important authority among the Smyrna rabbis, and he held that position until the end of the Ottoman period.

The five portraits of Smyrna figures drawn here faithfully represent a wide spectrum of community rabbis and leaders in the Ottoman Empire of the seventeenth century. They demonstrate how this Jewry was formed a century after the expulsion from Spain.

The great influence of the large Jewish communities of Istanbul and Salonika on the organization and leadership of the new community in

Smyrna is striking. From the standpoint of spiritual productivity, the important centers and study houses established by the Iberian exiles in the sixteenth century varied in their influence. Thus, Safed stands out, in addition to the two great centers mentioned above. Its influence was greatest in the area of halakha; the influence of Lurianic Kabbalah was not particularly striking during the first half of the seventeenth century and became important only after the Sabbatean crisis.

The fact that five figures portrayed here came from different cities in the Ottoman Empire (Ankara, Bursa, Smyrna, Salonika, and Istanbul) exemplifies the variety of Ottoman leadership. The figures discussed here faithfully reflect the appearance of the rabbinate and the leadership in the seventeenth-century Ottoman communities. We find in them a complex variety of characteristics and activities: believers and opponents of Sabbateanism, pilgrims to Erez Israel, authors of works in all areas of Jewish thought, different leadership types influenced by their various teachers of written texts and study houses.

IO

⬚

Sephardic Refugees in Ferrara: Two Notable Families

Renata Segre

The two or three generations of Iberian Jews who took refuge in the Italian peninsula beginning in the late fifteenth century introduced radical and long-term changes in the internal equilibrium and nature of Italian Jewry.[1] Although they all came from the same geographical area and for the most part all spoke the same language, these refugees from Spain and Portugal (the former Jews, the latter New Christians) did not regard themselves as members of a single "nation." The same feeling, namely, that there was a sharp cleavage among these newcomers, was also perceived by the governments and people among whom they settled.

Those expelled in 1492 who reached Italy without having been baptized were commonly termed Spanish Jews, and their origins and religious identity were not questioned. Although they in fact constituted a new presence, it was natural to group them together in a sole category under one name. This sweeping and clear-cut classification did not apply to those who had converted to Christianity, usually in Portugal. For them to proclaim allegiance to Judaism was a dangerous matter and only from time to time could certain rulers consent to it. Furthermore, the Christians among whom these converts settled were uneasy about the use of the term *Jew*. Therefore, adjectives and national qualifications multiplied and overlapped in a conflicting manner. As a rule, they were called Portuguese or Lusitanians, with or without the specification of Jews, but they were called Ponentines when they lived as Jews ignoring or denying their temporary and forced baptism, and they were termed marranos when the church or the lay authorities regarded them as apostates, and thus to be persecuted.[2]

The split between the Sephardic Jews, who never abandoned Judaism, and the New Christians, who reverted as soon as possible, was not due only to the policy of the princes and the church; hence the division did not generally disappear once the danger of persecution had passed.

Ferrara and Venice were two of the main—perhaps the major—centers of settlement for the Sephardim who entered Italy between the beginning of the 1540s and the turn of the 1570s, following the Christian victory at Lepanto. These were precisely the cities where the most prominent families of these two different worlds lived. The Abravanels had landed in the Kingdom of Naples at the end of the fifteenth century and then, after being expelled with their last coreligionists forty years later, settled in the Duchy of Este;[3] the Mendeses, or De Lunas, or Benvenistes, or Nasis (the variety of names is evidence of their uncertain and ambivalent identity) had moved from Portugal to Flanders under imperial protection, then escaped undercover to Venice and later to Ferrara, and finally emigrated "out of Christianity" to Constantinople to return publicly to their Jewish faith.[4] This was the first time that Italians in government and finance came in contact with such rich and powerful Jews, respected by the Christian sovereigns with whom they were often in personal, even confidential correspondence. Before this they had known only physicians, men of learning, and some bankers who had had access to the court and had earned the trust of a ruler; even then, it was always at an individual level, conferring no benefit on other members of their family. Now, however, there existed two real dynasties side by side, sometimes in confrontation with one another, each with its network of relations, servants, and clients. An investigation into their experiences during their stay in Italy offers us a glimpse into the mentality and lifestyle of the two nations.

II

Probably the most visible difference in behavior between the two families concerns religion, especially the way the two formulated their profession of faith. The oaths are particularly significant: whereas the Abravanels had no reason to remain silent about their allegiance, the Mendeses often introduced ambiguous clauses that would be acceptable to both religions. The formula employed by Isaac Abravanel in his lawsuit over his father's will ("more mosayco super libris Biblie per Deum Sabbaoth," that is, "according to Mosaic custom upon the books of the Bible for God Sabbaoth")[5] sounds almost ostentatious and is evidence of a quest for orthodoxy that would have been unusual even in some of the most notable rabbinical courts.

The attitude of the De Luna sisters toward religion is considerably more uneven, for they led a perilous life on the border between the two faiths. On May 28, 1546, Beatriz swears on the four gospels before the Venetian magistrate who will entrust her with the guardianship of her daughter and her niece.[6] But when in July 1550 she and Brianda agree to end their dispute, they confirm the settlement by an oath ("to touch corporally the Holy Scriptures")[7] that is quite ambiguous in meaning. During her stay in Italy Beatriz issues powers of attorney to the managers of the family business in Antwerp and Lyons, all of which end with the Christian oath. Her niece will be able to swear "per sanctam legem Moisis"[8] only after proclaiming openly on August 23, 1555, that she intends to live and die as a Jew, an act that led to her immediate departure from Venice. Her choice is definite, her name is now Gracia; nevertheless, to disavow the guardianship of her uncle Aries De Luna in 1558 she had to appeal to both the episcopal vicar and the rabbinical court (*chachaminis et doctoribus hebreis*) and had the deed drafted in Hebrew.[9]

The straightforward behavior of the Abravanels, who relentlessly affirmed their Jewish faith, was perhaps also an attempt to hold back the forces that threatened the family's creed. In September 1553 five Jews—two of them bankers, one a much revered rabbi, Benedetto Forti (alias Baruch Hazak/Hazacheto), and the two cousins Isaac and Jacob Abravanel—hand over their copies of the Talmud to the inquisitor in Ferrara.[10] Moreover, the same rabbi is often to be seen at their home, and the great Mose Basola is their trusted agent in the Marches.[11] Furthermore, in 1554 Isaac's signature appears at the end of the *takkanot*,[12] the rules by which the leaders of Italian Judaism sought to counteract some of the more distressing provisions enforced by the prelates of the Counter-Reformation. Nevertheless, the pressures brought to bear by the Christian world were felt even within the home of the Abravanels.

Conversion had also won over the Zarfati,[13] the family nearest to them both in consanguinity and in business, who still called themselves "Neapolitans," settled between the Marches and Rome, and held an eminent position at the Curia.

After the Christian victory at Lepanto, as the Sephardic community in Ferrara began to diminish, one of the Abravanels converted and took Duke Alfonso's name at his christening.[14] For the previous thirty to forty years, however, their family residence had been emblematic of the Sephardic Jewish presence and culture in Ferrara, even though it had at times housed a clergyman from Naples. This individual served as witness for several deeds relating to affairs that the Abravanels had not settled before leaving the kingdom. He seems rather out of place in that milieu: more an agent concerned with secular matters than a man of culture or a preceptor.[15]

The circumstances of the Mendes sisters in Venice and Ferrara were quite different. Even before leaving Portugal for Antwerp their family had been entitled to some of the most generous papal franchises awarded to New Christians, among them the right to maintain a private chapel (and a portable altar when traveling) and to appoint their own confessor.[16] These privileges, which were periodically reconfirmed by the Holy See, made it all the more difficult for both the local authorities and the inquisitors to control the practice of the Catholic faith within the walls of the Lusitanian homes. In April 1548 Cardinal Farnese instructed the nuncio in Lisbon to grant Beatriz's "pious and honest wish" to have the remains of her parents and her husband removed to Venice.[17] This echoed the frequent instruction in the wills of the New Christians that their heirs be allowed to choose how and where they should be buried, which meant as Jews, possibly even in the Holy Land. Brianda's palace, just outside the ghetto in Venice, was beyond the reach of prying eyes. She thought it preferable to call on three priests from neighboring churches to witness the series of notarial deeds that terminated the suit with her sister and recognized her guardianship over her daughter.[18] In that particularly tense moment she wanted to demonstrate her loyalty to Catholicism, but three years later, when her trusted agent, the "licenciate" Costa, was detained in the jails of the Inquisition, the parish priest of San Marcuola charged that she and her household "have never been seen at church" and that the only time he had stepped inside the main door of her palace he had seen no religious images in the portico.[19]

The two sisters, who were otherwise so dissimilar, shared a common attitude toward the Catholic faith; so too, with some small variations, did all the New Christians who chose to remain in Italy. Only after Beatriz had moved to Constantinople in August 1552[20] did they abandon this precautionary attitude, at least for the time being. Less than a year later the editors of the *Biblia en lengua española* wrote two separate dedications to their volume, one to the duke of Ferrara, signed with their Christian names (Jeronimo de Vargas and Duarte Pinel), and one to Beatriz, now called Gracia Naci, signed with their Jewish names (Yom Tob Atias and Abraham Usque).[21] They spoke briefly of their "love of the fatherland" and of the "merits" that Gracia had acquired toward "all of us." She was honored not only as head of the Portuguese nation (a reference to the distant homeland that resounded with the melancholy of the outcast) but also as promoter of the publication. So far no documentary evidence has been found to support the contention that Beatriz financed this expensive and risky enterprise, but her sponsorship of what was the most distinguished attempt to spread the knowledge of the Bible among those who could no longer read it in the original marks a high point in the religious standing of the marranos— as least as regards their outward behavior. This venture was not the only one intended to advance the re-Judaization of the Portuguese; at the same time the workshop that had printed the Bible also brought out the *Consolação às tribulações de Israel* by Samuel Usque, the most solemn lament for the persecutions that the Jews had endured and the most outspoken expectation of the messianic redemption. This text was dedicated to "Gracia Nasci," who was described as "the heart within the body" of "our Portuguese nation."[22] There is possibly herein a reference of the author to the yearlong conflict between the two sisters, which had also disrupted the life of their protégé, for we know that the poet was jailed in 1549 during the plague, at the request of Brianda and, in all likelihood, in defiance of Beatriz his protector.[23] Despite these internal feuds, however, the Portuguese continued to look to this great dynasty for guidance.

III

To assess the hegemony these two families exercised over their respective nations in Italy, we now turn to their relationship with the princes and the local authorities. In the autumn of 1541 a number of Jews who had been expelled from the Kingdom of Naples reached Ancona. Of those, some settled in the city, but the richer ("the major and best part," as the governor noted with great disappointment) went on to Venice and Ferrara, "among them a certain Samuel Barbanello, who stopped here a few days and who is among them lord and master."[24] According to the governor, he was heading toward Ferrara, where he had a long-standing invitation from Hercules II d'Este to come and settle.[25] Samuel conveyed the same impression a year and a half later, when the ducal secretary explained to his master that the newcomers "have arrived with that king of the Jews from the Kingdom of Naples."[26] This rather odd and exotic picture of a "royal" Jewish court will soon be dispelled by the Abravanels' robust participation in the Ferrarese society and especially in the Jewish one.[27]

Since March 1544 through the "procurator of the people of the New Christians" the De Luna sisters had been granted license by the Council of Ten to settle in Venice "together with their agents, possessions, and families up to thirty people."[28] Yet although the safe-conduct follows the usual form, it is recorded among the "secret" acts of the council— clear evidence that the issue was not considered an everyday matter by either the petitioner or the granter. The magnificent procession, which had departed from Antwerp eluding the strict surveillance of the imperial authorities, encountered obstacles and delays on its journey to Venice, in all likelihood only a stop on the way to the Levant.

In the spring of 1546, shortly after the arrival of the De Lunas, the Venetian government first encountered the sensitive issues that threatened the harmony of the family.[29] The dispute between Beatriz and her sister regarded the guardianship of Brianda's child, who was still a minor, and the management of her estate. The research of Paul Grünbaum Ballin has shown that the judicial courts of the Forestier and Petizion upheld Brianda's position,[30] and despite her husband's will, entrusted her with full power over their daughter.[31] The legal authorities decided against Beatriz, partly because of their adherence to the principle of natural descent, but mainly on account of Brianda's show of Catholic devotion, which had impressed the Senate.[32] Beatriz, however, refused to accept the ruling and, as her sister lamented in a petition to the Ten, "at nighttime secretly escaped with all the family possessions to Ferrara."[33] In reality, this was not a clandestine departure, for it had been carefully organized and involved her entire entourage. Early in 1549 Duke Hercules issued an ad hoc license to the heirs of his secretary Gerolamo Magnanini to let their house (*aedes seu palacium*) in the Giovecca district to Beatriz De Luna at the remarkable price of two hundred scudi for two years;[34] her chamberlain paid the rent in cash on January 11. A few days later a ducal decree put a quick end to the plea that the "magnificent and renowned lady" had submitted to his Council of Justice. Hercules declared that his decision to validate the will of Diego Mendes depended upon reasons of equity as much as upon appreciation of the lady (ob insignes animi sui dotes ingenuos mores . . . aliasque raras virtutes quibus eam Altissimus illustravit) the deceased Portuguese merchant had appointed his testamentary executor.[35] The words of praise used by the ducal chancellor in drafting the decree may be indebted to humanistic rhetoric, but they also reflect his master's assumption that Beatriz fully merited the appellations "noble" and "magnificent" normally found in her deeds. Thereafter she was entitled to issue powers of attorney to her agents in Portugal, Spain, Antwerp, and Lyons to run all the Mendes businesses, including those of her young niece.[36]

The warm welcome given to these newcomers reflected more than the yearlong relationship Diego had established with the duke of Este or his family's standing in the world of finance and trade.[37] The duke meant to benefit from the wealth and the abundance of cash that always accompanied Beatriz. Brianda, too, who had remained behind in Venice with her daughter, could not long resist on her own, and despite her formal legal rights she was soon to move to Ferrara, since her sister was still pulling the strings. Her only hope lay in a reversal of the duke's favors, and to this end she implicitly offered him a share in her daughter's riches.[38] From the moment that Beatriz settled in Ferrara, Hercules, acting as sovereign judge, sought to disentangle the many issues that had soured relationships within the Mendes family. His mediation lasted over a year, interrupted by the outbreak of plague, a plague that, despite Samuel Usque's vivid and sorrowful description,[39] had been assumed by many, even historians, to be a mere literary fantasy. Following the outbreak, the university closed and the duke sought refuge in the countryside with part of his court, while the more recent Portuguese immigrants—among them five prominent traders—were concentrated in the lazzaretto because "public rumor" held them responsible for spreading the disease, which had infected them on the way to Ferrara via the Brenner Pass and Verona. Even Beatriz's intervention proved of no avail and the duke refused to permit their dismissal from quarantine. From the daily briefings that he received from his secretaries on the situation in the capital, the duke was advised that the city regarded the Portuguese "with displeasure," and not only because some had died of the disease. What most concerned the Ferrarese, especially in time of pestilence, was their religious well-being; by contrast, the Portuguese, as the ducal chancellor reported to his master, "will never agree not to deny Christ."[40] Moreover, these wealthy and powerful merchants did not intend to settle permanently in Ferrara, for they were only willing to give "assurance" (that is, a financial guarantee) that they would stay for the next three years and not for the ten years Hercules had requested. The effect of the expulsion that followed the breakdown in the negotiations between the officials and the Portuguese reached well beyond the few traders for whom Beatriz had interceded. A series of shipping contracts shows that the leaders of their nation had envisaged transportation to Ragusa and Valona for at least three hundred marranos—men, women, and children with all their belongings.[41]

Thus, despite her prestige, Beatriz failed in her endeavors. Moreover, in the Mendes palace the plague is said to have broken out in the very rooms in which Brianda was living, to the latter's great anger. It was malevolence, Brianda claimed, a charge spread purposely by Beatriz to ruin her and her trusted servants and eventually secure their expulsion.[42]

As soon as the pestilence had abated the duke resumed his efforts to mediate between the two De Lunas, all the more vigorously since Brianda had promised him the enormous sum of forty thousand scudi if he succeeded in ousting Beatriz from the management of their estate and half that sum if he secured a settlement.[43] Hercules shrewdly chose the second alternative, and on July 4, 1550, in his private lodgings in Castelvecchio, the dispute between the two sisters was terminated by a notarial deed.[44] Among the many clauses of the agreement one is particularly difficult to read because of the many corrections to which it was subjected until the very last moment. It states that Beatriz, after producing the accounts of the management of the estate of her underage niece and providing warrants for Brianda's dowry, may depart for a land "outside Italy"; this expression replaces the previous text, which had read "out of Christianity."

The undoubted success of the duke, who had perhaps used more than just persuasion to secure agreement on all the issues, was unfortunately not definitive, for the European network of the Mendes's finances and trade could not be fully surveyed from Ferrara but had to be directed from both Venice and Constantinople.[45]

In the fall of 1551 the whole Mendes family had again settled in Venice, and the Abravanels reemerged in Ferrara, at the center of Hercules' economic and political concerns. This turn in the duke's interests seems to prove that he was inclined to favor either the Portuguese or the "Jewish Neapolitan" family, but not both at the same time—at times one, at times the other prevails. The flow of documentary evidence reflects this alternation; sometimes the information on both families is abundant and nearly daily; sometimes there is hardly a word about one of the two families but a plethora on the other.

Since 1541 the wealthiest notables of the Portuguese nation in Ferrara were partners with the ducal Treasury (Camera) in a company that by 1545 was showing poor profits. One year later the same group of "respectable sirs and erudite merchants" (*spectabiles viri et eruditi mercatores*), along with a few other nationals, guaranteed the duke that they would reimburse him the entire capital.[46] The only warrantee not of the nation was "solers mercator don Jacob," son of the late "Don" Samuel Abravanel, termed "Neapolitan Jew." The second son of Samuel (the first son of his second wife, Benvenuta) does not bear any distinctive or noble title, such as those attributed to the Mendes family, for he never denies his Judaism; yet in Ferrara the appellation "don" is used only in his Jewish family. The notary who drafted these deeds was perfectly at ease with social hierarchies, honorific titles, and qualifications. In what was apparently an act relating to a partnership but in effect a ducal safe-conduct for the Portuguese in Ferrara, the notary underlined that "Johanne Rodoricho medico," that is, Amatus Lusitanus, "Diego sive Didaco Pirho," that is, Didacus Lusitanus, also known as Flavius Eborensis, and Hesdra Vicino were not merely merchants but also men of learning, indeed famous university professors. He therefore classed them under the unusual heading of "erudite merchants."

The difference between the inclinations and the impact of the two families emerged in the role they played during the dramatic events in Ancona in 1555–1556, when Hercules' policy toward them varied according to circumstances. Since the late 1530s the main harbor city of the

Marches had become the site of redistribution for the Jewish refugees from southern Italy, who, as we have seen, looked upon Samuel Abravanel if not as a "king" at least as the undeniable leader of the exiled nation. Thanks to his endeavors these newcomers had been able to replace the Italian Jews in some local loan banks. This Neapolitan influx, which, with the notable exception of the Abravanels, consisted mainly of poorer people, was rapidly surpassed by the transit and settlement of Sephardic Jews, especially of marranos. Paul III was fully aware that other Italian rulers (especially in Venice and Florence) were open to welcoming these refugees, provided they were willing to take up residence for some years. In the 1540s the Portuguese were courted and granted franchises on their own merits, whereas the Neapolitans had to rely upon the prestige of the Abravanels to be awarded their charters.

A dramatic change in the climate was brought about by the election of Paul IV to the papal throne, and events in its aftermath bear witness to the political ability of the duke of Este. In December 1555,[47] while the conversos in Ancona were in prison awaiting their death sentence, Hercules granted the Portuguese living in his duchy a charter that explicitly recalled that granted by Julius III in January 1553. In effect the duke's aim was to attract the marranos who were fleeing the Papal state while simultaneously defending the conflicting interests of the Abravanels and the Mendes. In November Hercules had instructed his envoy at the Curia to secure the release of Abram Francese, the principal agent of the Abravanels in the Marches, and of his estate, with the argument that the detainee was not a marrano but a Levantine from Salonika.[48] Many New Christians who had dwelt in the Greek city or elsewhere in the Ottoman lands for part of their life were able to seek protection under Turkish rule. But this did not apply to the many agents and business partners of the Mendeses in Ancona who had been sentenced as outspoken Portuguese, that is, as re-Judaizers. Hercules could not act on their behalf as strongly as he did on behalf of Francese,[49] but he repeatedly claimed that the goods seized as theirs actually belonged to third parties, especially his ducal Treasury.

The documents from the Este archives have so far not provided evidence on the duke's attitude vis-à-vis the boycott of Ancona and the attempt to divert trade to Pesaro. Its aim was twofold: to retaliate against the brutal papal policy and to open a new and extensive trade center promoted and run by the Mendes business network. But the project ran contrary to the interests and perspectives of the Abravanels, who viewed Ancona's maritime function and mercantile connections with Salonika as vital.[50] They believed that the entrepôt was essential for maintaining the presence of the Jews in the Papal state, in the face of Paul IV's policy.

IV

To assess the Abravanels' assumption that Ancona's economy had to be preserved and bolstered for political reasons, we now turn from Ferrara to the other Italian principalities with which Samuel and his family had established relationships.

Via the friendship in Naples between Eleonora of Toledo (the daughter of the kingdom's governor and the future duchess de Medici) and Bienvenida (alias Benvenuta), the Abravanels gained access to the court in Florence and license to run five loan banks in the duchy.[51] Here, too, as in the Marches, the old establishment of Italian local pawnbrokers was faced with an unexpectedly tough competition from foreign coreligionists with solid financial and personal connections. Duke Cosimo de Medici bypassed the crisis that this shift in the capital market could not fail to produce, for his main endeavors were directed toward developing Tuscan ties with the Levant. Jacob Abravanel, who had for the last five years been very successful in his late father's business, worked out a detailed charter of privileges for the Levantine Jews,[52] which the duke signed, following the advice of his council of the Pratica Segreta and of the economic magistratures. The realization of the project was entrusted to Servadio of Damascus, a man whose origin was intended to allay all fears of marranism.[53] Although the sponsors probably had a say in the appointment of the Oriental trader and the establishment of the entrepôt, the initiative proved short-lived and the Abravanels never came to the forefront. To compete in the Ottoman market with the Salonikan woolen industry was an ill-conceived plan of the Florentine manufacturers. On political grounds Jacob also had meant to promote the role of Ancona; besides his often repeated appraisal of the city's relevance in regard to the Jewish settlement in the peninsula, he fully realized that as it stretched from the Tyrrhenian to the Adriatic coast, the Papal state was in a strategic position to check all Tuscan maritime moves. If this was his assumption in the early 1550s, it applied a fortiori to the papacy of Paul IV.

Jacob's Jewishness limited his ability to deal on behalf of the Italian princes; his role was thus restricted to that of financier. When in July 1557 Cosimo requested "master Jacob Jew in Ferrara" to advance five thousand scudi he owed Hercules II, it was the duke himself, not Jacob, who replied that the remittance could not be made on account of the "bad quality of the events."[54]

If some aspects of the relations between the Medici government and the Mendes look similar to those with the Abravanels, the political impact was quite different. In January 1549 Cosimo granted the Portuguese license to dwell and trade in Florence and the duchy; the deal was signed by two agents of the Mendes household (Antonio Lopez and Thomas Gomes) and doctor Ferdinando Mendes.[55] A near relative of the De Lunas and one of the few Portuguese to have attained high public office (in 1556 he was *uditore di rota*), he was a familiar figure at the ducal court, where he mingled with other Portuguese relations and friends, such as Enrico Nunes, a close acquaintance of Duchess Eleonora's brother, or Aries De Luna, the brother of Beatriz and Brianda.

Florence was also the headquarters of the Antinori, Salviati, and Panciatichi banking companies (to mention only a few), whose financial transactions and partnership with the Mendes went back to the 1530s and covered the exchange markets in Portugal, Spain, Antwerp, and Lyons. All of them had been hit equally hard by the unfortunate 1550 loan to the French crown. Again in December 1555 the Florentine bankers intervened to remit to the ever hungry papal Treasury in Rome the huge sum collected by the Portuguese (but actually cashed by the Mendes) to rescue the Ancona marranos from the stake. The money arrived too late,[56] and it was again up to the same banking companies to secure the release of the credits and estates confiscated from the Judaizers in Ancona, properties that Beatriz, now renamed Doña Gracia, claimed to be hers as an Ottoman subject.

V

At Rome the Mendes were in direct communication with the "procurators of the people of the New Christians," first Duarte de Paz and then Diego Fernandes Nieto, who in some circumstances acted as their emissaries. Francisco Mendes had already used this channel to funnel the much needed payments to the Curia, which provided the New Christians with briefs of pardon and delayed the establishment of the Holy Office in Portugal. If in this respect Beatriz managed to follow in her late husband's footsteps even after she moved from Lisbon to Antwerp, she was, however, no longer in a position to cultivate the warm relationship that Francisco had maintained with the nuncios in Portugal.[57] Despite the papal brief he had secured in 1531 in order to protect his family from religious harassment,[58] he could not prevent his brother Diego from running into serious trouble in Antwerp the following year. So, on becoming head of her household in 1543, Beatriz sought a papal safe-conduct to move to Rome with her entire family. As we know, she finally accepted the invitation to settle in Venice that the procurator of the New Christians had obtained from the Serenissima. Again, early in 1551,[59] either because she was no longer happy in Ferrara (where she had moved in the meantime) or because she was simply longing to leave for the Levant, Beatriz secured another papal letter-patent to take up residence with her household in Rome or elsewhere in the Papal state. Although she might have preferred to live in Ancona as a port of transit to the Ottoman Empire and a cherished shelter for many of her compatriots, she would have received a warm welcome in Rome as well, for Julius III had recommended her to some of the most powerful cardinals of the Curia (Alexander Farnese, John Dominic Cupi, John Salviati, and John Ricci). She also had important contacts with the diplomatic world, where one of her agents used to supply the Portuguese ambassador with up-to-date information from Cairo for his master.[60] Beatriz's wealth and reliability were acknowledged at the Curia, especially by the Florentine bankers, which enabled her to assist the duke of Ferrara whenever regular and timely payments of tithes and contributions to the Apostolic Chamber were required.[61]

João Miques also turned to Rome after his ill-fated abduction of his underage cousin Beatriz Mendes (Brianda's daughter) from her home in Venice. Besides invoking immunity, he also sought to establish diplomatic and economic connections that he could then exploit in Constantinople, where he finally settled in the spring of 1556.[62] Yet, when he sailed from Ancona for the Levant, time had not yet healed the wounds that the failure of the papal authorities to hand him over to the Serenissima had inflicted on their interstate relations.

VI

The doge is possibly the only other Italian ruler besides the pope to have played a decisive role in the fate of the New Christians during the Counter-Reformation. The Venice-Ferrara journey was familiar to the De Luna sisters. They traveled back and forth between the two cities three times, always hurriedly—in 1548 going south, when Beatriz was deprived of the guardianship of her niece, and again, in 1551, heading this time for Venice, where she hoped for a quick settlement of the family disputes so she could depart for the Levant—and finally in September 1555, when Brianda and her daughter, now officially declared to be Jews, were suddenly banned by their cherished republic. In the end Venice failed in its attempt to gain the maximum benefit from the presence of the Mendeses and the deposit of their capital at the mint. The appeal to Catholic orthodoxy and the private interests of the patriciate, which played off one sister against the other, prevailed over every political and financial motivation.

To the Abravanels the significance of Venice was economic, not political. The city on the lagoon was an essential market, especially in grain (in time of penury) and manufactured goods for the Este court. Jacob and Leone were Jewish merchants and financiers and within this framework managed their dealings on behalf of their Ferrarese customers and the ducal family as well.

VII

On the whole the Abravanels might seem to have been somewhat overshadowed. Yet, they still held eminent positions at court, despite their continuing adherence to their fathers' faith. In September 1550,[63] Benvenuta, by a solemn deed drafted in her mansion, in the presence of all her family, gave her son Jacob power of attorney to commit himself to pay fifteen thousand scudi to the noble Genoese Teodoro Spinola if he were to secure "from the invincible Roman Emperor Charles V a license, signed by the viceroy, allowing one hundred Jewish households, selected by Benvenuta, to settle freely in Naples and its Kingdom." Perhaps it is worth underlining, more than the project in itself, the right of choice that Benvenuta intended to retain for herself. One wonders what powerful reasons led her to believe that, thanks to the action

of the Spinolas at the imperial court, the advocates of the return of the
Jews to the kingdom would be in a position to reverse the ban of 1541,
of which she too had been a victim. By all accounts she seems to have
been convinced that don Pedro de Toledo, the viceroy to whom she had
had easy access in Naples, still harbored positive feelings toward her.
We know nothing of what went on behind the scenes or what if anything came of Jacob's power of attorney. The only conclusion we can
draw is that well into the 1550s the Abravanels still sided with the imperial party, despite its antiheretical and anti-Turkish belligerency and despite the anxiety this policy aroused among the other Sephardic nation,
the Portuguese New Christians.

On the other side, the French party enlisted alternately both Paul IV
and Hercules d'Este. The long-standing and traditional pro-Ottoman
policy of the French was congenial to the New Christians, who also had
other reasons to appreciate the conduct of Henry II. In 1550 he had
granted them a charter with considerable franchises and exemptions,
confirming the claim that France was a land of freedom. Again, there is
reason to believe that the financial power of the Mendeses was also behind this royal decree and that their investment in the consistent loan,
the so-called *grand partie du roy*, which the king had increasing difficulty to reimburse, was being repaid elsewhere.

This was not the case with the Abravanels, since the Jews had been
banned for the past two centuries; and when in 1552 Isaac and Jacob
went to Lyons,[64] their royal safe-conduct entitled them to the same
privileges granted to the Florentine nation, quite an exceptional treatment.

VIII

Three well-known episodes chronicle the relationship between the
Mendeses and the Porte. The first took place in the autumn of 1551,
when the sultan's envoy (the chiaus) failed to secure the De Lunas' departure for Constantinople after Brianda had proclaimed her Catholic
faith and refused to leave for the Levant. The second event, the tri-
umphal entry of Beatriz and her fabulous entourage into the Turkish
capital in the spring of 1553, has come down to us through the description of Andres Laguna.[65] The last fact centered on the Porte's ill-fated
commitment, on the instigation of the Mendeses, to save the marranos

in Ancona from the stake in 1556 and thereafter to boycott its port to the benefit of Pesaro. Out of the three, this is the only case of political significance.

Despite the failure of her Pesaro enterprise, Gratia De Luna (as she signed her correspondence in the Christian territories) continued to keep a close eye on events in Italy and was soon to achieve her most cherished goal, the reunification of her family in the Ottoman lands. In the summer of 1559 her niece Gratia Benveniste departed from Ferrara with her husband, Samuel Nasi, and sailed to Constantinople with all the riches in which both princes and claimants had taken such a keen interest.

This turn of events, unthinkable only four years before, brings us back to Hercules II and his Treasury, strained by the turmoil of the anti-Spanish war. Following the settlement of Brianda and her underage daughter in Ferrara, where they were greeted in the fall of 1555[66] with a generous ducal charter of safe-conduct, Gratia De Luna was again in a position to control them. Hercules lost no time in soliciting recognition for his act and urging the head of the household "to give proof of the goodwill you always meant to show me and keep your promise."[67] The response was the deposit of fifteen thousand scudi from the estate of Gratia Benveniste into the duke's personal chest in the castle in July 1556.[68]

Three months later Hercules addressed a new letter to "s.ra Gratia De Luna" in Constantinople, wishing her "all the best" and promising her that "he would decide according to her request" in a delicate matter,[69] namely, the confirmation of her nominees as guardians of her niece, following Brianda's death in July 1556.[70] A ducal decree appointed to the office the child's uncle and aunt,[71] Aries and Beatriz De Luna, with the latter's agent, Agostino Enriques, enjoying power of attorney in her absence. Just four days after the signing of the decree, on the explicit order of Beatriz, Aries and Agostino donated forty-three thousand scudi to the duke, to sustain his war efforts ("all the more so," the text reads, "as she is perfectly aware of the high expenditure His Excellency is facing in this turmoil . . . for the conservation of his State").[72] The accompanying letter from Gratia De Luna then recalls the "innumerable benefits" she had received from Hercules, both during her stay in Ferrara as well as after her departure. Besides protecting her and her possessions, "His Excellency has with his utmost care and diligence helped to save the estate" of her niece from foreseeable disruption, "since it consisted mainly in cash."

The donation was not free of obligations and carried some strings: the duke agreed to entrust the two guardians with the management of the child's properties and the authority to choose her husband "with the free consent" of the would-be bride. On the other hand, Hercules was given assurances that Gratia would continue to live in Ferrara for at least six years, even after her wedding, and that she would enter into a partnership with the ducal chamber. And this is the main point: we have here not an agreement involving individual franchises or business matters but a charter granting the marranos license to dwell in Ferrara for the same number of years (that is, "allowing the Portuguese nation to stay and live without any impediment on the part of the pope or others, and without being expelled, but upholding their safe-conduct").

On January 19, 1557, the duke signed the agreement attached to the donation, in the presence of his personal valet and the castle's captain. In a letter sent to the duke from "the vineyards of Pera" just a week later (but that reached Ferrara only on March 25) Josef Nazi, as he signed himself, asked his addressee to consent to the petition Agostino Enriques and Duarte Gomes were about to submit to him. In plain words he explained that, by so doing, the duke would "make us very obliged to him in our present deeds and anxious to be so also in the future" and concluded with "advice" from equal to equal:

> Your Excellency should bear in mind that there is no prince so great that he may never need a particular nor a man of low condition to do him some service. Your Excellency is a person of wide understanding and perfectly aware how more natural to God and the world and more honorific to him it is on this occasion to reach an agreement with the agents of my lady rather than with others.[73]

The message delivered by the two envoys announced to Hercules that Josef's brother, Samuel, had been designated to marry Gratia and that no other pretender would be welcome. The wedding took place in June 1557, and the *ketubbah* (marriage contract) in Hebrew was handed over to the bride;[74] it is quite possible that the medal with the famous portrait of Grazia by the sculptor Pastorini may have been done in celebration of this event.[75] Six months later the duke again addressed himself to his correspondents in Constantinople, requesting a loan "in this time of war."[76]

Immediately after the wedding, the bridegroom, "dominus Samuel Naci lusitanus,"[77] solemnly promised Hercules that he and his wife would live for the next six years in Ferrara and not depart without the duke's license. Yet, less than a year later, to please the sultan, on April 30, 1558,[78] the Council of Ten consented to the transit through Venice of Samuel, son of Samuel, "called Bernardo Miches" and his household on their way to Constantinople. He did not actually leave Ferrara until the summer of 1559,[79] although since May 16, 1558, he had been released from his commitment to live in the city and allowed to depart for the Levant with his household and estate. For the Portuguese in Ferrara, 1559 proved a crucial year, and the sudden death of the duke left them ever more exposed to the harassment of the Inquisition. Yet, the departure of the Nasis for the East had very little connection with the plight of their coreligionists. It was the happy conclusion of Gratia De Luna's scheme to recover control over her niece and estate by marrying her to a trusted person.

IX

What impact did the way of life of these two families, one Jewish and the other "Portuguese," who mixed with the international diplomatic and business society, have on their environment, and what adjustments did it entail? Through his dress the respected and wealthy Jew of the mid-sixteenth century tried his best to be acknowledged as a man of quality, his primary and most consistent perquisite being the exemption from the badge. The proceedings of the Inquisition record many descriptions of marranos, garbed as gentlemen, as evidence that they actually lived as Christians concealing their Jewishness.

Generally speaking, however, there was little distinction in terms of standard of living between Portuguese and Spanish Jews or, more specifically, between the two families we have been discussing. On her departure for Venice Beatriz De Luna sublet to the French envoy to the Este court the mansion the duke had designated as her residence. It was on two floors, decorated with marble on the facade and with painted and gilded ceilings in the living rooms, "two marble columns both carrying a statue of Hercules of fine metal" in the garden, an orchard and vineyard, a granary, a bakery, a furnace adjacent to the salami store, a cold room for butter, an armory, and so forth.[80] Beatriz's niece Gratia

Benveniste paid one hundred scudi (half her aunt's rent) for the two-floor house with garden, orchard, and stable in Giovecca,[81] in which she was to live after the wedding. So too did Samuel Abravanel in 1543, when he first settled in Ferrara in a mansion for which he had to pay for badly needed repairs and renovations. According to the definition in a notarial deed, the house in which Samuel's son Jacob lived and greeted the newlywed Gratia Benveniste was a "palace." It is therefore quite understandable that his brother Isaac should seek refuge from the 1549 plague in a country house that had a courtyard, orchard, hatchery, granary, and stable.[82]

In light of the charters that limited the employment of Christian servants and of licenses for loan banks (*condotte*) that simply mention agents and factors, it is not surprising to learn that an accountant, a valet, even a wet nurse, all of whom were Jews, lived at the Abravanels.'[83] The safe conduct granted by the Republic of Venice to the De Luna sisters included an extensive entourage. Although the function of most of its members was unspecified, six were allowed to carry arms for the protection of the household.[84] In Ferrara there were no limits placed on the number of people who could be employed by the Sephardic Jews, and slaves were also admitted. In Beatriz's household a special position was assigned to her personal physician and to her majordomo, who was responsible for all agents, factors, domestic servants, and personal maids. The language spoken by both the young valets and the orphan girls who waited on the "lady" was Portuguese.[85] The wages and the dowry of these persons was to be paid at the appropriate time by the most reliable of Beatriz's factors, namely, Guglielmo Ferdinando and Duarte Gomes.[86] Brianda, too, had to have her personal physician and her factor, known as the licenciate Costa (his role in her life was in fact crucial),[87] and her "servant" Rodrigo Nunes (who had opened the door to João Miques and the other kidnappers of his mistress's daughter in Venice). The lawsuit brought by the Council of Ten against Miques records other members of his household who were his accomplices,[88] among them at least two valets and one horseman (*cavallero*), all Portuguese, a sailor (*fante di nave*) and another horseman, both of whom were Christian, one from Venice and the other from Bologna. Thus, one of the most significant features of the marranos—on account both of their franchises and of their uncertain status—was their ability to employ Christian labor.

An even more consistent field of acknowledged "trade with the Christians" proved to be the cultural world. Beatriz's house in Ferrara was a meeting place, frequented by men of science, medical doctors, writers, and booksellers of her nation, and the most famous names at the university. For instance, Musa Brasavola, university professor and personal physician to the duke, is recorded among the witnesses of her notarial deeds and refers to her in his writings.[89] Marco Bruno dalle Anguille, a jurist and lawyer, recounted the legal details of the Mendes family with no trace of unease, taking for granted that the distinguished readers of his *Consilia*[90] knew who they were. It is no surprise then to find books dedicated to Beatriz and her nephew, João Miques. It would not be so easy to discover similar connections for the Abravanels, however, despite their acknowledged achievements in the fields of philosophy and literature, as is fully demonstrated by the fact that Leone *hebreo* ("the Jew") was a member of the family. But it is precisely this insistence on their Judaism that denied the Abravanels and the Spanish what the Mendes and the Portuguese were entitled to.

Nevertheless, books illustrating the Abravanels' service to the ducal family do appear, some of them years after the death of Hercules II. The publication of the plea made by the famous jurist Bartolomeo Ricci in 1546 in defense of Isaac Abravanel (nephew and son-in-law of Samuel) against charges of high treason twenty years after the event was a rhetorical exercise.[91] The accusation was based on letters to Venice on state affairs supposedly in Isaac's handwriting. According to Ricci the decisive proof of Isaac's innocence was the dialect used by the author of the documents. All the evidence suggested that he was a Venetian, whereas everyone agreed that Isaac spoke with a Neapolitan and later a Ferrarese accent.

To further illuminate the lives of the two Sephardic "nations" in mid-sixteenth-century Ferrara through the histories of its two great dynasties, we now turn to a conflict that split the Abravanel family after the death of Samuel in 1546. According to the terms of his will, Benvenuta was to become the head of his household. She had given birth to two sons, Jacob, who was very close to his mother, and Leone. But Isaac, son of Samuel's first wife, also lived and worked in Ferrara. His stepmother regarded him as an illegitimate son and, furthermore, disliked his friendly ties with the New Christians, which were highlighted in 1553 when the Enriques ("all Lusitanians," as they claimed, and close relatives of the Mendes) petitioned the duke to allow Isaac to arbitrate their hereditary dispute, "although he is a Jew."[92]

Isaac lived apart from the Abravanel household. In 1551, however, a monition from the "Jewish doctors" in Salonika demanded that the two factions submit to arbitration and make peace.[93] On July 25, 1551, the two arbitrators, Rabbi Mose Basola and Isaac Abravanel (the one who had been charged with treason and the uncle and brother-in-law of his homonym) handed down their ruling. But the disputing sides soon split again. In May 1552 Leone was jailed and his possessions seized at the request of his mother and his elder brother Jacob, who accused him of having contracted marriage with a Portuguese girl in Pesaro.[94] Benvenuta's will of February 17, 1553, is uncompromising.[95] Leone is to be deprived of all his hereditary rights, for not only has he had a love affair with a "Lusitanian Jew" but, perhaps even worse, he "is in relation" with Isaac, "claiming" to be an Abravanel. The family dispute was not readily settled,[96] but what is worth stressing here is that the struggle was essentially over the relationship between the Abravanels and the Portuguese New Christians.

If this protracted legal action and Benvenuta's angry provisions underline the sense of irreconcilability between the main branches of the Abravanels and the Portuguese, a document dated June 1558,[97] sheds light on the "fights and controversies" that had flared up between the two sides in Ferrara over the past years. The duke had ordered Jacob Abravanel and Enrico Nunes (the head of the Enriques household, protagonist of a famous trial before the Venetian Inquisition) to give their bond that they would "not offend one another or allow others to do so." The ducal councilors and the notary had "struggled hard" to compel the two sides to obey the duke's command, for Nunes claimed that his "commitment covers only Jacob and not his relatives" and questioned the proper definition of the clause in the bond that referred to his "relatives." Did this mean also "cousins and brothers-in-law," and if so, all of them? The Abravanels listed among their relatives only two Zarfatis, whereas Nunes attempted to prove that he was related not only to those people bearing his name but also to the Reinellis, to the Jacchias, and to Vita Barochas, the leader of the Portuguese community. Jacob would not agree to this, nor would he bow to Nunes's claim that Barochas "is a relative and even if he were not, he plays such a part in it that honestly he should be in the list." The ducal councilors were less interested in genealogies than in social order and ruled that the list of the Portuguese covered by the bond must remain unchanged.

While this struggle was going on, the last branch of the Mendes family, Gratia Benveniste and her husband, Samuel Nasi, severed its ties with Italy, leaving behind it in Ferrara a solidly established Portuguese "nation." The presence of the Abravanels in the Jewish society of the peninsula would continue for many years to come, but the deep rift that had occurred in the first half of the sixteenth century was to last even longer.

PART V

Continuity and Change in the Sephardic Diaspora:

Intellectual Pursuits

II

◼

Encounters Between Spanish and Italian Kabbalists
in the Generation of the Expulsion

Moshe Idel

Methodological Remarks

I would like to reflect here upon the relationship between a historical event, the expulsion from Spain, and its implications for the kabbalistic literature of the period immediately after the expulsion. There are two ways to approach the question: to consider the possibility that the historical event changed the very nature of the kabbalistic phenomenon, that is, affected the contents of Kabbalah; to ask whether the historical event affected the context of kabbalistic thought and writing and only indirectly contributed to a change in contents.[1] Let me try to define the terms *context* and *content*. *Context* refers to the new environments that served as background for the activity of the Spanish kabbalists after the expulsion: these environments included encounters with other cultural phenomena, with previously unknown forms of Kabbalah, and even with other Spanish kabbalists, and they include the spiritual challenges posed by these encounters. As such, the expulsion is the larger context of the postexpulsion Sephardic Kabbalah, which in turn generated smaller contexts, many of them expected and factually unrelated to the historical event. The expulsion, that is, should not be seen in isolation, but must be seen in relation to the events that followed it; these new geographical and cultural contexts then qualified the larger context.

It should be emphasized, however, that the Sephardic Jews who left Spain, especially the kabbalists, had a distinct sense of their own worth, fostered by their rich cultural legacy and tested and proved by the very fact that they resisted the temptation to convert. While acknowledging the importance of the contexts, therefore, I would nevertheless eschew the accepted view (though on another level) that context is the most formative factor in cultural and spiritual phenomena. Sephardic Jews were proud, sometimes even aggressive, despite their status as refugees, a fact that is exemplified by numerous and varied sources.[2]

As a dislocation and fragmentation of a major kabbalistic center, the expulsion, beyond doubt, had a dramatic influence on Spanish Kabbalah. In all the kabbalistic writings of the Spanish refugees it created, mutatis mutandis, new conditions and new contexts. Last but not least, the expulsion created new situations that could serve as hermeneutical grilles for new and different choices of topics to be emphasized. Even when certain topics were already present in earlier texts, the preference for one over the other emphasis now shifted. Since I assume that a new context fertilizes, the expulsion indirectly had an impact on content in many cases, by impinging on the topics chosen or by encouraging the consideration of new topics.

The situation is not a simple one, however, for many kabbalists had more than one new context: Portugal, Northern Africa, Italy, including a number of major cities, and, for some, even countries in the East. Moreover, it is quite reasonable to assume that a kabbalist writing in postexpulsion Jerusalem would react to previous contexts, such as Renaissance Italy, or messianic propaganda of an Ashkenazic "prophet" like Rabbi Asher Lemlein, who visited Jerusalem and then returned to Italy. Likewise, in some instances it is even possible to reduce the importance of the context to the status of pretext: namely, a kabbalist wrote a certain kabbalistic writing in a certain context, as the result of the requirements involved in his being there, without changing his views because of it. In other words, even if the context induces someone to compose a kabbalistic work, it does not necessarily mean that the context also inspired its content.

As to the possibility that the expulsion had a direct influence on the contents of Kabbalah, I am much more skeptical. Whenever a kabbalist indicates the connection between a topic he addresses and the historical context of his writing, I see, from the methodological point of view, no reason to dismiss such a confession. However, when such a confession is absent, as it seems to be in most of the writings on Kabbalah I am acquainted with, the scholar bears the responsibility for demonstrating a link between historical context and speculative content. He may offer his opinion as to the possibility or plausibility of such a nexus, he may attempt to adduce evidence in support of his speculation, but in the end it remains a hypothesis that may be more or less persuasive.

One possible way to convince a skeptical reader is to demonstrate the appearance of new kabbalistic concepts or new kabbalistic structures. If a scholar can argue on the basis of a comprehensive inspection of the extant material that a concept or a more comprehensive kabbalistic structure is found only in the aftermath of the historical event, then a hypothetical link between the two is compelling. My own perusal of the extant kabbalistic material and reading of the speculations embraced by modern scholarship dealing with it do not encourage me to pursue the line of inquiry linking historical events and allegedly novel kabbalistic concepts. The hypothesis of a single scholar all too easily became an established "fact" for many other scholars. In all the cases of which I am aware further research of neglected material has shown—convincingly in my opinion—that the alleged link was a premature speculation, certainly an undocumented one.[3] This is not to say that such speculations may not turn out to be correct, but rather that they will require the analysis of new neglected material or fresh methodological approaches.

As to the possibility that kabbalistic systems were restructured as the result of a traumatic historical event, this is still an open question. Although it is, in general, very difficult to deal with the emergence of comprehensive structures, which are more often systematic amalgams of already existing smaller systems and individual concepts, in order not to close possible future avenues of research I will suspend, methodologically, my skepticism. Therefore, what remains to be done is to attempt to address a topic that seems to be less controversial: how did a new context frame the literary activity of a kabbalist? To address this question of the context requires not only a knowledge of the kabbalistic thought of someone who arrived in a new place but also an acquaintance with the relevant intellectual ambience that served as a background for a Spanish kabbalist. Kabbalah, especially during the dynamic period we are dealing with, was not a static intellectual system; it was a changing entity whose various currents are to be understood by a relational analysis rather than by a description of its different trends as isolated currents. Thus, for example, the impact of the Renaissance was often neglected while addressing topics related to the history of Kabbalah during this period of time.

We shall address here only the cases of the Spanish kabbalists who went to Italy, although I hope in the future to expand this project to include cases of other geographical milieus pertinent to the kabbalistic efflorescence after the expulsion.[4] I begin with the situation of Kabbalah in Spain, insofar as it is relevant to our further discussions.[5]

A Theosophical Split in Spanish Kabbalah

The history of Kabbalah, like that of any spiritual movement that flourishes in many places over a long period of time, is to a certain extent the story of its ramifications. Splits are the most conspicuous signs of dynamic thought and of the involvement of human experience. Evidence of divergences between kabbalists abound from the very beginning of Kabbalah. By the second half of the thirteenth century significantly different schools of Jewish mysticism had emerged in Spain. We can speak of a deep split between the theosophical-theurgical Kabbalah that remained the dominant form of mystical theosophy in Spain and the ecstatic Kabbalah, which had been banned by Rabbi Shlomo ben Abraham ibn Adret (Rashba) from Spain but continued to develop in Italy, Sicily, the Byzantine Empire, and the Land of Israel. Nevertheless, even this purification of the Spanish Kabbalah, which was responsible for the attenuation of the mystical aspects of this lore, did not create a monolithic theosophy. At the end of the thirteenth century two different approaches to a central topic in kabbalistic thought were already articulated: the view that the Sefirot are the essence of the Godhead versus the view that these entities are the instruments and vessels of the divine operations and presence.

Shortly before the expulsion from Spain Rabbi Abraham ben Eliezer ha-Levi offered a relatively complex typology of the different understandings of the Sefirot among his kabbalist contemporaries.[6] Thus, while the Spanish Kabbalah can be described as strongly inclined to accept the centrality of the sefirotic system, together with the theurgical understanding of the commandments that was dominant in many of the Spanish kabbalistic writings, there was still room for creative divergences among the late fifteenth-century kabbalists. It is therefore very difficult to describe the Sephardic Kabbalah before the expulsion as a unified system. However, I would propose two common denominators shared by most of the kabbalistic literature produced in this generation in Spain.

First, *The Book of the Zohar*, either the part that is designated as the bulk of the *Zohar*, or the later layers, *Sefer Tikkunei Zohar* and *Ra'aya Mehemna*,[7] was growing in status as the most authoritative kabbalistic text. And second, Kabbalah was divorced from substantial interactions with philosophy, as thirteenth- and fourteenth-century kabbalistic writings in Spain were striving to establish Kabbalah as an independent religious phenomenon, and sometimes this distancing was accompanied by strong antiphilosophical critiques. Although neither characteristic was an innovation of the late fifteenth-century kabbalists—they are implicit in the *Zohar* itself[8]—they surfaced in a particularly compelling manner in Rabbi Shem Tov ben Shem Tov's *Sefer ha-'Emunot*.[9] Despite the fact that this book was practically unknown before the expulsion,[10] it seems that its major conceptual assumptions reflected an attitude that became much more dominant in the generation of the expulsion.

The acceptance of the authority of the *Zohar* does not mean that kabbalistic thought was homogeneous in nature; there was, after all, the deep split between the theosophy of the "bulk," which accepts the essential attitude toward the Sefirot, and the "instrumental" concept dominant in the theosophy of later layers.[11] Thus, the Spanish kabbalists who left Spain were not the tradents of one monolithic and sacrosanct theosophy; even as each of them was convinced beyond all doubt that the *Zohar* represented his particular position, in fact there were major divergences (nevertheless, almost all of them, I repeat, were convinced that his own conceptual stand, and his alone, is also the stand of the *Zohar*). The expulsion, whatever its subsequent relation to the content of Kabbalah, is beyond doubt a primary instrument in the export of a variety of theosophical systems that were connected to the *Zohar* and considered totally independent of philosophy. Centering on the various layers of the *Zohar* and distancing themselves from philosophy are but two different expressions of a closure of mind among the Spanish kabbalists. Limiting the range of the important kabbalistic texts and excluding altogether the interaction of Jewish and Christian philosophical thought created the mind-set and paradigm that would frame important reactions toward other spiritual phenomena in Italy.[12] While the Italian kabbalistic paradigm, both Jewish and Christian, was based upon the assumption that unknown, alien bodies of literature were important and helpful in clarifying the religious outlook in the Renaissance period, the Spanish kabbalists were engaged in polemics to discredit the other forms of thought. If Jewish and Christian Renaissance thought benefited from the theme of *prisca theologia*, which dramatically expanded their libraries and intellectual horizons, the Spanish kabbalists, especially in Italy, were actively engaged in reducing the size of the significant religious library by purifying it of even well-known kabbalistic texts.

The relative exclusiveness of the canonical text, which strengthened the religious life of the kabbalists among the expellees, at the same time provoked a particularistic vision that has been characteristic of the Oriental Kabbalah since the sixteenth century. It should be emphasized that adherence to a centuries-old canonical text is characteristic not only of the Spanish kabbalah. An examination of Jewish philosophy in Spain evinces, in my opinion, a similar canonical attitude to the twelfth- and thirteenth-century masters and masterpieces: Abraham ibn Ezra, Maimonides, and Averroës are the subject of commentaries that constitute a major part of the speculative literature of the Spanish Jewish thinkers. When compared to the Italian Jewish philosopher, their openness to new trends in scholastic thought is very limited.

Translatio Kabbalae

An understanding of the messages of Kabbalah consists in both the understanding of the common denominators of the various kabbalistic forms of literature, whenever those can be discerned, and the specification of each kabbalistic current and center. However, this desideratum is complicated by the fact that kabbalistic schools and centers flourished in splendid isolation. The contacts between the kabbalists belonging to different trends and the transmission of their writings create great difficulties for anyone looking to offer a simplistic typology of various kabbalistic currents. Emigrations of kabbalists, and not only the encounter with previously unknown writings, were crucial in the establishment and development of new spiritual types of dynamics. This is the case, in my opinion, with the arrival of Rabbi Isaac Sagi Nahor to Gerona from Provence;[13] the infiltration of Ashkenazic esoteric material into Spain during the thirteenth century shaped, to a certain extent, some trends in the Jewish mysticism in this country. Abraham Abulafia's arrival in Castile apparently influenced the linguistic Kabbalah of this province; his wanderings in Greece and Italy were instrumental in the establishment of Kabbalah in these countries.[14] In the fourteenth century Rabbi Shem Tov ibn Folia's arrival from Spain contributed to the deepening of this type of knowledge in the Byzantine Empire.[15]

However, none of these commutations of kabbalists from one country to another can be compared to the massive departure of kabbalists from the Iberian Peninsula during the two expulsions. Before analyzing the nature and impact of this departure, let me clarify the usage of this term. *Departure,* or *commutation,* is hardly representative of the terrible events associated with the expulsion, whether in the peninsula, at sea, or sometimes even in the territories where the expellees arrived. I nonetheless prefer to use more neutral terms that can temper the emotional implications that bring modern scholarship to the study of kabbalah in the aftermath of the expulsion. I am not sure, for example, whether the dramatic form of the departure, a forced and violent one both in 1492 and 1497, colored substantially the nature of the cultural interaction between a Spanish kabbalist and his new environment, as compared, say, with a similar encounter in 1491. I would like to emphasize that a forced departure or a voluntary one may, at least in principle, generate similar results.

The nature of the encounter is, in my opinion, shaped by even stronger factors than the specific reasons for the departure. Thus, I regard as crucial the structure of the kabbalistic paradigms that come in contact with one another: if they are drastically different, the tension created by the encounter will have nothing to do with the violence of the expulsion. Likewise, the extent of the receptivity of a certain environment toward a kabbalistic paradigm will condition the reaction of the representative of this paradigm in the new situation. Moreover, the arrival of the written material, even when disseminated by an expellee kabbalist, is not connected to the event that caused the departure from a certain place. The interaction between the non-Sephardic kabbalists and the new kabbalistic material stemming from Spain may have very little to do with the particular nature of the event of the expulsion and the vicissitudes of the transmitters' fate. It should be emphasized that most of the transmitted material was composed by kabbalists who wrote long before the expulsion and, consequently, this historical event could not be echoed in it.

Last but not least, the personality of the kabbalist—his ability to adapt to a new environment or, on the contrary, his reluctance to do so—will have much more of an impact on his writings than historical events. Of paramount importance will be the possibility that a particular kabbalist may seek a crisis to reinforce his preexisting eschatological proclivities whereas another kabbalist may not subscribe to such an apocalyptic attitude.[16] These observations notwithstanding, the above reservations should not detract from the centrality of the expulsion for the shape of subsequent Jewish history, especially that of the Sephardic community, neither are they intended to attenuate the traumatic impact it may have had on some of the individuals who suffered from its atrocities.

However, in order to make a credible evaluation of the possible significance of this rupture in the continuum of the Sephardic Jewish experience, it is necessary to enter into these details, which seemingly did not preoccupy modern scholarship insofar as kabbalistic issues were concerned. Attracted by large historical schemes, which inspired a monolithic reaction on the part of so many individuals to such a complex event, modern scholars preferred to look for the impact of the expulsion on the nature of Kabbalah—more precisely, on the dramatic change that allegedly affected its content—rather than to probe more pedestrian questions concerning disseminations of ideas, interactions between different paradigms, intellectual tensions, and even personal frictions. By postulating the emergence of a new messianic mood in Kabbalah as characteristic of this new phase, modern scholarship embarked upon an intensive detective project to uncover evidence of a messianism that was representative of the generation of kabbalists who experienced the expulsion.[17] The most classic formulation of the dominant line in the Scholemian school seems to be Scholem's own radical assumption that "it is easy to understand that the entire religious literature of the first generation after the expulsion from Spain is pervaded by this issue [messianism] being, as a whole, an actual hope for immediate redemption."[18] Nevertheless, Scholem indicates elsewhere that the expellees' kabbalah "did not contain any new points of view."[19] Let us, therefore, leave for a moment these very attractive, comprehensive, and highly influential speculations in favor of more pedestrian discussions of some kabbalistic texts that are, in my opinion, much more numerous and more representative of the Sephardic Kabbalah in the period under consideration.

Within this limited framework the processes that involved Kabbalah of Spanish extraction after the expulsion cannot be described in detail. Provided that the Kabbalah of this period is still extant (in numerous manuscripts that are, for the time being, not explored, many of them being of outstanding importance), any attempt to provide an alternative, general picture at this time will suffer from the same defects that the prevailing theories do. Therefore, it is methodologically more appropriate to study each center of Kabbalah on its own terms and resort to more general statements only when a much more detailed examination of the more important forms of Kabbalah is available. In general, I assume that the changes Sephardic Kabbalah underwent in Italy are different from those in the former Byzantine Empire or in Jerusalem and Safed. I assume that North Africa was an environment that differed substantially from Italy of the Renaissance period, and both of them affected the reception and the alterations experienced by Kabbalah in those places.

In the following I would like to address only one center of kabbalistic creativity after the expulsion: Italy. My working hypothesis is that the particular intellectual and spiritual ambience of Italy, which has no peer in this period, served as a vital background for the Italian Kabbalah as conceived by both Jews and Christians, and for the reaction to it by some Spanish kabbalists. By emphasizing the paramount importance of the different cultural contexts I assume that the prevailing assumption as to the traumatic and dramatic importance of the expulsion for the Kabbalah will be reconsidered in favor of a much more variegated theory, one that will explain the huge and unexpected creativity of the Spanish kabbalists as the result of many factors, varying from one country to another, or even from one kabbalist to another. The monolithic explanation, including the implicit assumption that the event of the expulsion was understood in the same way by all the refugees, across three continents, is but one example of the single-reason explanations that dominate the historiography of Kabbalah in modern scholarship.[20]

Spanish Kabbalists in Italy in the Generation of the Expulsion

There are few studies that detail the arrival of the Spanish Jews in Italy. Most of the discussions center around the more influential figures like Isaac Abravanel or Isaac Aramah.[21] I am not aware of any significant attempt to map and analyze in detail the influx of the kabbalists, although there is a consensus that no fewer than six kabbalists came to Italy and stayed there for a while between 1490 and 1500. They are (1) Rabbi Isaac Mor Ḥayyim, (2) Rabbi Yehudah Ḥayyat, (3) Rabbi Joseph ibn Shraga, (4) Rabbi Joseph Alkastiel,[22] (5) Rabbi Abraham ben Eliezer ha-Levi,[23] and (6) Rabbi Isaac ben Ḥayyim ha-Kohen.[24] At least one more kabbalist, Rabbi Abraham Saba, was reported to have visited Italy before his death, but more information is needed to confirm this.

The first three kabbalists wrote kabbalistic works in Italy and they will preoccupy us in the following. As for Alkastiel, it is still an open question as to whether his influential kabbalistic responsa addressed to Rabbi Yehudah Ḥayyat were composed in Italy, but this issue cannot be decided, at this time, and I shall refer to his text only tangentially. Rabbi Abraham ha-Levi visited Italy but apparently did not write anything on its soil. However, it seems that at least one short passage, to be discussed below, is relevant for understanding the relationship between Jewish kabbalists and their Christian contemporaries.[25] Rabbi Isaac ha-Kohen's knowledge of Kabbalah notwithstanding, it seems that he was not expert in this lore like the other figures mentioned above; I hope to deal with the kabbalistic material in his writings in a separate study.

I begin with the discussion of the most important Spanish kabbalist who wrote in Italy, Rabbi Yehudah Ḥayyat, as, in my opinion, he is the main representative of his generation of Spanish kabbalists. A review of the writings produced by the Spanish kabbalists in Italy demonstrates that only a few kabbalistic treatises were produced in the first generation after the expulsion. Quantitatively, much more was written by Sephardic kabbalists in the other centers of Jewish life: the Ottoman Empire, North Africa, and the Land of Israel. Despite their small numbers, however, most of the writings from Italy had a significant impact on the course of Kabbalah; Ḥayyat, especially, both before and after the printing of his *Minḥat Yehudah*, was a major kabbalistic figure whose deep influence is apparent throughout the kabbalistic literature, in Italy and elsewhere.[26] The epistles of Mor Ḥayyim, too, though they reach us in only a few manuscripts, left a deep imprint on the discussions on the nature of the Sefirot in the Ottoman Empire and in the Safedian Kabbalah.[27]

Rabbi Yehudah ben Yaakov Ḥayyat

In comparison with the fate of the other expellees, that of Rabbi Yehudah Ḥayyat is relatively well documented. In the preface to his *Minḥat Yehudah*, his only kabbalistic treatise, he took pains to report the events of his recent past, some of them including terrible experiences that occurred during his departure from the Iberian Peninsula and while in North Africa. Nevertheless, there are many crucial details we do not know, and they may affect our understanding of the formation of his thought. We do not know, for example, where he studied Kabbalah, who his main master was, or what his kabbalistic views were before the expulsion. His commentary on *Sefer Ma'arekhet ha-'Elohut, Sefer Minḥat Yehudah*, is our main source for his Kabbalah, but it was composed in Italy.

However, some indications are very helpful for reconstructing his avatars and the basis of his kabbalistic thought before the expulsion. His introduction provides some historical aspects: he was a Spaniard, though we do not know from which part of Spain he came. It seems that he was a respected figure already in Spain, since he presents himself as a teacher of an unspecified community; as he tells it, the reaction of the Sephardic people in Italy to his plight implies that he was already well-known in Spain.[28] From the fact that he left Spain from Lisbon, we may assume that he was a Castilian Jew, and not a Catalan one, since he preferred the Western trajectory to the Eastern one.

Sometime during the winter of 1492–1493 he left Lisbon with his family and some two hundred others. Because of the plague that had spread throughout the boat, they wandered for four months and then were forced to anchor in Malaga because no other port would let them dock. The boat was then robbed by Basques. The persuasive efforts of the Christian authorities or, according to another version, the priests and the famine convinced hundreds of the expellees to convert; some of the others, including Ḥayyat's wife, died. They were then kept for two more months in Malaga before they were allowed to leave. When Ḥayyat arrived in Fez, in North Africa, a Muslim acquaintance initiated a libel suit, the precise nature of which is not totally clear. Ḥayyat,

apparently, had organized a celebration on the occasion of the defeat of
the Muslims that also included some form of denigration of Islam. He
was rescued by the Jews, to whom he gave two hundred books in return
for the ransom. After a stay in Fez he left for Naples in the autumn of
1493 (under totally inhumane conditions) where he witnessed the
French invasion in 1494; he then left for Venice, where he was very well
received by the "nobles," the Spanish refugees.

Sometime in the middle of the decade Ḥayyat reached Mantua,
where he met another famous expellee, Rabbi Joseph Yaaveẓ, a conservative thinker and author of several theological and exegetical treatises.[29]
Yaaveẓ and other "nobles and wise men" entreated him to write a commentary on *Sefer Ma'arekhet ha-'Elohut* because "their soul desired to
contemplate the delight of the Lord and visit his palace"[30] He in turn
composed his commentary, in order not to "prevent them from learning" and because he greatly esteemed the book. According to Ḥayyat,
this book opened the gate to kabbalistic issues not disclosed by other
books of Kabbalah. Ḥayyat also mentions that another kabbalist,
whose name he did not know,[31] had already commented on this book,
but in an inappropriate manner. Nevertheless, he indicates the commentary was widespread in the province of Mantua.[32]

The kabbalist thus offered three different reasons for writing his
commentary—the request of the Jews of Mantua, the intrinsic value of
the book, and his critique of the existing commentary—none of which
is related to the expulsion or to any messianic expectations whatsoever.
This kabbalist then, who probably has suffered more than any of the
other kabbalists from the vicissitudes of the expulsion, does not offer
that event as a rationale for his kabbalistic activity.

Let us now return to the autobiographical information in the preface. While in Spain Ḥayyat began his study of Kabbalah, which he pursued for some time and with some success. He collected pieces of the
book of the *Zohar* from various places and was able to put together
most of the literature connected to it.[33] As he expressly put it, he was
confident that it was this devotion to the book, and to Kabbalah in general, that had sustained him throughout the ordeals of the expulsion.
Indeed, all the details he adduces are intended to demonstrate the
apotropaic function of the *Zohar*, which had saved him throughout
these trials. He recounted the extended and evocative portrayal of his
vicissitudes only to emphasize the sanctity of the *Zohar*, a fact that

should be recalled by anyone looking to the preface for evidence of the attitude of the expellees toward history. Scholars must read the personal story of the kabbalist in its context, namely, as an illustration of the nature of the *Zohar*, a book relatively well known in Spain but almost unknown in Italy. History, to the extent it is mentioned, is introduced to prove the uniqueness of the mystical classical book, not vice versa. If I can guess at Ḥayyat's intention, it concerns his desire to demonstrate that the holiness of the Kabbalah prevails even in the face of terrible ordeals.

Ḥayyat quotes mainly from part of the book called *Tikkunei Zohar*, which is the major source for the views and quotations that permeate the commentary.[34] The *Zohar* is described in his introduction as practically unknown by the earlier kabbalists, including some important ones.[35] He explains this fact by citing a theory, found in one of the later layers of the book of the *Zohar,* that the book will be revealed during the last generation, namely, the generation of the Messiah.

Ḥayyat indicates this is his generation. Moreover, he argues, study of the *Zohar* will bring the Messiah. Prima facie, this confession of the eschatological role of the study of the *Zohar* may seem to support the views of those scholars who emphasize the importance of the messianic change in kabbalah as the result of the expulsion. In my opinion, however, such a reading is at least an exaggeration: Ḥayyat collected the various parts of the book while in Spain before the expulsion. Whether messianic hopes nourished his activity cannot be established on the basis of our knowledge today. However, if indeed messianism played a significant role in his kabbalistic activity he never related it to his experience of the expulsion. Moreover, the argument concerning the eschatological effect of the study is certainly not Ḥayyat's innovation but the rehearsal of a view he quotes from the *Tikkunei Zohar*. Ḥayyat did not initiate the "actualization" of the Zoharic view in the generation of expulsion; though he wrote his book even earlier than it was assumed,[36] it seems that already in the circle of *Sefer ha-Meshiv*, the relationship between the study of the *Zohar* and redemption had been adapted from earlier sources.[37]

Ḥayyat did not plunge into a project of bringing the Messiah by printing the *Zohar* or by disseminating it. His brief two sentences concerning the eschatological role of the *Zohar* had no echoes in the bulk of his single masterpiece, *Sefer Minḥat Yehudah*. There seems to be no evidence whatsoever to connect the one statement in the introduction and the other tens of folios of his kabbalistic writings.[38] Indeed, the assumption that a change in the nature of his kabbalistic thought transpired, or that it included some novel elements related in one way or another to his terrible personal experiences, is to be proven by scholars that would like to make such a connection not by merely stating this nexus as a fact but by pointing to specific shifts in the details of his thought. In any case, the burden of proof lies with those who argue that one sentence indicates that the ethos of a book was changed.[39]

However, the occurrence of the name of the *Zohar* in another context may clarify somewhat the function of Ḥayyat's praises of the book. At the end of the introduction he compiled what is in effect the first Jewish index: a list of titles of the kabbalistic writings that should not be studied and another list of books of Kabbalah that Ḥayyat recommended. The analysis of these two lists follows.

Good and Bad Kabbalistic Books

The Spanish kabbalist made the following proposal:

> These are the books that you shall approach [*tikrav 'eleihem*]: *Sefer Yeṣirah*, attributed [*ha-mekhuneh*] to Rabbi Akiba, blessed be his memory; *Sefer ha-Bahir*, attributed to Rabbi Neḥuniah ben ha-Kanah, should be a diadem to your head; the book of the *Zohar* "should not depart from your mouth,"[40] and the books of Rabbi Joseph Gikatilla and those of Rabbi [Moshe ben] Shem Tov de Leon, you "shall tie about thy neck"[41] and the secrets of Nahmanides, should be written upon the table of your heart, and the books of Rabbi Menahem Recanati, "thou shall bind them for a sign upon thy arm;"[42] and *Sefer Ma'arekhet ha-'Elohut* with my present commentary, "shall be as frontlets between thy eyes" and then you will be successful in your ways and then you will be illuminated.[43]

These titles represent the classical theosophical-theurgical trend of Kabbalah, which dominated Spanish Kabbalah since the second half of the thirteenth century. With the exception of *Sefer Yeṣirah*, which was understood by the Spanish kabbalists as a theosophical treatise as well,[44] the other books reflect the creativity of kabbalistic thought that tended to the theosophical. The list reflects Ḥayyat's historical conception. Abraham the patriarch, Rabbi Akiba, and R. Simeon bar Yoḥai, the alleged author of the *Zohar*, precede the medieval kabbalists. The use of the biblical verses are intended, I assume, to impart canonical status to these books. These writings represent the real sources for most of *Sefer Minhat Yehudah*; they do not deal with a theoretical program. Seen as such, the exaltation of the *Zohar* is in line with the general trend of Hayyat's Kabbalah, beyond the fact that he had collected parts of it while still in Spain. However, the list is much more than a disclosure of sources or of some idiosyncratic predilections. It is also to be preferred to the other kabbalistic books that he had just enumerated and criticized. Hayyat admits that the anonymous commentary on *Sefer Ma'arekhet ha-'Elohut* was circulated in "this province."[45] However, its danger lay in its interpretation of the kabbalistic text "according to philosophical presuppositions [*hakdamot be-filosofiah*]; but this is not the way, neither is this the city."[46] He then expatiated on the other books "that were spread in this province, kabbalistic books that confuse the pure mind."[47] What are these kabbalistic books Hayyat was so eager to warn against?

> The divine sage, Rabbi Isaac ibn Latif, blessed be his memory, the author of *Sefer [Sha'ar] ha-Shamayim*[48] and *[Zurat] ha-'Olam*[49] and *Zeror ha-Mor* and *Sefer Ginzei ha-Melekh*, whose words are more precious than gems; but insofar as his words concern the science of Kabbalah, one of his feet is within while the other without [Kabbalah]. Consequently, you should see only a small part of them, but not see all of them. And if God will tell me to do it, I shall distinguish the fine flour from the chaff.

Although Hayyat's attitude to ibn Latif as a religious thinker is very positive, this relates only to the latter's writing about nonkabbalistic issues. One should avoid his kabbalistic work. Unfortunately, Hayyat did not elaborate, and we can only guess, on the basis of the content of the books mentioned, that he considered ibn Latif too philosophical a writer to represent genuine kabbalistic thought.

Much more severe is the critique of Abraham Abulafia. Hayyat's assault on the views of this controversial kabbalist is virulent without qualification. Although he admits to having seen "many[50] books" by Abulafia, he refers to only three of them, *Sefer 'Or ha-Sekhel*, *Sefer Hayyei ha-'Olam ha-Ba'*, and one of Abulafia's commentaries on the *Guide of the Perplexed*. The founder of ecstatic Kabbalah is described, inter alia, as "mad," and his books as "replete with imaginary things and fakes invented by his heart."[51] Ḥayyat refutes Abulafia's attempt to interpret Maimonides according to his Kabbalah, which, says Ḥayyat, is a false one. Maimonides himself is introduced by Ḥayyat as "ha-ḥakham ha-'Elohi,"[52] namely, the divine sage. Thus, it is not philosophy, or at least not Maimonides' philosophy that is the main target of the critique, but the synthesis of philosophy and Kabbalah.[53]

Finally, Ḥayyat writes about "the sage Matut; you should pay attention to his ways, neither come close to the entrance of his door, since he has a wicked rod in his hand, in order to cause you to deviate from the right way and go to the crooked one."[54]

There are two common denominators to these three authors and the anonymous commentary on *Sefer Ma'arekhet ha-'Elohut*. First, all combine Kabbalah with philosophy (a mixture that is absent in the works favored by Ḥayyat). He describes them as books that "confuse the pure mind," a characterization, I assume, that has something to do with the composite nature of the kabbalistic systems presented in these books. Second, all the aforementioned books, according to Ḥayyat, were disseminated in the area of Mantua. Their particular brand of Kabbalah can be discerned in the writings of a Mantuan kabbalist who flourished at precisely the time of Ḥayyat's stay in Mantua. Rabbi Yoḥanan Alemanno was born in Mantua, was educated there, and probably returned to this city after a stay in Florence; he is the exponent of a sustained effort to explain Kabbalah in a more rational way,[55] even using the phrase "the Kabbalah that is understood by reason."[56] Moreover, he probably encountered Ḥayyat's book very soon after its composition and seems to be the first author who quoted from it. We shall return later on to Alemanno and Kabbalah. For our purposes it is sufficient to point out that Ḥayyat's emphasis on the centrality of the *Zohar* is part of a sustained effort to counteract a type of Kabbalah found in Italy by presenting Spanish Kabbalah as the sole appropriate alternative. The *Zohar*, however, played a rather marginal role in the fabric of the Italian Kabbalah during Ḥayyat's lifetime. Alemanno, as well as his contemporary Italian kabbalists, was not well-acquainted with the *Zohar* and quotes it only rarely, often in Hebrew translations.[57]

Ḥayyat's *Minḥat Yehudah* insists on the centrality of the *Zohar*, to judge by the frequency of quotations from this book. Its study, according to Ḥayyat, may hasten the redemption, but this is not primarily an eschatological statement. Rather it is much more an attempt to exploit the eschatological conception related to the *Zohar* in order to strengthen the study of the *Zohar*. Indeed, in general, *Minḥat Yehudah* otherwise ignores messianic topics;[58] the eschatological quote should be understood, in my opinion, in its larger context, as part of a confrontation between two types of Kabbalah. This explains not only its occurrence in the introduction but also the dominant role played by the *Zohar* in *Minḥat Yehudah* and the absence of the messianic overtones throughout the book.

Approaching the above question from another angle, the choice of the book to be interpreted was not entirely Ḥayyat's. He contends that it was the Mantuan nobles who selected the work. A perusal of *Minḥat Yehudah* shows that despite the nice words about it whenever it contradicts the *Zohar* he accepted the approach of the latter. So, for example, he writes: " I shall stand up and strengthen myself in order to struggle against the Rabbi [namely, the author of *Ma'arekhet ha-'Elohut*] concerning the topic.[59] Ḥayyat wonders why the anonymous author followed Nahmanides, R. Shlomo ibn Adret, and their disciples, who differed with the *Zohar*. Even a long list of famous kabbalists could not convince Ḥayyat to accept a position that conflicted with the *Zohar*. He was eager to promote the *Zohar* to the exclusion of any other kabbalistic text. In other words, Ḥayyat, with his mythical orientation informed by the Zoharic theosophies,[60] challenged the philosophically oriented interpretation of *Sefer Ma'arekhet ha-'Elohut*, as found in Rabbi Reuven Ẓarfati's commentary, as well as the views of the text itself.[61] Ḥayyat's work is much more of an elucidation of the views of the *Zohar* than of *Sefer Ma'arekhet ha-'Elohut*. The very fact that Ḥayyat wrote a commentary on a book whose spiritual messages he did not always accept is telling, a reflection of the basic situation faced by a Spanish kabbalist in Italy. The *Zohar* itself was not of sufficient interest to the Italian Jewish kabbalists; they were concerned with *Ma'arekhet ha-'Elohut*, however, and Ḥayyat used it in order to inject a great dose of mythical Kabbalah under the pretext of clarifying a relatively antimythical text.[62] However, by structuring his kabbalistic discourse around this specific book, with its systematic approach to Kabbalah, Ḥayyat implicitly adopted the format dominant among the Italian kabbalists, that is, discussions on the nature of the divine world and the questions concerning the essence of the divine manifestation. This systematic, almost scholastic, form of espousing their own view is dominant among the Italian kabbalists but less so among scholars of the Spanish preexpulsion Kabbalah.

Finally, Ḥayyat is unhappy with the views of another Italian kabbalist, whose name he does not mention.[63] However, as Ephraim Gottlieb has indicated,[64] it is reasonable to assume that the individual in question was Rabbi Eliahu of Gennazano, who flourished in the decade before Ḥayyat arrived in Italy. The critique centers on divergences between Ḥayyat's "instrumental" view of the Sefirot and the "essentialistic" one adopted by Gennazano and the assumption of the Italian kabbalist that Ein Sof is identical to the first Sefirah.[65] This is yet another example of the uneasiness felt by the Spanish kabbalists toward the work of their Italian counterparts.

Kabbalah and Philosophy in the Generation of the Expulsion

As we have proposed, we assume that the polemical tone of the Spanish kabbalists resulted from their encounter with a different kabbalistic paradigm. The regnant Spanish view of the fifteenth century assumes that pure Kabbalah is not a philosophically oriented type of lore, whereas the contemporary Italian Kabbalah combined a variety of intellectual trends: Kabbalah, philosophy, and magic.[66] Was the clash between the two paradigms—the purist and the particularist, the synthetic and the universalistic—the product of the expulsion? Was the particularistic approach, that is, the outcome of the pressures of the terrible events that occurred in the peninsula? I would answer in the negative. Before the expulsion, as well as afterward, Spanish kabbalists betrayed antiphilosophical attitudes. A circle of kabbalists, to be referred to as the circle of *Sefer ha-Meshiv*, was fervently opposed to philosophy in general, again both before and after the expulsion.[67] However, since members of this school were not active in Italy, I shall not address their critique within the framework of the present discussion. However, the more moderate views of another Spanish kabbalist, Rabbi Isaac Mor Ḥayyim, may indicate that the situation and the reaction of Yehudah Ḥayyat are independent of the crisis of expulsion. He will serve as a point of reference that will allow a better understanding of Ḥayyat's position.

Two years *before* the expulsion, Rabbi Mor Ḥayyim visited Italy on his way to the Land of Israel.[68] In Italy he met at least two people interested in Kabbalah and wrote two letters to one of them, Rabbi Isaac of Pisa, who was apparently staying in Pisa or Florence. The second person, mentioned en passant, was a certain Rabbi Yoḥanan who had close relations with Rabbi Isaac. I would identify him with Rabbi Isaac's teacher, Rabbi Yoḥanan Alemanno.[69] In his letter Mor Ḥayyim expresses the hope that whenever his views differ "from the view of Rabbi Yoḥanan, let God safeguard him, I am sure that you will find, because of the quality of your mind, the reason for my deviance."[70] He then becomes much more insistent:

> When you inquire into these matters, you should not follow the [views] of those sages who regarded the *intelligibilia* as the root [of their speculations] and interpret the kabbalistic matters so that they agree with philosophy [*'iyyun*]. But you shall regard Kabbalah as your root and you shall make an effort to make the intellect will agree with it. But if your excellency will not be able to do it, you should know that there is a limit to the intellect, but the Kabbalah, which was received from the mouth of a prophet, is higher than the intellect, so that it can correct whatever the intellect has distorted."[71]

Mor Ḥayyim's warnings are his attempt to neutralize the "pernicious" influence of Alemanno's philosophization of Kabbalah. It seems that he considered any effort to introduce speculative approaches to the interpretation of Kabbalah to be dangerous. In another epistle, written some months before that quoted above, he declares that his views on the nature of the Sefirot can be ascertained by reading "all the books that agree with the view of R. Simeon bar Yoḥai regarding the emanation of the Sefirot and their expansion.[72] But the rational inquiry concerning these matters is something forbidden to us."[73]

It seems that Yoḥanan Alemanno was not alone in taking a philosophical approach. His younger contemporaries (and perhaps also companions), Rabbi David Messer Leon and Rabbi Abraham de Balmes,[74] and the kabbalistic epistle that may have been written by Rabbi Isaac of Pisa combined Kabbalah and philosophy.[75] While Alemanno was inclined to introduce Neoplatonic concepts, in addition to the Aristotelian ones brought to the fore by medieval thinkers, the other two Renaissance kabbalists were definitely more sympathetic to the various forms of Aristotelianism. In the case of Messer Leon the impact of Thomism in general and also in matters of theosophy is evident, too, as has been shown in the recent studies by Hava Tirosh-Rothschild.[76]

Last but not least, the Christian kabbalists understood Jewish Kabbalah as tradent of and pregnant with a theological message that adumbrated Christianity while also according with philosophical stands, Platonic and Neoplatonic, hermetic and "Zoroastrian." At least in one case Pico della Mirandola compared a certain kind of Kabbalah to the "catholic philosophy," namely, the universal philosophy.[77] However, much more explicit, and instructive, is the manner in which Johannes Reuchlin approaches Kabbalah. For him, as for Pico—and for many modern scholars of Kabbalah—it mattered little whether a kabbalist was an Italian Jew or a Sephardic one. Their belief in the single message of a transspacial Kabbalah blurred the differences between the developments in the two countries. Thus, seduced by the image of the greatness of the Spanish Kabbalah, Reuchlin invented an imaginary encounter in Frankfurt between a Spanish kabbalist, named Simon, and two other persons, a Pythagorean thinker named Philolaus and a Muslim named Marranus. Since the names are overtly symbolic and not historical, I assume that the use of the name Simon ben Eleazar for a kabbalist is related to the figure of R. Simeon bar Yoḥai, the alleged author of the *Zohar*, despite the fact that Reuchlin does not quote from this book. The explicit purpose of the dialogue between these figures is to introduce Pythagoreanism to Germany, a mission that consumed Reuchlin throughout *De Arte Cabalistica*. He wanted, in the line of Ficino, who introduced Plato in Italy, and Jacques Faber d'Etaples, who "has brought out Aristotle" in France, to "bring about a rebirth of Pythagoras in Germany." And Kabbalah was, according to Reuchlin, one of the sources of Pythagoras's thought:[78] "I have only been able to glean from the Hebrew Kabbalah, since it derives in origin from the teachers of Kabbalah and then was lost by our ancestors, disappearing from Southern Italy [*Magna Graecia*] into the kabbalistic writings."[79]

This is a fascinating reversal of the medieval Jewish complaint about the loss of the sciences among the Jews as the result of the exile. The Christian kabbalist argues that Kabbalah preserves ancient philosophy that otherwise would be lost; for this reason Reuchlin wrote about the symbolic philosophy of the art of Kabbalah, to bring Pythagorean doctrine to the attention of scholars.[80] Reuchlin was invited by his interlocutors to explain the philosophical method of Kabbalah.[81] Whatever his kabbalistic inventions,[82] he was convinced from his visit to Italy and his encounter with Pico, and perhaps also with Jewish Italian kabbalists, that Kabbalah was consonant with Pythagoreanism. The reputation of Sephardic greatness in matters of Kabbalah combined with the Italian conception of Kabbalah to produce a hybrid in Reuchlin's writing. It is very ironic indeed that this view was attributed to a Sephardic kabbalist. On the basis of the writings of the Spanish kabbalists one may assume that they would have vehemently protested against such an understanding of their mystical lore.

The speculative similarities between the Jewish and Christian conceptions of Kabbalah in Italy may indicate that there was a certain osmotic influence.

The Italian kabbalists in the period under discussion are self-taught, few if any of them having studied with authoritative figures. Thus, one might expect a certain diffidence vis-à-vis their Sephardic critics. This was not the case, however. The Italians respected the positions of the Italian kabbalists but were not ready to yield to their authority. I am inclined to attribute this attitude to their feeling that their speculative and open trend, and not the Sephardic reticence from philosophy, was the one more attuned to the spirit of their age, as expressed by the renascence of philosophy and the emergence of the philosophical understanding of Kabbalah among the Christians.[83]

The *Zohar* and Italian Kabbalah

Like Yehudah Ḥayyat, Mor Ḥayyim also assumes that the *Zohar* is the ultimate authority in matters of Kabbalah and is reticent insofar as philosophy may be involved in its translation.[84] Again, as with his compatriot, Mor Ḥayyim complains that "the book of the *Zohar* is not available in its entirety in any one province but is dispersed throughout all the provinces. This passage I have copied from the book of the *Zohar* that I have found in the academy of Rabbi Eliezer, let God safeguard him, in the city of Lisbon."[85]

Such a confession is meaningful only in a country where the *Zohar* was very little known. Had considerable parts of this book been available in Italy, there would have been no reason to mention the specific Portuguese academy in which he copied one of the most profound and important parts of the *Zohar*. Mor Ḥayyim's analysis of the Zoharic passage was intended to counteract the view, represented by Rabbi Menaḥem Recanati, that the Sefirot are not identical to the divine essence.[86] Mor Ḥayyim interprets the text of the *Zohar* as pointing, correctly in my opinion, to the opposite view, that the Sefirot are identical with the divine essence. This interpretation is posited as his Kabbalah and the Kabbalah of the sages of Sefarad, blessed be their memory, since all of them decided that the Sefirot are not created [entities].[87] *Kabbalat kol ḥakhmei Sefarad* is a highly instructive phrase; it stands for the more mythical kabbalistic view, that the Sefirot are part of the divine essence, indeed they form it, in opposition to the stand of Recanati, who was, at least by his name and influence, an Italian. The awareness of the existence of a Sephardic Kabbalah is crucial for our discussion. It reflects an awareness, very similar to that of Ḥayyat later on, that his mystical tradition is representative of Spanish Jewish thought. Indeed at the end of his two letters, Mor Ḥayyim mentions the epithet Sephardi after his name.[88] He seems to criticize only Recanati alone but it is likely that this kabbalist was not his sole target.[89] As mentioned above, Mor Ḥayyim also refers to Rabbi Yoḥanan Alemanno, who, in my view, was also in the camp of those who believed that the Sefirot are instruments of the divine activity but not of divine essence. This is indeed the view of Alemanno, and I assume that he was aware of this veiled attack, because he reacted very strongly. He copied the Zoharic text that was translated into Hebrew and interpreted by Mor Ḥayyim and, without mentioning the Spanish kabbalist's interpretation, Alemanno offered another, very different interpretation.[90]

The strong nexus between the Zoharic Kabbalah and Spain, and the relative ignorance of this seminal book in Italy is, however, exemplified by even more substantial evidence. A perusal of the voluminous books of Yoḥanan Alemanno shows that the role played by the *Zohar* in his earlier thought was marginal. Some of the few quotations he adduced from the *Zohar* appear in his later works, sometimes in Hebrew, and many of them were influenced by Rabbi Menahem Recanati and Ḥayyat's *Minḥat Yehudah*. In his program of study, in which he enumerated several kabbalistic writings to be studied by the ideal student, the *Zohar* is not mentioned at all.[91]

The *Zohar* is also absent from the writings of Rabbi Asher Lemlein, as E. Kupfer has already noticed.[92] However, even more persuasive are the statements of Rabbi Isaac Mor Ḥayyim to his Italian addressee, Rabbi Isaac of Pisa, himself a kabbalist. In his first letter he copied a passage from the *Zohar* in its original Aramaic. Unfortunately, we do not have the answer of Isaac of Pisa, but we do have the second letter of Rabbi Isaac Mor Ḥayyim, who wrote, "Since we are not accustomed in this country[93] to the Jerusalemite Targum,[94] I decided to translate it into Hebrew word by word, then I shall divide the passage into paragraphs and explain each one separately, to the extent I am able to do it."[95]

There is no reason to doubt this evidence: in Italy, even the kabbalists were unable to read the *Zohar*. Furthermore, even the Aramaic dialect in which it was written was unknown to them. Finally, even the translation into Hebrew is not sufficient, and the translated text had to be explained in detail. In the other side Alemanno testifies that "the sages of Israel were already divided between themselves and were confused concerning the question whether the Sefirot are the essence of the Godhead or whether they are separate from Him, as it can be seen from a passage attributed [*meyuḥas*] to Rashby [R. Simeon bar Yoḥai] in the book of the *Zohar*, found [in the hands of some] few persons, in addition to the translation into Hebrew, because of its profoundness in the language of the Jerusalemite [Talmud]."[96]

Since the small fragment discussed by Alemanno is identical to that sent to and translated for Isaac of Pisa, we see the paucity of Zoharic literature available to those Italian intellectuals interested in Kabbalah. The kabbalistic sources used by Rabbi David Messer Leon seems to confirm the above conclusion, as does the corpus of the kabbalistic literature translated by Flavius Mithridates for Pico della Mirandola. Despite the very massive project of translations, which I believe reflects the kabbalistic literature extant and studied in Italy, and much less in Spain, no Zoharic significant passage was translated. To the extent the book was known or cited, it was through the quotes in Rabbi Menahem Recanati's *Commentary on the Pentateuch*.[97] Even later on, in the kabbalistic writings of Johannes Reuchlin, composed at the end of the fifteenth century and the beginning of the sixteenth century—precisely the period under consideration here—the *Zohar* plays only a marginal role.[98] By contrast, the *Zohar* was quoted by Spanish converts to Christianity who wrote about Kabbalah; they even adduced Zoharic texts that are not found in the extant Zoharic corpus.[99] It is thus evident that even among the Christian kabbalists the dichotomy between Spain and Italy remains significant insofar as the *Zohar* is concerned.

Against the neglect, not to say ignorance, of the central book of Spanish Kabbalah, the insistence of the two Spanish kabbalists on its importance is much easier to understand.

Italian Kabbalah and Abraham Abulafia

The Spanish Kabbalah has its classic book: the *Zohar*. The Italian kabbalists did not focus on one central book, although some of them had their predilections, as is easily discerned from the list of the pernicious books discussed above. However, we should also compare its content to other data in order to be able to paint a more nuanced picture of the Italians' preferences for the three kabbalists; Isaac ibn Latif emerging as the least threatening. The attack on Shmuel ibn Matut (or Motot) is obvious, but it is not so vicious as that against Abraham Abulafia. We may hypothesize that the stronger the attack leveled by Ḥayyat, the more dangerous he considered the author to be. By this criterion, Abulafia was considered the most dangerous among the kabbalists, Matut less so, and ibn Latif the least so. Ḥayyat's evaluation that the writings of these three kabbalists were influential in Northern Italy was certainly correct; he did not engage in a battle with imaginary problems.

Yoḥanan Alemanno was acquainted with and attracted to all the kabbalistic writings mentioned by Ḥayyat; Ḥayyat may even have compiled a response to Alemanno's study program. One can easily reconstruct Alemanno's preference among the three: his curriculum moves from the earlier to the later, so that a text or author that is mentioned earlier would represent a less important stage in the education of an ideal student, while a text to be studied later on would be conceived as a more advanced and more esteemed form of Kabbalah. Matut, who influenced several passages in Alemanno's writings was nevertheless not even included in Alemanno's study program.[100] Ibn Latif, by contrast, is mentioned at a relatively early stage of the study of Kabbalah, and all his writings mentioned by Ḥayyat were quoted in Alemanno's various writings. Abulafia's books are to be read at the very end of the study of Kabbalah.[101] An inspection of Alemanno's texts shows that he knew at least two out of the three books by Abulafia that were on Ḥayyat's list.[102] Consequently, we may conclude that Ḥayyat's critique would apply to Alemanno's predilections.

Rabbi Asher Lemlein was also very fond of Abulafia's Kabbalah. Whereas he did not mention Matut and ibn Latif at all, traces of Abulafia's views are conspicuous in his writings. In any case, he mentions *Sefer Ḥayyei ha-ʿOlam ha-Baʾ* three times, always in very laudatory terms.[103] As for Pico della Mirandola's knowledge of Kabbalah and the translations made for him, as I tried to show elsewhere,[104] he was acquainted with ibn Latif's *Shaʿar ha-Shamayim*, though this book was not translated into Latin. It seems that he was not familiar with Matut. However, as far as Abulafia is concerned, the situation is quite different. Many of his books were translated by Mithridates, and as has been convincingly shown by Wirszubski, they were deeply influential on Pico's Kabbalah. And, as Robert Bonfil has indicated, *Sefer 'Or ha-Sekhel*, one of Abulafia's main mystical handbooks and one of the writings criticized by Ḥayyat, was well-known in Italy.[105] Indeed, the great number of Italian manuscripts of Abulafia's works demonstrates the appeal of his Kabbalah in Italy.

However, in addition to the direct influence of Abulafia's own writings, Italian kabbalists before the generation of the expulsion had been influenced by his thought and indirectly disseminated it. The most important of these seems to be Rabbi Reuven Ẓarfati, the author of the *Commentary on Sefer Maʿarekhet ha-'Elohut*.[106] This kabbalist, who probably flourished in the fourteenth century, is one of the first to synthesize ecstatic and theosophical Kabbalah, and his commentary was widespread in Italy.[107] Ẓarfati accepted Abulafia's numerological techniques, his theory about combinations of letters, his philosophical epistemology, and, to a certain extent, his metaphysics. Thus, Ẓarfati's commentary displayed some of the most representative features of ecstatic Kabbalah. The split between the ecstatic Kabbalah, and the theosophical, which took place at the end of the thirteenth century, allowed the two trends to develop independently in the different geographical areas. However, with the expulsion of the kabbalists from Spain they were forced to confront in Italy and in the East an unfamiliar Kabbalah; they reacted with antagonism. It was not only the decree of R. Shlomo ben Adret that was instrumental in distancing them from Abulafia's thought: they found the very essence of his kabbalistic vision to be alienating: his rapprochement between Kabbalah and philosophy, especially that of Maimonides, his anomian attitude, namely, his heavy reliance on techniques that had nothing to do with the halakhic regulations, and the ideals he cultivated, ecstatic and unitive experiences that were not the focus of the Spanish Kabbalah.

Rabbi Joseph ibn Shraga and Rabbi Asher Lemlein

The two Spanish kabbalists mentioned above expressed their reservations and critiques of the Italian kabbalists in rather mild terms. However, another refugee from Spain through Portugal adopted a different attitude. Rabbi Joseph ibn Shraga was less known, less important, and less influential on the course of Kabbalah.[108] He nevertheless enjoyed a very great reputation during his lifetime.[109] Sometimes referred to as the kabbalist from Agrigento,[110] he composed a commentary on the liturgy and several small kabbalistic explanations on different topics, all of them still in manuscript. Several folios containing kabbalistic commentaries on some pericopes are extant in two manuscripts; these writings were dedicated to Rabbi Leon Sinai of Colonia, the son of Rabbi Shmuel of Bologna. According to a manuscript note, this book was not completed because the author took ill and died.[111] One finds no great originality in these still unpublished writings; they rely heavily on the theosophy of the *Zohar*, including views from *Tikkunei Zohar* that are quoted amply. Ibn Shraga occasionally adopted texts that were composed in Spain long before he was born,[112] a fact that reflects not only on his personality but also on the state of the knowledge of Kabbalah in Italy. We shall analyze an affair in which he was involved in terms of our particular interest here; it has already attracted the attention of scholars.[113]

Early in the sixteenth century the elderly Rabbi Moshe Ḥefeẓ, whose identity still requires some research, had asked Rabbi Asher Lemlein some questions related to the kabbalistic concept of metempsychosis. Rabbi Asher's answers were brought to the attention of ibn Shraga, who, though not asked to respond, composed a strong critique of Rabbi Asher's somewhat eccentric understanding of the topic. I will not enter into the details of the divergences between the two kabbalists;[114] Suffice it to adduce here several of the vitriolic expressions used by ibn Shraga against Rabbi Asher. It seems, moreover that such tones also characterized the writings of Asher Lemlein himself,[115] in speaking about Spanish practice and thought. Lemlein's sources are ancient mystical texts, from the Heikhalot literature, Ḥasidei Ashkenaz, and ecstatic Kabbalah—

none of them vital for understanding the Spanish Kabbalah's view of metempsychosis.[116] Indeed, this encounter between the Ashkenazic-Italian author and a contemporary Spanish kabbalist represents rather graphically the chasm between these two Jewish cultures.[117] Here we can address only the rhetorical aspect of the controversy, without entering into matters of substance, which require detailed analyses.

From the outset, ibn Shraga depicts the views of Rabbi Asher as "an inverse world,"[118] using a phrase from the Talmud.[119] For this reason he feels that he must respond. Drawing heavily from the *Zohar* and *Tikkunei Zohar*, ibn Shraga rejects each of Rabbi Asher's solutions to Rabbi Ḥefeẓ's questions, calling them "damaging,"[120] destructive to the whole of Torah,[121] and consisting of "vain things."[122] At the end he pretends that he offered this response to Lemlein, in order to show that there is Torah in Israel.[123] Just as in the case of Ḥayyat's total disagreement with the contemporary Italian Kabbalah, so it is with ibn Shraga's, who does not accept even one of the kabbalistic answers provided by Lemlein.

Rhetoric and Facts

We have delved into the two principles that characterized the Spanish kabbalists and were expressed by them explicitly when confronting the Italian Kabbalah. The assumption that two kabbalistic paradigms met with the arrival of the Spanish kabbalists in Italy seems instructive, since it may explain the clashes between Mor Ḥayyim and Ḥayyat and the Italian Kabbalah. Nevertheless, despite their critiques, the Spanish kabbalists did not totally reject even the views that they so openly and vehemently opposed. Ḥayyat, while critical of the commentary on *Ma'arekhet ha-'Elohut*, also acknowledges that he is going to quote some passages from it—an entirely understandable statement, since there is plenty of material in the commentary that would be consonant with Ḥayyat's positions. What is surprising, however, is the fact that some of the quoted fragments display the conspicuous influence of none other than Abraham Abulafia. At least in one case, the quote from Ẓarfati's commentary may either stem from a lost text of Abulafia or simply reflect Abulafian thought very faithfully.[124] Indeed, I see no reason to refrain from using one of these quotes in order to better understand some points in Abulafia's kabbalistic thought.[125]

The two elements criticized by Ḥayyat are easily visible in these quotes: the combinations of letters and the gematria, which were described in Ḥayyat's introduction as imaginary or fantastic, and many philosophical terms that recur in Abulafia's books. I wonder whether Ḥayyat misunderstood the type of Kabbalah he was importing into his own commentary. It seems that even as he criticized Abulafia and the commentary on *Maʿarekhet ha-'Elohut* he still absorbed some themes representative of ecstatic Kabbalah, albeit in a very few cases.

One finds a similar situation with Mor Ḥayyim. Despite his vehement protests against introducing philosophy into matters of theosophy, he himself did it, in at least in one case by quoting a text that may stem from Plotinus and that has conspicuous philosophical implications.[126] Aristotle, too, is quoted, in a way that suggests a scholastic understanding of his thought.[127] These quotes, as part of a larger passage, present precisely the viewpoint that he himself opposed. It seems then, that despite the strong critique of the views and practices of their Italian counterparts, the Spanish kabbalists were not totally closed to them.

However, these few instances of openness should be compared to the much greater openness of the Italian kabbalists to the kabbalistic texts brought from Spain. Alemanno immediately cited long passages from *Tikkunei Zohar*, copied from *Minḥat Yehudah*, while other Italian kabbalists at the beginning of the sixteenth century integrated the *Zohar* as an important book. This receptivity to the new texts that had just arrived from Spain shows that they accepted very willingly, but not submissively, the authority of the Spanish kabbalists and the importance of the new parts of the sacrosanct *Zohar*. This was in keeping with the Renaissance attitude that what is older is better; thus, the Italian Jewish kabbalists, too, could enjoy their share in the enrichment of their spiritual horizons, just as their Christian contemporaries did with the ancient corpora of literature just translated by Marsilio Ficino.

However, despite this openness, and what can be called an insinuation of the mythical texts into Italian Kabbalah, coming from the West,[128] there remained a singularly Italian attitude to Kabbalah in general, and also to the Safedian Kabbalah, manifested in the continued attachment to the views of Abraham Abulafia,[129] and even more so in the philosophical interpretations of kabbalistic texts.[130]

The Silence About the Christian Kabbalah

When the first Spanish kabbalists arrived in Italy in the period under discussion here, Christian Kabbalah was already taking its first steps. Some Spanish converts had already produced Christological interpretations of kabbalistic themes, most notably Abner of Burgos, Pedro de la Caballería, and Paulus de Heredia.[131] The last in particular was well acquainted with kabbalistic texts and probably forged some passages or short treatises; at the end of his life he was active in Italy.[132] Rabbi Abraham Farissol, a reliable source for the intellectual life in Renaissance Italy, was acquainted, at the end of the fifteenth century, with other kabbalistic forgeries produced by converts in Spain.[133] Flavius Mithridates, a native of Sicily,[134] translated the huge collection of Jewish kabbalistic writings.[135] Pico della Mirandola printed his kabbalistic conclusions, and other Jews who were acquainted with kabbalistic concepts had already converted years ago.[136] Some of them were Ashkenazic; Mithridates, as mentioned, was a Sicilian. Others, like Alemanno, cooperated with Pico, though they remained practicing Jews. This was indeed a unique phenomenon, as the particularistic conception of Kabbalah that was dominant in Spain encountered a much more cosmopolitan variant in Italy.[137] Nevertheless, this phenomenon, which was deeply related to the philosophical understanding of Kabbalah, at least insofar the Italian converts were concerned, was not mentioned in the critiques of the Jewish Italian Kabbalah put forth by the Spanish kabbalists living in Italy. This silence is striking especially since other kabbalists, Italian and Sephardic, living in the Land of Israel did openly react to it (though these reactions appeared mainly during the second generation after the expulsion).

Rabbi Elijah Menahem Ḥalfan, a rabbi and kabbalist in Venice in the first part of the sixteenth century,[138] and probably a student of Rabbi Joseph ibn Shraga, describes what happened in his generation:

> Especially after the rise of the sect of Luther,[139] many of the nobles and scholars of the land [namely, the Christians] sought to have a thorough knowledge of this glorious science.[140] They have exhausted themselves in this search, because among our people there are but a small number of men expert in this wisdom, for, after the great numbers of troubles and expulsions,[141] only a few remain. So seven learned men [namely, Christians] grasp a Jewish man by the hem of his garment and say, "Be our master in this science."[142]

At least in this epistle an Italian Jew seems to be somewhat positive about the possible consequences of this dissemination of Kabbalah, although he himself was much more reticent about the subject in another text he wrote.[143] However, two Spanish kabbalists expressed other feelings; Rabbi Abraham ben Eliezer ha-Levi wrote in his eschatological *Commentary on the Prophecies of the Child*: "Everyone who discloses this secret to a Gentile,[144] who is not[145] a faithful member of our covenant and a keeper of our law, will not see the delight of the Lord, neither will he visit His palace."[146]

This kabbalist took a more explicit stand in an epistle to Rabbi Abraham of Perugia in Italy, whose authorship was established recently by Abraham David.[147] He wrote (c. 1520):

> In my opinion there is a danger in sending you this commentary, since we have said that our brethren, the sons of Esau, study Hebrew and these matters are ancient,[148] and whoever will write[149] anything there, it may, God forfend, fall in their hands. And despite the fact that those who study are faithful to us, nevertheless it is reasonable and compelling to conceal these matters from them, and there is also a severe ban concerning it.[150] In any case, I have refrained[151] from sending to you these treatises constituting the *Epistle of the Secret of the Redemption*[152] and you, my masters, those who conceal the wisdom and the secret of the Lord, are the fearers of God;[153] the participants in the covenant will contemplate it, but this will not be accessible to every gentile.[154]

Like his Italian contemporary, the Sephardic kabbalist does not consider the study of Hebrew as negative. Nevertheless, he would not like to see his eschatological secrets divulged to the Christian Hebraists, and that is the main reason he not prepared to send his own writings to his Italian Jewish correspondents.[155] Within thirty years, however, the moderate attitude toward the Christian Hebraists gave way to another very extreme approach. Those who studied Kabbalah in Italy, priests and other Christians, were severely attacked by Rabbi Moshe Cordovero, the great kabbalist of Safed, but his views belong to another kabbalistic center.[156]

Since it is obvious that some other Jews and kabbalists did react negatively to the spread of Kabbalah among the Christians, why was there such a silence among the three Sephardic kabbalists who lived in Italy and took issue publicly with the Jewish Kabbalah as it was studied there? I see at least two answers to this quandary. First, I assume that their status as refugees (in the case of Ḥayyat and ibn Shraga) and their awareness of the danger that could result from criticizing Christian thinkers kept them from doing it. Second, and equally important, there is the fact that some of the precedents among the converts had nothing to do with Italian Kabbalah; not only were some of the converts of Spanish provenance but it was also rather difficult to point out a direct filiation between the philosophical stand of their Italian contemporaries and conversion. After all, neither Alemanno nor Elijah Levita, who apparently taught Kabbalah to Pico and Aegidius Viterbus respectively, converted.

Literary Genres of Spanish Kabbalists in Italy

One way to detect a change in the content of kabbalistic thought is to look for shifts in the literary genres used to express it. So, for example, Abulafia's technical handbooks reflect his emphasis on the experiential aspect of Kabbalah. By contrast, the popular nature of Cordoverian Kabbalah reflects the exoteric drift of that circle. An examination of the genres used by the Spanish kabbalists is thus in order.

Ḥayyat's *Minḥat Yehudah* is a commentary on another kabbalistic book, *Sefer Ma'arekhet ha-'Elohut*. As we learned from Gershom Scholem's description of the commentaries on this book, it was hardly a novelty; it had been preceded by Rabbi Reuven Zarfati's major commentary, which influenced Ḥayyat. As far as we know, commenting upon *Ma'arekhet ha-'Elohut* was not a typical genre of the Spanish Kabbalah, and Ḥayyat's confession that the Mantuan nobles requested his writing may indicate that they were eager to learn about the Sephardic perspective on this book. It is therefore likely that the Italian background and conceptual details informed his writing.

Joseph ibn Shraga's writings reflect the same conservative mood: his commentary on the prayer, his fragments of homiletic commentaries on some of the portions of Genesis, and his interpretation of kabbalistic secrets, as well as his eschatological text, faithfully reflect Sephardic literary genres that were prevalent before the expulsion. The two kabbalistic epistles of Rabbi Isaac Mor Ḥayyim were sent before the expulsion, and they reflect the same scholastic attitude toward clarification of theological issues that was dominant in Italy among the Italian kabbalists. Therefore, at least insofar as these three kabbalists are concerned, it is very difficult to detect any significant change in literary genres vis-à-vis those cultivated in Spain and Italy. Since all these genres were in use before the expulsion, there is no case for arguing that something in this event pushed the kabbalists to contemplate other modes of expression. This conclusion regarding the Sephardic kabbalists in Italy seems to hold to a very great extent also for Sephardic kabbalists who were active elsewhere.

Of particular importance is to distinguish between the various types of Kabbalah found in Italy in the generation of the expulsion, since it can operate on different levels and in different ways. It can be, as it was in the writings of the Spanish kabbalists, a particularistic, antiphilosophical, and conservative kind of lore. In the Italian version, both Jewish and Christian, it was much more universalistic, more inclined to magic and to the use of various philosophical jargons.[157] A generic vision of such a variegated literature obfuscates the proper understanding of its own nature and of the different roles it played in the Italian culture.

The above analyses and reflections have sought to demonstrate that Spanish kabbalists and Italian kabbalists held very different attitudes toward Kabbalah. One can even speak of "collective mentalities" that would define more comprehensive paradigms rather than simply of divergences on some few topics. These postulated mentalities framed the types of the interaction between persons and paradigms to a much greater extent than we can infer from assuming the impact of the historical upheaval. As a result, in lieu of pursuing an understanding of the cultural developments of Sephardic Jewry as the result of one major event that induced one major spiritual change it would be much more fruitful to allow for the possibility that various spiritual crosscurrents shaped intellectual events in different directions. An array of processes (and recall that we have discussed above only one single type and center of interaction) would account for the complexity of the religious situation much better than a monolithic explanation assuming the centrality of one type of religious orientation—in this case, messianism. However, even in the case of sixteenth-century messianism, especially when it was not expressed by Sephardic thinkers, there is no reason to attribute it to one factor, the expulsion from the Iberian Peninsula. Thus, we find that most of the academic thought on this topic has been informed by one main historical factor that produced one major effect, as elucidated by one major scholar.

For all that I have said here, I would not like to be misunderstood as affirming a total divorce between history and mentality. In fact, I assume that the different mentalities regnant in Spain and Italy were actually nourished by different cultural and social conditions. What I am reluctant to agree to is the formative role attributed to a historical event, dramatic as it may be, before also examining all the other alternatives and without adducing pertinent evidence for such an influence from the writings of the kabbalists themselves. I believe that close examination of the extant writings of most of the kabbalists betrays an indifference, from the speculative point of view, toward the event of the expulsion. On the other hand, they are acknowledging the reasons for the writing and the tendencies they prefer or oppose, sometimes in relatively open and clear terms, so that the scholarly speculations as to a "hidden" or more "profound" agenda of Kabbalah in this period are to be proven by adducing some evidence. A survey of the extant kabbalistic literature composed in Italy in the generation of the expulsion reveals, among both the Spanish and the Italian kabbalists, a rather theological inclination, not a historical one.

Another major outcome of the above discussion is the need to investigate the minutiae of the activity of the Spanish kabbalists in their new environments. They were not simply transmitting their mystical lore to ignoramuses or creating in a vacuum, nor did they respond explicitly to a historical crisis. They had rather to cope with new, unexpected, and sometimes very disturbing cultural challenges in order to make their point clear,[158] either by dismissing or by rejecting openly cultural tendencies that deviated from their own spiritual patrimony.

Last but not least: also significant, at least early on, is the reticence of the Italian kabbalists toward the mythical theosophy and dynamic theurgy as represented by the *Zohar* and disseminated by the Spanish.[159] Some of the Italian kabbalists, however, had proclivities toward a much more magical interpretation of this lore.[160] In a period when ancient and pagan mythologies were returning to the center of interest in some Christian intellectual circles in Italy, among both thinkers and artists, the Jewish Italian kabbalists preferred a more philosophical understanding of Kabbalah, which attenuated the mythical facets of their sources. This discrepancy is, however, superficial. What is more, in

Christian circles the ancient myths were not accepted literally but were adopted in accordance with the hermeneutical grilles en vogue throughout the Renaissance.[161] As Jean Seznec has sensitively formulated it, "Mythology still plays a considerable role (even more so than in the past) but is fatally submerged in allegory."[162] In both cases Renaissance thinkers appropriated ancient material in a manner that fit their intellectual orientations, and the mythical elements were more often reduced to ahistorical speculative truths. Both the Spanish mythical Kabbalah and the ancient Greek myths informed Italian thought in the Renaissance period by adapting to the mind-set of their recipients.

12

▨

The Ultimate End of Human Life in Postexpulsion Philosophic Literature

Hava Tirosh-Samuelson

The Expulsion from Spain

The Travails of Time

Time with his pointed shafts has hit my heart
and split my guts, laid open my entrails,
landed me a blow that will not heal
knocked me down, left me in lasting pain.
Time wounded me, wasted away my flesh,
used up my blood and fat in suffering,
grounded my bones to meal, and rampaged, leapt
attacked me like a lion in his rage.
He did not stop at whirling me around,
exiling me while yet my days were green
sending me stumbling, drunk, to roam the world,
spinning me dizzy round about the edge—
so that I've spent two decades on the move
without my horses ever catching breath—
so that my palms have measured oceans, weighed

the dust of continents—so that my spring
is spent—
                    no, that was not enough:
He chased my friends from me, exiled
my age-mates, sent my family far
so that I never see a face I know
father, mother, brothers, or a friend.
He scattered everyone I care for northward,
eastward, or to the west, so that
I have no rest from constant thinking, planning—
and never a moment's peace, for all my plans.
Now that I see my future in the East,
their separation clutches at my heels.
My foot is turned to go, but my heart's at sea;
I can't tell forward from behind.[1]

Written in 1503 by Judah Abravanel, these verses commence a long
Complaint About Time (*Telunah 'al ha-Zeman*) that captures the painful
experience of Iberian Jews at the close of the fifteenth century. Fusing
the conventions of a medieval poetic genre,[2] the principles of medieval
Aristotelianism,[3] and the Renaissance reflections on Fortune,[4] Judah
Abravanel recounted the harrowing experience of his family.[5] The
wealthy, well-educated, and well-connected Abravanels probably endured the physical hardships of the expulsion better than other Jews, but
their suffering and anguish was no less. For all Iberian Jews who chose to
remain loyal to Judaism, 1492 spelled displacement, humiliation, loss of
possessions, dangerous travel, harassment and abuse, captivity, starva-
tion, disease, rape of women, breakup of families, and death.[6]

The expulsion from Iberia concluded a tumultuous century that
began with the persecution of 1391. From that time professing Jews had
to cope with acerbic attacks on Judaism, mounting pressures to convert, the mass apostasy of fellow Jews, and the many economic, social,
and legal problems occasioned by the rise of the converso class. Given
the choice of conversion or persecution, a continued loyalty to Judaism
was anything but self-evident. It required a constant reaffirmation and
a reasoned rebuttal of Christian triumphalism.

With that terrible background, professing Jews faced yet a more
painful choice: conversion or expulsion! The despair grew deeper.

Many succumbed and converted.[7] And those who chose exile over conversion could not avoid asking themselves painful questions: Why did
God let us, His faithful believers, suffer, while our apostate brethren
prosper? Which sins brought upon this particular punishment? When
will we be rewarded for our faithfulness to God? When will God re-
deem us from the misery of exile? What can and should we do to hasten our redemption?

Explicitly and implicitly these questions preoccupied Sephardic intellectuals in the decades after the expulsion.[8] Those leaders of nascent Sephardic communities in Italy, North Africa, and the Ottoman
Empire took upon themselves a mission: to make sense of the painful
historical experience for themselves and for their communities; to rationalize continued belief in the merciful God of Israel against voices of
frustration and disbelief; to provide strategies for renewal to overcome
personal tragedies and national defeat.

Messages of Consolation

Indeed, in the postexpulsion period Sephardic thinkers articulated several messages of consolation that inspired religious renewal. These men
varied in intellectual makeup, temperament, and education, but their
messages were not mutually exclusive. A given thinker, or a group of
scholars, could combine these strategies in a variety of ways that defy
simple classification. All, however, had this in common: the profound
desire to transcend the cruel accident of time, to go beyond the perpetual changes of history to a perfect, eternal spiritual reality in which
Time has no dominion and evil is no more.

In the matrix of Jewish religious symbols, the vicissitudes of Time
exemplified the travails of exile. Therefore, the quest for transcendence
was inextricably intertwined with the Jewish hope for redemption, be it
collective and political or individual and spiritual.[9] Those who emphasized the collective dimension of traditional Jewish hopes highlighted
the imminent coming of the Messiah. Thus, Isaac Abravanel consoled
the suffering exiles by rebutting the Christian reading of the Bible, asserting the innate superiority of the Jewish people and calculating the
date for the arrival of the Messiah.[10] Others—for example, the kabbalists Abraham ben Eliezer Halevi, Joseph ibn Shraga, and the anonymous authors of *Kaf ha-Ketoret* and *Galya' Raza'*—not only determined

the date for the Messiah's arrival but also depicted the dramatic events of the eschaton that would forever subdue the powers of evil.[11] And the messianic activists Solomon Molkho and David Reubeni expressed their intense expectation of the messiah in political action. Inspired by Christian millenarianism and by Kabbalah, they actually tried to usher in the posthistorical messianic age.[12]

Yet for most Sephardic intellectuals the suffering of the expulsion led neither to apocalyptic visions nor to political activism. Rather, most exiles intensified their pursuit of holiness, or spiritual perfection, within the parameters of halakhah.[13] Through Torah study, punctilious observance of the mitzvot, and habitual acts of personal piety, the devotee could sanctify himself and the community at large, making Israel worthy of divine redemption in some undisclosed future time. Thus traditional Jewish life itself was invested with salvific expectations not dependent on the imminent coming of the Messiah.

Some scholars infused the pursuit of spiritual perfection with kabbalistic theosophy and mysticism.[14] Those who viewed Kabbalah as the main pathway of Jewish spirituality conferred theurgic and mystical meaning on the performance of the mitzvot. By deploying their knowledge of divine mysteries (that is, kabbalistic theosophy) in their religious life, the kabbalists attempted to unify the masculine and feminine aspects of the Godhead—to repair and re-pair the Deity. Then would the sacred triumph over the profane, redeeming all levels of reality—divine, cosmic, national, and individual.

For most of the sixteenth century, however, philosophy and not Kabbalah charted the path to spiritual perfection. Schooled in the categories of medieval rationalism, the philosophers thought and taught that the disciplined acquisition of moral and intellectual virtues enables the individual not only to withstand the vicissitudes of time but also to liberate the soul from its corporeal conditioning, restoring it to its heavenly abode.[15] In the afterlife the saved soul enjoys the infinite everlasting delight of a mystical union with God (*devekut*), the bliss of personal immortality. By thus focusing on individual salvation, the philosophers muted the collective, public, historical, and dramatic aspects of traditional Jewish messianism. To put it differently, the emphasis on individual salvation enabled Jewish intellectuals to come to terms with the historical conditions of the dispersed Jewish nation without losing hope and without undermining traditional Jewish theodicy.

This paper addresses the question of how expulsion from Iberia affected Jewish culture by exploring the quest for transcendence in postexpulsion philosophic literature written in the Ottoman Empire. It discusses works by Meir Aramah, Joseph Garson, Solomon Almoli, Joseph Taitatzak, Isaac Aderbi, Isaac Arroyo, Moses Almosnino, Solomon ben Isaac Halevi, and Abraham ibn Megash, focusing in particular on their understanding of the ultimate end of human life (*ha-takhlit ha-'aharon*), which they defined as happiness, felicity, or beatitude.[16] Reflections on the ultimate end of human life and the road to it loom large in their biblical commentaries,[17] commentaries on Tractate *'Avot*,[18] commentaries and references to Aristotle's *Ethics*,[19] treatises of systematic theology,[20] sermons,[21] and practical manuals for good conduct.[22] I argue that the discourse on happiness sheds light on the ability of Iberian Jewry to regenerate itself after the traumatic expulsion as well as on the transition from Aristotelianism to Kabbalah in Jewish intellectual history.

Cultural Renewal

A Hebrew Renaissance

The expulsion from Iberia was undoubtedly traumatic, but it did not exterminate either Sephardic Jewry or Sephardic culture. Moshe Idel views the expulsion as a crisis that ultimately salvaged Sephardic Jewry from cultural stagnation.[23] Indeed, Spanish religious nationalism had suffocated Jewish culture for nearly half a century. The expulsion did unleash long-suppressed creative energies and did facilitate a fruitful interaction with contemporary Renaissance culture outside of Iberia.

This forced release from Christian persecution proved especially good for the Sephardim who settled in the multiethnic and multireligious society of the Ottoman Empire. Islamic law granted them more freedom and protection, and since they considered contemporary Turkish culture to be beneath them, they could focus on preserving and developing their own heritage—a continued conversation with their beloved homeland—without fear of Christian backlash.

The Sephardic cultural renewal in the Ottoman Empire was impressive indeed. Within a few decades of the expulsion the Sephardim not only overpowered other Jewish subgroups (the Romaniote, Musta'arabi, Italian, and Ashkenazic Jews) but could also boast unprecedented productivity in halakhah, biblical hermeneutics, homiletics, poetry and prose, Kabbalah, philosophy, and theology.[24] Quantitatively and rhetorically the Sephardic literary output was so dazzling that Yosef Yahalom calls it "a Hebrew Renaissance."[25] That is no hyperbole.

As Joseph Hacker has shown, Sephardic culture took root in the determination of the exiles and their descendants to preserve and even enshrine the glorious past, be it real or imagined.[26] The Sephardim had brought from Spain a strong aristocratic self-perception, a sense of cultural superiority, a courtier class committed to patronage of scholars and artists, a tradition of large-scale philanthropy for public and private education, a wistful nostalgia for the lost past, and a resolve to pass on their legacy to their children. Their new home provided not only relative freedom but also two more concrete factors: the printing press and the rise of an urban middle class eager for learning. As a result, Sephardic culture blossomed in the Ottoman Empire, not in a radical departure from preexpulsion trends, but in conservation and embellishment of past achievement.

Philosophy in Context

Philosophy and science had been the hallmark of Judeo-Hispanic culture. The culture that the Iberian exiles imported to their new havens was suffused with the rationalist approach to Judaism, derived from the incorporation of philosophy and its related arts and sciences into Jewish education. Human reason was employed in the interpretation of the divinely revealed tradition, and the knowledge of God was emphasized as the purpose of Jewish worship.[27] Precisely because rationalism was so deeply entrenched in Judeo-Hispanic culture, exiles and their descendants did not, and indeed could not, excise philosophy from their endeavor to re-create the past. Notwithstanding the antiphilosophic sentiment of some famous exiles, such as Joseph Yaavez and Isaac Aramah,[28] the study of philosophy and its related liberal arts and natural sciences flourished during the second and third quarters of the sixteenth century.

Sephardic exiles in the Ottoman Empire brought philosophy to the heart of Judaism, to rabbinic training. In fifteenth-century Spain, Isaac Canpaton and his disciples, Isaac Aboab, Isaac De Leon, and Samuel Valensi, had pioneered the use of Aristotelian logic as a tool for studying Talmud.[29] In the numerous yeshivot that flourished in the Ottoman Empire, Sephardic exiles and their descendants refined that tool. God's Word could now be understood with scientific precision! The scholar would thus actualize his rational potential and gradually progress toward intellectual perfection and ultimately union with God. The pursuit of truth through halakhah was but another expression of the Sephardic exile's yearning for transcendence and spiritual perfection.

On a more worldly note, mastery of Aristotelian logic as it applied to halakhah brought a rabbi social status among a Jewish populace taken with philosophy and its related fields. Many a celebrated halakhic authority was called *ḥakham kolel* (literally, a comprehensive scholar), an honorific title that designated mastery of the broad philosophic-scientific curriculum in addition to rabbinic scholarship.[30] These well-rounded scholars wielded much power and influence either in their capacity as official congregational rabbis (*marbiẓ Torah*) or as respected physicians.

For the Jewish elite in the Ottoman Empire, philosophy and its related arts and sciences were not "alien wisdoms"; they were the very core of Sephardic cultural identity and its claim to fame and power. The social status of Jewish diplomats, physicians, financiers, and astronomers who rendered professional services to the government depended not only on personal wealth and business contracts but on philosophic-scientific knowledge as well. In the circles of the Nasi, Hamon, Ibn Yahya, Ben Banvenist, Abravanel, and Ibn Yaish families, educated Jewish courtiers wrote philosophic texts, engaged in philosophic conversations with rabbinic scholars, and funded the dissemination among Ottoman Jews of philosophic knowledge,[31] secular poetry and prose, and rabbinics. Joseph Nasi, a former converso, exemplifies this phenomenon.[32] So too do brilliant, university-trained scientists such as Amatus Lusitanus and Aharon Afiyah. When they returned to the Jewish fold, they introduced their new coreligionists to philosophic texts, academic debates, and cultural trends current in sixteenth-century Europe.[33]

No less than Italian scholars, Sephardic scholars in the Ottoman Empire knew of and responded to contemporary scientific discoveries and the expansion of Europe's geographical horizons.[34] Moses Almosnino, the celebrated rabbi of Salonika, is a case in point. He received his philosophic and scientific training from the former converso Aharon Afiyah. The two scholars collaborated on the translation of and commentary on two astronomical works, *Tractatus de Sphaera* by the thirteenth-century English astronomer John Sacrobosco[35] and *Theorica Novae Planetarum* by the fifteenth-century Austrian astronomer Georg Peurbach.[36] It is very likely that the discovery of the Americas, to which Almosnino refers in both works,[37] inspired the two Jewish scholars to rethink and reaffirm the Aristotelian-Ptolemaic astronomy and cosmology. That they defended the validity of medieval cosmology indicates that Jewish philosophers in the middle of the sixteenth century stood at the end of an intellectual epoch rather than at the beginning of a new one.

The classes that cultivated philosophy in the Ottoman Empire also enjoyed secular poetry and prose, invigorated by the Sephardic Jews' increased familiarity with European vernacular literature and with local literary traditions. Professional poets such as Isaac and David Onkenierra, Moses Abbas, and Saadia Longo not only perpetuated a poetic tradition transplanted from Muslim and Christian Spain but even claimed to have surpassed the achievement of their Iberian forbears.[38] Sephardic Jews enjoyed medieval Hebrew secular prose, now available in print: romances, dramas, philosophic dialogues, and historical narratives written by Jews and non-Jews in Spain and Italy, either in the vernacular or in Hebrew translation.[39] Sephardic Jews also composed their own secular prose in Ladino and Castillian. As Yosef Yerushalmi has demonstrated, while this literature was intended primarily for the education of the returning conversos, it also reflected contemporary European literary and aesthetic standards.

Philosophic Literature

Sephardic scholars in the Ottoman Empire systematized and summarized philosophy, along with halakhah and aggadah, thus popularizing all these fields, making serious study easier, and creating greater access for nonscholars. These philosophic summaries, or digests, preserved and categorized five centuries of Jewish philosophic-scientific activity. One example of such a philosophic encyclopedia is Solomon Almoli's *Me'asef le-Khol ha-Maḥanot*.[40] Written in Constantinople a decade after the expulsion by a scholar who failed to gain congregational employment,[41] this encyclopedia summarized the accumulated knowledge in the following disciplines: grammar, logic, mathematics, music, geometry, measurements and weights, optics, astronomy, physics, medicine, talismanic magic and alchemy, ethics, and metaphysics.[42] Almoli insisted that mastery of these sciences was a necessary precondition to the correct understanding of the entire received tradition that for him included the Hebrew language, the twenty-four books of the Bible, the dogmas of Judaism, Kabbalah, and halakhah. Almoli was convinced that the dissemination of philosophy would perfect the community at large and thereby hasten the messianic age.[43] Concomitantly, he rejected the notion (apparently common among Sephardic exiles) that one attains immortality through children.[44] Children, he said, secure only the perpetuation of the species (*kiyyum ba-min*), not the immortality of the personal soul (*kiyyum ba-'ish*). Only wisdom can ensure the survival of the personal soul after death. Echoing the humanists of his generation, Almoli linked personal immortality to the perpetuation of one's name through writing. He expressly states that his philosophic encyclopedia will secure his reputation long after his children have perished.[45] Almoli's preoccupation with the survival of his name reflected a profound awareness of human finitude and the miseries of earthly life as well as his struggle to assert his social position in a society obsessed with nobility and lineage. As an orphaned refugee with no family connections or lineage to boast, he had to rely on his own intellectual prowess. In this he was helped by the newly available technology—printing.

The invention of printing stood behind this literary upsurge.[46] It was now physically possible to teach philosophy directly to the masses.[47] The most popular philosophic works in print were Baḥya ibn Pakuda's *Ḥovot ha-Levavot*, Maimonides' *Moreh Nevukhim*, Yedayah Bedersi's *Beḥinat 'Olam*, Shem Tov ibn Shaprut's *'Even Boḥan*, and Joseph Albo's *Sefer ha-'Ikkarim*.[48] Printing, of course, compromised the old Maimonidean elitism toward philosophy. The hesitancy about publishing philosophic texts was not unlike the debate on the publication of kabbalistic books, especially the *Zohar*.[49]

In his introduction to *Sha'ar 'Adonai he-Ḥadash,* Solomon Almoli voiced some apprehension about printing philosophical works. Torn between a desire to raise the intellectual level of the many and a fear that philosophy could be harmful to those ill equipped to study it, Almoli decided to print the introduction but keep the body of the text only in manuscript. Thus, the general public could read the chapter headings of philosophic wisdom, but only serious students could gain access to the core text and, one hopes, pay handsomely for it.[50]

Along with philosophic digests, new commentaries on philosophic texts also appeared. Such commentaries were a medieval genre through which the student of philosophy could demonstrate his erudition. For example, Moses Almosnino wrote a commentary on al-Ghazzali's *The Intentions of the Philosophers*, entitled *Migdal 'Oz*,[51] the basic textbook for the study of Aristotelian logic, physics, and metaphysics in the Ottoman Empire,[52] a commentary on Aristotle's *Nicomachean Ethics*,[53] and a supercommentary on Averröes' *Long Commentary on Aristotle's Physics* (no longer extant).[54] In his *Regimiento de la Vida* Almosnino encouraged Jews to study the logical treatise of Ibn Bajja, Avicenna, and al-Ghazzali, Ptolemy's *Almagest*, and the *Long Commentaries* of Averröes on Aristotle's works in natural philosophy, that is, physics.[55] We can surmise that the works of these Muslim philosophers were readily available in the Ottoman Empire and mastery of Arabic easily gained in regions where it was a spoken language among Musta'arabi Jews and Muslims.

Under the influence of Renaissance humanism, Almosnino devoted much effort to determining the correct text of Aristotle's *Ethics*. Almosnino consulted two Hebrew commentaries written in the fifteenth century: that of Joseph ibn Shem Tov,[56] which was based on the translation of Meir Alguades,[57] and that of Baruch ibn Yaish, composed in the 1480s.[58] Ibn Yaish's commentary was based on two new fifteenth-century translations of the *Ethics* by the humanists in Italy into Latin: the translation of Leonardo Bruni from the version of Robert Grosseteste[59] and from the Greek original by the Byzantine humanist scholar John (Ioannes) Argyropoulos in 1457.[60]

Almosnino's concern went beyond determining the original text of the *Ethics;* he also sought to understand what Aristotle meant and so consulted the commentaries of the late Scholastics on the *Ethics*. He often refers to the commentaries of Eustratius,[61] Albert the Great, Thomas Aquinas,[62] Geraldus Odonis,[63] John Buridan,[64] Walter Burley,[65] Faber Stapulensis Jacobus (Jaques Lefevre d'Etaples),[66] and Agostino Nifo.[67] This list alone attests not only to Almosnino's philosophic erudition and the availability of these texts in Salonika but also to the expansion of the Judeo-Muslim Aristotelian tradition to include late medieval scholastic philosophy as well as humanist scholarship.

Although Moses Almosnino was the most talented among Salonika's scholars, he was by no means unique. His older contemporary, Joseph Taitatzak, as the late Joseph Sermoneta has documented, was also a well-trained philosopher who studied and taught Latin scholastic sources.[68] Almosnino's younger contemporaries, Solomon ben Isaac Halevi and Abraham ibn Megash, were also conversant with non-Jewish classical, medieval, and Renaissance philosophic sources.[69] Salonikan scholars applied these non-Jewish texts to the most Jewish activity of all—the interpretation of Scripture. Taitatzak, for example, based his commentary of Ecclesiastes on a creative misreading of Boethius, Thomas Aquinas, and Giles of Rome, and Almosnino frequently cites Aristotle's *Ethics* in his commentaries on the Five Scrolls, his commentary on *'Avot,* his sermons and his manual of moral training, *Rigimiento de la Vida.*

Philosophy And Hermeneutics

Reasons and Faith

The popularization of philosophy might lead us to conclude that postexpulsion Jews were turning secular. They were not. The most favored mode of Jewish self-expression for postexpulsion philosophically trained scholars, and the major vehicle for the dissemination of post expulsion philosophy, was not the digest or the commentary but traditional Jewish hermeneutics, the genre of scriptural exegesis and homily, both oral and written.[70] Philosophers wrote many biblical commentaries and homilies and creatively interwove philosophy with rabbinic aggadah and Kabbalah.[71]

The shift from exposition of philosophic texts, more prevalent before the expulsion, to philosophic exegesis of sacred texts, more prevalent after the expulsion, reflected this conscious theological position: revealed religion perfects natural human reason and the divinely revealed Torah contains all human wisdom because it is identical with the infinite wisdom of God.[72]

The seeds of that position were sown before the expulsion by Sephardic scholars such as Joseph Albo, Abraham Rimoch, Joseph ibn

Shem Tov, Abraham Shalom, Abraham Bibago, Joel ibn Shuaib, Joseph Ḥayyun, Isaac Aramah, and Isaac Abravanel, who were frequently cited in the works of postexpulsion philosophers. As I have demonstrated elsewhere,[73] Sephardic thinkers had harmonized their religious beliefs and the truth-claims of philosophy in a way that enabled them to legitimize the study of philosophy, on the one hand, while proving the superiority of Judaism over Christianity and philosophy, on the other hand. Although they credited the synthesis to Maimonides, it actually developed under the influence of Christian scholasticism, especially the works of Thomas Aquinas.

Following Aquinas, these Jewish thinkers had asserted the primacy of theology over philosophy, of faith over reason. They argued as follows: natural human reason is inherently limited because its knowledge is derived from sense data of created beings. On its own, human reason fails to provide the knowledge necessary for individual salvation and personal immortality. Only divine grace can reveal salvific knowledge. Human beings may nevertheless affirm revealed truths on faith and then explore them through human reason, despite its limitations. Properly understood, divine revelation does not contradict human reason but completes and perfects it. The apparent contradictions were caused by the errors of finite human reason and could be avoided by subordinating rational human knowledge to the suprarational knowledge of divine revelation.

The synthesis of reason and faith arose from the debate on the ultimate end of human life that had raged within the preexpulsion Iberian Jewish community and between Jewish and Christian scholars.[74] Following Aquinas, the late fifteenth-century Jewish philosophers held that the ultimate end of human life lies neither in temporal happiness derived from wealth, fame, honor, or sensual pleasures—as many Jewish apostates apparently believed—nor in the acquisition of philosophic wisdom—as radical rationalists thought.[75] The final aim of human life consists of the beatific vision of God in the world to come, namely, in the infinite bliss of personal immortality.

That logic presented Jewish philosophers with a problem: since the final end of life is predicated on the revealed grace of God, they had to assert that Judaism was the one and only divine revelation. This was in essence a nonphilosophic claim, so it had to be asserted as a cardinal dogma of the Jewish faith, the denial of which entails forfeiture of the greatest reward of all—individual salvation.[76] Thus, fifteenth-century

Jewish philosophers asserted that ultimate happiness came through neither philosophy alone, nor Christianity, but through faith, the performance of the revealed law, and the subordination of philosophy to revealed theology. The revealed Torah alone is salvific.

Postexpulsion thinkers endorsed this position to address their own theological concerns. The Jewish particularist tenor was especially meaningful in a period of growing doubts about God's everlasting covenant with Israel, and its otherworldly emphasis, particularly relevant in a period of intense misery and suffering. Elaborating on fifteenth-century trends, the postexpulsion scholars cultivated philosophy while emphasizing its limitations.

They continued to revere Maimonides as the single most authoritative Jewish thinker, referring to him as "the Master" (ha-Rav) and to his Guide as the "wondrous book" (ha-sefer ha-mufla') or the "honorable book" (ha-sefer ha-nikhbad). They continued to reinterpret Maimonides in accordance with the views of late fifteenth-century thinkers. Thus, even though they often disagreed with Maimonides, they still found it necessary to ascribe their views to him.[77] This continued veneration not only ensured the perpetuation of philosophic discourse but also accounted for the recurrence of the Maimonidean controversy throughout the sixteenth century.[78]

Perhaps paradoxically, as the wave of philosophy spread out into postexpulsion Jewish society its intellectual force declined. Philosophy became the handmaiden of popular hermeneutics. The philosopher's task was to apply his human wisdom (culled from the study of philosophy) to interpret suprarational, supranatural divine revelation. To merely understand—let alone enjoy—sermons and biblical commentaries, one had to be familiar with philosophic vocabulary and themes. The very inclusion of references to philosophic texts, authors, concepts, and theories in the interpretation of sacred texts made philosophy (albeit a diluted version) a household commodity. But, in the end, the divinely revealed text won out and medieval Jewish rationalism waned.

Affirming the primacy of sacred texts over philosophy led to the gradual emergence of Kabbalah as the official Jewish theology and the dominant interpretation of the rabbinic tradition at the expense of Maimonideanism. Kabbalah had begun to enter the framework of medieval Jewish Aristotelian philosophy before the expulsion, but the fusion of Kabbalah and philosophy flourished thereafter.

Postexpulsion philosophers had a positive attitude toward Kabbalah, even though they were creative kabbalists. They took at face value that Simeon bar Yoḥai wrote the *Zohar*, which led to the following chain of reasoning. Midrash was an integral part of the revealed rabbinic tradition, that is, *kabbalah* broadly defined; the *Zohar* was rabbinic midrash; therefore the *Zohar* was a sacred suprarational knowledge that was qualitatively superior to demonstrative philosophy.[79] Consequently these postexpulsion scholars had to harmonize philosophy with the views of the *Zohar*. And the *Zohar*'s views shaped the philosophic discourse about the nature of the human soul and the ultimate end of human life.[80]

The impact of Kabbalah on philosophy was most evident in the philosophic conception of Torah. Following the kabbalists, the philosophers identified the Torah with God's essence (*'azmut*) and accordingly viewed the revealed Torah as the corporeal manifestation of a transcendent, supernal, perfect Torah that the philosophers identified with the infinite Wisdom of God.[81] With the kabbalists, the philosophers stated that the Torah consists of the Names of God.[82] According to the philosophers, the infinity of Torah guarantees that it alone is salvific.

This conception of Torah had an important practical result that underscored the expansion of philosophic hermeneutics in the Ottoman Empire. The wisdom of God is infinite. If the Torah is identified with it, then multiple readings of the same verse or rabbinic pericope are permissible, with no need for logical consistency; they can be simultaneously correct. Although the source material remained finite and limited, the philosopher-exegete could nonetheless churn out new material unlimited in its quantity or imaginativeness. He could thereby meet the demands of a market that features increasing competition among suppliers and increasing rhetorical sophistication among consumers. It is no wonder that even a well-trained scholar such as Solomon ben Isaac Halevi was anxious about his ability to satisfy his audience's thirst for hermeneutic innovation[83] or that by the 1580s Abraham ibn Megash expressed exasperation with the wordiness of Jewish preachers in Salonika.[84]

This hermeneutical activity was a prominent feature in the philosophic quest for individual salvation. Still loyal to Aristotelian hierarchal cosmology, the philosophers located the supernal Torah "above Time" (*le-ma'alah me-ha-zeman*), that is, in the realm of immaterial beings that are not governed by the laws of motion and change whose measurement is Time. Thus Isaac Arroyo avers: "Since our holy Torah is His Wisdom, Blessed be He, and His Wisdom and Essence are one and the same, the Torah is above the celestial spheres [*ha-shamayim*] and does not fall under [the category of] Time [*ve-'einah nofelet tahat ha-zeman*]."[85] Similarly Isaac Aderbi holds that "the very excellence [*segulatah*] and essence [*mahutah*] of the Torah does not fall under Time . . . and therefore it alone can ensure survival [after death] [*hish'arut*] and immortality [*nizhiyyut*] for Man."[86] Identified with God's Wisdom, the supernal Torah is the intelligible order of the universe (*defus ha-nimzaot*), the paradigm that God consulted when he brought the universe into existence. By cleaving to the revealed Torah (that is, through Torah study and the performance of the mitzvot) the religious devotee can attain spiritual perfection, overcome the limits of human corporeality and particularity, and enjoy the spiritual rewards of the world to come, i.e., a mystical union with God. Almosnino summarized this position when he states: "There is only one thing that transcends Time, that does not fall under the category of Time and is, in fact, above Time—the perfection of the intellect [*shlemut ha-sekhel*]; and it is predicated on cleaving to God: he who cleaves to God transcends Time [*'oleh le-ma'alah me-ha-zeman*].[87]

The Influence of Renaissance Humanism

An exegetical unveiling of the infinite meanings of Scripture required linguistic sophistication and rhetorical versatility. It is here that the quest for spiritual perfection, the kabbalistic conception of Torah, and the impact of Renaissance culture converged to create the so-called Hebrew Renaissance. The efflorescence of philosophic hermeneutics was accomplished through a selective (and largely polemical) adaptation of the Renaissance cult of rhetoric.[88]

Rhetoric—the art of effective communication and ornamental speech—stood at the core of the Renaissance resurrection of classical civilization and the educational reforms of the humanists. The early humanists were attracted to rhetoric because of its flexibility in addressing all human concerns in their ever-changing, infinite particularity. Rhetoric thus undermined the fixed hierarchies of medieval cosmology, replacing them with Man as the center of the universe, and articulated a new view of Man as a mysterious bundle of psychic energies—sensual, emotional, intellectual, and spiritual. And because rhetoric lacked a fixed philosophic substance it could be used to advance diverse ideological positions, to gloss over logical inconsistencies, and even to obfuscate shallowness of thought.

As Renaissance humanism progressed, its assumptions changed and with them its attitude toward language and the *studia humanitatis*. By the 1480s the Florentine humanists, most notably Marsilio Ficino and Pico della Mirandola, had developed a certain distrust of human language, especially in regard to the richness of divine Truth. Along with the ancient poets and the Jewish kabbalists, the humanists understood that the infinite truths of God were manifested in many ways that could only be approached indirectly, through riddles, allegories, and hints. The humanist's task was to recover all aspects of ancient wisdom in order to fathom the infinite richness of divine revelation, culminating in the spiritual truths of Christianity.

Renaissance humanism had begun to make inroads into Spanish culture by the 1440s, when the House of Aragon gained control of the Kingdom of Naples.[89] During the 1480s, under the active patronage of Isabella, Italian humanist scholars settled in Spain and Sephardic scholars went to study in Italy. The Spanish perceived humanism not as antagonistic to Christianity but as a vehicle for Christian renewal. Inspired by millenarianism, they employed humanism to restructure higher education in Spain and in particular to refocus on the biblical text itself. (That enterprise was accomplished with the active involvement of conversos.)[90]

The spread of humanism in Spain did not elude Jewish scholars. As the works of Isaac and Judah Abravanel attest, Jewish scholars before the expulsion were familiar with the humanist recovery of ancient literature and the humanist interest in Kabbalah.[91] Sephardic familiarity with humanist scholarship increased after the expulsion both in Italy and in the Ottoman Empire. Sephardic scholars in the Ottoman Empire learned and maintained an interest in Renaissance humanism through contacts with exiled Italian Jewish scholars in the Ottoman Empire, social and business ties between branches of extended Sephardic families, joint ventures with Italian publishing houses, and contacts with former conversos who brought the masterpieces of Spanish and Italian letters.

While Sephardic scholars in the Ottoman Empire could not boast direct contact with Renaissance humanists (as did some of their coreligionists in Italy), they could indirectly participate in the Renaissance recovery of ancient civilization because of their very presence on Greek soil. Their indigenous Greek-speaking Romaniote Jews made access to the Greek language easier, enabling Sephardic scholars such as Moses Almosnino to read Greek philosophy and literature in the original.[92] And Greek philosophy came alive, so to speak, because references to the people, places, and anecdotes could be visualized in their actual geographic context, in the same way that living in the Land of Israel helped contextualize biblical and talmudic stories.[93] Needless to say, even though Jewish scholars enjoyed reading classical literature, their primary concern was not to recover the Greek and Roman past but to articulate a Jewish response to the challenge of the Renaissance.

The Hebrew Bible anchored that response. Jewish scholars viewed the Bible not only as the record of the Jewish ancient past but also as the repository of revealed ancient Jewish wisdom. That wisdom, in turn, encompassed all human sciences including those dear to the humanists—grammar, rhetoric, poetics, history, and moral philosophy.[94] The very attempt to prove that the Bible equals the aesthetic, moral, and intellectual achievements of the ancients necessitated a rereading of the Bible against a humanist background. Thus King Solomon was presented as the embodiment of the Renaissance ideal *homo universalis* and the wisest of all ancient sages,[95] and the religious poetry of King David was favorably compared to Greek and Roman poetry.[96] So too the moral teachings of King David and King Solomon—recorded in Psalms, Proverbs, and Ecclesiastes and interpreted by rabbinic sages— surpassed the moral wisdom of Aristotle, Seneca, and Cicero, and the other ancient moral philosophers.

In their humanist rereading of the ancient Jewish sources, postexpulsion philosophic commentaries created a distinct discourse of moral philosophy that fused Jewish, Aristotelian, Platonic, and Stoic elements.[97] By interpreting Jewish sacred texts, the postexpulsion Jewish thinkers shared the humanist focus on the individual, the primacy of grammar and rhetoric over scientific rationalism, and the cultivation of *virtu* as the answer to the unpredictability of *fortuna*. In the ancient Jewish sources the Jewish philosophers found the humanist emphasis on the dignity and worth of the human personality, the primacy of the human will, and the striving for personal immortality through cultivation of moral virtues. As much as the intense suffering made Iberian Jews receptive to the humanist emphasis on human emotions and passions, so did the Bible provide them with evidence that the virtuous man who lives by the Torah is able to transcend Time.[98]

The purpose of the Jewish moral inquiry was not to solve metaethical problems but to guide the Jewish public toward the attainment of human perfection. In a society of immigrants ravaged by communal and interpersonal disputes and diverse interpretations of moral values, the philosophic commentaries filled an important civic function: they molded the inchoate Jewish masses into a genuine community seeking spiritual perfection. Though the philosophic moral discourse reflected a dialogue with non-Jewish systems of thought, its overall tenor was highly particularistic and ethnocentric. It was the dignity of Israel (rather than the dignity of Man), the personal immortality of Jews (rather than the survival of non-Jews), and the divine perfection of Torah (rather than the claims of other religions) that concerned the Jewish scholars in the Ottoman Empire. In short, the discourse on the ultimate end of human life was an answer to Jewish perplexity after the expulsion from Iberia.

The Pursuit of Holiness

Sephardic intellectuals reflected on the ultimate end of human life within the contours of the Maimonidean tradition.[99] But they transformed the medieval discourse on happiness by reviving the mythic elements of rabbinic Judaism that Maimonides had attempted to purge and by incorporating Platonic themes into the framework of medieval Aristotelianism. If Maimonides "*demythologized*" Judaism, as Kenneth Seeskin succinctly put it,[100] postexpulsion thinkers *remythologized* Jewish philosophy in order to address their religious and existential concerns.

Psychological Dualism

The Aristotelian conception of happiness presupposed a certain view of human nature or, more precisely, a psychological theory that explains the relationship between the mental and the physical aspects of the human species. Postexpulsion Sephardic philosophers fused Aristotelian and Platonic psychological theories. When they spoke about the human species at large, they employed Aristotelian theories: the soul is the form *of* the body, the organizational principle of the physical and mental functions of the human organism.[101] But when the philosophers reflected on the soul-body nexus in the case of Jews, they adopted the Platonic two-substance theory: the soul is a Form *in* a body.

The "Platonization" of the Aristotelian tradition is understandable given the dissemination of Kabbalah (whose doctrine presupposed Platonic ontology and psychology), the resurgence of Jewish and Muslim Neoplatonic philosophy, and the blossoming of Renaissance Platonism. But beyond the circumstances of culture lay the realization that Platonic doctrines were more compatible with the traditional Jewish beliefs in personal immortality and divine retribution than were Aristotle's views.[102] By applying Platonic psychology exclusively to Jews, the philosopher rationalized continued allegiance to Judaism: Jews alone can enjoy the bliss of immortality because their soul is by nature a preexistent eternal substance.

Under the sway of Kabbalah, Taitatzak, Arroyo, Almosnino, Aderbi, and others held that the souls of Jews are literally divine; they are a part of the divine essence, or a "particle of God" (*ḥelek mimenu*).[103] Israel's soul "was carved from under the Throne of Glory" (*kiseh ha-kavod*) and was "infused" (*mushpaʿat*) into the human body by God.[104] As a divine substance, the soul of Israel is holy and eternal. Prior to its descent into the body, the soul resides in a special realm (*ʿolam ha-neshamot*) to which she will return after the demise of the body, provided she perfects herself on earth.[105] Precisely because the soul of Jews is literally a divine spark, Israel alone can be said to have been created in the image of God. Therefore, whenever Scripture uses the word *man* (*ʾadam*), it refers exclusively to Israel rather than to the human species at large.[106]

If the soul of Israel is a preexistent, holy substance, the human soul is but "an incorporeal substance with a propensity for intellection" (*ʿeẓem ruḥani mukhan ʾel haskalah*).[107] The human soul is "generated" (*mithavah*) in the realm of the Separate Intelligences (*sekhalim nifradim*) and requires an association with the body in order to actualize its potential for intellection. By abstracting intelligibles from perception of sensible things, the human soul can perfect itself. It can acquire moral and intellectual virtues, culminating in philosophic wisdom, as Aristotle teaches. But precisely because the postexpulsion philosophers believed that the "way of investigation" (*derekh ha-ḥakirah*) is inherently imperfect, they argued that philosophic wisdom can at best constitute earthly happiness; it falls short of ensuring the survival of the individual soul.[108] Lacking a divine soul and devoid of the grace of divine revelation, Gentiles are barred from the afterlife.

The pursuit of perfection or happiness varies with Jews and non-Jews. Because Israel received a revelation from God, Jews need not rely on the imperfect "path of investigation" but walk instead in "the path of faith" (*derekh ha-'emunah*) that makes known the true beliefs and just actions necessary for transcendent happiness.[109] The two paths differ from each other not only in terms of content and ultimate end but also in terms of epistemic procedure. Whereas the "path of investigation" consists of abstracting intelligible universals from perception of sensible particulars, the "path of faith" consists of "recollection" (*hizakhrut*) of truths that the divine soul possessed prior to its descent into the body, precisely as Plato had taught.[110] The full significance of this view will become apparent below. For now suffice it to say that according to Moses Almosnino and Isaac Arroyo, for example, the absolute verity and certitude of the "path of faith" means that a Jewish child who has just learned to read Torah and can understand its literal meaning is wiser and closer to the attainment of immortal life than is a non-Jewish adult who studied philosophy all his life.[111]

The acquisition of knowledge is a mental activity that requires the mediation of the body. Since the soul of Jews is literally a divine substance, Jews experience a very acute conflict between the spiritual soul and the corporeal body. The corporeal body naturally seeks sensuous pleasure (derived primarily from food and sex) and seduces the soul to pursue apparent goods such as wealth and honor. The sense appetite (*ha-koaḥ ha-margish*) is the power of sensation and perception and the appetitive part (*ha-koaḥ ha-mit'orer*) is the location of all desires and passions that are aroused as a result of the information provided by the senses. Both powers are bodily dependent and as such are the source of the human tendency to sin. Therefore, the body and the physically related functions of the soul function as a "partition" or "divided barrier" (*meḥizah*; *masakh mavdil*) between the spiritual soul and her divine origin, alienating the soul from God.[112] If left to satisfy its own desires, the body could hinder the return of the soul to the supernal world. The task of the soul, therefore, is to gain control over the body, spiritualize it through the acquisition of virtues, and direct it toward the attainment of the ultimate end of life—the love of God.

Ideally, says Moses Almosnino, there should be "peace between the matter and the form" of man (*shelom ha-ḥomer ve-ha-ẓurah*).[113] Such peace indicates the attainment of mental health. Yet this inner balance is not the harmonious coexistence of two equal partners but rather is a hierarchial relationship in which the soul dominates the body. The perfect man (*ha-shalem*), says Almosnino,

> subdues and subordinates the corporeal part (*ha-ḥelek ha-ḥomri*) to the rational part (*ha-ḥelek ha-sikhli*). When one subdues (*yashpil*) the material [principle] man elevates (*yinaseʾ*) the formal [principle], one removes himself from all inequities (*peḥitut)* and ascends in the ladder of perfections.[114]

A failure of the soul to control the body manifests a sickness that requires healing (*refuʾah)* no less than physical sickness.[115] As recipients of divine revelation, Israel already possesses the best and the only true medication for the sickness of body and soul, the divine Torah.[116] Those who cling to the Torah through study and performance of its commandments attain the desired inner balance and experience happiness in this world and immortality in the next.

Even though God revealed the path that enables the soul to regain her spirituality, the process itself is painful, suffused with misery and anguish. The soul experiences her temporary association with the body not merely as a form of imprisonment (as Plato taught) but rather as a dangerous exile.[117] The soul desperately seeks to liberate herself from the body and regain her initial spirituality and holiness. No one understood the yearnings of the soul and her anguish better than King David, whose celebrated Psalms expressed the profound truths of the human condition in a poetic language. Those who penetrate the meaning of the Psalms could gain a deeper understanding of the ultimate end of human life and focus on its attainment.[118] The Sephardim, as we noted above, instituted the ritualized study of the Psalms (along with Proverbs, Ecclesiastes, and Tractate *ʾAvot*) as part of a rigorous program for ethical-religious training. By virtue of that program, the soul of the believer could "polish and purify" (*le-zakekh u-le-marek*) herself from the contaminating influences of the body,[119] preparing the believer to encounter God during the reenactment of Sinaitic theophany on the festival of Shavuot.

Postexpulsion thinkers understood pain and suffering positively, as a cathartic means of self-purification. Adversity and pain cleanse the body from its natural inclination to enjoy physical pleasure and cleanse the soul from the polluting influences of the body.[120] Yet philosophers such as Almosnino and Solomon ben Isaac Halevi were no ascetics. Unlike the kabbalists of Safed,[121] they did not institute practices for the mortification of the body in order to reach a higher level of spirituality. As members of wealthy families, these philosophers enjoyed material comfort and endorsed Aristotle's claim that human perfection requires the presence of certain external goods as well as human association.[122] But Almosnino, for example, repeatedly exhorted his audience to accept suffering *be-sever panim yafot*, that is, with a positive attitude and even with joy (*simḥah*).[123] This acceptance of adversity reflects the impact of Stoic attitudes (derived primarily from the writings of Cicero and Seneca) at least as much as it suggests the impact of Bahya ibn Pakuda's ascetic teachings on contemporary Kabbalah.[124] According to Almosnino, the acceptance of suffering indicates that the soul has already neutralized the passions of the body and has reached the desired control over the body so that it is no longer perturbed by the body.[125] Those who perfect themselves through clinging to the Torah can release their soul from its embodied conditioning while they are still alive. In other words, they can attain communion with God (*devekut*) in this world.[126]

Not unlike Abraham Abulafia, the Sephardic philosophers in Ottoman Turkey advocated a nonpolitical individualistic interpretation of the messianic ideal.[127] The redemption (*ge'ulah*) to which the Jews aspire is not the gathering of the exiles in the Land of Israel but freedom (*ḥerut*) of the individual soul from its exile in the body.[128] This is true freedom from the travails of Time and from the determinism of natural causality (*ma'arakhah*).[129] By psychologizing the historical experience of exile, postexpulsion philosophers took the sting out of the bite of history and articulated a hopeful message: redemption is within the reach of each and every Jew in this life, despite the vicissitudes of Time.

Human Perfection and Hermeneutics

It is here that psychology, ethics, moral training, and hermeneutics converge in the discourse on happiness. Postexpulsion thinkers viewed the pursuit of happiness (both earthly and transcendent) as a fundamental Jewish activity, that is, the creation of midrash. One can become perfect only through the hermeneutical act of interpretation that unveils the inner, esoteric meaning of the sacred text. But if for Maimonides the inner meaning of the Torah consisted of abstract philosophic truths of physics and metaphysics, for postexpulsion thinkers the esoteric core of the Torah was the essence of the Divine Self. The revealed Torah is not only the most perfect law, the observance of which assures perfection of body and soul, but a sacred medium through which the human self and the divine self can encounter each other. In Almosnino's words, "The Torah is the intermediary [*'emza'i*] through which Israel can communicate with God by doing God's Will.[130]

As indicated above, the Sephardic philosophers endorsed the kabbalistic doctrine that the esoteric Torah is the essence of God, comprised of infinite permutations of the divine name. Since the soul of Israel is also "carved" from the essence of God, it follows that God, the supernal Torah, and the souls of Israel are one and the same, precisely as the *Zohar* teaches.[131] This is why the study of Torah and the acquisition of knowledge are two sides of the same endeavor, two aspects of the process of self-knowledge. The pursuit of perfection consists of two parallel moves of removing the veils of corporeality—from the believer and from the Torah. In the human believer the veil of corporeality is the body; in the revealed Torah the veils of corporeality are the figurative expressions that unclothe the esoteric divine truth in metaphors, narratives, and laws.[132] The attainment of union between the divine and the human requires the believer to spiritualize himself through the study of Torah and the performance of its laws. The better Jews understand themselves and purify themselves by doing what God wants of them, the deeper they can penetrate the infinite mysteries of the Torah, which paradoxically conceal and reveal the divine Self.

To understand what one must do to become perfect, one must have a conceptual vocabulary (or a theory) about the ultimate end of human life. That conceptual vocabulary was articulated by the philosophers and especially by Aristotle's *Ethics*. Maimonides, of course, was the first

to argue that the *eduaimonian* ethics of Aristotle is consistent (though
not entirely identical) with the moral and religious ideals of the rabbis.[133] Postexpulsion thinkers perpetuated the Aristotelian tradition that
viewed ethics as a practical science (*ḥokhmah maʿasit*) whose goal was the
formation of good character through habitual practice of good deeds.
On the level of praxis there was no significant conflict between Aristotle
and Jewish tradition. This is the purpose of Almosnino's commentary on
the *Ethics, Penei Mosheh*. He shows that the anecdotes on rabbinic sages
in Talmudic aggadot and their moral aphorisms in Tractate *ʾAvot* verify
Aristotle's moral philosophy and, conversely, that a correct interpretation of biblical and rabbinic texts illuminates the obscure or disputed
points in Aristotle's *Ethics*. By so reading Aristotle, Almosnino in fact invested the science of ethics with a religious import: whoever acquires the
virtues in accord with Aristotle's moral philosophy and the teachings of
the rabbis could attain the desired level of spirituality and encounter
God in the verses of the revealed text. Whether or not a given person in
fact devotes his or her life to the Torah depends largely on the will,
which freely decides whether to follow divine commands or not.

From Intellectualism to Voluntarism

The Maimonidean tradition put a premium on the intellect. Following
Aristotle, Maimonides conceptualized God as a perfect intellect that is
absorbed in eternal self-contemplation and insisted that creation in the
image of God refers to the rational potential of man. Maimonides further depersonalized God by denying from God any volition and desire.
Because God is absolutely perfect, there is neither want nor desire in
God. God wills only to the extent that God knows Himself. In contrast
to God, created human beings are endowed with a free will and are responsible for their choice. Despite his reaffirmation of rabbinic belief in
human freedom, Maimonides no less than Aristotle[134] reduced volition
to the cognitive activity of practical reason. Human beings desire only
that which their intellect judges to be good (whether this good is real or
apparent). A given choice is good if it promotes human happiness, and
it is bad if it leads man to pursue apparent goods. When one chooses
badly, it is a failure of the intellect rather than the weakness of the will.

The bitter confrontation between Judaism and Christianity and the
mass apostasy of the Iberian Jews compelled Jewish Aristotelians to re-

consider the Maimonidean approach to human choice and pay closer attention to the role of will in human conduct. Especially after 1391 a Jewish philosopher could no longer explain why some Jews remained loyal to Judaism while others converted to Christianity. A mere conviction of the intellect was not enough to account for the new historical situation. The trauma of the expulsion further underscored these problems, because in 1492 the choice to profess Judaism was clearly not the most rational course of action. It was rather a voluntary act of faith that expressed the believer's love of God and the willingness to suffer pain in the sanctification of God's name (*kiddush ha-Shem*). As Sephardic intellectuals took a closer look at the role of the will in the pursuit of human perfection, they resorted to the rich scholastic literature on the subject, gleaning from it subtle distinction and sophisticated arguments.[135]

The works of Moses Almosnino (especially *Penei Mosheh*) illustrate the shift from intellectualism to voluntarism during the postexpulsion period.[136] By this I do not mean that Almosnino denied the teleological and intellectualist parameters of Maimonideanism. To have done so would have undermined the entire study of philosophy as well as his conception of Torah and his own cultural identity. Rather, Almosnino's works suggest a certain softening of Maimonidean intellectualism by agreeing with Crescas that God is the supremely good Will, that the pursuit of human perfection depends on the perfection of both the intellect and the Will, and that the ultimate end of human life is a combination of both the knowledge and the love of God.

Almosnino's voluntarism is evident in his conception of God. He shared the premises of the Maimonidean tradition that God is the First Cause of the universe, the Necessary Being whose essence is identical with His existence. But instead of dwelling on the unity of essence and existence in God, Almosnino talked about the goodness of the divine Will: "The divine Will is the Good that is desired for its own sake and that is not subject to change."[137] In accordance with this personalist conception of the God, Almosnino reinterpreted Maimonides' teachings on divine attributes.

Maimonides stated that the "Ways" that God Revealed to Moses are the attributes of action. While the Torah speaks of these attributes as interpersonal terms (for example, lovingkindness and justice), in truth, these attributes of divine action are revealed in the realm of nature. God's love for His creatures is manifested in the regularity of nature and the knowability of its laws. The better one understands the laws of nature (through the study of physics and metaphysics), the more one avoids mishaps and errors, thereby appearing to enjoy God's special favors. Similarly, Maimonides interpreted miracles naturalistically: miracles are not manifestations of supernatural divine intervention in nature but the preprogrammed exceptions to natural laws, built into nature at creation.

Almosnino departed from Maimonides' intellectualist naturalism when he stated that the Ways are the perfect character traits (*middot*) of the supremely good divine Self.[138] The hidden core of the divine Torah, therefore, does not consist of the fixed laws by which God governs the universe, but the infinite, dynamic perfections of God that the kabbalists call Sefirot. Human perfection is possible because God revealed His perfections in the Torah. By revealing His perfections to Israel, God enables those who love him to imitate Him and attain happiness in this world and immortal life in the next. Those who freely cling to God's Torah and love God unconditionally—the love of the noble for its own sake[139]—become like God and enjoy earthly as well as transcendent happiness. Such love, however, manifests the perfection of the will, which for Almosnino is a distinct power within the faculties of the soul.

Human excellence (*maʿalat ha-ʾadam*), says Almosnino, lies in the freedom of the will to determine whether one will be as happy as God or as unhappy as beasts.[140] The human will is by nature rational and free. The will is rational because it acts in accordance with information provided by the intellect, but it is free because it can either will the known object, will against it, or not will it at all.[141] The will is superior to the intellect not only because the known object cannot compel the will in any way but also because the will is free to act or not to act. The intellect's freedom is more limited than the freedom of the will because the intellect is bound by the teleological structure of the universe. Hence, the freedom of the intellect is limited only to doing something for its own sake rather than for the sake of something else.[142]

In the hierarchy of the soul the will belongs to the appetitive power. Located between reason and the sense appetite, the will carries out the soul's task of "taming" or subduing the body's natural inclinations. The freedom of the will entails two things: it can ignore the information provided by the intellect and it can freely choose to pursue evil, an idea that both Aristotle and Maimonides would have found self-contradictory.

The human desire to sin is neither uncommon nor merely a result of mistaken judgment by the intellect. Rather, it reflects the imperfection of the will or the sickness of the will.

Finally, the freedom of the will is evident even within the act of cognition. The human intellect does not engage in cognitive activity at all times. What moves the intellect to do so is a command by the will to cognize this or that object. Moreover, the will can even prevent the progression of the intellect from premises to conclusions through syllogism, so that the acquisition of knowledge is a free activity that lacks either compulsion or necessity. And after the intellect has already acquired a certain piece of knowledge, it is the will that determines whether the intellect would reflect it or not. The act of mental concentration (*hitboddedut*) is therefore not solely the domain of the perfect intellect; it is also a contemplative act that requires the involvement of the will as well.[143] Almosnino summarizes the arguments in favor of the primacy of the will by saying that the intellect acts as a "counselor" (*yo'ez*) to the will but the will is free either to accept or to ignore the information provided by the intellect, exactly as a king can either accept or reject the advice of his ministers.[144]

The upshot of Almosnino's analysis of the interplay of the will and the intellect is that human happiness requires the perfection of both.[145] Wisdom (*ḥokhmah*) is the perfection of the intellect and love is the perfection of the will. Almosnino therefore concludes that the unlimited end of human life must consist of "contemplation [of God] combined with love" (*'iyyun be-ẓeruf 'ahavah*).[146] Unlike Maimonides, who considered the love of God an intellectual activity that reflects the perfection of theoretical reason, Almosnino and his contemporaries viewed love as the perfection of the will and therefore the perfection of practical reason. The love of God thus belongs to the realm of praxis (*ma'aseh*) rather than *theoria* (*'iyyun*).

The Primacy of Praxis

The Aristotelian tradition (and indeed Greek and Hellenistic moral philosophy in general) emphasized the intrinsic link between intellectual perfection and moral goodness. The wise man must be morally good by habitually practicing just acts toward other persons, and, conversely, moral goodness exhibited in the social sphere presupposes knowledge about the Supreme Good. The thrust of Aristotelian ethics was to develop the moral personality that lives intelligently by curbing desires and practicing virtuous acts toward other persons, governed by a worthwhile end, that is, happiness. Aristotle posited the faculty of practical reason (*phronesis*) as the middle ground between the theoretical and the moral life.

According to Aristotle, the man of practical reason (*phronimos*) deliberates with a view not merely to particular goals but to the good life in general, with a view to the best and with a view to happiness. Concomitantly, the prudent man is concerned not only with universals, such as the good life in general, but also with particular actions in concrete situations.[147] By perfecting practical reason, one can act "just right" in them. That is, one act according to the rule of the mean, doing the right amount of good, at the right time, in the right manner, toward the right object, and for the right reason. Moral training thus involves the discovery of the mean between two extreme vices: overindulgence on the hand and abstinence on the other hand. But moral goodness arises not through mere following of abstract rules but through practice and cumulative experience in interpersonal relations.

Maimonides incorporated these ideas into his analysis of Jewish law in his attempt to show that the Torah perfects body and soul. Yet Maimonides had relatively little interest in practical reason per se because he invested the moral life with only instrumental value. Moral perfection is but the means to the attainment of a higher perfection, that is, theoretical wisdom that culminates in the knowledge of God. Moreover, Maimonides' own analysis of halakhah (the praxis of Judaism) rendered the discussion of practical reason almost unnecessary. The one who lives by halakhah (as interpreted by Maimonides) was to attain perfection of body and soul.

Postexpulsion philosophers such as Almosnino took a different approach to the cultivation of moral virtues. For them moral life is not only a means to an end but the very core of religious life in this world. The moral life that is guided by practical reason is informed by the values of the religious tradition. By imitating divine perfections revealed in the Torah, the devotee can acquire the moral virtues and attain the necessary self-spiritualization that leads to *devekut* in this world and eternal life after death. Moreover, for Almosnino the moral life of action is the very arena in which one manifests the perfection of the will and the total devotion to God. Hence, the highest virtue in this life is not the intellectual virtue of philosophic wisdom but rather the virtue of prudence. Such an approach is closer to the Christian understanding of the moral life than is Maimonides' understanding of it.

Borrowing from Buridan's commentary on the *Ethics*, Almosnino posited prudence as the supreme virtue.[148] The man of practical reason (*ha-navon*) is the wise man who has acquired all moral virtues;[149] the one who has attained the virtue of prudence (*tevunah*), the most important of the four cardinal virtues.[150] The prudent man is religiously perfect because he lives by the divine commands of the Torah. The prohibitions of the Torah (*mitzvot lo ta'aseh*) enable the good man to subdue the passions of the body and move away from sin and the positive commandments of the Torah (*mitzvot 'aseh*) facilitate the acquisition of moral virtues through habitual practice of good deeds. The man who acquires prudence knows how to distinguish between real and apparent goods. He realizes that bodily pleasures, wealth, honor, glory, and fame do not constitute true happiness even though a modicum of material goods is necessary for the performance of good deeds toward others (for example, charity).

The perfection of practical reason encompasses the perfection of the will, that is, the love of the good for its own sake. Since the Supreme Good is the divine Will, the prudent man who knows "divine things" is also the one who unconditionally loves God. Maimonides was indeed correct, says Almosnino, in teaching that the more one knows God the more one loves God. But Almosnino reinterprets the meaning of the love of God. Love is not the perfection of theoretical intellect but rather the perfection of the will, the inner dimension of praxis (*ma'aseh penimi*).[151] The man of prudence is therefore the one who diligently performs the mitzvot not because they are instrumental to the theoretical knowledge of God but because they have an intrinsic value as the expression of God's Will. In short, the felicitous man (*ha-me'ushar*) who has acquired the virtue of prudence is the human ideal about whom King David sang in Psalms, whom King Solomon praised in Ecclesiastes and Proverbs, and whom the Tannaim portrayed in Tractate 'Avot. He is the one who is rewarded with happiness on earth and with immortal life in the world to come.

The Love of God

The love of God is the ultimate end (*ha-takhlit ha-'aharon*) of human life.[152] The love of God is the love of the honorable that enables the human will to resist the passions. In any perfect virtue there is love of the honorable, which leads to right reasoning and right choice and connects that love to the other virtues. With each choice of every virtue the love of God is reinforced. Hence, it is through love of God that one attains the perfection of all virtues in this world and for which one is rewarded with eternal life. The love of God is everlasting and inexhaustible because it is an unconditional love.[153] Almosnino agrees with Maimonides and all those who followed him that the love of God is commensurate with knowledge. But for Almosnino the love of God is not a communication between two perfect intellects that share the identity of universals but rather the love of the infinite "details of the beloved" (*pirtei ha-davar ha-ne'ehav.*)[154] Only a perfect will that can discern the infinite variations of particulars can love God, the most perfect Will, unconditionally.

The ultimate end of human life is blissful union of the separated soul with God. The perfected soul that removed from herself vestiges of corporeality embraces God in a mystical union (*hithabrut, hit'ahadut*) in which the known, the knower, and the act of knowing are one and the same, as Maimonides taught in the *Guide*, 1:68. Transcending Time, Nature, and Evil, the separated soul of Israel becomes one with God and the supernal Torah as she was before her descent into the body. Enjoying an incomparable spiritual delight (*ta'anug*), the soul finds repose and completion whose religious symbol is the Sabbath.[155]

Those Jews who devote themselves to God and His Torah could experience the bliss of immortality despite the continuation of political exile and the waiting for the Messiah. Almosnino and his cohorts did not ignore the traditional hope for the coming of the Messiah. They depoliticized it by spiritualizing its meaning. The messianic age is not a historical period of the ingathering of Jews in the Land of Israel but the total transformation of human existence from corporeality to spirituality. In the messianic age all Jews will envision the "face of the Shekhinah" during their lifetime because their body will no longer be a material entity.[156]

The bliss of personal immortality is reserved for perfect Jews. Surprisingly, however, the community of the perfect now includes both men and women. In a remarkable departure from the Maimonidean tradition, postexpulsion thinkers discussed in this article stated that women can enter the world to come even though their intellect is naturally imperfect.[157] Precisely because ultimate felicity depends not on philosophic wisdom but rather on faith, the perfection of the will, and the actual performance of *mitzvot*, women can enjoy the bliss of immortality. Even though postexpulsion thinkers continued to regard women as intellectually inferior to men and charged with the task of facilitating the perfection of their husbands, they did agree that as religious devotees women are equal to men.[158]

In conclusion, I have argued that the expulsion from Iberia was no caesura in Sephardic cultural and intellectual life. The Sephardic cultural renewal in the middle of the sixteenth century encompassed philosophy along with halakhah, aggadah, and Kabbalah. The cultivation of philosophy was an essential ingredient in the pursuit of transcendent happiness that constituted the spiritual response to the trauma of the expulsion. In direct continuity with fifteenth-century intellectual trends, philosophy was considered a necessary, though not sufficient, condition in the attainment of the ultimate end of human life, that is, personal immortality. The subordination of philosophy to the revealed tradition went hand in hand with the expansion of the revealed tradition to include Spanish Kabbalah.

Kabbalah invigorated philosophic hermeneutics but also clipped its wings. Philosophy waned to become only one voice in the interpretation of God's infinite, multivocal, multitalented, symbolic, verbal self-revelation. Philosophic hermeneutics came to reflect a conscious response to and a selective adaptation of Renaissance humanism; it in turn created a distinct discourse in moral philosophy. The very efflorescence of rhetoric enabled the Sephardic intellectuals to find new meaning in the sacred texts that justified their continued allegiance to Judaism, despite the pain and the suffering.

Within the framework of the Aristotelian discourse on happiness, postexpulsion thinkers transformed the orientation of Jewish philosophy. They remythologized the conception of God; they endorsed the dualism of body and soul; they paid greater attention to the noncognitive dimensions of the human personality; they highlighted the importance of the will in human conduct; they recognized the religious value of moral action through the performance of mitzvot; they diminished the importance of theoretical wisdom and focused instead on practical reason; they posited the love of God as the ultimate end of life and envisioned ultimate felicity as a mystical union with God. As a result of these changes the very scholars who studied philosophy also paved the way for the emergence of Kabbalah as the dominant interpretation of Judaism.

PART VI

Continuity and Change in the Sephardic Diaspora:

Cultural Dimensions

13

▦

Hebrew Manuscripts and Printed Books Among the Sephardim Before and After the Expulsion

Menahem Schmelzer

The production of Hebrew manuscripts[1] and printed books[2] flourished in the second half of the fifteenth century in Spain and Portugal. Indeed, several features of Hebrew bookmaking were unique to Sephardic Jewry at the time and not found in other Jewish centers. These features made the decades prior to the expulsion extraordinary in the history of the Hebrew book.[3]

One of these features was the assumed existence of a workshop for creating Hebrew manuscripts in Lisbon. Unlike Christian manuscripts, the production of which took place mostly in scriptoria, Hebrew manuscripts in the Middle Ages were written by individual scribes and not in workshops.[4] A possible exception is a Lisbon workshop that flourished between the 1460s and 1490s. This atelier produced attractive illuminated Hebrew manuscripts, mainly Bibles and prayerbooks, but also a *Mishneh Torah* of Maimonides and calligraphically beautiful, although nonilluminated, manuscripts of Kimhi's grammar, Nahmanides' commentary on the Pentateuch, and Joseph ibn Shem Tob's commentary on Aristotle's *Ethics*.[5] Unfortunately, there are no external sources about the history of this atelier, its inner workings, and its personnel. The evidence is in the manuscripts themselves, in their style and in the occasional laconic statements in the colophons relating to the place and date of their writing and to the identity of the copyists. It is noteworthy that it was on the Iberian Peninsula that the appreciation for aesthetically pleasing, fine manuscripts led to what was apparently the only institutionalized undertaking among medieval Jews for the production of Hebrew codices. Manuscript making in Lisbon also influenced the newly introduced art of printing by movable type, which began there in the 1480s. The Hebrew manuscripts of the Lisbon school and the printed books of the Lisbon Hebrew press bear some similarity in the character of letters and in the layout and decoration of the pages.[6]

Another phenomenon found among Sephardic Jewry was perhaps similar to the organized effort for the writing of Hebrew manuscripts in the Lisbon workshop. There are some references in colophons to manuscripts copied in the rabbinic academies of Spain.[7] In Seville the scribe Jacob ben Joshua Frontino copied manuscripts in 1471 and 1474 in the synagogue called Ibn Yaish. One manuscript contained a halakhic work, *Ḥazeh ha-tenufah*, and the other the Book of Proverbs, with commentaries by Ibn Ezra, Kimhi, and Gersonides. Joseph ben Joshua Frontino, most likely a brother of Jacob, was active as a scribe of Hebrew manuscripts in the Jewish quarter of Fez, probably after the expulsion.[8] Fez, as we shall soon see, was the site of organized scribal and printing activity in the second decade of the sixteenth century. The involvement of the Frontino brothers in scribal work in the Ibn Yaish synagogue in Seville and later in the *mellah* of Fez, seems to indicate not only the continuation of a family tradition but also that of an established and perhaps institutionalized endeavor of Hebrew book production. In Saragossa, in 1471, Moses Narboni's commentary on al-Ghazzali's *The Intentions of Philosophers* was copied in the academy of Rabbi Abraham Bibago.[9] A manuscript of Judah Halevi's *Kuzari* was written in 1490 by a Spanish scribe in the academy of Rabbi Moses ibn Habib of Lisbon, in the Southern Italian city of Bitonto.[10] The Responsa of Asher ben Jehiel were copied in the academy of Rabbi Isaac Aboab in Guadalajara in 1491.[11] Guadalajara was the site of a Hebrew press, too.[12] This tradition was apparently transported by the exiles from the Iberian Peninsula to their new home in Fez. Members of a society of scholars (*ḥavurah*) that was established in Fez by a Castilian exile, Rabbi Judah Uzziel, were engaged as scribes of Hebrew manuscripts.[13] Other Iberian traditions of bookmaking were carried out in this city. It is well known that Abudraham's commentary on the prayerbook, originally printed in Lisbon in 1489, was reprinted in Fez in 1516 and followed the layout and typographical arrangement of that of the Lisbon edition to the letter.[14] Similarly, fragments of editions of the Talmud published in Fez closely resembled their earlier Iberian counterparts.[15]

In one of the few elegies on the expulsion that has come down to us, the author, Abraham ibn Bukrat, mourns the destruction of book-filled academies. He referred probably to the existence of extensive libraries in the yeshivot of Sepharad. Still, he may have wanted to imply that the yeshiva had also served as a place for the organized production of Hebrew books.[16]

There seem to have been two kinds of scriptoria in Sepharad, the Lisbon type, on the one hand, and various academic types, on the other hand. Further, the Lisbon atelier served the needs of well-to-do laypeople, producing mainly lavish illuminated Bibles and prayerbooks, while the academies provided manuscripts for scholars in the areas of halakhah, philosophy, and other disciplines.

The introduction of one of mankind's greatest inventions, printing by movable type, occurred in Spain and Portugal in the waning years of Jewish life there. As a result of the abrupt end of the Jewish community on the Iberian Peninsula, Hebrew printed books from there are far less known and far more scarce than Hebrew books printed in the same period in Italy. Generally, Italy is regarded as the cradle of the Hebrew printed book and the name of the Soncinos, the preeminent Hebrew printers, is familiar even to the lay public. Hebrew incunabula from Italy have been thoroughly researched for a long period of time, whereas the history of Iberian Hebrew incunabula is much more obscure. If not for the expulsion, Hebrew printing in Sepharad would have become as significant as that of Italy. The first Hebrew book in Spain was probably printed in 1476, just one year after the printing of the first dated Hebrew book in Italy.[17] In the following years Hebrew presses were established in Zamora, Hijar, Leiria, Faro, and Lisbon, and perhaps also in Montalbán and Toledo.[18] The products of these presses yield considerable knowledge on various aspects of Jewish life and learning. In addition to the names of the printers, frequently members of well-known families, and the dates and places of printing,[19] the colophons also reveal attitudes toward the new art. The Iberian printers, like their Italian colleagues, expressed their amazement about the seemingly miraculous quality of the new art to which they refer as a divine gift, heavenly work, and deriving from God.[20]

Allusions to historical events are also found in the colophons. In a Leiria incunabulum, the 1494 Bible, there is explicit mention of the expulsion and its effects on Hebrew printing. The printer speaks about the great anguish that befell the Jewish community as a result of the decree of expulsion. Among its devastating results he counts the decline of Hebrew printing: this glorious, heavenly work suffered its downfall when the Jews were compelled to leave Spain.[21]

Because of this dislocation, alongside easily identifiable incunabula from Spain and Portugal, there exists a puzzling load of unidentified printed fragments of Sephardic origin. Among these are leaves from tractates of the Babylonian Talmud, of Isaac Alfasi's *Halakhot,* and of Maimonides' *Mishneh Torah.* The first discovery of these Sephardic fragments was made at the end of the nineteenth century, and since then they have continued to pose a scholarly quandary. Because of the fragmentary nature of these remnants and because of the similarity between paper and type used on the Iberian Peninsula and that used by exiles in Fez, Constantinople, and Salonika, scholars could not determine which of the fragments were preexpulsion and which were postexpulsion. Recently, however, as a result of painstaking research, new criteria were established for classifying the material with greater accuracy. This made it possible to know what tractates of the preexpulsion Sephardic edition of the Babylonian Talmud are extant and to identify printed editions of various other works, among them printed fragments of preexilic editions of the *Mishneh Torah.*[22] The latter were printed in square letters resembling the monumental square Hebrew script so familiar from medieval Spanish synagogue inscriptions and from formal biblical codices. The anonymity of these leaves, the lack of any identifying features such as place, date, and name of printer, led to the suggestion that the books represented by these fragments were produced clandestinely by Marranos. In archival sources mention is made of a Marrano, Juan de Lucena, and his daughters, who, according to the accusations of the Inquisition, were producing Hebrew books set in Hebrew type. Although no actual book from this alleged press can be identified with certainty, the assumption that the anonymous *Mishneh Torah* fragments were the work of Juan de Lucena is quite alluring.[23]

Other fragments, most significant among them leaves of the first illustrated printed Haggadah, may have been produced in Spain before the expulsion and not, as was previously assumed, in Constantinople in the second decade of the sixteenth century.[24]

Despite some of the uncertainty regarding the attributions of these unidentified fragments as the products of the Hebrew printing presses of Spain and Portugal, there is no doubt that right up to the expulsion there existed on the Iberian Peninsula a rich and varied printing activity, alongside the continued making of Hebrew manuscripts. Indeed, as Joseph Hacker has amply documented,[25] the exiles mention an abundance of Hebrew books possessed by Jews of Spain and Portugal, but they also refer to the fact that they were able to take their books with them on their wanderings. Abraham ibn Yaish[26] and Abraham Saba[27] both speak about innumerable books that were lost during the flight from the Iberian Peninsula. David ibn Yahya, another exile, relates that he had lost three-quarters of his collection of four hundred books.[28] Isaac Abravanel tells us that he had sent "whatever the hail has left" (Exodus 10:12) from his books to Salonika.[29]

The combined number of Hebrew manuscripts from the Iberian Peninsula and of Hebrew codices written in Sephardic script by scribes from Spain and Portugal in Italy and in Byzantium is, surprisingly, greater than the number of Hebrew books copied by native scribes in Italy, long considered to be the "homeland" of Hebrew manuscripts.[30] The popularity of Spanish Hebrew manuscripts in Italy can be seen from the humorous description by Immanuel of Rome of the Italian adventures of a bookseller from Toledo in the fourteenth century.[31] The basic point of the story, that Hebrew manuscripts from Spain were highly desirable in Italy and that Italian Jews were ready even to commit mischief in order to obtain them, is probably valid for the fifteenth century as well.

The expulsion put an end to a rich and productive tradition in the area of scribal and printing activity. Hebrew books became the target of banning, burning, and confiscation or were victims of loss and abandonment.[32] Despite these adversities, as mentioned above,[33] many exiles managed to take their books with them.

There are two manuscripts in the library of the Jewish Theological Seminary that include on their pages the account of having been taken from Spain and from Portugal at the time of the expulsion. A manuscript Bible records the following colophon:

> This volume, which contains the twenty-four sacred books, was written by the learned Rabbi Abraham Calif in the city of Toledo, in Spain. It

was finished in the month of Nissan 5252 [1492]. And on the seventh day of the month of Av in the selfsame year, the exiles of Jerusalem who were in Spain, went forth dismayed and banished by the royal edict. And I, Ḥayyim ibn Ḥayyim, have copied therein part of the Masorah and the variants in the year 5257 [1497] in the city of Constantinople.[34]

Hence, it is clear from this colophon that the unfinished manuscript was taken from Spain in 1492 and was completed five years later in Constantinople. The other manuscript is Shem Tob ben Shem Tob's *Sefer ha-'Emunot*, an anti-Maimonidean polemic against philosophy. Because of its controversial nature, this work had been copied only rarely. In 1497 the Portuguese ruler, King Manuel, issued a decree forbidding Jews to possess Hebrew books. He ordered that they be surrendered and deposited in synagogues. The JTS manuscript of *Sefer ha-'Emunot* was among books that ended up in a synagogue in Lisbon, where it was locked up and made inaccessible to its former Jewish owners. Somehow exiles managed to remove the manuscript and take it with them on the journey to Constantinople or Salonika. Thus was the manuscript of *Sefer ha-'Emunot* saved. The story of its vicissitudes is told on the margin of the manuscript, concluding with the words: "It was brought here to the Ottoman Empire by the exiles from Spain and Portugal.[35]

The exiles not only tried to save their books and bring them to their new homes, but very soon after their arrival—indeed, even at a time when they had not yet had a permanent home—they resumed their activities as scribes and as printers, as preservers and transmitters of knowledge.

The manuscript of Joseph ibn Shoshan's commentary on the *Sayings of the Fathers* was written in Tunis, in 1496. The scribe, an exile from Spain, states in the colophon: "I, the unfortunate, a man of suffering, copied these commentaries, while on the shores of Tunis, in the house of eminent and righteous people in a room in the attic that they put at my disposal. And as we were expelled from our homeland . . ."[36] There are other testimonies in which scribes mention the fact that they were exiles from Spain and Portugal, and in a few instances they indicate the year the manuscript was copied by counting from the expulsion, for example, "year two of the Spanish exile."[37]

Hebrew manuscripts continued to be written in the new communities, but the introduction of printing by Iberian exiles in Constantinople, Salonika, and Fez made the printing press the dominant instrument of publishing, with far-reaching effects on Jewish religious and cultural life. Perhaps the most telling example of the introduction of printing in the newly established communities is the story of the printing, by Spanish exiles, of Jacob ben Asher's 'Arba'ah Turim in Constantinople. Despite the fact that there is an explicit date, 1493, in the colophon, scholars have long debated when this edition was actually published. Alexander Marx and his brother, Moses Marx, took the date at face value and emphasized its meaning for demonstrating how speedily the Spanish exiles began the reconstruction of their cultural and religious life. After all, to print a bulky volume such as the 'Arba'ah Turim just one year after the expulsion, in a faraway location, is a sign of great vitality and a proof of strong determination to start the rebuilding of the community. Others, however—De Rossi, Steinschneider, Goldschmidt, and Yaari—doubted that it was possible to print such a major work just one year after the expulsion. They argued that the printers needed time to arrive in the Balkans from the Iberian Peninsula, and considerable time was also required for setting up an operation capable of carrying out a project of such magnitude. Accordingly, these scholars maintained that the explicit date was a typographical error, and they suggested a later date: 1503. A. K. Offenberg, on the basis of the evidence of the paper and its watermarks and the typographical material, proved that the book was indeed printed in 1493, and this is the year when Hebrew printing in Constantinople started.[38]

After the printing of the 'Arba'ah Turim, the nascent Hebrew press of Constantinople issued a series of major works: the Bible with commentaries by Rashi, David Kimḥi, and Abraham ibn Ezra, in 1505–1506,[39] the Halakhot by Isaac Alfasi in 1509,[40] and the Mishneh Torah by Maimonides in the same year.[41] These were monumental undertakings, large, multivolume, copious folio productions, efforts that required a great deal of technical skill, scholarship, and financial investment. The printers and the people associated with them were fully aware of the importance of their historical mission: transplanting Jewish learning from the Iberian Peninsula to the new Jewish centers established by the exiles. This sense of mission is clearly expressed in the lengthy colophon of the 1505–1506 Bible. The colophon was written by Abraham ben Joseph ibn Yaish, the editor and corrector of the work, an exile from Spain and a well-known rabbi:

> From the day that God had confounded the speech of the whole earth through the bitter and impetuous exile, the exile from Sepharad, all good things have abandoned us. . . . The few survivors were compelled to wander from country to country. . . . In the wake of the terror of the persecutions the books, too, were gone. . . . People neglect to teach their children because of the vicissitudes of the times and the unavailability of books. . . . When one finds a copy of the Torah, the Targum will be lacking, and if there is available a copy of the Targum, the Commentary [that is, Rashi's] will be missing. . . . Suddenly, God provided a remedy. A few survivors, coming from many directions . . . found their way to Constantinople, among them two brothers, David and Samuel Nechamias, who were blessed by God to be great experts in the art of printing. . . . They decided to spread the knowledge of Torah among Israel, to make up, even though only to a small extent, for the innumerable books that were destroyed on land and on sea.[42]

In the 1509 edition of Maimonides' *Mishneh Torah*, the printers bemoan the destruction of the Jewish communities of Sepharad, the forced exile imposed upon them, and the consequences of these dislocations, including the loss of books and the diminution of learning and scholarship. In view of these vicissitudes they regard their own activities in spreading knowledge through printing as the "restoration of the fallen tabernacle of the Torah."[43]

In the subsequent decades the printing presses of the cities of the Ottoman Empire, operated mainly by Iberian exiles, were churning out Hebrew books in large number and in many subject areas. Again, a comparison with Italy may be helpful. It is noteworthy that it was in Constantinople and Salonika that the first editions of midrashim and midrashic anthologies appeared in print.[44] The *Midrash Rabbah*, the halakhic midrashim, the *Tanḥuma'*, the Midrash on Psalms and Proverbs, *Pirke de-Rabbi 'Eliezer*, the *'Ein Ya'akov*, the *Haggadot ha-Talmud*, and so on, all were printed for the first time by Spanish exiles in Constantinople and Salonika, followed only decades later by Italian editions. The reason for including these titles among the early editions produced by Sephardic printers may have been related to the importance of sermons in the newly established exile communities. Sermons provided solace and guidance following the recent traumas. Indeed, a large number of collections of sermons, some printed but many more in manuscripts, have come down to us from this period.[45] Since the sermons were, of course, based on midrashic sources, it is plausible to assume that the practical needs of the rabbis for appropriate source material for their homiletic activity was what prompted the printing of midrashim and midrashic anthologies in the first two decades of the establishment of Hebrew presses in the Ottoman Empire.

Alongside the traditional literature—Bible and commentaries, rabbinic classics and their commentaries, codes, philosophy and ethics— other subject matter, such as belles lettres, poetry, grammar, medicine, mathematics, history, and travel, were also represented among the books published. The wide-ranging intellectual interest of the exile communities is attested also by the report that many copies of al-Ghazzali's writings were circulating in Salonika in the sixteenth century.[46] Al-Ghazzali's works on logic may have been much in demand because of the dominance of the philosophical-logical method of Talmud study that was practiced by many talmudists in the period.[47] This prolific printing activity was aided and stimulated by the existence of great private collections of Hebrew manuscripts and printed books. Jacob ibn Habib, in the introduction to his 'Ein Ya'akov, writes that although he had planned to publish this collection of talmudic *aggadot* for a long time, he had to delay his work on it because he lacked the books needed for it. But in Salonika, with the help of the extensive libraries owned by members of the Benveniste family, he could finally carry his project to completion.[48] Samuel di Modena and Joseph ben Leb also mention books that they had found in the private libraries of the same family.[49] An elegy included in the Ninth of Av liturgy of an Ashkenazic *mahzor* printed in Salonika mourns the losses from a great fire that devastated Salonika in 1545. Among these, the destruction of Samuel Benveniste's collection of books occupies a prominent place. We learn from this elegy that Don Samuel used to hire scribes to copy for him "innumerable" copies of the books of the Talmud, codes, and commentaries. The author, Benjamin ben Meir ha-Levi Ashkenazi, refers to "hibburim . . . penimiyyim ve-hizoniyyim," perhaps meaning writings not only by Jewish but also by non-Jewish authors, such as al-Ghazzali, just mentioned. He also speaks about the physical beauty of the books, some of which were copied on fine parchment.[50] Indeed, it is noteworthy that among the earliest books printed in Constantinople and Salonika a disproportionately large number were produced on parchment, a clear sign of interest in bibliophilic, aesthetically pleasing editions.[51] In this connection mention should also be made of Rabbi

David ibn Zimra, the Radbaz, who possessed a large library in Cairo and who encouraged scholars to copy works that he owned.[52]

This survey has attempted to demonstrate the centrality and diversity of the Hebrew book in the life of Sephardic Jews in a time of great historical upheaval. The Hebrew book, in its physical form and as an idea, became, as at so many other times in Jewish history, a symbol of memory, survival, continuity, and vitality.

14

A Converso Best-Seller:
Celestina *and Her Foreign Offspring*

Dwayne E. Carpenter

There are, perhaps, no more striking examples of continuity and change within the literary arena than the converso Fernando de Rojas and his masterpiece *Celestina*. Rojas, whose life spanned the last quarter of the fifteenth century and nearly the first half of the sixteenth, witnessed not only the persistence of religion in daily life, the progressive power of the printed word, and the unremitting drive toward national unity but also Spain's profound social transformations, its heightened role in an expanding world, and its novel artistic expressions.[1] *Celestina* stands as a bridge between a rural society based on traditional honor and an urban one preoccupied with material ostentation,[2] between the moralizing concerns of the Middle Ages and the heady sensuality of the Renaissance.

The book begins with a passionate declaration of love by the young nobleman Calisto to the enchanting Melibea in the latter's garden (or, some critics allege, in a church). When she spurns his advances, the disconsolate Calisto returns home and pours out his woes to Sempronio, one of his two servants, who encourages Calisto to retain the services of Celestina, "former whore, now brothel keeper, witch repairer of broken maidenheads, peddler of cosmetics and quack medicines."[3] As the work progresses, Celestina enlists the support of Calisto's servants, both of whom are tempted by the carnal rewards promised by Celestina as well as by the material riches that the lovesick Calisto is only too willing to dispense to acquire his prize.

In order to gain entrance to Melibea's house, Celestina arrives as a peddler and, once inside, explains that Calisto is afflicted with a malady that only prayer to Saint Apollonia and a belt that has touched holy relics can cure. The compassionate—and curious—Melibea offers her belt to Celestina, who in turn presents it to the deliriously happy Calisto, from whom she receives a gold chain for her success. Calisto's servants insist on sharing in the spoils and, when Celestina resists, they murder her. Both servants are then summarily executed.

Unconcerned with the untimely demise of either Celestina or his servants, Calisto initiates a month-long series of clandestine rendezvous with Melibea. On one of these nocturnal trysts, Calisto, who is ascending a ladder to reach his beloved, slips and falls to his death. The distraught Melibea climbs to the tower of her house and, after confessing the story of the couple's illicit love to Pleberio, her father, casts herself to the ground. The work concludes with a lament by the disillusioned Pleberio on the cruelty of the world and fortune.

Fernando de Rojas, the author of this profoundly moral but nonetheless pessimistic text, reveals himself in an acrostic spanning eleven octaves: "EL BACHJLLER FERNANDO DE ROYAS ACABO LA COMEDJA DE CALYSTO Y MELYBEA Y FVE NASCJDO EN LA PVEBLA DE MONTALVAN" ("The Bachiller Fernando de Rojas Completed the 'Comedy of Calisto and Melibea' and Was Born in La Puebla de Montalbán").[4] This ostensibly innocuous disclosure obliges us to confront the thorny problem of authorship, since Rojas claims in his introductory letter to an anonymous friend ("El autor a un su amigo") that he discovered the first act of the *Comedia* already written and, recognizing its great merit, resolved to complete the work during a fifteen-day break from his legal studies.[5] Scholars have endeavored to identify this unnamed writer as Juan de Mena or Rodrigo Cota or, alternatively, to deny Rojas's assertion of the existence of another author. The critical dust has yet to settle on this issue, although it appears to me that, barring further evidence to the contrary, Rojas's claim of dual authorship should be accepted.

As already noted, Fernando de Rojas was born around 1475 in La Puebla de Montalbán, in the province of Toledo, and it is here that he spent his childhood. His most assiduous biographer, the late Stephen

Gilman, estimated that he left for Salamanca to begin his university studies when he was perhaps eighteen years old and that he completed his bachelor of law degree and remained there until 1501 or 1502.[6] By this time, he had seen the *Comedia* published, and he had presumably finished the *Tragicomedia*, although the editio princeps is no longer extant. After returning to La Puebla de Montalbán, where he spent some five years, Rojas moved to Talavera de la Reina, in Castile, to set up his legal practice. Gilman speculates that Rojas envisioned Talavera to be a more hospitable locale for a young converso professional than, for example, Toledo. About this same time, that is, 1507, Rojas married Leonor Alavarez, who brought him a dowry of eighty thousand maravedís and then bore him seven children. Rojas spent the remainder of his prosperous life in Talavera, serving for a brief period as *alcalde mayor*. Apparently never again did Rojas exercise his exceptional literary talents; furthermore, despite the renown of *Celestina*, its author enjoyed only local notoriety. Rojas died in early April 1541 and was buried in the convent of the Mother of God, wrapped, as he had requested, in a Franciscan habit.

Within these spare biographical details concerning Fernando de Rojas we have only hinted at the pivotal feature of his existence and the touchstone for a good deal of *Celestina* criticism during the past two decades: Rojas's converso status and its implications for our understanding of *Celestina*. Inquisitorial documents involving Rojas were first brought to light by Manuel Serrano y Sanz in 1902 and were later supplemented by the investigations of Fernando del Valle Lersundi, a descendant of Rojas, who also published Rojas's will and described the contents of his library.[7] These documents include the transcript of the 1525 trial of Rojas's father-in-law, Alvaro de Montalbán, and a seventeenth-century patent of nobility.[8] Gilman used this and other material to weave a complex tapestry of the life and times of Rojas, in which he sought to reveal the precariousness of converso life in general and that of Rojas in particular. According to this view, *Celestina* can be rightly understood only within the context of converso insecurity, alienation, and anguish. Indeed, much of the irony and skepticism permeating the work is explicable in terms of Rojas's own disenchantment with the world around him, a world poisoned by mutual suspicion and fear, a world in which even ostensibly innocuous acts could produce mortal consequences.

It will hardly come as a surprise that Gilman's provocative thesis, perhaps inspired by the same muse that had animated his teacher, Américo Castro, engendered both passionate assent and rancorous demurral. Defenders argued that *Celestina* accurately and movingly reflects the atmosphere of uncertainty and pessimism that dogged conversos and their descendants, whereas critics discounted much of Gilman's thesis, labeling his work self-indulgent, partisan, and impressionistic.[9]

In any event, rarely has an academic holiday proved more fruitful than the fifteen days Fernando de Rojas alleged to have devoted to the composition of his *Comedia de Calisto y Melibea*.[10] Although it is improbable that Rojas, at the time a law student at the University of Salamanca, penned his masterwork in but little more than a fortnight—Clara Louisa Penney sniffed that it was not "the product of a student's brain"[11]—what is undeniable is the instant success of his literary venture. The first extant edition of the *Comedia*, containing sixteen acts, was printed by Fadrique de Basilea in Burgos, probably in 1499.[12] During the next two years, the *Comedia* appeared in Toledo, Seville, and possibly Salamanca; today only three exemplars exist, and each presents the text in a somewhat different manner.

The public's enthusiastic reception of the *Comedia* encouraged Rojas to take up his pen once again and add five more acts to the original sixteen. The enlarged and revised work now displayed a new title—*Tragicomedia de Calisto y Melibea*—and was published sometime between 1502 and 1504, perhaps in Seville, although no copy of this edition survives. Readers' appetites were insatiable; in the course of the next fifteen years, the *Tragicomedia* appeared in Seville, Toledo, Salamanca, Saragossa, and Valencia, and by 1634 some 109 Spanish editions had been published.[13]

Nowhere is it more true than in publishing that success breeds excess; thus, the Spanish literary world was treated in 1526 to a twenty-two-act version of the *Tragicomedia*, the additional—mediocre—act having been authored by an enterprising but rather obscure writer, perhaps Sanabria.[14] Fourteen years later, Juan Sedeño, a jurist, put the entire *Tragicomedia* into rhymed couplets.[15] About the same time, another jurist composed, as lawyers are wont, an extensive gloss on the work, in the process providing a unique contemporary perspective.[16] And, as if anticipating Hollywood's motto that one should go with a winner, literary sequels to *Celestina,* as the work was commonly known, included *La segunda Celestina, La tercera Celestina,* and *La hija de Celestina* (The Second Celestina, The Third Celestina, and Celestina's Daughter).[17] Given the abundance of editions and offshoot works dedicated to *Celestina,* not even the hugely successful *Don Quixote* would achieve such a publishing triumph by its first centenary. And we have yet to mention those foreign offspring!

The *Tragicomedia's* fortune was largely due to the allure of the work's main character, Celestina. In fact, in the Seville edition of ca. 1518, Celestina appears alongside Calisto and Melibea in the newly titled *Libro de Calixto y Melibea y dela puta vieja Celestina* (Book of Calisto and Melibea and of the Old Bawd Celestina). During the next few years, well-known writers, such as Luis Vives and Juan de Valdés, began to refer to the work simply as *Celestina.* By 1595 the priority of Celestina had become so firmly established that the title page now read *Celestina. Tragicomedia de Calisto y Melibea* (Celestina. Tragicomedy of Calisto and Melibea). Today, Celestina's literary apotheosis is complete, and many editions are known by the concise title *[La] Celestina.*[18]

Celestina's appeal to generations of Spaniards is by now evident; at least as striking is the book's fascination for a broader European public. In 1505, a mere six years after the appearance of the first Spanish edition, "Alphonso de Hordognez, nato hispano," a writer associated with that epitome of Renaissance patrons, Pope Julius II (1503–1513), translated the *Tragicomedia* into Italian and witnessed its publication in Rome the following year.[19] Within a year or two, Yosef ben Shmuel Zarfati, likewise attached to the household of Julius II, rendered *Celestina* into Hebrew, probably basing it on Ordóñez's Italian version. This text will be discussed in greater detail at the conclusion of this brief survey of non-Spanish editions.

In 1520, in Augsburg, Christof Wirsung published the first of his two German translations (the second, *Ainn recht liepliches Buechlin,* appeared in 1534), likely based on a 1519 Venice edition, with the enchanting title *Ain hipsche Tragedia.*[20]

The first English translation of *Celestina,* actually a verse arrangement of the opening four acts, debuted around 1530 as *A new comodye in englysh in maner of an enterlude.*[21] This truncated adaptation, attributed to its printer, John Rastell, is flawed by an utterly incongruous ending, aptly summarized by Penney:

After Celestina's interview with Melebea, the father of the heroine appears with an account of a dream, in which he has seen her lured by a 'foule roughe bych' to the brink of a foul pit. Thereupon, Melebea interprets the dream, and repents aloud of her sins, while her father points the moral in a long discourse upon the efficacy of prayer, the importance of youthful training and the remedial function of wise laws.[22]

British interest in *Celestina* continued to manifest itself in the curious—and no longer extant—late sixteenth-century *The delightful history of Celestina the faire*, culminating in the sprightly 1631 translation by James Mabbe, also known as Diego Puedeser, *Celestine or the Tragick-Comedie of Calisto and Melibea*.[23]

Celestina first appeared in French in 1527 simply as *Celestine*, the work of an anonymous translator, and went through twenty-two more editions, up to the bilingual Spanish-French edition in 1634 of Charles Osmont Roven.[24] The first Flemish version, *Celestina. Ende is een Tragicomodie van Calisto eñ Melibea*, is from 1550, and was followed by three more sixteenth-century editions.[25]

Surely the most curious translation of *Celestina* is Kaspar von Barth's Latin version, *Pornoboscodidascalvs latinvs*, which Theodore S. Beardsley, Jr., observes "is not Classical Latin but rather a string of Greek words, Latinized, and then built on German word formation."[26] Beardsley's English rendition of the title is "Exposé of a Redlight House Keeper." To date, Barth's translation has been cited most often within the context of the polemic concerning putative didacticism in *Celestina*.

In sum, by the mid seventeenth century, *Celestina* had enjoyed at least one translation into Latin, four into German, four into English, five into Flemish, nineteen into Italian, and twenty-four into French.[27] Although *Celestina* suffered a decline in popularity after 1650, the present century has witnessed an international resurgence of interest, as evidenced by translations into Arabic, Croatian, Czech, Danish, Hebrew, Hungarian, Japanese, Polish, Romanian, and Russian. In addition to these linguistic transformations, *Celestina* has metamorphosed, in ways that would make Ovid blush, into ballads, ballets, poems, operas, theater, and, of course, films, the last a risqué Spanish production titillatingly titled *Los placeres del sexo* (The Pleasures of Sex).[28]

The foregoing provides some idea of the extraordinary plenitude both of *Celestina*'s Spanish progeny and of her foreign offspring. In the case of *Celestina*, as in real life, her children did not all enjoy the same fate. Some have vanished completely, the only record of their passing being the succinct bibliographic entry of an impassive scholar; others have fallen in with false friends and unsavory companions—those editors, playwrights, translators, and their ilk—who have corrupted the text and ravaged the message; still others of *Celestina*'s children have prospered, that is to say, they survive as university texts, while the obscure offspring were unable to enter even the academic world.

Notwithstanding the appeal of many of *Celestina*'s foreign children, my personal favorite is one that survived but a short time. I refer to the aforementioned Hebrew translation by Yosef ben Shmuel Zarfati.[29] Zarfati, also known as Giuseppe Gallo, belonged to an illustrious Jewish family renowned for its medical services to four popes, including the bellicose Julius II and the prodigal patron of the arts Leo X (1513–1521). In addition to his role as papal physician, Zarfati cultivated philosophy and mathematics and was admired for his linguistic prowess in Hebrew, Aramaic, Arabic, Greek, and Latin. He was recognized as the author of celebrated Hebrew love poetry and scintillating Latin orations, evidence of the classical milieu in which bright young Jewish literati distinguished themselves, much as did their Christian counterparts. We see in Zarfati the Renaissance ideal of the *homo universalis*, as well as the *ḥakham kolel*, the comprehensive scholar, one who was as comfortable with secular learning as with rabbinic Judaism.[30] Zarfati befriended an astonishing spectrum of people, from David Reubeni, the messianic pretender, to Pope Clement VII, with whom Zarfati shared his home for a brief time, when the pope found his own palace intolerably noisy. After a lifetime of adventures, Zarfati met an untimely death by plague during the sack of Rome in 1527.

Zarfati's translation of *Celestina*, the first comedy to appear in Hebrew, was completed in 1507 or 1508, less than a decade after the appearance of the first extant Castilian edition of the *Comedia* and only two or three years after Ordóñez had completed the first Italian version of the *Tragicomedia*.[31] Zarfati's rendition is, unfortunately, no longer extant, and we must therefore be content with his sixty-two-line introductory poem.

At the outset, the poet exhorts the reader to heed the plight of lovers caught in the tangle of Love and to beware the seditious servants, whose feet are swift to commit violence, as well the crafty crones, who ensnare their victims (11.1–15). Zarfati then details Love's calamitous effects: She fills men's hearts with fear, She abases the haughty, and She burdens young men and old with Her yoke (11.16–28). Alas, only extravagant presents will soften a woman's heart (11.29–37). Moving abruptly from his cynical criticism of acquisitive women to the praise of modest maidens, Zarfati returns to a zealous condemnation of feminine wiles (11.38–50). Citing Melibea by name and alluding to Calisto, the poet proclaims them to be examples for all who love and desire. The conclusion of the poem (11.51–62) identifies the author and reveals his purpose in translating *Celestina*.

Despite its brevity, Zarfati's poem is replete with biblical, talmudic, and liturgical allusions, most of which were identified by Moshe David Cassuto in his 1935 edition and study of the poem.[32] These passages are often used to underscore the destructive tendencies of love, the coercive power of wealth, and the dangers of evil women. The mere presence of didactic material, however, does not necessarily signify didactic intent. Indeed, Zarfati reveals toward the end of the poem that he translated *Celestina* "to gladden the poor, the downcast to soothe" (1.55). Anticipating his detractors' censure, the poet thunders: "The scoffers against me amassed / Shall receive the same as they give. / And when they are brought to account, / Hell shall not allow them to live" (11.57–58). And, as if to dispel any lingering hopes of those seeking a didactic end, Zarfati encourages his audience to abandon itself to the pursuit of the (vicarious?) amorous experience embodied in the succeeding words: "May God grant you good gifts, and may / Your radiance soon be displayed / When that graceful one lights your heart, / And in fervid flames you hover. / Awaken, and hurry as one; / Hark, friends, to the war of lovers" (11.60–62).[33]

A Poem Composed by the Poet for the Translation of "The Treatise of Melibea and Calisto"[34]

1. Hark, friends, to the war of lovers
Entrapped in Passion's tempting snare;

2. The discourse, too, as both debate
With honeyed words and fables fair;

3. The fierce rage and dread of maidens,
In whom reproof and love combine;

4. The dulcet words to charming girls,
Which on impassioned lips recline.

5. Behold the arms they wield in their desire,
As well the servants' scorn and schemes.

6. Their arms are arms of violence;
Destruction and distress their dreams.[35]

7. They plot to steal their master's name;
Revolt each moment they prepare.

8. And there you'll find the cunning crones,[36]
and how they lay their traps e'erwhere;

9. And there the words maidservants speak,
Aflame in lovers' hearts to light.

10. Their mistresses they state with gall
And wormwood; suspicions they ignite.

11. And there the voice of lovers sad, in pain;
Limbs rent asunder, they cry out.

12. Their bitter tears, their pleas for help;
Wretched, they roam among the rout.

13. And there you'll find their cries, their sighs,
and how they quaver with each blow.

14. So too their pangs of sorrow and grief;[37]
Like outcast poor they vent their woe.

15. A brazen vamp despoils Calcol,[38]
Along with all men wise, renowned.

16. Oppressed, unshod, they wander by
The thousands, scattered all around.

17. I shall tell their tales and travails;
The myriad hardships they bear;

18. Weary, they stumble and perish
From onerous burdens unshared.

19. There is no wisdom nor advice;
No one to correct nor direct

20. The feet of a man in fetters,
Secured by maids with wrath unchecked.[39]

21. On what will lovers fix their eyes?
And where will lovers find support?

22. In love there's none who pities nor
Is kind; nowhere a sheltered port.[40]

23. She'll break and then entomb a man;
She'll fill with fear a warrior's heart;

24. She'll chasten and bring low the proud;
She'll rip a strong man's pride apart.

25. Enraged, She'll cast men wise and famed
Outside of Reason's lofty hall;

26. Enslaved, officials young and old
Beneath her baneful yoke do crawl.

27. The fools deceitfully intone
Their chants; Love's praise they sing in vain;

28. Her deeds are nought but barren winds
And clouds on high bereft of rain.[41]

29. For naught are songs to win *les femmes*,
And mothers' plaints o'er their lost sons.[42]

30. Gifts of silver and of raiment touch
The young belles' hearts; all else they shun.

31. And gold exalts, enchants the swain,
And brings forth spikenard from each thorn;

32. Gold is a prince, ennobling men
And bringing joy to aged and newborn.[43]

33. Hard hearts will melt with presents rich,
And necklaces will calm fierce ire.

34. Grant gifts and favors to young girls;
To comely women fine attire.

35. For bracelets are the price of love,
And nose rings anger will allay.

36. With these, her lover she'll desire,
And kiss, and satisfy in every way.[44]

37. No longer brazen, she'll prepare
The food to slake his appetite.[45]

38. Howbeit, modest ones, 'tis best
To turn aside from her delights.

39. David and Solomon attest
To you of women's guile and bonds;

40. In them reside angels of death,
As well a devil and his throngs.

41. Each day they carry off the sons
Of men; all creatures they oppress.[46]

42. Escape their charms; discern their flaws,
Polluted flesh in comely dress.

43. Abhor their looks, for in the end
They'll thrust a skewer through your heart.[47]

44. Fools are they who yield to them,
And from their worship ne'er depart.

45. Young lovers, all, observe the case[48]
Of Melibea and her friend:

46. Veer from the path of Gentile lust;[49]
Above all, flee its fiery end.

47. Snuff out the flame that burns your heart;
Expunge it from your very core.

48. O remnant company, rejoice,
Incline your ears, give heed, therefore:

49. Is it wise, my friends and noble lords,
To be shamed, in maidens' traps to land?

50. Or be like deer without their horns?
Or rams bound by a woman's hand?

51. I am Joseph, son of Rav Samuel,
Prince of those who serve the one God;[50]

52. A spring of wisdom and counsel;
Support for the tent of Yaacov.[51]

53. He is called Ẓarfati, servant
Of the most exalted of sovereigns:

54. Julius, high priest of the nations,
Who destroyed the pride of the vain.

55. Truly, my tongue has rendered this work
To gladden the poor, the downcast to soothe.[52]

56. Its essence alone I arrange
And transmit to my fellow Jews.[53]

57. The scoffers against me amassed
Shall receive the same as they give.

58. And when they are brought to account,
Hell shall not allow them to live.

59. Judge me kindly, O my people,
Pious ones in finery arrayed.

60. May God grant you good gifts, and may
Your radiance soon be displayed,

61. When that graceful one lights your heart,
And in fervid flames you hover.

62. Awaken, and hurry as one;
Hark, friends, to the war of lovers.

שיר חברו המשורר על העתקת חבור מֶליבֵיאה וקלִיסטו

‎‑ ‑ ‑ ◡ ‑ ◡ ‑

פְּנוּ, דּוֹדִים, לְמִלְחֶמֶת יְדִידִים,   אֲשֶׁר הֵמָּה בְּפַח חֵשֶׁק לְכוּדִים,

וּמַעְנֵיהֶם בְּהִנָּכַח שְׁנֵיהֶם   בְּטוּב מִלִּים וּבִמְשָׁלִים חֲמוּדִים,

וְעֹז חֵמוֹת וְאֵימוֹת הָעֲלָמוֹת,   מְרִיבָתָן וְאַהֲבָתָן צְמָדִים,

וּמַמְתַּקִּים אֲשֶׁר בִּשְׂפַת חֲשׁוּקִים   בְּדַבְּרָם אֶל־בְּנוֹת הַחֵן נְגִידִים,

5   כְּלִי נִשְׁקָם בְּהָאָבְקָם בְּחָשְׁקָם,   וּמַהְתַּלּוֹת וְתַחְבּוּלוֹת עֲבָדִים,

וְנִכְלֵיהֶם כְּלֵי חָמָס כְּלֵיהֶם,   לְשׂוּם שֶׁבֶר בְּלֵב נָבָר וּפִידִים,

וְקִשְׁרָם עַל־כְּבוֹד בַּעַל לְגַנְּבוֹ,   וּמֹרְדִים בּוֹ בְּכָל־עִתּוֹת מְרָדִים;

וְשָׁם עָרְמוֹת וּמִרְמוֹת הַזְּקֵנוֹת,   וְאֵיךְ פְּרֵשׂוֹת בְּכָל־חוּצוֹת מְצוֹדִים,

וְשָׁם שִׂיחוֹת תְּדַבֵּרְנָה שְׂפָחוֹת   לְהַדְלִיק אֵשׁ בְּלֵב דּוֹדִים וְאוּדִים,

10   וְתַרְנֶינָה גְבִירוֹת רֹאשׁ וְלַעֲנָה   בְּהַרְבּוֹתָן, בְּקִרְבָתָן, חֲשָׁדִים,

וְקוֹל אֹהֲבִים בְּמַכְאוֹבִים עֲצֵבִים   יְצוּרֵיהֶם בְּצִירֵיהֶם פְּרוּדִים;

בְּכִי דִמְעָם, נְהִי שַׁוְעָם, וְשַׁבְעָם,   בְּאַף זַעַם בְּנִבְזֵי עָם נְדוּדִים,

וְצִוְחָתָם, וְאַנְחָתָם, וְאֵיךְ הֵם
וְנֵם־חַבְּלָם בְּצִיר הַבְלָם וְאָבְלָם,
15 וְשָׁבַת כָּל־נְבוֹנֵי עָם כְּכָלְכָל
מְנֻגָּפִים יַחְפִּים לַאֲלָפִים,
אָחוּ שִׂיחָם, נְדוֹד אָרְחָם, וְטָרְחָם
וְהָעֵת יִכְשְׁלוּ, יִבְלוּ וְיִכְלוּ,
וְאֵין בִּינָה, וְאֵין עֵצָה נְכוֹנָה,
20 לְנָבָר גָּבְרוּ עָלָיו עֲלָמוֹת,
וּבַמֶּה יִשְׁעֵנוּ שָׁעִים בָּאֹהֲבִים,
וְאֵין בָּאַהֲבָה מַחְסֶה וּמִכְסָה,
וְהִיא תְשַׁבֵּר גְּוִיַּת אִישׁ וְתִקְבֹּר,
וְהִיא תַשְׁפִּיל גְּבֹהַּ רוּחַ וְתַפִּיל,
25 מָתַי הַשֵּׁם וְהַשֵּׂכָל תְּנֵרְשֵׁם
וּמֵעֶדְנָה וְעַד־זִקְנָה וְשֵׂיבָה
שְׁבָחֶיהָ בְּכָל־עֵת הָאֱוִילִים
אֲדָמָה פָּעֲלָה הֶעְדֵּר גְּשָׁמַי
וְשָׁוְא שִׁירוֹת לְפַתּוֹת הַגְּבִירוֹת,
30 וְאַךְ כָּסָף לְבַב יַעֲלוֹת יֶאֱסַף,
וְהַזָּהָב יִנַּשֵׂא דוֹד וְיִרְהַב,
וְהוּא נָשִׂיא וְהוּא יַשִּׂיא אֲנָשִׁים,
וְרֹב מַשְׂאוֹת יְשִׁיבוּן לֵב צְבָאוֹת,
תְּנוּ מָנוֹת וּמַתָּנוֹת לָעֲפָרוֹת,
35 הֲכִי קִצְפָּן יָרַף נָזֵם בְּאַפָּן,
וְכֵן עָפְרָה בְדוֹד תַּחְשֹׁק וְתֶחְשַׁק,
וְלֹא תָזִיד כְּדַרְכָּהּ עוֹד, וְתָזִיד
אֲבָל מַה־טּוֹב וּמַה־נָּעִים, צְנוּעִים,
לְנִכְלֵיהָן וְכֵכְלֵיהָן שְׁלֹמֹה
40 בְּקָרְבָּן מַלְאֲכֵי מָוֶת יָגוּרוֹן,
וְאֵלֶּה שֵׁדִים יוֹם יוֹם בְּנֵי אִישׁ
בָּרַח יָפָן, רְאֵה דָפָן, הֲכִי הֵן

בְּכָל־רָגַע בְּכָל־פֶּגַע חֲרֵדִים,
בְּתַת מִלִּים כְּמוֹ דַלִּים מְרוּדִים,
בְּיַד אִשָּׁה, בְּלִי בוּשָׁה, שְׁדוּדִים,
וְנִדָּפִים בְּכָל־פִּנּוֹת וְנָדִים.
בְּסָבְלָם מַעֲמַס אַלְפֵי פְרָדִים,
בְּמַשּׂוֹאוֹת מְאֹד מֵהֶם כְּבֵדִים.
וְאֵין מַכְשִׁיר וְאֵין מַיְשִׁיר צְעָדִים
וְשָׂמוּ בָחֲרִי רַגְלָיו בְּסַדִּים.
וְאֵיפֹה יִמְצְאוּ סָמָךְ סְעָדִים?
וְאֵין חֹמֶל, וְאֵין גֹּמֵל חֲסָדִים.
וְהִיא תִצְבֹּר בְּלֵב גִּבּוֹר פְּחָדִים,
וְהִיא תַעֲבִיר גְּאוֹן מַגְבִּיר גְּדוּדִים.
בְּאַף, מִהְיוֹת בְּבֵית עֶלְיוֹן פְּקִידִים;
בְּעֶלָּה יַעַבְדוּן לָהּ פְּקוּדִים.
בְּשֶׁקֶר עֶרְכִים נֶגְדָּהּ וּבַדִּים;
וְשָׁמַי מָלְאוּ רוּחוֹת וְאֵדִים.
וְרִיק לַהֲמוֹת כָּאֻמּוֹת עַל יְחִידִים,
וְתַת רֵעִים צְעִיפִים עִם רְדִידִים,
וְיַצְמִיד בְּכָל־חֹחַ נְרָדִים,
וְהוּא יַנְעִים יָשִׂישִׂים עִם יְלָדִים,
וְרֹב חָרוֹן עֲלֵי נֶרוֹן רְבִידִים.
וְלַיְפוֹת חֲלִיפוֹת כָּל־בְּגָדִים!
וְתַת דּוֹדָן עֲלֵי יָדָן צְמִידִים.
תְּרַוְּנֻהוּ כְחָפְצֵהוּ מְנָדִים,
כְּמֵאָנְתּוּ לְשָׁבְעָתוֹ נְזִידִים.
נְטוֹת מָנָה, וְסוּר אֶל הַצְּדָדִים!
וְדָוִד הֵם שְׁנֵיהֶם לָךְ שְׁהֵדִים.
וְשָׂעִיר עִם הֲמוֹן שָׂדוֹת וְשֵׁדִים,
בְּכִשְׁפֵיהֶן, וְכָל־חַי מַאֲבִידִים.
כְּלֵי נֵדֶה בְּסוּת חָמְדָה אֲפוּדִים.

מָאַס צֹפָן, הֲכִי סוֹפָן צְנִינִים

כְּסִילִים הֵם אֲשֶׁר נַעֲנִים אֲלֵיהָן,

45 וּמַלִּיבֵיאָה לְכָל-רַעְיָה, וְדוֹדָה

וְיִטּוּ מִנְתִיב חֵשֶׁק לְאָמִּי,

וּמַלְבָּם יְכַבּוּהוּ וְקִרְבָּם,

פְּנֵה אֵלַי, וְהֵט אֹזֶן לְמֵלַי,

הֲטוֹב תִּהְיוּ לְבוּז, רֵעַי וְשׁוֹעַי,

50 בְּאֵין אֱיָל וְקַרְנִי עֹז, כְּאַיִל

אֲנִי יוֹסֵף בְּנוֹ הָרַב שְׁמוּאֵל,

מְקוֹר חָכְמָה וּמַעְיָן כָּל-מְזִמָּה,

וְצָרְפָתִי יְכַנּוּהוּ, הֲלֹא הוּא

אָדוֹן יוּלְיוֹס, וְכֹהֵן רֹאשׁ לְאָמִּים,

55 אֱמָת הָעָתִּיק לְשׁוֹנִי זָה, לְהַמְתִּיק

וְרַק עִנְיָן אֲנִי מַעְתִּיק, וְעֵרֶךְ

עֲדַת לַצִים אֲשֶׁר נֶגְדִּי חֲלוּצִים

וּבְעֶרְגָה בָם לְלֹא חִנָּם נֵיהִנָּם,

וְדִינוּנִי בְזֹאת לִזְכוּת, הֲמוֹנִי,

60 וְחִישׁ יִזְרַח עֲלֵי רֹאשְׁכֶם מְאוֹרְכֶם,

בְּהַדְלִיק אֶת-לְבַבְכֶם יַעֲלַת-חֵן,

כְּאָחָד מַהֲרוּ עוּרוּ וְסוּרוּ,

שְׁנוּנִים בָּךְ, וְתוֹךְ לְבָךְ שְׁפוּדִים.

מְשֻׁנָּעִים אֲשֶׁר כְּרֵעִים וּמוֹדִים.

לְנֵס אָקִים לְכָל-חֲשֵׁקִים וְדוֹדִים.

וְאֵשׁוֹ יִבְרְחוּ מִכָּל-יְקוֹדִים,

וְשָׁרְשָׁיו יְעֹרוּ עַד יְסוֹדִים.

וּבִי תִצְהַל, עֲדַת וּקְהַל שְׂרִידִים.

בְּחַרְמֵי יַעֲלוֹת יַחְדָּו אֲגוּדִים,

וְכִתְיָשִׁים בְּיַד נָשִׁים עֲקוּדִים?

נְשִׂיא לַמְיֻחָדִים, דָּת מַעֲמִידִים,

לְאֹהֶל יַעֲקֹב מִשְׁעָן יְתֵדִים,

אֲשֶׁר שֵׂרַת גָּדוֹל מֹשְׁלִים וְרֹדִים,

אֲשֶׁר הַשָּׁמַיִם גְּאוֹן רָמִים וְזֵדִים.

עֲנִי רָשִׁים וְלֵב אִישִׁים טְרוּדִים,

פְּאֵר שִׂיחִי לְאַחַי הַיְהוּדִים.

הֲלֹא יִהְיוּ בְּמִדָּתָם מְדוּדִים,

אֲשֶׁר שָׁם הֵם לְתֵת הַדִּין עֲתִידִים.

חֲסִידִים כָּל-עֲדֵי חֶמְדָּה עֲנוּדִים;

וְיִזְבָּדְכֶם אֱלֹהִים טוֹב זְבָדִים,

וְתִחְיוּן תּוֹךְ יְקָר חֵילִים וְאֵידִים.

פְּנוּ, דוֹדִים, לְמִלְחָמַת יְדִידִים.

תם נשלם תל"ח.

15

Sephardic Ceremonial Art: Continuity in the Diaspora

Vivian B. Mann

Basic to any understanding of continuities between the Jewish ceremonial art of the Iberian peninsula and the ceremonial art of the Sephardic diaspora is a reconstruction of the corpus of peninsular Judaica. Unlike the hundreds of Hebrew manuscripts that were carried into exile,[1] only eleven works of ceremonial art are extant, half the result of planned or chance excavations.[2] Still a larger corpus is discernible on the basis of four types of evidence:

1. The small group of eleven extant objects.
2. A somewhat larger series of genre illustrations in fourteenth-century Haggadot depicting Passover rituals in the home and synagogue.[3]
3. Texts of Spanish responsa that mention ritual objects.[4]
4. Types of objects common only to the communities of the Sephardic diaspora and unknown in Ashkenazic congregations of the same period. These include the split skirt mantle and the decorated marriage contract, to be discussed below.

Often, the existence of a particular sort of object is attested to by more than one type of evidence, providing a fuller picture of its appearance and use by the Spanish community.

Extant Objects

Eleven ceremonial objects remain from Jewish Spain. The earliest is a trough from the fifth century that is decorated with symbols commonly found on Jewish ritual objects dating from the Roman Empire: the menorah, the tree of life, and a form that has been interpreted as both a shofar and a ram's horn (fig. 15.1).[5] The exact purpose of this 56.5 × 46 cm trough found in Tarragona is uncertain. It may have been a child's sarcophagus or a water basin for ritual ablutions.

With one exception, the remaining works are all late-dated to the fourteenth and fifteenth centuries, and most are made from base materials. The exception with regard to date is a twelfth-century horizontal Hanukkah lamp of stone that was quarried at St. Beat in the Pyrenees.[6] A bronze Hanukkah lamp, also of northern Spanish or southern French manufacture, was discovered in the old Jewish quarter of Lyons (and must date from before 1394, when the Jews of that city were expelled),[7] and three fragmentary fifteenth-century ceramic Hanukkah lamps were found in Teruel during excavations of the *juderia* conducted in 1977 (fig. 15.2).[8] (Presumably, future excavations will enlarge the corpus presented here.)[9]

Another ceramic piece is a seder plate in the Israel Museum (fig. 15.3),[10] which is similar in form and decoration to other fifteenth-century plates made for Christians and Muslims.[11] Many of these plates bear bastardized inscriptions that may indicate the ignorance of the potters or some other deliberate purpose. One Haggadah illustration suggests that chargers like the Jerusalem Passover Plate were used to dis-

FIGURE 15.1. Basin with trilingual inscription, Tarragona, fifth century, marble. Museo Sefardi, Toledo. *Photo courtesy the Museo Sefardi.*

FIGURE 15.2. Hanukkah lamp fragment, Teruel, fifteenth century, ceramic. I. G. 7.167. Museo de Teruel. *Photo courtesy the Museo de Teruel.*

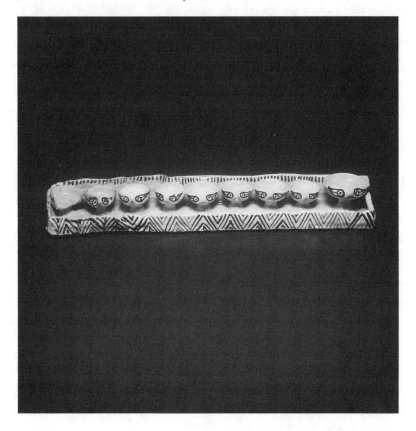

tribute matzot to the community before the seder, rather than at the seder itself, just as some of the Christian chargers were used for the distribution of candles.[12] Also extant is an intriguing Teruel ceramic plate that is today in the Museu de Ceramica in Barcelona (fig. 15.4).[13] It is not included in the census of extant objects, however, since it was not scientifically excavated, and it does not bear Hebrew inscriptions; nor is any plate of this type depicted in the Haggadot. Still, its unique form, without parallels in Islamic or Christian art, indicates it may have been a seder plate: five small containers, a suitable number for the symbolic foods of the seder, rise from the surface, each decorated with a ḥamsa.

FIGURE 15.3. Passover plate, probably Valencia, ca. 1480, ceramic. Israel Museum, Jerusalem. *Photo courtesy Nachum Slapak.*

A less convincing case for Jewish usage of a museum object without significant known provenance has lately been made for a tower-form receptacle that has been in the Victoria and Albert Museum since 1855.[14] Its horseshoe arches indicate an Iberian origin; but it may have been a monstrance, a reliquary, rather than a Jewish spice container for havdalah, the ceremony that separates Sabbaths and holy days from ordinary workdays. The several depictions of the havdalah ceremony in Spanish Haggadot do not include such a container,[15] and the only literary source prior to the thirteenth-century date ascribed to the object is an Ashkenazic one.[16] Further, Sephardic Jews are known to have used

myrtle branches, rather than dried spices, for the aromatic substance required in the havdalah ceremony.[17]

Literary sources, in particular responsa, aid in identifying another
rare work from medieval Spain as a synagogue furnishing. This example
is the rug, found in a church in the Tyrol in 1880, which is the oldest relatively complete Spanish rug in existence (fig. 15.5).[18] Today measuring
125 × 37 inches, its main decoration is the "sacred tree" composition,
well-known from Islamic art. What is unusual are the forms of the
flowers: gabled, horned shrines with paneled bivalve doors. There are no
parallels for this motif in Islamic art, but there are in Jewish art, particularly the synagogue mosaics of the Byzantine period, such as the one at
Beit Alpha.[19] Although this parallel was long cited in art historical literature,[20] some Islamicists were reluctant to ascribe Jewish patronage to

FIGURE 15.4. Passover plate?, Teruel, fifteenth century, ceramic. Museo de
Ceramica, Ajuntament de Barcelona. *Photo courtesy the Museo de Ceramica.*

FIGURE 15.5. Synagogue rug, Spain, fourteenth century, wool. I. 27. Staatliches Museen zu Berlin, Islamisches Museum. *Photo courtesy the Staatliches Museen zu Berlin, Islamisches Museum.*

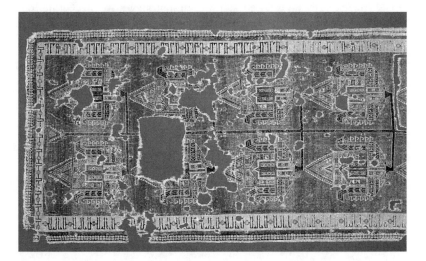

the rug, since they could not imagine any use for such an object in the synagogue.[21] A responsum of Rabbenu Asher, however, dated between 1304 and 1327 (the dates of his arrival in Spain and his death), discusses the use of rugs in the synagogue for two purposes: hanging beside the Torah ark as decoration and for seating.

> You inquired about the matter of the small mat that is called *sajjada* in Arabic, on which it is the custom of the Muslims to pray and that bears an image resembling a black weight, whether it is permitted to hang it in the synagogue next to the ark. . . . In Toledo, they were accustomed to forbid placing such a rug in the synagogue in order to sit on it; certainly it is forbidden to hang it at the side of the ark.[22]

The long, narrow shape of this rug suggests it was used for seating, as were similarly shaped Muslim rugs of the fifteenth century.[23]

Without its Hebrew inscription, it would be difficult to recognize a work in the Cluny Museum, Paris, as a piece of Sephardic Judaica (fig. 15.6). Its form and material are similar to mortars made by Muslims,[24] but the Ladino inscription carved into the stone mentions the year 1319–1320, Queen Esther, and King Ahasueros, suggesting that this may have been a container for the alms collected as part of the ritual requirements of the holiday of Purim.[25]

Hebrew inscriptions also distinguish a pair of fifteenth-century silver finials (fig. 15.7),[26] now set atop processional staves in the Cathedral Treasury of Palma de Mallorca, from other stave ends like the slightly later examples from Valencia in the Victoria and Albert Museum.[27] In late fifteenth-century Spain there appears to have been a fashion for stave ends made in architectural tower forms symbolic of heavenly

FIGURE 15.6. Alms box, Spain, 1319, stone, carved. Cl. 12974. Musée national du Moyen Age des Thermes de Cluny, Paris. *Photo © Reunion des musée nationaux.*

FIGURE 15.7. Torah finial (*rimmon*), Camarata, Sicily, fifteenth century, silver and semiprecious stones. Palma de Majorca, Cathedral Treasury. *Photo courtesy the Jewish Museum, New York, Frank Darmstadter Photo Archives.*

Jerusalem.[28] Perhaps their similarity to church furnishings ensured the survival of the Palma de Mallorca *rimmonim;* following the expulsion they were easily integrated into ecclesiastical furnishings.

Finally, there are decorated Jewish marriage contracts (*ketubbot*) in a number of Spanish archives, both entire documents and fragments, that we will count as one type in the census of extant Spanish Judaica because of their similarity of form and decoration.[29] The oldest is a contract of 1300 written in Tudela (fig. 15.8);[30] its decoration, though crude, is noteworthy in light of a responsum of Rabbi Simon ben Zemah Duran (1361–1444), who praised the practice of decorating ketubbot because it limited the possibility of later tampering with the text.[31]

FIGURE 15.8. Decorated Jewish marriage contract (*ketubbah*), Tudela, 2 Elul 5060 (August 19, 1300), ink and watercolors on parchment, 28 x 56 cm. Caja 192, no. 2. Gobierno de Navarra, Departamento de Educación, Cultura y Deporte, Archivo Real y General, Pamplona, Cámara de Comptos. *Photo courtesy Gobierno de Navarra, Departamento de Educación, Cultura y Deporte, Archivo Real y General, Pamplona.*

The expulsion was, of course, the major factor in the loss of all other Jewish ceremonial art from Spain. Forbidding Jews to exit with gold and silver affected not only individuals and families but also communities.[32] Communal property, including synagogue furnishings, was confiscated by crown commissions who often ceded a portion to local authorities as compensation for lost revenue. The Spanish responsa refer to Torah ornaments, finials, and crowns as being of silver.[33] Sources from Saragossa refer to the melting of such objects as well as the melting of synagogue textiles embroidered with gold and silver in order to extract the bullion.[34]

Another factor affecting the survival of Judaica was the common nature of many of the objects, the result of a lack of specificity in relevant halakhot (Jewish laws). For example, the halakhot concerning kiddush cups require that they contain a certain volume, but their form is not mentioned.[35] Material, decoration, and shape are unspecified. The seder scenes of the Spanish Haggadot show people using metal or glass goblets or beakers.[36] There are no Hebrew inscriptions evident on the cups that would identify them as kiddush cups for later generations. A responsum of the Rashba', Rabbi Solomon ben Abraham Adret (c. 1235–c. 1310) indicates that Spanish Jews used the same cups, or *tazza* (the Spanish term appears in the text), on Passover as they did during the year, after "kashering" them by immersion in scalding water.[37] These cups were not restricted to ritual purposes but were used for everyday drinking. This text suggests one interpretation of the kiddush cups in the Haggadot illustrations and may explain why no Spanish kiddush cups have survived. In effect, there were no cups used exclusively for benedictions, so that at the time of the expulsion cups that had been used for kiddush could easily be taken over by the general population, much as the Nazis confiscated the silver candlesticks of Jewish families.[38]

It is also important to remember that the size of the corpus of Spanish Judaica is smaller than might be expected because various forms of Jewish ceremonial art were not invented until after the expulsion; for example the Torah shield first appears in the sixteenth century.[39] Individuals, similarly, owned few material goods during the Middle Ages compared with later centuries, so that it is not surprising to find few objects represented in seder scenes or in the eating scenes of Christian art from the same period.[40]

Continuity in the Diaspora

Of the eleven Judaica objects extant, only four types continued to be produced in the diaspora: the bronze Hanukkah lamp with architectural backplate,[41] the tower-form rimmonim,[42] rugs,[43] and decorated ketubbot.[44] The lamp type is found, for example, in Italy and Morocco, in both cases reflecting local architecture, while the tower-shaped rimmonim are found in Italy, Holland, and later in Morocco. Italian church traditions similar to those in Spain and the existence of Italian silver workshops producing commissions for both Catholics and Jews encouraged continuity with the late Sephardic pair that were made in Sicily while it was under Spanish rule.[45] Italian tower-form rimmonim then became a model for those of North Africa.

The history of rugs made for Jewish ritual purposes is an interesting one, a case of artistic development dependent on the art of the majority culture.[46] The next extant Jewish rug after the Spanish example is a transitional Mamluk-Ottoman Torah Curtain (fig. 15.9) that appears to have been created by a craftsman from Cairo who worked with a Paduan model either in Padua, where the synagogue still owns the rug, or in Cairo.[47] The gate depicted on it is based on the frontispiece of a Hebrew book printed in Padua in 1567 and the inscription from Psalms (118:20), "This is the gate of the Lord; the righteous shall enter here," is commonly found on other Hebrew books printed in Italy in the sixteenth century, as is the motif of the menorah. The remainder of the decoration is derived from Mamluk and Ottoman sources. The commissioning of such a Torah curtain may have been inspired by the general European "passion" for oriental rugs or as the result of an immigrant Sephardic patron wishing to re-create the synagogue furnishings of Spain.[48]

Since knotted pile rugs were not part of the Italian artistic tradition, their manufacture in Italy was short-lived among Jews and non-Jews. The Sephardim who immigrated to the Ottoman Empire, however, found a rich artistic genre, with the result that rugs for Jewish purposes continued to be produced there into the late nineteenth and early twentieth centuries. One of the earliest is also the finest, the early seventeenth-century rug now in the Textile Museum. It was produced in an Ottoman court atelier similar to that which created the late sixteenth-century Ballard Prayer Rug in the Metropolitan Museum of Art.[49]

FIGURE 15.9. Torah curtain, Padua?, ca. 1550, wool. Padua, Comunita Israelitica.

Following Muslim usage, Ottoman Jews of the eighteenth century also commissioned rugs as bier covers, for example, a rug dated 1789–1790.[50] In the Ottoman Empire, then, rugs used for Torah curtains and other ritual purposes had a long history because the artistic tradition to which they belonged was supported by the host culture.

A similar development took place in Italy in regard to decorated marriage contracts. Shalom Sabar has shown that the earliest decorated Italian contracts can be tied to the settlement of the Sephardim in Venice in 1589.[51] At first, the decoration resembles Spanish manuscripts, as can be seen in a comparison of a 1614 contract written for a groom from the Abravanel family and a bride from the De Paz family, all prominent Sephardim, with the decoration of Spanish Hebrew Bibles.[52] Gradually, the painters adopt motifs and subjects from Italian baroque art. The decorated ketubbah had a long history and rich development in Italy until the present day, whereas in other countries with Sephardic settlement ketubbah decoration tends to be repetitive and uninventive.[53] The different history of Italian ketubbah decoration may be ascribed to the Italian practice of elaborately decorating all kinds of documents, both personal and official, for example, medical school diplomas.[54]

The Evidence of the Haggadot

More extensive evidence for the continuity of Sephardic ceremonial art in the diaspora comes from a comparison of the genre illuminations in fourteenth-century Haggadot with the Judaica of diaspora communities.

The Split Skirt Torah Mantle

In all settlements of the Sephardic diaspora where mantles are used to cover the Torah scroll, the mantle flares outward from the top, is split up the back, and fringed along the edges. Examples from Italy, the Ottoman Empire, Holland, and England are known and suggest a common prototype in Sephardic Spain.[55] Three such mantels are depicted on folio 34r of the Sarajevo Haggadah whose subject is the departure after reading the Haggadah in the synagogue on the eve of Passover (Barcelona, second quarter of fourteenth century; Sarajevo, National Museum; fig. 15.10).[56]

Crown and Finial Sets

The same miniature depicts the scrolls adorned with both crown and finials, the opposite of Ashkenazic usage, but the custom followed in the Sephardic diaspora, for example, in Italy and the Ottoman Empire.[57] Actual diaspora examples were made as units, with crown and finials linked by common decorative motifs, materials, and forms.

FIGURE 15.10. "Synagogue Scene," The Sarajevo Haggadah, Barcelona, second quarter of the fourteenth century, ink and gouache on parchment. Fol. 35r. Sarajevo, National Museum. *Photo courtesy the Jewish Museum, New York, Frank Darmstadter Photo Archives.*

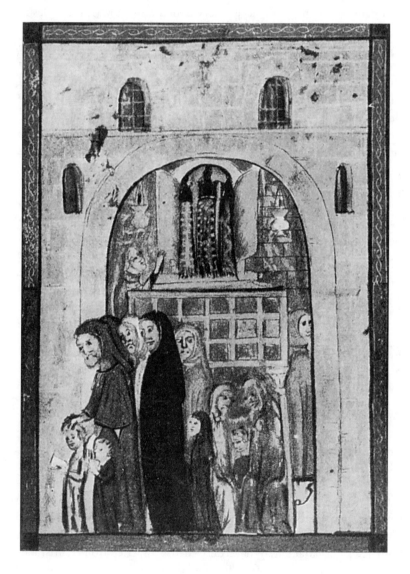

Fruit-Form Rimmonim and Rimmonim for the Reader's Desk

Another synagogue scene of the reading of the Haggadah on Passover eve in the Sister of the Golden Haggadah (British Library, Or. 2884, fol. 17v.) centers on the lector atop the wooden almemor (reader's desk), whose posts are covered with silver, piriform (pear-shaped) rimmonim (fig. 15.11). Rabbinic texts from Spain refer to Torah finials as *tapuḥim* (fruit),[58] suggesting that their shape was bulbous. The oldest Ottoman rimmonim, which date 1601–1602 and were found in Budapest, are of this form and bear an inscription stating they were dedicated to the Holy Community of the Pest Sephardim.[59] Later examples can be found throughout the Sephardic diaspora. Piriform rimmonim are a variation of this type; they existed in Spain, as can be seen from this miniature, and were particularly popular in the Ottoman Empire.[60]

In the Sister of the Golden Haggadah, finials decorate the almemor, possibly reflecting Muslim influence, through works like the minbar from the Kutubiyya Mosque in Marrakesh, which was made in Cordoba in 1125–1130.[61] The practice of decorating the reader's desk with finials was followed in both the Ottoman Empire and Italy. The almemor of the Ohrid Synagogue, established in Constantinople before the conquest of 1453, was adorned with piriform rimmonim prior to its recent restoration.[62] In the Spanish synagogue of the Venice ghetto, the practice was to adorn the reader's desk prior to the reading of the Torah and to remove the finials once the reading was completed.

Tikim

Two Haggadot include miniatures showing an officiant of the synagogue holding a Torah scroll encased in a *tik* (a rigid cylindrical container): the Barcelona Haggadah (London, British Library, Add. 14761, fol. 65v) and the Kaufmann Haggadah (Budapest, Hungarian Academy of Sciences, Kaufmann Collection, Ms. 422, p. 72; fig. 15.12). This alternative method of protecting the Torah is especially widespread among Jews of Arab lands and may reflect the continuing influence of the Islamic practice of storing the Koran in a box or other rigid container. Both Jews and Arabs may have derived this practice from Christians, whose earliest box shrine for the Bible dates to the seventh century.[63] The oldest published tik is a Samaritan example in Mamluk style dated

FIGURE 15.11. "Synagogue Scene," Sister of the Golden Haggadah, Barcelona, fourteenth century, ink and gouache on parchment. Ms. Or. 2884, fol. 17v. London, British Library. *Photo courtesy the Jewish Museum, New York, Frank Darmstadter Photo Archives.*

1565 that is now in the collection of the Jewish Museum, New York (S21).[64] It lacks the conical top shown in the Spanish miniatures, but, interestingly, three sixteenth- and early-seventeenth-century Koran "boxes" in the Museum of Turkish and Islamic Art, Istanbul, are close in form and decoration to the painted tikim.[65] Whether this form of

FIGURE 15.12. "Synagogue Scene," Kaufmann Haggadah, Spain, last quarter of the fourteenth century, ink and gouache on parchment. Ms. A422, page 72. Budapest, Hungarian Academy of Sciences. *Photo courtesy the Jewish Museum, New York, Frank Darmstadter Photo Archives.*

Koran box existed in Ottoman lands prior to the arrival of the Sephardim or whether it reflects the influence of their tikim remains to be studied.

Whatever population figures are accepted for the Jews of Spain,[66] it is obvious that the surviving works of ceremonial art are but a minuscule percentage of what must have existed. Objects made of precious materials, gold, silver, or silk woven with metallic threads or decorated with metallic embroidery were particularly vulnerable to the depredations of pogroms and the expulsion.[67]

The fact that all of the extant works of Sephardic religious art, with the one exception of the fifth-century trough, date to the last three centuries of Jewish life on the peninsula suggests that the late Middle Ages was the beginning of a creative period in the history of Jewish ceremonial art. The factors behind this development can only be surmised: perhaps an increase in wealth in the middle and upper classes, the same groups able to commission elaborately illuminated manuscripts like the Haggadot, or the increased influence of the now more prevalent Christian culture, which had a greater number of ceremonial objects in comparison with Islam. Similarly creative developments occur among Ashkenazim in the mid sixteenth century and, undisturbed by cataclysmic conversions and expulsions, continue in the seventeenth century and later.

In one sense, Sephardic ceremonial art continued in the diaspora. We can point to types of objects used in places like Italy and Rhodes that are the same as those known to have been used in Spain. But their style changed over time, losing the unique mixture of Islamic, Jewish, and Christian elements that constituted the mudejar art of the peninsula. At some point, the object ceased to be Sephardic and became Italian, Moroccan, Ottoman, or Dutch. New types of Judaica were invented, enlarging the body of ceremonial art in use at one time. In the diaspora, the Sephardic portion of that corpus became smaller but never disappeared.

Notes

2. Secular Hebrew Poetry in Fifteenth-Century Spain

1. Heinrich Graetz, *Geschichte der Juden*, 4th ed. (Leipzig, 1873–1900), 8:411; Ezra Fleischer, "The 'Gerona School' of Hebrew Poetry" in Isadore Twersky, ed., *Rabbi Moses Nahmanides (Ramban): Explorations in His Religious and Literary Virtuosity* (Cambridge, Mass, 1983), p. 37.

2. Among the poets' defenders are: Raphael Patai, *Misefunei ha-Shira* (Jerusalem, n.d.), 67–85; Arye Tauber, "Sefer 'Imri No'ash le-R. Shelomoh Dapiera," *Kiryat Sefer* 1 (1924–25),62–66; 139–141; Hayim Brody, *R. Shelomoh Dapiera: Devarim 'Aḥadim 'Odotav ve-'Odot Sefarav 'Im Toẓe'ot Misifro "Shir Hashirim"* (Berlin, 1892–93); S. Bernstein, *Diwan Shelomoh Ben Meshulam Dapiera* (New York, 1942).

3. For an inventory of the poets, see Moritz Steinschneider, "Poeten und Polemiker in Spanien um 1400," *Hebräische Bibliographie* 14 (1874) 77–79, 95–99, 15 (1875), 54–60, 78–84, 107–111, 16 (1876) 86–88, 17 (1877) 129–131.

There has been much confusion about the identity of the poets variously named Vidal (ben Benvenist) de la Cavalleria and Don Vidal Benvenist. I am satisfied now that Mati Huss has proved conclusively that (1) these were indeed two distinct individuals who knew and exchanged poems with each other; (2) the former was called Joseph ben Lavi in Hebrew, Vidal de la Cavalleria in Spanish, and bore the Hebrew patronymic ben Benvenist; (3) the former converted to Christianity, adopting the name Gonzalo; (4) the latter is always and exclusively called Don Vidal Benvenist except for occasional scribal errors; (5) the latter is not known to have converted to Christianity; (6) the latter composed both the poems edited by Tirzah Vardi and the story *Meliẓat 'Efer ve-Dinah*; see Mati Huss, "Meliẓat 'Efer ve-Dinah: Mahadurah Bikortit," masters thesis, Hebrew University, 1993–94, 29–70.

It is often said that these poets belonged to a formally constituted society for the propagation of poetry called *kat hameshorerim* or *'adat nogenim*. So far I have found the former term only once in a medieval source, and that source gives no certain indication that the term designates such a society; I have not encountered the second term at all. The earliest reference in scholarly literature to such a society or school that I have found is Steinschneider, "Poeten und Polemiker," *Hebräische Bibliographie* 14 (1874), 78, though even Steinschneider does not use the Hebrew terms. The matter calls for further investigation.

4. Full bibliographies are included in "Meliẓat 'Efer ve-Dinah"; and Tirzah Vardi, "Shire Don Vidal Benvenist," masters thesis, Hebrew University, 1986–87. See also Eliezer Gutwirth, "Solomon Bonafed's Social Criticism and Its Historic Background," *Sefarad* 45 (1985), 23–53; idem, "The World Upside-Down in Hebrew," *Orientalia Suecana* 30 (1981), 141–47; idem, "A Muwashshah by Solomon Bonafed," in F. Corriente and A. Sáenz-Badillos, eds., *Poesía estrófica* (Madrid, 1991), 137–44.

5. Tova Rosen-Moked, *Le'ezor Shir: 'Al Shirat Ha'ezor Ha'Ivrit bi-Yemei ha-Benayim* (Haifa, 1985) does not mention any of our poets. Gutwirth, on the other hand, in "The World Upside-Down" gives the impression that many *muwashshaḥāt* were written in this period. My impression that the *muwashshaḥ* was little cultivated in the period is based on a partial perusal of the manuscripts and a complete survey of the published materials; those that were written seem mostly to have been panegyrics, like Hebrew poetry of the period in general.

6. A muwashshaḥ is a strophic poem employing a specific pattern of changing and recurring rhymes; the form came into Hebrew from Arabic in the Golden Age; the fullest discussion of the Hebrew muwashshaḥ is Rosen-Moked's *Le'ezor Shir*. For a nonstandard muwashshaḥ, see Gutwirth, "The World Upside-Down." For nonmuwashshaḥ strophic poems, see Da Piera, *Diwan*, nos. 7 and 9.

7. Aharon Kaminka, "Hadiwan le-R. Shelomoh Bonafed," *Mi-Mizraḥ u-mi-Ma'arav* 2 (1895) 114–15, no. 1; Hayim Brody and Meir Wiener, *Mivḥar ha-Shira ha-'Ivrit* (Leipzig, 1922), 329–30.

8. Its meter is *hamitpasheṭ* and it is monorhymed.

9. Historians will note that I interpret the poem and its superscription differently from Yitzhak Baer in *A History of the Jews in Christian Spain* (Philadelphia, 1966), 2:213–14. I translate the superscription as follows: "When I was in Tortosa at the time of the disputation, the spirit—the spirit of poetry—was present there like flowing water, for most of the poets of the Kingdom [of Aragon] were present with the other sages. Among them was Don Vidal ben Lavi, who

passed between the parts and did not stand. The sage En Bonastruc Demaestre greeted him with precious poems, and he replied to him with ready inspiration in splendid words. Nor did I hide my face from finding favor with him, for I sent him this poem, speaking in the language of his own poem, crying bitterly about the bitter waters and making the voice of lament to pass through the camp of the Hebrews, as follows." The words "who passed between the parts and did not stand" could refer to de la Cavalleria's conversion, but that must have occurred *after* the poem was written; the superscription was written many years later, when Bonafed compiled his *dīwān*, and when the past tense was appropriate, with the meaning, "who [later] passed between the waters."

Perhaps Baer was partly misled to interpret the poem as a rebuke to de la Cavalleria because he did not take seriously enough its qaṣīda form. The opening of such poems is ordinarily about a different (though often complementary) subject from the main theme, which is reached only by means of the takhalluṣ. The opening lines quoted by Baer lament the condition of the Jews at Tortosa in terms of a standard complaint about Time, and do not refer directly to the addressee. In the second part, the panegyric proper, not one word is spoken in reproach to de la Cavalleria. Kaminka too apparently read the poem as being in praise of de la Cavalleria; see his note to line 16.

10. See my article "The Hebrew *Qasida*" in Stefan Sperl, ed., *The Qasida* (Leiden, 1996). There are only a few examples of this technique in the poetry of the Golden Age, most of them in religious poems using Arabic prosody. Ibn Gabirol's "Bi-Yemei Yekuti'el 'Asher Nigmaru" (Hayim Schirmann, *Ha-Shira ha-'Ivrit bi-Sefarad u-ve-Provans*, 2d ed. [Jerusalem and Tel Aviv, 1960], 1:196–201) and Halevi's "Zot ha-Tela'ah le-Val Eshkaḥ Meẓarehah" (H. Brody, *Dîwân des Abû-l-Hasan Jehuda ha-Levi* [Berlin, 1896–1930], 2:93–99) are two rare nonliturgical poems that use it. The practice became a common one with such thirteenth-century poets as Meshulam Da Piera and Todros Abulafia, but it became normative in the fourteenth century. It is so routine in our period that a poem lacking such a return is suspect of being incomplete. This can be verified in one case, Vidal's poem no. iii in Vardi, "Shire Don Vidal," part 3, p. 58, a formal ode that lacks the expected return; the poem is accompanied by an epigram, called *siman*, indicating that it originally had thirty-two verses instead of the extant thirty-one.

11. "Tevel ke-Khala Ta'ade Keleha," poem no. 118 in Vardi, "Shire Don Vidal," part 2, pp. 62–65. In one place in Vidal's *dīwān*, he is called Meir Shneur. According to Avraham Gross, "Hameshorer Shelomoh Bonafed u-Me'ora'ot Doro," in Barry Walfish, ed., *The Frank Talmage Memorial Volume* (Haifa, 1993), 35–61, Shneur b. Meir was a correspondent of Bonafed. It is not clear if Meir Shneur and Shneur b. Meir are the same person.

12. "Ereẓ ke-Yalda Hayeta Yoneket," in Schirmann, *Ha-Shira ha-'Ivrit bi-Sefarad*, 1:454.

13. The rhyme is not actually the same; but Vidal's rhyme, like Halevi's, is partly formed by a feminine grammatical suffix (Halevi, *neket*; Vidal, *leha*) that depends on the girl of the poem's opening. This rhyme is one of the notable features of the craftsmanship of Halevi's poem.

14. See R. P. Scheindlin, *The Gazelle: Medieval Hebrew Poems on God, Israel, and the Soul* (Philadelphia, 1991), pp. 3–4.

15. The opposition of garden to patron, here taken as a reversal of the values of the Golden Age, is adumbrated at the very beginning of the Golden Age by Dunash ben Labrat, in his panegyric on Hasdai Ibn Shaprut beginning "Know wisdom, O my heart," "De'e Libi Ḥokhma," (Schirmann, *Ha-Shira ha-'Ivrit bi-Sefarad*, 1:35–40). In Dunash's poem, as in Vidal's, gardens of pleasure are depicted in loving detail and then rejected in favor of the patron and his wisdom. But Dunash's poem was written at the very beginning of the Golden Age, before the attitudes that were to become characteristic of it were fully assimilated. His other famous poem describing a garden party, "Ve-'Omer 'Al Tishan" (Schirmann, *Ha-Shira ha-'Ivrit bi-Sefarad*, 1:34–35), is a veritable debate on the propriety of sensual pleasure. See Ross Brann, *The Compunctious Poet* (Baltimore, 1991), pp. 32–34, for these two poems and one by Isaac Ibn Khalfun.

16. "Kalah Temol Haytah ke-Mit'abelet," poem no. 11, Vardi, "Shire Don Vidal," part 3, pp. 11 ff.; Schirmann, *Ha-Shira ha-'Ivrit bi-Sefarad*, 2:599 ff. Vardi gives opening word as *dala*, as in most of the manuscripts, but the reading of Oxford 2769 seems preferable because of Vidal's evident desire to allude to Halevi's poem.

17. Halevi's words are "The earth, like a girl-child, was sucking the rains of winter yesterday, while the cloud was her nurse"; the poem never mentions winter. Vidal begins, "A bride that yesterday was like a woman in mourning (now) wears scarlet, crimson, linen, and purple," and continues to dwell on the misery of winter for a full eight verses before devoting a full verse to spring.

18. The same person as the one addressed by Bonafed in our first example.

19. There is some reason to think that the poem is incomplete. In this period most serious poems of any length end with a "return" line, as mentioned earlier; the return is absent here. The poem was part of an exchange of poems, all of which have this feature and all of which are considerably longer. Finally, there is no siman indicating the number of lines as have the other poems in the exchange; perhaps when the end of the poem was lost the scribes dropped the siman as well to obscure the fact that the poem is incomplete.

20. Dvora Bregman, "The Emergence of the Hebrew Sonnet," *Prooftexts* 11 (1991), 231–39.

21. "Zeman Hika be-Ḥeẓ Shanun Levavi" in Hayim Schirmann, *Hashira ha-'Ivrit be-'Italya* (Berlin: Schocken, 1934), pp. 217–22; trans. R. P. Scheindlin in "Judah Abravanel to His Son," *Judaism* 41 (1992), 190–99. Though written in Italy

at the dawn of the sixteenth century (1503), it is the product of a man who lived to maturity in the Iberian Peninsula.

22. Bonafed's assertion that he studied logic in Latin is in Neubauer, *Catalogue of the Hebrew Manuscripts in the Bodleian Library* (Oxford, 1886–1906), MS 1984, no. 47 (column 673), the source for Kaminka, "Hadiwan le-R. Shelomoh Bonafed," p. 110; the passage about Albertus Magnus, from the same manuscript, is quoted by Gross, "Hameshorer Shelomo Bonafed." His vernacular poem is known from his own account, quoted in Schirmann, "Ha-Pulmus Shel Shelomo Bonafed be-Nikhbede Saragosa," *Kovez 'Al Yad* n.s. 4 (1945/46), p. 12, and picked up by Gutwirth, " "Solomon Bonafed's Social Criticism," p. 27, who adds "probably in Hebrew characters intermingled with Hebrew words; of the sort known to us from documents by the community's 'romanzador.' " On his knowledge of Spanish and Arabic, see Kaminka, "Hadiwan le-R. Shelomoh Bonafed," p. 110; Gutwirth, "Solomon Bonafed's Social Criticism," p. 27.

23. The Latin poem in S. Bernstein, "Shire Don Vidal Yosef Ben Lavi," poem no. 4, *Tarbiz* 8 (1937), p. 355, quoted by Gutwirth, "Solomon Bonafed's Social Criticism," p. 27. The translation of Cicero, in Baer, *A History*, 2:211. The Arabic medical book had been composed in Arabic on the instructions of Vidal/Joseph's father, Benvenist b. Solomon de la Cavalleria, and the translation was done also at his demand. It is entitled *Gerem hama'alot*. See Moritz Steinschneider, *Die Hebräischen Übersetzungen des Mittelalters und die Juden als Dolmetscher* (Berlin, 1893), p. 762.

24. The poem to Astruc Rimokh is in Bernstein, *Diwan*, pp. 87–88 (poem no. 91, especially line 9). See also Steinschneider, "Poeten und Polemiker," *Hebräische Bibliographie* 15 (1875), 79. The testimony of Vida Benvenist is in Vardi, "Shire Don Vidal," p. 15 (no. 16, line 20). Da Piera's lament in Bernstein, *Diwan*, p. 11 (poem no. 2, line 24). On the letter received by Moshe Abbas, see Steinschneider, "Poeten und Polemiker," *Hebräische Bibliographie* 14 (1874), 79.

Baer, *A History*, 2:173, lists a number of Jews who knew Latin and were acquainted with scholasticism. If I understand him correctly, these include Zerahia Halevi and Moses Ibn Abbas, both of whom exchanged poems with members of the Saragossa circle, and others.

25. For Ibn Ṣaqbel, see the interpretation offered in my article "Fawns of the Palace and Fawns of the Field," *Prooftexts* 6 (1986), 189–203. For Jacob ben Eleazar, see my "Sipure ha-'Ahavah Shel Ya'akov Ben 'Ele'azar: Ben Sifrut 'Aravit le-Sifrut Romans" [The Love Stories of Jacob ben Elezar: Between Arabic and Romance] in *Proceedings of the Eleventh World Congress of Jewish Studies,* division C (Jerusalem, 1994), 3:16–20. For Todros, see Angel Sáenz-Badillo's "Hebrew Invective Poetry: The Debate Between Todros Abulafia and Phinehas Halevi," in *Prooftexts* 16 (1996), 49–73. For Ibn Zabara, see my review article, "Sefer Sha'ashu'im: Makama 'O Roman Hithankhut Yemeybenaimi?" *Hadoar*, October 3, 1986, pp. 26–29; and

Dan Pagis, "Variety in Medieval Rhymed Narratives," *Scripta Hierosolymitana* 27 (1978), 79–98.

26. Schirmann, *Ha-Shira ha-'Ivrit bi-Sefarad*, 2:582; idem, "Hebräische Poesie in Apulien und Sizilien," *Mitteilungen des Forschungsinstitute für hebräische Dichtung* 1 (1933), 135.

27. Juan Luis Alborg, *Historia de la literatura española: Edad media y renacimiento*, 2d ed. (Madrid, 1970), p. 321.

28. Ibid., p. 325.

29. Ibid.

30. George Ticknor, *History of Spanish Literature* 3 vols., 6th ed. (New York, 1965), 1:346; Roger Boase, *The Troubadour Revival: A Study of Social Change and Traditionalism in Late Medieval Spain* (London, 1978).

31. See note 4 above. Steinschneider saw the possibility that the circle of Hebrew poets resembled the consistory, for he described the putative Hebrew society or school as a kind of *gaya saber*. But he does not cite his sources for the existence of a formally constituted group of Hebrew poets, and I have not been able to discover them.

3. 1492: A House Divided

1. Colette Sirat, *A History of Jewish Philosophy in the Middle Ages* (Cambridge, 1985), 345–96.

2. Isaac Barzillay, *Between Reason and Faith* (The Hague, 1967), 72–132.

3. Tertullian, *Prescription Against the Heretics*, in Jason Saunders, ed. and trans., *Greek and Roman Philosophy After Aristotle* (New York, 1966), 343–51.

4. Most notably D. Z. Phillips, *Religion Without Understanding* (Oxford, 1976).

5. Isaac Abravanel, *Commentary on Exodus*, Parshat Yitro, 78 ab, repr. (New York, 1959).

6. Isaac Abravanel, *Commentary on Deuteronomy*, Parshat Zot ha-Berakha, repr. (New York, 1959), 157–59.

7. Isaac Abravanel, *Commentary on I Kings* (Jerusalem, 1953), chap. 3.

8. Aristotle, *Posterior Analytics*, 1:13; *Physics*, 1:1, in John Herman Randall, Jr., *The Career of Philosophy* (New York, 1962), vol. 1, chap. 11.

9. Aristotle, *Posterior Analytics* 2:19.

10. Karl Popper, *The Logic of Scientific Discovery* (New York, 1958).

11. Abravanel, *Commentary on I Kings*, 468b; John Locke, *An Essay Concerning Human Understanding*, ed. A. Z. Woozely (New York, 1974), book 2:23, 31.

12. Aristotle, *Metaphysics*, trans. W. D. Ross (Oxford, 1929), 4:4, 7.

13. Isaac Abravanel, *Commentary on I Kings*, 469b, 474b–75a.

14. Isaac Abravanel, response to the letter of Rabbi Saul Ha-Cohen Ashkenazi, included in his *Responsa and Miscellaneous Essays on Maimonides' Guide of the Perplexed*, repr. (Jerusalem, 1967).

15. Norman Malcolm, "The Groundlessness of Religious Belief," in Stuart C. Brown, ed., *Reason and Religion* (Ithaca, 1977), 143–57.

16. Augustine, *On Free Choice of the Will*, trans. Anna Benjamin and L. H. Hackenstaff (Indianapolis, 1964), book 2:5–6.

17. Seymour Feldman, "Abravanel on Maimonides' Critique of the Kalam Arguments for Creation," *Maimonidean Studies* 1 (1990), 5–26; idem, "Abravanel's Defense of Creation ex nihilo," *Proceedings of the Eleventh World Congress of Jewish Studies*, div. C (Jerusalem, 1994), 2:33–40.

18. Abravanel, *Commentary on I Samuel*, 25:29, 284b–85a. See also his *Commentary on Deuteronomy*, Parshat Ki Teẓe, 107b–109a, and his messianic treatise *Yeshuat Meshiḥo*, (Koenigberg, 1861), 36. Avicenna, "The Deliverance, Psychology," from *Avicenna's Psychology*, in Arthur Hyman and James Walsh, eds., *Philosophy in the Middle Ages*, trans. Faziur Rahman (Indianapolis, 1983), 255–62.

19. Averroës, *The Incoherence of the Incoherence* (Tahafut al-Tahafut), trans. S. van den Bergh (London, 1954), vol. 1:15; idem, *Long Commentary on Aristotle's De Anima*, book 3, selection in Hyman and Walsh, *Philosophy in the Middle Ages*, 324–34.

20. Gersonides, *The Wars of the Lord* (Philadelphia, 1984), vol. 1 book 1 passim; Seymour Feldman, "Gersonides on the Possibility of Conjunction with the Agent Intellect," *Association for Jewish Studies Review* 3 (1978), 99–120.

21. Hasdai Crescas, *'Or 'Adonai* (Vienna, 1859), book 3, Second and Third Principles.

22. Abravanel, *Mif'alot 'Elohim* (Lemberg, 1853), book 1, chap. 1; book 8, chap. 1.

23. Maimonides, *Guide of the Perplexed*, trans. Shlomo Pines (Chicago, 1963), 2:19, 24.

24. Thomas Aquinas, *Summa Theologiae*, in Anton Pegis, ed., *Introduction to St. Thomas Aquinas* (New York, 1945), 1, question 46, article 2, pp. 252–257.

25. Gersonides, *The Wars of the Lord*, book 6, part 1, chap. 17.

26. Crescas, *'Or 'Adonai*, book 1; Harry Wolfson, *Crescas' Critique of Aristotle's Physics* (Cambridge, Mass., 1929), proposition 1, parts 1–2.

27. Abravanel, *Mif'alot 'Elohim*, book 9.

28. For the most complete and recent account of Judah Abravanel's life, see Menahem Dorman's introduction to his Hebrew translation of the *Dialoghi d'Amore* (Jerusalem, 1983). See also Santino Caramella's Italian edition (Bari, 1929), which contains Italian translations of Judah's Hebrew poetry. C. Gebhardt's edition (Frankfurt am Main, 1929) contains the Hebrew text of the poems and a German translation of them.

29. Benzion Netanyahu, *Isaac Abravanel* (Philadelphia, 1972).

30. Dorman, *Dialoghi d'Amore*, 58–70.

31. David Ruderman, "The Italian Renaissance and Jewish Thought," in A. Rabil, Jr., ed., *Renaissance Humanism* (Philadelphia, 1988), 1:407.

32. T. Anthony Perry, *Erotic Spirituality* (Alabama, 1981), 25 ff.

33. Dorman, *Dialoghi d'Amore*, 52–58; Moshe Idel, "Origins of the Image of the Circle in Dialoghi d'Amore," *Iyyun* 28 (1978–79), 156–66; Arthur Lesley, "The Place of the *Dialoghi d'amore* in Contemporaneous Jewish Thought," in K. Eisenbichler and O. Z. Pugliese, eds., *Ficino and Renaissance Neo-Platonism* (Ottawa, 1986), 69–86.

34. Dorman, *Dialoghi d'Amore*, gives an excellent account of this issue; see pp. 86–95.

35. Perry, *Erotic Spirituality*, 25 ff.

36. Shlomo Pines. "Medieval Doctrines in Renaissance Garb?" in Bernard Cooperman, ed., *Jewish Thought in the Sixteenth Century* (Cambridge, Mass., 1983). Pines tries to draw a connection between Leone and Avicenna's treatise of Love. But, as he himself admits, Avicenna's essay is not known to have been translated into Hebrew or Latin.

37. Arthur Lesley, "Circumcising Pagan Myths: Leone Ebreo's Methods of Interpretation." Paper presented at a conference on Jewish-Christian Cultural Contacts in the Renaissance, University of Chicago, April 1989.

38. Leone Ebreo, *The Philosophy of Love*, trans. F. Friedeberg-Seeley and Jean H. Barnes (London, 1937), 277–78; Italian edition of Caramella (1928), 236–37.

39. Although various Plotinian ideas were known, indeed adopted, by medieval thinkers, Plotinus himself was not. Several of Plotinus's *Enneads* had been translated into Arabic and then into Latin, but they were known as *The Theology of Aristotle*. Some of Proclus's *Elements of Theology* were also rendered into Arabic and then into Latin and entitled *The Book of Causes*. But it was only with Ficino's translation of Plotinus's *Enneads* that Western philosophy became directly acquainted with the real Plotinus. Probably the first mention of Plotinus by a Jewish author is found in Yoḥanan Alemanno, a teacher of Pico. See Moshe Idel, "The Magical and Neo-Renaissance Interpretations of the Kabbalah in the Renaissance," in Cooperman, *Jewish Thought in the Sixteenth Century*, 216–19.

40. Leone, *The Philosophy of Love*, 296 (Caramella, 246). Samuel Hugo Bergmann, *A History of Modern Philosophy* (in Hebrew) (Jerusalem, 1970), 1:80.

41. Leone, *The Philosophy of Love*, 295–96 (Caramella, 250–51). Gersonides, *The War of the Lord*, vol. 3, book 6, part 1, chap. 17; book 6, part 2, chap. 8.

42. Leone, *The Philosophy of Love*, 295, 336, 387 (Caramella, 250, 284, 324).

43. Plato, *Timaeus*, in Edith Hamilton and Huntington Cairns, eds., *Plato, Collected Works* (Princeton, 1961), 34b–37c.

44. Leone, *The Philosophy of Love*, 387–88 (Caramella, 325–26).

45. Plato, *Timaeus*, 29ab.

46. Philo, *On the Creation of the World According to Moses*, in *Philo's Works*, trans. F. H. Colson and G. H. Whitaker, Loeb Classical Library (Cambridge, Mass., 1929), vol. 1, 16–20, 24–25.

47. Leone, *The Philosophy of Love*, 278, 284 (Caramella 236–37, 242).

48. Augustine, *City of God* (New York, 1984), 11:4.

49. Leone, *The Philosophy of Love*, 285, 303 (Caramella, 242, 256).

50. Plotinus, *Enneads*, trans. A. H. Armstrong, Loeb Classical Library (Cambridge, Mass., 1966), vol. 2, 2.4.15–16; John Rist, *The Road to Reality* (Cambridge, 1967), 117–19.

51. Leone, *The Philosophy of Love*, 285 (Caramella, 242). Plato, *Timaeus*, 50d; Aristotle, *On Generation of Animals*, trans. A. L. Peck, Loeb Classical Library (Cambridge, 1953), 2:3–5.

52. Leone, *The Philosophy of Love*, 303, 305, 413–15 (Caramella, 256, 258, 345–47).

53. Ibid. 415 (Caramella, 348).

54. Ibid.

55. Ibid., 416, 420–21 (Caramella, 351–52).

56. Ibid., 424 (Caramella 355).

57. Philo, *On Drunkenness*, trans. F. H. Colson and Rev. G. H. Whitaker, in *Philo's Works*, Loeb Classical Library (Cambridge, Mass., 1930), 3; *On Flight*, trans. F. H. Colson and Rev. G. H. Whitaker, in *Philo's Works*, Loeb Classical Library (Cambridge, Mass., 1934), 5. Bergmann, *A History of Modern Philosophy*, 80.

58. *Midrash Rabbah*, Genesis 1:1 (New York, 1951).

59. In this way he is also able to reconcile Plato with himself. For in the concluding book of the *Republic* Plato says that God created Forms (597 bc).

60. Leone, *The Philosophy of Love*, 277–78 (Caramella, 236–37). Maimonides, *Guide of the Perplexed*, 3:51.

61. Paul Kristeller, *Renaissance Thought and Its Sources* (New York, 1979), chap. 10.

62. Pietro Pompanazzi, *On the Immortality of the Soul*, trans. William Henry Hay, revised by John Herman Randall, Jr., in Ernst Cassirier, Paul Oscar Kristeller, and John Herman Randall, Jr., eds., *The Renaissance Philosophy of Man* (Chicago, 1948), 280–381.

63. Leone, *Philosophy of Love*, 45 (Caramella, 41–42).

64. Alexander of Aphrodisias, *The De Anima of Alexander of Aphrodisias*, trans. A. P. Fotinus (Washington, D.C., 1979), 117.

65. Leone, *The Philosophy of Love*, 46 (Caramella, 43).

66. Ibid., 43 (Caramella, 40–41).

67. Ibid., 426 (Caramella, 357).

68. Ibid., 51, 427, 439–40, 456 ff. (Caramella, 46–47, 357, 367–70, 382–83).

69. Ibid., 467 (Caramella, 391).

70. I. Barzilay, *Between Reason and Faith*, 79; Moshe Idel, "Kabbalah and Philosophy in R. Isaac and Judah Abravanel," in Menahem Dorman and Zeev

Levy eds., *The Philosophy of Love of Judah Abravanel* (in Hebrew) (Tel Aviv, 1985), 73–112; Abraham Melamed, " 'Let not the wise man glory . . . ,' Philosophical Interpretations of Jeremiah 9:22–23 in Medieval and Renaissance Jewish Thought" (in Hebrew), *Jerusalem Studies in Jewish Thought*, 4 (1984–85), 60–75; Eric Lawee, "On the Threshold of the Renaissance: New Methods and Sensibilities in the Biblical Commentaries of Iaaac Abravanel, *Viator* 26 (1995), 283–319.

71. Jakob Guttmann, *Die Religionsphilosophen Lehren des Isaak Abravanel* (Breslau, 1916), 41; my translation.

72. Idel, "Kabbalah and Philosophy," 73–79; idem, "The Magical and Neoplatonic Interpretations of the Kabbalah in the Renaissance," in Cooperman, *Jewish Thought in the Sixteenth Century*, 186–242.

73. Raymond Klibansky, *The Continuity of the Platonic Tradition During the Middle Ages* (Oxford, 1939). Kristeller, *Renaissance Thought and Its Sources*, chap. 3, 8.

74. Judah Halevi, *Le Kuzari: Apologie de la Religion Meprisée*, trans. Charles Touatl (Louvain-Paris, 1994), 1:67.

75. Plato, *Phaedrus*, 245c–246a.

76. Plato, *Republic*, in Edith Hamilton and Huntington Cairns, eds., *Plato, Collected Works* (Princeton, 1961), 620a ff.; *Phaedo*, in Edith Hamilton and Huntington Cairns, eds., *Plato, Collected Works* (Princeton, 1961), 81e.

77. Isaac Abravanel, *The Deeds of God* (Jerusalem, 1988), 8:6.

78. Augustine, *City of God*, 8:11.

79. Isaac Abravanel, *Commentary on Genesis,* Parshat Bereshit (New York, 1959), 43a.

80. Isaac Abravanel, *Response to R. Saul Hacohen Ashkenazi* (Venice, 1574), 12b; Moshe Idel, "Jewish Kabbalah and Platonism," in Lenn E. Goodman, ed., *Neo-Platonism and Jewish Thought* (Albany, 1992), 332.

81. Abravanel, *Commentary on Genesis,* Parshat Bereshit, 24b.

82. Aristotle, *On the Heavens,* trans. W. K. C. Guthrie, Loeb Classical Library (Cambridge, Mass., 1960), 2:7–8.

83. Samuel Sambursky, *The Physical World of Late Antiquity* (Princeton, 1962), 142 ff.

84. Isaac Abravanel, *The Wells of Salvation* (Jerusalem, 1959), 8:2, 6, 11:6; Guttmann, *Die Religionsphilosophen Lehren*, 42.

85. Abravanel, *The Deeds of God*, 8:6.

86. Proclus, *Elements of Theology*, trans. E. R. Dodds, 2d ed. (Oxford, 1963), propositions 196, 208.

87. Guttmann, *Die Religionsphilosophen Lehren*, 41.

88. Idel, "Jewish Kabbalah and Platonism," 320–22.

89. Abravanel, *The Deeds of God*, 2:3.

90. Ibid.

4. On Converso and Marrano Ethnicity

1. Haim Beinart, "The *Converso* Community in Fifteenth Century Spain," in R. D. Barnett, ed., *The Sephardi Heritage* (New York, 1971), 441.

2. By "racialist" I mean the tendency to treat culture and ethnicity as if transmitted from generation to generation by heredity. Such essentialism has characterized mainstream Spanish medievalism in the twentieth century (e.g., Ramón Menéndez Pidal, Claudio Sánchez Albornoz) until quite recently. See my comment in *Islamic and Christian Spain in the Early Middle Ages* (Princeton, 1979), 6–13.

3. On boundary-maintaining mechanisms, see Thomas F. Glick and Oriol Pi Sunyer, "Acculturation as an Explanatory Concept in Spanish History," *Comparative Studies in Society and History*, 11 (1969), 136–54.

4. Pierre van den Berghe, *Race and Ethnicity* (New York, 1970), 150.

5. On modern Chuetas, see Kenneth Moore, *Those of the Street: The Catholic-Jews of Mallorca* (Notre Dame, 1976); Eva and Juan F. Laub, *El mito triunfante: Estudio antropológico-social de los Chuetas mallorquines* (Palma de Mallorca, 1987). See also Dan Ross, *Acts of Faith: A Journey to the Fringes of Jewish Identity* (New York, 1982). His chapter on Chuetas (52–66) is in part a reflection of my views.

6. Miquel Forteza, *Els descendents dels jueus conversos*, 2d ed. (Palma de Mallorca, 1970), 14, 20–25.

7. Juan Riera, *Carlos III y los Chuetas mallorquines* (Valladolid, 1975).

8. Forteza, *Els descendents,* chaps. 13 (institutional parallelism), 15 (ethnic stereotypes), 18 (self-hatred), and 19 (professional structure). Forteza, a Chueta himself, was a particularly accurate witness to all these phenomena.

9. Francesco Riera Montserrat, *Luites antixuetes en el segle XVII* (Palma de Mallorca, 1973).

10. R. A. Schermerhorn, *Comparative Ethnic Relations: A Framework for Theory and Research* (New York, 1970), 81–83. In place of Schermerhorn's abstract physical terms, the concepts intended by "centripetal" and "centrifugal" are rendered more intelligible by substituting "integrative" and "segregative," respectively.

11. Norman Roth makes this case eloquently in his *Conversos, Inquisition, and the Expulsion of the Jews from Spain* (Madison, 1995).

12. For a discussion of similar situations of ambivalence, see Leonard Broom and John I. Kitsuse, "The Validation of Acculturation: A Condition to Ethnic Assimilation, *American Anthropologist* 57 (1955), 44–48. The authors stress that if access to participation in the society's dominant institutions is denied to a minority, then full assimilation is impossible, no matter how much progress there has been toward acculturation. Lessening of cultural distance, therefore, may not inevitably lead to a lessening of social distance.

13. I doubt, however, whether it is justified or accurate to describe Old Christians as centrifugal in orientation, in spite of the significance of limpieza de

sangre. Limpieza fulfills one of the requirements of a centrifugal mode: it rejects acceptance of conversos as fully assimilated equals. But it lacks another requirement—that the conversos be autonomous. Therefore, in spite of some misgivings, I think the Old Christian mode in sixteenth- and seventeenth-century Spain should be read as centripetal, with the recognition that limpieza statues were used as mechanisms to prevent the recruitment of conversos into the elite without compromising the basic strategy of assimilation.

14. Schermerhorn, *Comparative Ethnic Relations*, 193.

15. There is no agreement on what constitutes minimal Judaism. Baruch Braunstein, for example, kept changing his mind in the same volume: at one point he says circumcision, at another, observance of Yom Kippur, at another, the conviction that salvation was attainable through belief in Mosaic law. See Baruch Braunstein, *The Chuetas of Majorca* (New York, 1970).

16. The point is made in the biographies of marranos fleeing to France, Italy, or Holland in the seventeenth century with virtually no knowledge of normative Judaism.

17. Miguel de la Pinta Llorente and José María de Palacio y de Palacio, *Procesos inquisitoriales contra la familia judía de Juan Luis Vives* (Madrid, Barcelona, 1964), 1:80: "No pot dir segons lo comte dels christians en quin any fonch, perque no sabia lo compte."

18. Stephen Gilman, *The Spain of Fernando de Rojas* (Princeton, 1972), 81.

19. I use the term *Moorish* rather than *Muslim* here to indicate that morisco culture included more than purely religious elements.

20. Robert A. Levine and Donald T. Campbell, *Ethnocentrism: Theories of Conflict, Ethnic Attitudes, and Group Behavior* (New York, 1972), 33.

21. Ibid., 39

22. Of course, this is a truism. Cf. Américo Castro, *La realidad histórica de España,* rev. ed. (Mexico City, 1962), 43: "El judío . . . engrano con el cristiano mucho mas que el moro." That much is clear, although why that should have been so needs explication. The point is made often and is frequently polemical, because it suggests a rationale for the conversion of so many Jews, particularly intellectuals. On the relationship of "cultural coincidence" to assimilation, see David Rothstein, "Culture Creation and Social Reconstruction: The Socio-Cultural Dynamics of Intergroup Contact," *American Sociological Review* 37 (1972), 673–74.

23. Mark Meyerson suggests that the moriscos were more highly enclosed, paradoxically, than were the Mudejars of the fifteenth century: *The Muslims of Valencia in the Age of Fernando and Isabel* (Berkeley, 1991), 8.

24. Continuous concentration of Chuetas in the same quarter may have accounted for their atypical cohesiveness.

25. Benjamin N. Colby and Pierre L. van de Berghe, *Ixil Country: A Plural Society in Highland Guatemala* (Berkeley, 1969), 20.

26. See Andre Adam, "Berber Migrants in Casablanca," in Ernest Gellner and Charles Micaud, eds., *Arabs and Berbers* (London, 1973), 325–43, esp. 334.

27. F. K. Lehman, "Who Are the Karen?" in Charles F. Keyes, ed., *Ethnic Adaptation and Identity* (Philadelphia, 1979), 215–53, at 234.

28. Miguel de Cervantes, *Don Quixote*, trans. Samuel Putnam, 2 vols. (New York, 1949), 2:862–65, part 2, chap. 54.

29. Brian Pullan, *The Jews of Europe and the Inquisition of Venice, 1550–1670* (Totowa, N.J., 1983), 221.

30. Brian Pullan, " 'A Ship with Two Rudders': 'Righetto Marrano' and the Inquisition in Venice," *Historical Journal* 20 (1977), 25–58, at 45.

31. Glen F. Dille, *Antonio Enriquez Gomez* (Boston, 1988), 10–20; Constance H. Rose, "The Marranos of the Seventeenth Century and the Case of the Merchant Writer Antonio Enriquez," in Angel Alcala, ed., *The Spanish Inquisition and the Inquisitorial Mind* (New York, 1987), 53–71. According to Rose (64), Enriquez Gomez "wanted to be both Spanish and Jewish in a country which held such divided loyalty to be treasonous."

32. Yosef Kaplan, *From Christianity to Judaism: The Story of Isaac Orobio de Castro* (Oxford, 1989), 223–34.

33. His declaration is provided by Julio Caro Baroja, *Los judíos en la España moderna y contemporanea*, 3 vols. (Madrid, 1962), 3:332–36. See Pullan, *The Jews of Europe*, 204.

34. Benzion Netanyahu, *The Marranos of Spain from the Late Fourteenth to the Early Sixteenth Century* (New York, 1966), 147; Pullan, *The Jews of Europe*, 233.

35. Pullan, "A Ship with Two Rudders," 37 (the words of Giovanni Giacomo, formerly Leo the Jew).

36. Yosef Kaplan, "The Jewish Profile of the Spanish-Portuguese Community of London During the Seventeenth Century," *Judaism* 41 (1992), 229–47, at 235.

37. Lehman, "Who Are the Karen?"

38. Ibid., 247.

39. Yosef Kaplan, "The Self-Definition of the Sephardic Jews of Western Europe and Their Relation to the Alien and the Stranger," in this volume.

40. Kenneth R. Stow, "Ethnic Rivalry or Melting Pot: The Edot in the Roman Ghetto," *Judaism* 41 (1992), 286–96.

41. Cecil Roth, "The Role of Spanish in the Marrano Diaspora," in Frank Pierce, ed., *Hispanic Studies in Honor of I. Gonzalez Llubera* (Oxford, 1959), 299–308.

42. Dan Pagis, *Hebrew Poetry of the Middle Ages and the Renaissance* (Berkeley, 1991), 36–37.

43. Eleazar Gutwirth, "On the Hispanicity of Sephardi Jewry," *Revue des études juives* 145 (1986), 347–57.

44. Yirmiyahu Yovel, *Spinoza and Other Heretics: The Marrano of Reason* (Princeton, 1989), 49.

5. Order of the Expulsion from Spain

1. See Haim Beinart, "The Great Conversion and the Converso Problem," in *Moreshet Sepharad: The Sephardi Legacy* (Jerusalem, 1992), 346–82.

2. See Haim Beinart, *Conversos on Trial* (Jerusalem, 1981).

3. See Fritz Baer, *Die Juden im Christlichen Spanien* (Berlin, 1936), 2:281 ff.

4. See Tarsico de Azcona (O.F.M-Cap.) *Isabel la católica* (Madrid, 1964), 333 ff.; Marvin Lunenfeld, *The Council of the Santa Hermandad* (Coral Gables, Fla., 1970)

5. See Haim Beinart, "The Jewish Badge in Spain and the Enforcement of the Decree of the Badge Under the Catholic Monarchs" (in Hebrew), in Shmuel Almog et al. eds., *Israel and the Nation: Essays Presented in Honor of Shmuel Ettinger* (Jerusalem, 1987), 29–42.

6. See Haim Beinart, "The Jewish Living Quarters in Spain and the Order of Separation" (in Hebrew), *Zion* 51 (1986), 61–85.

7. See de Azcona, *Isabel la católica*, 388 ff.

8. See Haim Beinart, "La Inquisición española y la expulsión de los judíos de Andalucía," in Yosef Kaplan, ed., *Jews and Conversos* (Jerusalem, 1985), 103–23.

9. See Haim Beinart, "The Expulsion of the Jews from Valmaseda" (in Hebrew), *Zion* 46 (1981), 39–51.

10. Yitzhak Baer, *A History of the Jews in Christian Spain* (Philadelphia, 1961), 2:381.

11. See Azriel Shochet, ed., *Shevet Yehudah* (Jeruslaem, 1947), 127. Lately it has been proved that many of the Jews and conversos who left Spain headed for the Holy Land. See Haim Beinart, "A Hebrew Formulary from Fifteenth-Century Spain"(in Hebrew), *Sefunot* 5 (1961), 75 ff.

12. See G. A. Bergenroth, *Calendar of Letters, Despatches, and State Papers Relating the Negotiations Between England and Spain Preserved in the Archives at Simancas and Elsewhere*, vol. 1, *Henry VIII, 1485–1509* (London, 1862), xxxiv ff.

13. By the year 1491 the Jewish communities of Castile paid 1,637,320 gold castellanos (or 794,100,200 marevedís; 1 castellano of gold was worth 485 maravedís). See Luis Suárez Fernández, *Documentos acerca de la expulsión de los judíos* (Valladolid, 1964), 65–72.

14. See Baer, *A History of the Jews*, vol. 2, n. 10, s.v. Reg.

15. In Saragossa on April 29, 1492. See Rafael Conde y Delgado de Molina, *La expulsión de los judíos de la Corona de Aragón* (Saragossa, 1991), 41–44.

16. See Haim Beinart, "Did Micer Alfonso de la Caballería Intervene on Behalf of the Jews Against Their Expulsion? (in Hebrew), *Zion* 50 (1975), 265–74.

17. See Conde y Delgado de Molina, *La expulsión*, 44–46; Miguel Angel Motis Dolader, *The Expulsion of the Jews from Calatayud, 1492–1500, Documents and Regesta* (Jerusalem, 1990), 150. There is testimony on the promulgation of the order from Daroca, Calatayud, Tarazona, Borja, Mallén, Magallón, Ejea de los Caballeros, Tauste—all within the Kingdom of Aragon.

18. For the text of Ávila see F. Fita, *BRAH* 11 (1887), 412–528; Jose Amador de los Rios, *Historia política, social y religiosa de los judíos en España y Portugal,* repr. (Madrid, 1960), 1003–5; Henry Charles Lea, *A History of the Inquisition of Spain* (New York, 1906), 509–71; Manuel Serrano y Sanz, *Orígenes de la dominación española en América* (Madrid, 1918), 1:ccccxcii; appendix document 41; Baer, *Die Juden im Christlichen Spanien,* 2:407–8; Pilar León Tello, *Judíos de Ávila (Ávila, 1964), 91–95;* Suárez Fernández, *Documentos acerca de la expulsión de los judíos,* 391–95; Antonio Rumeu de Armas, *Nueva luz sobre las capitulaciones de Santa Fe de 1492* (Madrid, 1985), 138–41. For the text of Burgos, see AGS Patronato Real leg. 28, fol. 6; Elena Romero, ed., *La vida judía en Sefarad* (Madrid, 1991), 307. For the text of Toledo, see Archivo de la cancillería, Pleitos civiles F. Alonso Fenecidos C. 540–7 fol. 7 ff.; Haim Beinart, *The Expulsion from Spain* (in Hebrew) (Jerusalem, 1995), 41–44.

19. Conde y Delgado de Molina, *La expulsión;* Moshe Orfali and Miguel Angel Motis Dolader, "An Examination of the Texts of the General Edict of Expulsion" (in Hebrew), *Peamim* 46–47 (1992), 148–68.

20. See Rumeu de Armas, *Nueva luz,* 28–35.

21. For this formula, see Rumeu de Armas, *Nueva luz,* 31. He was not the only secretary of the royal household. Mention should be made of Fernán Alvarez de Toledo, of converso descent, Hernando del Pulgar, secretary and later royal chronicler, also of converso ancestry, Juan de la Parra, Alonso del Marmol, Christóbal de Vitorio, Fernando de Zafra, and, later, Gaspar de Grizio. See María de la Soterraña Martín Postigo, *La cancillería castellana de los Reyes Católicos* (Valladolid, 1959), s.v. Reg.

22. See José Cabezudo Astraín, "La expulsión de los judíos de Ejea de los Caballeros," *Sefarad* 30 (1970), 349–63.

23. This order mentions, for instance, usury and usurious moneylending as a cause for the expulsion. However, this reason was omitted in the text extant for Castile. See Conde y Delgado de Molina, *La expulsión.*

24. For the documents issued to Sardinia, see Mauro Perani, "Appunti per la storia degli Ebrei in Sardegna durante la Dominazione Aragonesa," *Italia* 5, no. 1–2 (1985), 138–39; Conde y Delgado de Molina, *La expulsión,* 75 ff.; For Sicily, see Conde y Delgado de Molina, *La expulsión,* 68 ff.; Beinart, *The Expulsion from Spain,* 48 ff.

25. For an English translation of the order, see Haim Beinart, *Atlas of Medieval Jewish History* (New York, 1992), 83.

26. See Beinart, *Conversos on Trial.*

27. See Suárez Fernández, *Documentos acerca de la expulsión de los judíos,* 65–72.

28. See Benjamin R. Gampel, *The Last Jews on Iberian Soil: Navarrese Jewry 1479/1498* (Berkeley and Los Angeles, 1989).

29. Luis de Santángel was of converso descent. He was "escribano de racion" of Aragon and considered very trustworthy by royalty. So was Francisco Pinelo, an active member of the city council of Seville. He too was of converso descent.

30. See Beinart, *Moreshet Sepharad,* vols 1–2 (Jerusalem, 1992).

6. Expulsion or Integration?

1. *Livro do Almoxarifado de Silves (século XV)* (Silves, 1984), 48.

2. A.N.T.T., *Chancelaria de D. João II*, vol. 15, fols. 36v, 42.

3. Maria José Ferro Tavares, *Os judeus em Portugal no século XV* (Lisbon, 1982), 1:423–27, 444–47.

4. Ibid., 437–39.

5. Maria José Ferro Tavares, "Judeus, cristãos novos e os descobrimentos portugueses," *Sefarad* (Madrid) 48 (1988), fasc. 2, pp. 302–3.

6. A. D. Évora, *Livro 3° de Originais,* fols. 205–6v; Ferro Tavares, *Os judeus em Portugal no século XV,* 435–37.

7. Antonio de la Torre and Luis Suárez Fernández, eds., *Documentos referentes a las relaciones con Portugal durante el reinado de los Reyes Católicos* (Valladolid, 1958), 2:406–8; Luis Suárez Fernández, ed., *Documentos acerca de la expulsión de los judíos* (CSIC, 1964), 487–89.

8. Jerónimo Münzer, "Viaje por España y Portugal en los años 1494 y 1495," trans. Julio Puyol, *Boletin de la Real Academia de Historia* (Madrid, 1924), 84:207–8.

9. A.N.T.T., *Chancelaria de D. Manuel,* vol. 10, fols. 26–26v, vol. 31, fol. 60.

10. Évora, *Livro 3° de Originais,* fols. 151, 159; G. H. C. Porto, *Livro Antigo de Provisões,* fol. 87. We have not yet found the document sent to the council of Lisbon.

11. Lx., A.H.C.M., *Livro 1° de D. Manuel,* fol. 12; Évora, *Livro 3° de Originais,* fol. 133; Porto, *Livro Antigo de Provisões,* fol. 66; Fundação Calouste Gulbenkian, *Ordenações Manuelinas,* vol. 2, tit. 41.

12. F. Cantera Burgos and Carlos Carrete Parrondo, *Las juderías medievales en la provincia de Guadalajara* (Madrid, 1975), 180.

13. A.N.T.T., *Foral de Torres Novas,* N.A. 373, fol. 1.

14. A.N.T.T., *Ordem de Cristo, Inquisição de Tomar,* B-51-26, fol. 34.

15. Damião de Góis, *Crónica de Felicissimo rei D. Manuel* (Coimbra, 1949), 41–42; Samuel Usque, *Consolaçam às tribulaçoens de Israel* (Coimbra, 1906), 3d dialogue, 30.

16. A.N.T.T., *Inquisição de Évora,* no. 3948.

17. A.N.T.T., *Inquisição de Évora,* nos. 8447, 6791; *Inquisição de Lisboa,* no. 12509; *Inquisição de Évora,* no. 7794, 6117, 9627, 11262, respectively.

18. A.N.T.T., *Místicos,* vol. 5, fols. 49–49v; *As Gavetas da Torre do Tombo* (Lisbon, 1964), 4:172–73.

7. The Exiles of 1492 in the Kingdom of Navarre

1. For a treatment of the Castilian and Aragonese Jews who emigrated to Navarre in 1492, based mainly on a variety of Navarrese sources, see Benjamin R. Gampel, *The Last Jews on Iberian Soil* (Berkeley and Los Angeles, 1989), 89–119.

See also Miguel Ángel Motis Dolader, "La emigración de judíos aragoneses a Navarra en las postrimerías del siglo XV," in *Primer congreso general de historia de Navarra* (Pamplona, 1988), 537–51.

2. Miguel Ángel Motis Dolader, *La expulsión de los judíos del Reino de Aragón*, 2 vols. (Saragossa, 1990).

3. Archivo de los Protocolos de Tudela (hereafter A.P.T.), Juhan Martínez Cabero, 1491–92 fol. 89v, par. a. See Gampel, *The Last Jews*, 115 and 198, n. 130.

4. Archivo Histórico de Protocolos de Zaragoza (hereafter A.H.P.Z.), Protocolo de Jaime Malo, 1492, cisterno, fol. 15v as discussed in Motis, *Aragón*, 2:215. The date of Ezmel's departure is noted by Motis (2:40), who cites A.H.P.Z., Protocolo de Jaime Malo, 1492 fols. 15v–23v. Jaime Malo is described by Motis (1:249) as a *notario del reino*; and as a Saragossan public notary (2:17, 65). A map of the routes that Aragonese Jews took to enter Navarre can be found in Motis (2:183).

5. Motis, *Aragón*, 2:36–40. On p. 39 Motis discusses Archivo de la Corona de Aragón (hereafter A.C.A.), Real Cancillería, Registro 3563, fol. 180v, a document of April 30, 1497, which lists the property that was confiscated from a number of Aragonese Jews and notes the date on which these actions were effected.

6. Motis, *Aragón*, 2:41.

7. Ibid., 2:42–51.

8. A.P.T., Juhan Martínez Cabero, 1493, fol. 10v. On debts owed Abnarrabi in Juslibol and that were confiscated, see Motis, *Aragón*, 2:45. It is of course possible that the debt was incurred after the expulsion.

9. A.P.T., Pedro Latorre, 1492–98, fol. 6r, par. a and the margin. This is a *comanda*; it is likely that Ezmel was speculating in hemp. Generally, on debts owed Jews who lived in Navarre, see Gampel, *The Last Jews*, 33–40.

10. A.P.T., Pedro Latorre, 1492–98, fol. 39r–v.

11. A.P.T., Sancho Ezquerro, 1480–1500, fols. 372v–73r.

12. A.P.T., Martin Novallas, Cascante, 1489–96; 1490–94, fol. 102r.

13. A.P.T., Pedro Latorre, 1492–98, fols. 110v–11r.

14. A.P.T., Pedro Latorre, 1492–98, fol. 30lv and in the margin. On April 30 a review was submitted of the properties taken from the expelled Aragonese Jews. The review had been in the custody of the royal Aragonese official mosén Domingo Agostín; the assets of Ezmel Abnarrabi also figured in it prominently. See note 3 above.

15. Archivo General de Navarra (hereafter A.G.N.), Cámara de Comptos, Documentos, Caj. 165 no. 80, fol. 63v, par. 1. On conflicts between *foranos* and *nativos*, see Gampel, *The Last Jews*, 113.

16. The relevant documents, respectively, are A.G.N., Cámara de Comptos, Documentos, Caj. 165 no. 80, fol. 64r, par. 6; Caj. 166 no. 7 fols. 18v, par. 1 and 21v, par. 5; and Caj. 165 no. 80, fol. 64r, par. 6. I have identified Rabí Çarça with Açac Çarça; see Gampel, *The Last Jews*, 194, n. 93.

17. Archivo Diocesano de Zaragoza, Libro de Actos comunes y de Ordenes,1492–97, fol. 153v as summarized in Motis, *Aragón*, 2:173.

18. The distances are listed in Motis, *Aragón*, 2:224, 260, 281.

19. Motis quoted from and discussed A.H.P.Z., Proceso contra Johan Sánchez, justicia de Biel, 1495–1496. See, for example, his *Aragón*, 155–56, 167, 168, 177–78, 203, 215, 225.

20. Yosef ha-Kohen's report can be found in his *Sefer Divrei ha-Yamim le-Malkhei Ẓarefat u-Malkhei Beit Ottoman ha-Togar* (Amsterdam, 1733), part 1, 49a and b; and idem, *Emek ha-Bakha*, ed. M. Letteris (Cracow, 1895), 101–2. Ferdinand's permission to Jewish exiles is in Antonio de la Torre, *Documentos sobre relaciones internacionales de los Reyes Católicos* (Barcelona, 1962), 4:137–40. In 1489, after Málaga had fallen to the armies of Ferdinand and Isabella, Jewish captives were allowed to travel through Andalusia, from which Jews had been expelled in 1483. Since these captives were not able to speak Castilian, Jews from Castile were permitted to accompany them. The relevant documents were first published in Fritz Baer, ed., *Die Juden im Christlichen Spanien* (Berlin, 1936), 1:391–393, part 2, no. 366, and again by Luis Suárez Fernández in his *Documentos acerca de la expulsión de los judíos* (Valladolid, 1964), 315–17. See also Baer, *Die Juden*, 393–94, and Suárez, *Documentos*, 327–29.

21. Shem Tov Gamil's account was published by Y. M. Toledano in *Hebrew Union College Annual* 5 (1928), 403–9. The text is discussed in Gampel, *The Last Jews*, 130–31. The text has now been translated into English in David Raphael, *The Expulsion 1492 Chronicles* (North Hollywood, Cal., 1992), 116–21.

22. A.C.A. Real Cancillería, Reg. 3567, fol. 104v, as quoted in Motis, *Aragón*, 2:412–13.

23. See what I argued in Gampel, *The Last Jews*, 119.

24. A.P.T., Pedro Latorre, 1492–1498, fol. 200r (and cf. 99v where he is mistakenly called Habran).

25. See the documents numbered 3, 5 (which involves Brahem as well), 11, 43 and 55, in Miguel Ángel Motis Dolader, ed., *The Expulsion of the Jews from Calatayud, 1492–1500: Documents and Regesta* (Jerusalem, 1990), 49–50, 52–54, 68, 71–72.

26. Both documents are summarized in Gonzálo Maximo Borrás Gualis, "Liquidación de los bienes de los judíos expulsados de la aljama de Calatayud," *Sefarad*, 29 (1969), documents 9 and 10, pp. 39–40; and now also briefly in Motis, *Calatayud*, documents 102, 106, pp. 117–18.

27. The document in which Çadoque was released from his obligation is A.P.T., Sancho Ezquerro, 1480–1500, fol. 385r. It has now been published in Motis, *Calatayud*, 188 as no. 244. Since Motis has the name as Simuel Çado (he separated the "Çado" and the "que"), he did not identify this individual with Simuel Çadoch. Çadoch changed his name to Alonso Daybar; see A.P.T., Pedro

Latorre, 1492–98, fol. 348r-v. The *comanda* contract with his uncle is described in three texts in A.P.T., Sancho Ezquerro, 1480–1500, fols. 385v–86r. On Simuel Çadoque, see Gampel, *The Last Jews*, 73, and the notes thereto. Property of Simuel Çadoch, which he owned with Mosse Paçagon, was still the object of transfer by those involved in processing the expulsion; see the document dated August 5, 1494, reprised in Motis, *Calatayud*, no. 243, pp. 187–88.

28. The documents respectively are in A.P.T., Pedro Latorre, 1492–98, fols. 279r–v; fol. 300r and in the margin. fol. 348r–v records the promise Mastre Andreo had made to repay the debt by the end of March.

29. A.P.T., Juhan Martinez Cabero, 1493, fol. 2v for the document of April 25 of the year. This source has now been summarized in Motis, *Calatayud*, no. 176, pp. 151–52. The source for Çulema's and Abram's whereabouts on March 2, 1492, is A.H.P.Z., Protocolo de Antón Maurán, 1492, cuaderno suelto, which is summarized in Motis, *Calatayud*, no. 37, p. 65. The matter at hand was a rental paid by the Muslim *aljama* of Jatiel, which was sold to Moses Paçagon on April 11, 1469, and was inherited by Çalema and Abram. The "Juderia of the castle of Tudela" is explained in *The Last Jews*, 18–19.

For the list of the Paçagons in Calatayud, see Motis, *Calatayud*, 318–19 and his comment on the difficulties in creating a genealogy of this family. Motis does not attempt to resolve any of the issues that he raised, nor has he carefully combed the documents he himself published for all the clues therein.

30. The July 11 source which is A.H.P.C., Protocolo de Pedro Díaz, 1486–92, fols. 436v–437v, was first summarized by Borrás Gualis, "Liquidación de los bienes de los judios expulsados de la aljama de Calatayud," no. 14, pp. 40–41; and also now briefly in Motis, *Calatayud*, no. 116, pp. 124–125. In a reference therein to a document appointing him as *procurador* on January 28, 1490, Çalema is identified as a Jew of Calatayud. In his notes, Motis, *Calatayud* adds references to other related documents. Another such power of attorney was registered on August 25, 1483; again see the note that Motis added to no. 152, p. 141. The document of July 18 is A.H.P.C., Protocolo de Pedro Díaz, 1486–92, fols. 455v–456, and is summarized in Borrás Gualis, no. 37, p. 46, where the date given is July 17; and in Motis as no. 138, p. 135. That of July 25 is encapsulated by Motis as no. 331, pp. 242–43. Çalema was still negotiating *aljama* business on July 27; see Motis, nos. 379, 386 on pp. 283–84, 286–87.

31. Motis, *Calatayud*, no. 157, p. 143; Açac and Jaco were two other Paçagon brothers mentioned in the document. The notary was the royal Navarrese notary and Tudelan Pedro de Castelroys (to be identified with Pedro Jiménez de Castelruiz). The August 12 document is A.H.P.Z., Protocolo de Martin de la Çayda, 1492, fols. 1051r–1056v, and published in Motis, no. 159, pp. 144–45. The September 1 sale is in A.H.P.Z., Protocolo de Martin de la Zayda [*sic*]. Motis has

the name of this notary spelled differently in these documents, 1492, fols. 103v–4v, summarized in Motis, no. 161, p. 146.

32. A.P.T., Pedro Latorre, 1492–98, fol. 5r for 1493 and fols. 16v–17r for 1494. On the activities of the *comisarios* of the Aragonese monarchy who dealt with the property of the exiled Jews and the many other officials involved in the expulsion and its aftermath, see generally, Motis, *Aragon*, 1:180–191 passim.

33. A.P.T., Pedro Latorre, 1492–1498, fol. 109v. A document of August 11, 1495, from the notarial archives in Calatayud incidentally helps us understand who "the molones" were. They are listed in A.H.P.C., Protocolo de Pedro Díaz, 1495, fols. 57v–58r as the officials in charge of the debts that Çalema Paçagon left behind when he traveled to Navarre. The Calatayud source is summarized in Motis, *Calatayud*, no. 297, p. 221.

34. A.C.A. Real Cancillería, Registro 3567, fols. 134v–136v, published in Motis, *Calatayud*, as no. 271, pp. 204–7. In the years immediately after the expulsion, Ferdinand and Isabella had issued calls to Jews who traveled to Portugal and Navarre as a result of the 1492 edict to return to their homes as Christians and, presumably, to recover all their property. See for example, Archivo General de Simancas Registro del Sello. 1492-XI, fol. 40 and 1493-VII, fol. 51, as published in Luis Suárez Fernández, *Documentos*, nos. 231, 258, on pp. 487–89 and 526–27, respectively. A direct order from Ferdinand, such as the erstwhile Çalema Paçagon had received, would ensure that his property be returned quickly and not be subject to all the entangling legal problems that usually attended such attempts.

35. There are other references to Çalema's property in the documentation from Calatayud; see, for example, Motis, *Calatayud*, no. 257, pp. 194–97, and no. 361, p. 268.

36. The record of the baptism is in A.P.T., Juhan Martinez Cabero, vol. 1498, fol. 5v, and is discussed in Gampel, *The Last Jews*, 132. It has now been published in Motis, *Calatayud*, no. 363, p. 269, and there cited as fol. 70v of the same notarial volume (there are conflicting paginations in this as well as other Tudelan notarial registers). Brahem's release of his brother from his obligation is in A.P.T., Pedro Latorre, 1492–98, fol. 109v. margin. See note 33 above.

It is interesting to note that the documents of October 18, 1493, and of January 13, 1494, recorded by Pedro de la Torre were witnessed by Johan de Berrozpe. We can speculate whether this individual was a relative who had converted earlier. The Paçagons and another New Christian family that appears in Navarre, the Daybar clan, were related. See Motis, *Calatayud*, nos. 382 and 383, p. 285. On the Daybar family, see Gampel, *The Last Jews*, 72. There I suggest that Johan Miguel de Munarriz of Tudela might have been a New Christian. Johan de Munarriz, "menor de dias," was one of the witnesses to Brahem's release of his brother from debt in late 1498.

8. Self-Definition of the Sephardic Jews

1. On the special economic function of the Sephardic diaspora in Western Europe in this period, see the pertinent parts of Jonathan I. Israel, *European Jewry in the Age of Mercantilism, 1550–1750* (Oxford, 1985).

2. On the attitude of the Sephardic community in Amsterdam toward Ashkenazic Jews, see Yosef Kaplan, "The Portuguese Community in Seventeenth-Century Amsterdam and the Ashkenazi World," in Jozeph Michman, ed., *Dutch Jewish History* (Jerusalem, 1989), 2:23 ff.

3. See in *Livro de Ascamoth* A in the archives of the Portuguese community of Amsterdam (henceforth; GAA, PIG), no. 19, fol. 70. The regulations of the merger of 1639 were published by Wilhelmina Chr. Pieterse, *Daniel Levi de Barrios als geschiedschrijver* (Amsterdam, 1968), 155–67; on these regulations, see Arnold Wiznitzer, "The Merger Agreement and Regulations of Congregation Talmud Torah of Amsterdam, 1638–39," *Historia Judaica* 20 (1958), 109–32.

4. On the Portuguese Jews in Hamburg and the nearby communities and on their connections with Ashkenazic Jews, see Hermann Kellenbenz, *Sephardim an der untern Elbe* (Wiesbaden, 1958). For a general survey of the Sephardic Jews in Germany during the seventeenth century see idem, "History of the Sephardim in Germany," in R. D. Barnett and W. M. Schwab, eds., *The Sephardi Heritage* (Grendon, Northants, 1989), 2:26–40.

5. A photocopy of the *Livros de Ascamoth* of the Beth Israel community in Hamburg from the years 1652–1683 is to be found in the Central Archive for the History of the Jewish People in Jerusalem, and I have used this photocopy for the present study (henceforth *Ascamoth Hamburg* A, B); and see ibid., A, fols. 28, 32.

6. The first book of *Ascamoth* of the *Sahar Asamaim* community in London was published in English translation by Lionel D. Barnett, *El Libro de los Acuerdos, Being the Records and Accompts of the Spanish and Portuguese Synagogue of London from 1663 to 1681* (Oxford, 1931), 3. On the relations of the Sephardic community in London to Ashkenazic Jews, see Albert M. Hyamson, *The Sephardim of England* (London, 1951), index.

7. See in *Livro do Mahamad*, in the Archives of the Sephardic Community of London (MS 103), fol. 6v.

8. Ibid., fol. 14r.

9. Ibid., fol. 64r.

10. See Arnold Wiznitzer, *Jews in Colonial Brazil* (New York, 1960), 131.

11. S. Dubnov, ed., *Pinkas ha-Medina o Pinkas Va'ad ha-Kehilot ha-Rishonot bi-Medinat Lita* (Berlin, 1925), p. 17, par. 99.

12. On the apologetic struggle within the Western Sephardic diaspora against the ethnocentrism within Spanish thought at that time, see Yosef Hayim Yerushalmi, *From Spanish Court to Italian Ghetto: Isaac Cardoso. A Study in*

Seventeenth-Century Marranism and Jewish Apologetics (New York and London, 1971), 352 ff.; cf. Yosef Kaplan, *From Christianity to Judaism: The Story of Isaac Orobio de Castro* (Oxford, 1989), 173 ff.

13. On views of this kind in Spanish literature at that time, see esp. Henri Méchoulan, "L'altérité juive dans la pensée espagnole (1550–1650)," *Studia Rosenthaliana* 8 (1974), 31–48, 171–203; idem, *Le sang de l'autre ou l'honneur de Dieu* (Paris, 1979).

14. See Isaac Orobio de Castro, *Respuesta a un cavallero francés*, MS Ets Haim 48 D 6, fol. 307r.

15. Kaplan, *From Christianity to Judaism*, 324 ff.

16. Yosef Kaplan, "Political Concepts in the World of the Portuguese Jews of Amsterdam during the Seventeenth Century: The Problem of Exclusion and the Boundaries of Self-Identity," in et al., eds., *Menasseh Ben Israel and His World* (Leiden, 1989), 57 ff.

17. GAA, PIG 19, fol. 173.

18. Ibid., fol. 224.

19. See Menasseh ben Israel, *Esperanza de Israel* (Amsterdam, 5410 [1650]), 118.

20. Juan Huarte de San Juan, *Examen de ingenios para las ciencias* (Baeza, 1575). I quote from the critical edition of Esteban Torre (Madrid, 1976), 237 ff., see also 241, 245.

21. Menasseh ben Israel, *To His Highnesse the Lord Protector of the Common-Wealth of England, Scotland and Ireland. The Humble Addresses* (London 1655), fol. 1. See the facsimile edition of that work in Lucien Wolf, *Menasseh ben Israel's Mission to Oliver Cromwell* (London, 1901), 81, 103.

22. See Yshac Cardoso, *Las excelencias de los hebreos* (Amsterdam, 1679), 364.

23. I discussed this entire matter in Yosef Kaplan, "Jewish Refugees from Germany and Poland-Lithuania in Amsterdam During the Seventeenth Century" (in Hebrew), in Roberto Bonfil, Menahem Ben Sasson, and Joseph Hacker, eds., *Culture and Society in Medieval Jewry, Studies Dedicated to the Memory of Haim Hillel Ben-Sasson* (Jerusalem, 1989), 587–622; on assistance to the communities of Eastern Europe during the persecutions between 1648 and 1660, see ibid., 604 ff.

24. Cf. *Ascamoth Hamburg* A, fol. 462 (emphasis added); *Ascamoth Hamburg* B, p. 59: "Considerando devemos primeiro acudir ao desempenho de nossa congrega que ao de outras."

25. See GAA, PIG 19, fol. 426.

26. Ibid

27. *Ascamoth Hamburg* A, fol. 152.

28. On changes in the size of the Jewish population of Amsterdam during the seventeenth century in general and on the relation between Sephardim and Ashkenazim in particular, see Yosef Kaplan, "Amsterdam and Ashkenazic Migration in the Seventeenth Century," *Studia Rosentaliana* 23 (1989), 23–44.

29. See Kaplan, "The Portuguese Community," 41 ff.

30. Ibid., 28 ff.

31. *Ascamoth Hamburg* A, fol. 35.

32. See *Livro de Mahamad*, 6 Adar 5439 (1679).

33. See GAA, PIG 19, fol. 375.

34. See, for example, *Ascamoth Hamburg* A, fol. 59.

35. He is mentioned in various documents as "Ers semas das mulheres." In addition to his salary, he at first also received contributions from the community charity fund. On him, see GAA, PIG no. 172, fols. 210, 249, 296; no. 173, fols. 75, 162; no. 174, fols. 218, 224, 227, etc.

36. On this phenomenon, see Yosef Kaplan, "Eighteenth Century Rulings by the Rabbinical Court of Amsterdam's Community and Their Socio-Historical Significance" (in Hebrew), in Jozeph Michman, ed., *Studies in the History of Dutch Jewry* (1988), 5:37–40. I intend to publish a comprehensive article on this subject in the near future.

37. GAA, PIG 19, fol. 20.

38. Ibid., fols. 430–31.

39. Ibid. fol. 533.

40. See *Ascamoth Hamburg* A, fol. 256.

41. See ibid., B, fols. 372, 377.

42. In the first half of the seventeenth century there was a tendency to send the poor eastward, to the Ottoman Empire, including Palestine. See Israel Bartal and Yosef Kaplan, "Emigration of Indigent Jews from Amsterdam to Erez Israel (Palestine) at the Beginning of the Seventeenth Century" (in Hebrew), *Shalem 6* (1992), 177–94. With the establishment of Jewish settlements in the New World, especially in the Caribbean, the poor of the community were sent there, especially to Surinam, Curaçao, Barbados, and Jamaica. See Robert Cohen, "Passage to a New World: The Sephardi Poor of Eighteenth-Century Amsterdam," in Lea Dasberg and Johnathan N. Cohen, eds., *Neveh Ya'akov: Jubilee Volume Presented to Dr. Jaap Meijer* (Assen, 1982), 31–42.

43. On that society, see, inter alia, Pieterse, *Daniel Levi de Barrios als geschiedschrijver*, 132; GAA, PIG 19, fols. 109–12.

44. De Pinto's work appeared anonymously in two editions: Amsterdam (1762) and Paris (n.d.). The Paris edition bears the title *Apologie pour la nation juive. Réflexions critiques sur le premier chapitre du viie tome des oeuvres de monsieur de Voltaire au sujet des juifs.* This is also the subtitle of the Amsterdam edition. On De Pinto's response to Voltaire, see Arthur Hertzberg, *The French Enlightenment and the Jews* (New York, 1970), 180 ff.

45. See GAA, PIG 19, fol. 643.

46. Ibid., 20, fol. 230; emphasis added.

47. Ibid., fol. 510.

48. See Jozeph Michman, "Between Sephardim and Ashkenazim in Amsterdam," (in Hebrew), in Issachar Ben-Ami, ed., *The Sephardi and Oriental Jewish Heritage* (Jerusalem, 1952), 136, n. 7; D. S. van Zuiden, "Een eigenaardige begrafeniskwestie in 1825, Portugeesch contra Hoogduitsch," *De Vridagavond* 6 (1930), 395–96.

49. All of the documents on this matter have already been mentioned in Yosef Kaplan, "The Attitude of the Spanish and Portuguese Jews to the Ashkenazic Jews in Seventeenth-Century Amsterdam" (in Hebrew), in Shmuel Almog et al., eds., *Transition and Change in Modern Jewish History: Essays Presented in Honor of Shmuel Ettinger* (Jerusalem, 1987), 406–8; cf. Herman Prins Salomon, "Myth or Anti-Myth? The Oldest Accounts Concerning the Origin of Portuguese Judaism at Amsterdam," *LIAS* 16 (1989), 275–316, also published in his work, *Deux etudes portugaises. Two Portuguese Studies* (Braga, 1991), 105–61.

50. On this issue, see A. A. Sicroff, *Les controverses des statuts de "pureté de sang" en Espagne du XVième au XVIIième siècle* (Paris, 1960).

9. Prototypes of Leadership in a Sephardic Community

This paper was completed during my tenure as a research fellow at the Institute for Advanced Studies at the Hebrew University of Jerusalem during the academic year 1991–1992.

1. Jacob Barnai, "The Origins of the Jewish Community in Smyrna in the Ottoman Period" (in Hebrew), *Pe'amim* 12 (1982), 47–58; idem, "Portuguese Marranos in Smyrna in the Seventeenth Century" (in Hebrew), in Menahem Stern, ed., *Nation and History* (Jerusalem, 1983), 1:289–98.; idem, "Congregations in Smyrna in the Seventeenth Century" (in Hebrew), *Pe'amim* 48 (1991), 66–84; Daniel Goffman, *Izmir and the Levantine World, 1550–1650* (Seattle, 1990), 77–92.

2. Barnai, "Portuguese Marranos"; idem, "The Sabbatean Movement in Smyrna: The Social Background," in Menahem Mor, ed., *Jewish Sects, Religious Movements, and Political Parties* (Omaha, 1992), 113–22.

3. Jacob Barnai, "A Document from Smyrna Concerning the History of Sabbatianism" (in Hebrew), *Jerusalem Studies in Jewish Thought* 2 (1982), 118–31.

4. Abraham Yaari, "The Hebrew Press in Smyrna" (in Hebrew), *Aresheth* 1 (1959), 101, nn. 3, 4, 9, 11, 12.

5. R. Joseph Escapa, *"Rosh Yosef" Responsa* (Frankfurt-am-Oder, 1709); Meir Benayahu, "Information About the Printing and Distribution of Books in Italy" (in Hebrew), *Sinai* 3 (1954), 165–67.

6. Salomon Rosanes, *History of the Jews in Turkey and the Eastern Countries* (Sofia, 1934–35), 4:168; Leah Bornstein, "The Jewish Communal Leadership in the Near East from the End of the Fifteenth Century Through the Eighteenth Century" (in Hebrew), Ph.D. diss., Bar-Ilan University, 1978, 128.

7. Barnai, "Congregations in Smyrna in the Seventeenth Century," 78–79.

8. Meir Benayahu, "The Sabbatian Movement in Greece," *Sefunot* (Book of Greek Jewry, IV) 14 (Jerusalem, 1971–77), 338, n. 66.

9. R. Abraham Palagi, *'Avraham 'Ezkor* (Smyrna, 1879), 35–36; Barnai, "A Document"; Gershom Scholem, *Sabbatai Ṣevi: The Mystical Messiah* (Princeton, 1973), 379, n. 104.

10. Scholem, *Sabbatai Ṣevi*, 124, n. 331.

11. Ibid., 123.

12. Aron Freimann, *Issues About Sabbatai Ẓevi* (in Hebrew) (Berlin, 1913), 142.

13. Ulker Necmi, "The Rise of Izmir, 1688–1740," Ph.D. diss., University of Michigan, 1974, 254.

14. Barnai, "A Document," 123–24.

15. Benayahu, "Information About the Printing," 188–89.

16. Ibid.; Jacob Spiegel, "Rabbi Solomon Algazi: Biographical and Bibliographical Observations" (in Hebrew), *'Alei Sefer* 4 (1977), 117–36.

17. Scholem, *Sabbatai Ṣevi*, 374, 389–90.

18. Moshe Idel, "One from a Town and Two from a Clan: The Diffusion of Lurianic Kabbalah and Sabbatianism: A Re-Examination," *Jewish History* 7 (1993), 79–104.

19. R. Solomon Algazi, *Me'ulefet Sapirim* (Istanbul, 1660), preface.

20. Scholem, *Sabbatai Ṣevi*, 414–15.

21. Spiegel, "Rabbi Solomon Algazi," 117–25.

22. Ibid., 132.

23. Jacob Barnai, "Connections and Disconnections Between the Sages of Turkey and of Poland and Central Europe in the Seventeenth Century" (in Hebrew), *Gal-'Ed* 9 (1986), 23, n. 53

24. Samuel Werses, "Rabbi Elijah Hacohen of Smyrna" (in Hebrew), *Yavneh* 2 (1942), 156–73; Gershom Scholem, "Rabbi Elijah Hacohen Ha-Itamari and Sabbatianism" (in Hebrew), *Jubilee Volume in Honor of Alexander Marx* (New York, 1950), 451–70; David Tamar, *Studies in the History of the Jews in Palestine and the Oriental Countries* (in Hebrew) (Jerusalem, 1981), 105–6; Benayahu, *The Sabbatian Movement*, 338 n. 66.

25. Barnai, "Connections," 23, nn. 54–55.

26. Scholem, "Rabbi Elijah Hacohen."

27. Jacob Barnai, "The 'Yishuv' in Palestine During the Years 1740–77 and Its Connections with the Diaspora" (in Hebrew), Ph.D. diss., Hebrew University, 1975, 195; idem, *The Jews in Palestine in the Eighteenth Century*, trans. N. Goldblum, (Tuscaloosa, 1992), 35.

28. Isaiah Tishby, *The Paths of Belief and Heresy* (in Hebrew) (Ramat Gan, 1964), 163–67.

29. Werses, "R. Elijah Hacohen," 166–69.

30. R. David Konforti, *Kore' ha-Dorot* (Berlin, 1846), 46.

31. R. Haim Benveniste, *Ba'ei Ḥayyai, Ḥoshen Mishpat* (Salonika, 1788), p. 119b, part 1, par. 105; Joseph Hacker, "The Jewish Community of Salonika from the Fifteenth to the Sixteenth Centuries" (in Hebrew), Ph.D. diss., Hebrew University, 1978, 159–220; Goffman, *Izmir*, 78–84.

32. Jacob Barnai, "R. Joseph Escapa and the Smyrna Rabbinate" (in Hebrew), *Sefunot* 18 (1985), 56.

33. R. Joseph Escapa, *Rosh Yosef, 'Oraḥ Ḥayyim* (Smyrna, 1658); idem, *Ḥoshen Mishpat* (Smyrna, 1659); idem, *"Rosh Yosef" Responsa*.

34. R. Raphael Joseph Ḥazan, *Ḥikrei Lev, Ḥoshen Mishpat* (Salonika, 1832), part 2, 37a.

35. R. Joshua Abraham Judah, *'Avodat Masa'* (Salonika, 1846), editor's introduction.

36. Ibid.

37. Ibid., author's introduction, 55b.

38. Ibid., 56b.

39. R. Joseph ben Ezra, *Masa' Melekh* (Salonika, 1600).

40. See, e.g., Judah, *'Avodat Masa'*, 4a, 59b.

41. Barnai, "R. Joseph Escapa," 56–58.

42. Leah Bornstein, "The Jewish Communal Leadership," 15–56.

43. Barnai, "R. Joseph Escapa," 58–70; Hacker, "The Jewish Community," 218; H. J. Zimmels, *Ashkenazim and Sephardim* (London, 1958), 199–204; Mosheh Amar, *'Eẓ Ḥayyim by Rabbi Haim Gaguine* (in Hebrew) (Ramat Gan, 1987), 67 ff.

44. Barnai, "R. Joseph Escapa," 70–75.

45. Hacker, "The Jewish Community," 265–75.

46. Hacker, "The Jewish Community," 92–98.

47. Hacker, "Ottoman Policy Toward the Jews and the Jewish Attitude Toward Ottomans During the Fifteenth Century," in B. Lewis and B. Braude, eds., *Christians and Jews in the Ottoman Empire* (New York, 1982), 117–26; idem, "The Ottoman System of *Surgun* and Its Influence on Jewish Society in the Ottoman Empire" (in Hebrew), *Zion* 55 (1990), 27–82.

48. Barnai, "R. Joseph Escapa," 75–81.

49. Scholem, *Sabbatai Ṣevi*, 138–51, 174–77.

50. Ibid., 378–80; Tamar, *Studies*, 119–135.

51. Tamar, *Studies*, 106.

52. Fernand Braudel, *The Mediterranean and the Mediterranean World in the Age of Philip II* (New York, 1966), 280, 284, 733, 746; Meir Benayahu, "Moses Benveniste: Court Physician to the Sultan, and Rabbi Judah Zarko's Poem on His Exile to Rhodes" (in Hebrew), *Sefunot* 12 (1971–78), 123–44.

53. Scholem, *Sabbatai Ṣevi*, 389–416; Tamar, *Studies*, 119–35; J. Barnai, "R. Haim Benveniste's Road to the Smyrna Rabbinate" (in Hebrew), 151–91, in Minna Rozen, ed., *Days of the Crescent* (Tel Aviv, 1996).

54. There are many sources for this episode; only the most important ones are listed here: R. Moses Benveniste, *Pnei Moshe* (Istanbul 1719), part 3, 3a; Palagi, *'Avraham 'Ezkor*, 35a; R. Haim Benveniste, *Knesset ha-Gedolah, Ḥoshen Mishpat* (Smyrna, 1734), part 2, 217b; R. Aaron Lapapa, *Bnei 'Aharon* (Smyrna, 1674), 104a; R. Haim Benveniste, *Ba'ei Ḥayyai, Ḥoshen Mishpat*, part 1, 27b. I intend to enlarge upon this issue elsewhere.

55. J. Barnai, "Messianism and Leadership: The Sabbatean Movement and the Leadership of the Jewish Communities in the Ottoman Empire," in Aron Rodrigue, ed., *Ottoman and Turkish Jews* (Bloomington, 1992), 170–74.

56. Palagi, *'Avraham 'Ezkor*, 35.

57. R. Haim Benviste, *Ba'ei Ḥayyai*, part 1, par. 105, p. 119b.

58. R. Abraham ben Ezra, *Batei Knesiyot* (Salonika, 1846), 20b.

59. Barnai, "Messianism and Leadership."

60. R. Benveniste wrote two volumes of his commentary on this book; they are called *Dinah deḤayyai*, 2 vols. (Instanbul, 1742). See also R. Haim Beveniste, *Knesset ha-Gedolah, 'Oraḥ Ḥayyim* (Livorno, 1791), introduction.

61. He calls them *The Collected Responsa*. Three volumes of them have been preserved in manuscript, some of them autographs, in the archives of the Jewish Theological Seminary of New York, nos. R1385/AB and R1386. R. Haim Benveniste, *Knesset ha-Gedolah* (Livorno, 1685; Istanbul, 1716), vols. 1–8. See also M. Benayahu, The Book *Bet Yosef* and the Turning Point in Halakhic Literature" (in Hebrew), *'Asufot* 3 (1989), 136–37.

62. Yaari, "The Hebrew Press in Smyrna," 98; J. Hacker, "An Emissary of Louis XIV in the Levant and the Culture of Ottoman Jewry" (in Hebrew), *Zion* 52 (1987), 31–38; Tamar, *Studies*, 123.

63. R. Haim Benveniste, *Knesset ha-Gedolah*, 1b.

64. R. Haim Benveniste, *Ba'ei Ḥayyai* (Salonika, 1788–89), vols. 1–4.

65. R. Haim Benveniste, *The Responsa of Ḥaim Benveniste* (Istanbul, 1743).

66. Here are a number of places where the Zohar and kabbalistic traditions are mentioned in R. Benveniste's writings (the problem in general requires a separate discussion): *Knesset ha-Gedolah, 'Oraḥ Ḥayyim*, 1a, 3a, 7a, 13a, 32a, 32b, 41b; *Sheyyarei Knesset ha-Gedolah* (Istanbul, 1729); *'Oraḥ Ḥayyim*, 1a, 12b, 16a, 45a, 47b–48a, 52a, 120a.

67. R. Abraham ben Ezra, *Batei Knesiyot*, 21a.

68. R. Haim Palagi, *Lev Ḥayyim* (Salonika, 1823), 1:31b.

69. R. Haim Palagi, *Ḥikkekei Lev* (Salonika, 1840), part 1, 58b.

10. Sephardic Refugees in Ferrara

1. ASA (Archivio di Stato, Ancona); ASC (Archivio storico comunale); ASF (Archivio di Stato, Ferrara); ASFI (Archivio di Stato, Firenze); ASM (Archivio di Stato, Modena); ASV (Archivio di Stato, Venezia); BAV (Biblioteca Apostolica

Vaticana); CD (Cancelleria ducale); Not. (Notarile); b. (busta); fz. (filza); matr. (matricola). The bibliography on the Abravanels in Ferrara is scanty; their genealogy (see *Encyclopedia Judaica*, vol. 2, cols. 103–4) is not definitive and requires further research. Much more is already known about the Mendes/De Luna/Nasi family, thanks mainly to the work of Paul Grünbaum Ballin, *Joseph Naci duc de Naxos* (Paris, 1968); and Cecil Roth, *The House of Nasi: Dona Gracia* (Philadelphia, 1948). Reference will be made to these books only in specific cases.

2. The term was not always used in a deprecatory way; at least until 1555 (when Cardinal Carafa ascended the papal throne) it maintained a matter-of-fact meaning. But it is a word that has not yet been sufficiently investigated. For a general picture, see Renata Segre, "Sephardic Settlements in Sixteenth Century Italy: A Historical and Geographical Survey," *Mediterranean Historical Review*, 6 (December 1991), 112–37.

3. V. Bonazzoli, "Gli ebrei del Regno di Napoli all'epoca della loro espulsione," *Archivio storico italiano* 137 (1979), 495–559; 139 (1981), 179–287. For new data on the Abravanels, and especially Samuel under the rule of the Aragonese, see Cesare Colafemmina, *Documenti per la storia degli ebrei in Puglia nell'Archivio di Stato di Napoli* (Bari, 1990), esp. 308–9. It is perhaps worth mentioning a certain merchant, called Didaco (alias Diogo) Consalves Abravanello "de Rinchon vicinus Lisbone," in Venice in 1556 and in Ferrara in 1557, whose family relation with the Abravanels may only be surmised for the time being. ASF, *Not.*, matr. 584, Giacomo Conti, b. 7, September 30, 1556, January 5, 1557.

4. Ibid., matr. 493, Battista Saracco, b. 29, July 4, 1550.

5. Ibid., matr. 534, Andrea Cocapani, b. 9, November 2, 1557; another formula of oath was "tactis scripturis sacre Biblie hebrayce per legem datam Moysi in monte Synay." Ibid.

6. ASV, *Giudice di petizion*. Terminazioni, reg. 63, fols. 134r-35v, 160v.

7. ASF, *Not.*, Battista Saracco, b. 29, July 4, 1550.

8. For the episode see ASV, *Consiglio dei Dieci*. Secrete, fz. 9, ed. P.C. Ioly Zorattini, *Processi del S. Uffizio di Venezia contro ebrei e giudaizzanti, 1548–1560* (Florence, 1980), 347. On that occasion Brianda made two statements illuminating her insight: she claimed that she had fled her fatherland only for fear of the Inquisition "ché io stava bene lì"; and she wished to be allowed to remain in Venice and live in the ghetto "with the other Jews."

9. ASF, *Not.*, Giacomo Conti, b. 8, October 20, 1558.

10. Ibid., b. 7, September 26, 1553.

11. Renata Segre, "Nuovi documenti sui marrani d'Ancona (1555–1559)," *Michael* 9 (1985), 152.

12. Louis Finkelstein, *Jewish Self-Government in the Middle Ages* (New York, 1924), 303.

13. The renunciation of the former Jew Gian Silvio, the youngest son of "ser" Abram Zarfati, to all his estate in favor of his brothers is in ASF, *Not.*, matr. 619,

Cesare Sacrati, May 27, 1549. The duke instructed his ambassador in Rome to assist Salomon Ẓarfati, agent of Isac and Jacob Abravanel, and very capable negotiator at the Curia on behalf of the Jews living in the Papal states. ASM. *CD,* Ambasciatori. Rome, January 22, 1551.

14. The only relative mentioned in the will of Alfonso Abravanel, merchant in Venice, is his brother "don Lion," who is to inherit all his wealth and jewels. ASV, *Not.* Testamenti, Ottavio Novelli, b. 751, August 21, 1591; Atti, b. 10532, October 16, 1590. In a petition to Cardinal Sirleto (protector of the catechumens) Alfonso claimed that his elder brothers moved to the Levant right before his baptism in order to deprive him of his family possessions. BAV, *Ott. Lat. 2452,* fol. 124r. So far I have been unable to identify the neophyte: the youngest son of Samuel was Leone, and therefore not the would-be convert.

15. ASF, *Not.,* Cesare Sacrati, b. 1, February 17, 1547, "rev. do presbitero don" Francesco de Gaudis of Naples.

16. Shlomo Simonsohn, *The Apostolic See and the Jews: Documents, 1522–1538* (Toronto, 1990), doc. 1851, pp. 2084–87. It applies also to Didaco/Diogo Mendez Benvenisti's brother Gundissalvo/Consalvo, his wife, Anna Mendez, and their children, February 22, 1538.

17. C. M. de Witte, *La correspondance des premiers nonces permanents au Portugal, 1532–1553* (Lisbon, 1980), 2:588–89. Cristoforo Manuel (and Duarte Pires), "clerici sive laici Ulixbonenses," as they were qualified in the papal safe conduct, were entrusted with the task: their briefs also cover facts of heresy, apostasy "et alios quoscumque, etiam maximos errores." Simonsohn, *The Apostolic See and the Jews: Documents, 1546–1555* (Toronto, 1990), docs. 2641, 2788, 2753, pp. 2554, 2622–23. On Manuel's return Beatriz acknowledged his accomplishments in Spain (Burgos and Medina de Campo), Lisbon (from where his partner Jacob Alvares was about to move to Ferrara), and Lyons. ASF, *Not.,* matr. 582, Gian Battista Codegori, b. 8, March 20, 1549.

18. The parish priests of San Felice, Santa Maria Formosa, and San Marziale, all near her residence in Santa Caterina. ASV, *Not.* Atti, Paolo Lioncini, b. 7818, fols. 180v–81r. The final agreement between the two sisters (ibid., fols. 176r–195r) does not differ in the essential from that of July 4, 1550 (ASF, *Not.,* Battista Saracco, b. 29), negotiated through the good offices of Hercules II, but, to his great disappointment, not ratified by the Venetian authorities. ASM, *CD,* Ambasciatori. Venezia, b. 37, 40, 41, among others.

19. ASV, *Consiglio dei Dieci.* Secrete, fz. 9, ed. Ioly Zorattini, *Processi . . . 1548–1560,* 261.

20. After settling all her main pending questions she sailed from Venice a few days later, on a vessel provided by the republic. ASV, *Collegio.* Notatorio, reg. 28, fol. 111r; *Not.* Atti, Paolo Lioncini, b. 7818, fols. 192v–94v.

21. Renata Segre, "Contribución documental a la historia de la imprenta Usque y de su edición de la Biblia," in I. M. Hassan, ed., *Introducción a la biblia de*

Ferrara. actas del simposio internacional, Sevilla, noviembre de 1991 (Madrid, 1994), 225–26.

22. Samuel Usque, *Consolação às tribulações de Israel* (Ferrara, 1553) repr., intro. Yosef Hayim Yerushalmi and Jose V. de Pina Martins (Lisbon, 1989), fol. IIr. It is acknowledged that the messianic expectations of the Iberian Jews, sustained by the *Consolaçao* by Usque and the trilogy (*Ma'ayane ha-Yeshu'a, Mashmi'a Yeshu'a, Yeshu'ot Meshiḥo*) by Isaac Abravanel, prompted the kabbalistic studies in the lands of exile.

23. ASF, *Not.*, Giacomo Conti, b. 4, September 22, 1549. One of the two witnesses at the deed was "domino" Fernando Mendes "lusitano," resident in Beatriz De Luna's house. See also note 55 below.

24. ASPR, *Carteggio farnesiano,* b. 173, governor Lionello Pio to Cardinal Farnese, Ancona, December 10, 1541.

25. Andrea Balletti, *Gli Ebrei e gli Estensi* (Reggio Emilia, 1930), 78.

26. ASM, *CD,* Carteggio di consiglieri, segretari e cancellieri, b. 8b, Bartolomeo Prospero to the duke, Ferrara, June 17, 1543.

27. "Don Samuel of Naples and his sons" are listed among the members of the Jewish community in Ferrara pardoned by the duke on payment of a "compositione." ASF., *Not.*, matr. 535, Maurelio Taurino, b. 6, September 17, 1544.

28. The patent letter is in ASV, *Consiglio dei Dieci.* Secrete, fz. 9, ed. by Ioly Zorattini, *Processi . . . 1548–1560,* 341–42.

29. ASV, *Capi del Consiglio dei Dieci,* Lettere comuni, fz. 48, n. 600, December 30, 1545. Notifying his king that "os Benvenistis" had arrived two months before in Venice, the Portuguese envoy explained their flight with their fear that King John III and Emperor Charles V might confiscate their wealth. *Corpo diplomatico portuguez . . .* por L. A. Rebello da Silva (Lisbon, 1884), 6: 14–15, Baltasar de Faria to King John III, Rome, February 16, 1546.

30. See esp. Grünbaum Ballin, *Joseph Naci,* 48–52.

31. The section of Diego's will concerning the appointment of his commissioners, his sister-in-law Beatriz (and, in case of her death, Agostino Anriques), Guglielmo Fernandez, and Giovan Micas is in Italian. ASF, *Not.*, Battista Saracco, b. 29, about January 28, 1549. Diego died between June 27 (date of his will) and July 4, 1543 (its publication). ASV, *Not.* Atti, Paolo Lioncini, b. 7818, fol. 177r.

32. ASV, *Senato.* Deliberazioni secrete, fz. 24, November 17, 1551.

33. Ibid., *Consiglio dei Dieci.* Secrete, fz. 9, ed. Ioly Zorattini, *Processi . . . 1548–1560,* 342. According to the earliest recorded evidence of Beatriz's arrival in Ferrara, on December 10, 1548, she was living with Sebastiano Pinto in contrada Sant'Agnese. ASF, *Not.*, matr. 569, Gerolamo Bonsignori, b. 3.

34. Ibid., Maurelio Taurino, b. 8, January 11, 1549. Hieronimo Dies was "majordomo" of the "splendidissima ingenii predita domina Beatrix ex Luna nobilis Lusitanie": the contract was renewed until Easter 1552, but since the tenant moved

to Venice before its expiration, the house was sublet on October 14, 1551, to the lord of Termes, "cavalier maggiore di Sua M.tà C. ma" and French envoy at the Este court for the rest of the time. Ibid., March 19, 1551.

35. Ibid., Battista Saracco, b. 29, about January 28, 1549.

36. Ibid., Gian Battista Codegori, b. 8 ff.

37. An autograph letter of "s.or Diego Mendez" to the duke, Antwerp, October 9, 1538, in ASM, *Lettere particolari*, b. 885.

38. Ibid., the original undated draft of a ducal safe-conduct in favor of Brianda and her daughter; owing to certain elements within the document, it may be assigned to their first transfer to Ferrara and not to that of the autumn 1555. A curiosity: on the verso appears "salvo conduto" in Hebrew characters. See below, n. 68.

39. *Consolação*, fol. CCXVIr–v, and the remarks by Yerushalmi, 1:69–70.

40. ASM, *CD*, Carteggio degli ufficiali camerali, b. 2 ff. (between September 14 and 27, 1549, for the plague and the negotiation of the charter; up to December for the contagion in Brianda's entourage). Actually the pestilence continued to rage in 1550: in fact the university rolls indicate that no lecture was held in that year ("propter suspitionem epidemie pestis que a mense augusti 1549 usque ad dictum tempus [feria quarta cineris 1550] merere affecit animas incolarum huius alme urbis Ferrare"). Jacob Abravanel returned to live in town in March 1550, whereas his brother Isac, who had sought refuge in the countryside in November, gave the farm back to its landlord over a year later, on April 17, 1551. ASF, ASC, *Serie finanziaria*, b. 14; *Not.*, Andrea Cocapani, b. 4, November 4, 1549. Balletti, *Gli Ebrei*, 78.

41. ASF., *Not.*, Giacomo Conti, b. 4, September 24 through October 22, 1549; matr. 576, Annibale Boldrini, b. 2, October 5–7, 1549.

42. The bad relationship between the two sisters was aggravated by Beatriz's decision to dismiss the licenciate Costa and his daughter, suspected of being contagious. The two headed for Bologna, whence Brianda managed to recall them. Another victim of the feud was Brianda's physician, who was forced to embark for the Levant. All this information comes from three autograph petitions Brianda addressed to the duke in the midst of the mediation he was attempting between the two De Luna sisters. ASM, *Lettere particolari*, b. 747. See also note 39 above.

43. ASF, *Not.*, Battista Saracco, b. 31, May 21, 1550.

44. Ibid., b. 29.

45. The duke, perhaps in an attempt to keep Beatriz in Ferrara, wrote to Diane de Poitiers on her behalf ("to assist such a person, especially in an issue involving a widow and underage girls, not only is pious and praised by God but makes me ever more obliged to Your Excellency, for I must assure her my protection in matters pertaining to justice since she has settled in my city, where she lives honorably" [deleted: "and performs many good deeds"]). The undated document contains no

indication of whether it preceded or followed the confiscation of Beatriz's estate to the benefit of the favorite of King Henry II. ASM, *Lettere particolari*, b. 885. Actually, a royal decree, dated Amboise, April 30, 1551, and registered by the parliament of Paris, acknowledged Beatriz's claims. ASF, *Not.*, Giacomo Conti, b. 5, September 17, 1551.

46. Ibid., Maurelio Taurino, b. 6, April 7 and 26, 1545; February 5 and April 5, 1546; although the company had been dissolved on December 24, 1548, Jacob's guaranty was still required. Actually, in the first deed the five-thousand-scudi security was in the name of his father, Samuel.

47. Abramo Pesaro, *Appendice alle Memorie storiche sulla comunità israelitica ferrarese* (Ferrara, 1880; repr. Bologna, 1967), 13. A copy of the papal brief may be found in the dossier on Brianda's expulsion from Venice (see note 66) with the indication that it had been granted at the request of David Caravon: in all likelihood the document was in the private "archive" of the De Luna sisters.

48. ASM, *CD*, Ambasciatori. Roma, b. 60. In a power of attorney of May 1555 he is termed a "Portuguese Jew" living in Ancona; in any case, he was still alive in 1559. ASF, *Not.*, Andrea Cocapani, b. 9, May 8, 1555, September 7, 1559. On the confiscation of his possessions in Ancona, see Segre, *Nuove testimonianze*, 202.

49. Ibid., 152–53.

50. At the end of 1556 the most active agent of the Abravanels in Ancona was Isac Fidalgo of Salonika, who availed himself of power of attorney (registered in Salonika on December 3, 1555, and in Ragusa [now Dubrovnik] on February 15, 1556) of *rubi* (i.e. Rabbi) Isac Abarbanel "Levantine Jew," resident in his same city. ASA, *Not.*, fz. 234, November 19, December 11, 1556; fz. 737, January 25, 1557. In the months of dire struggle between the advocates of the entrepôt in Ancona and its opponents, and as late as the 1560s, Pesaro was the place of residence and business of another of Samuel's sons, Juda alias Leone, to the great disappointment of his family. See also note 94 below.

51. The struggle for power between the two leading Jewish Tuscan groups (the Da Rietis, on one side, the Abravanels and their partners, the Da Pisas, on the other), is well illustrated by Bernard Dov Cooperman, "A Rivalry of Bankers: Responsa Concerning Banking Rights in Pisa, 1547," in Isadore Twersky, ed., *Studies in Medieval Jewish History and Literature* (Cambridge, Mass., 1984), 2:49, 64–65, 70.

52. Umberto Cassuto, *Gli Ebrei a Firenze nell'età del Rinascimento* (Florence, 1918; repr. Florence, 1965), 88–89. ASFI, *Mediceo del Principato*, b. 2879, August 8, September 12, 1557. A letter of warm recommendation written by the duke of Florence to the cardinal of San Vitale on his behalf, ibid., b. 3721, fol. 356r, October 15, 1552.

53. Cassuto, *Gli Ebrei a Firenze*, 173–76.

54. Ibid., 384–85.

55. For news on him and his family and the honors conferred on him by Cosimo de Medici and his successors, see Rita Mazzei, *Pisa medicea. L'economia cittadina da Ferdinando I a Cosimo III* (Florence, 1991), 31, 79–80; B. Casini, "I portoghesi aspiranti a essere ammessi tra i cavalieri del sacro militare Ordine di S. Stefano papa e martire," *Bollettino storico pisano*, 59 (1990), 287–23. See also note 23 above.

56. ASF, *Not.*, Giacomo Conti, b. 7, August 7, 1556.

57. Witte, *La correspondance des premiers nonces*, 2:31, about October 1533.

58. Ibid., 32.

59. Simonsohn, *The Apostolic See, 1546–1555*, doc. 2981, pp. 2771–74, Rome, March 17, 1551.

60. *Corpo diplomatico portuguez* (1884), vol. 7, Afonso de Alencastro to the king, Rome, June 20, 1554, pp. 356–57; Rome, the same to the queen, Rome, October 24, 1556, pp. 494–95.

61. Alessandro Guarini, factor general and ducal secretary (as his official title runs), counseled his master to remit the papal tax to the Curia through "signora Beatrice . . . who assured me that if we give her the money here in cash, she will have it transferred to Rome in due time at no additional cost." ASM, *CD*, Carteggio di consiglieri, segretari e cancellieri, b. 10b, May 26, 1551.

62. *Corpo diplomatico portuguez*, vol. 7, Afonso de Alencastro to the king, Rome, November 11, 1553, pp. 273–74. F. Gaeta, ed., *Nunziature di Venezia* (Roma, 1967), vol. 6 passim. The cardinal secretary of state wrote to the nuncio in Venice that the pope had been offered ten thousand scudi in case he would order that the *putta* be sent over to Rome instead of returned to her mother. BPP, *MS Pal. 1024/3*, January 29, 1553.

63. ASF, *Not.*, Giacomo Conti, b. 4, September 24, 1550.

64. Archives départementales du Rhône. Lyon, BP.3640, fol. 213r–v, Paris, January 20, 1552.

65. Marcel Bataillon, "Andrés Laguna, autor del "Viaje de Turquia" à la luz de las recientes investigaciones," *Estudios Segovianos*, 15 (1963), esp. 25–26, 39–41.

66. Brianda and her daughter left the Serenissma at the end of September, for they could not secure a delay to their one-month notice, despite the intervention of the French ambassador with the doge. On September 20, 1555, while still in Venice, they liquidated the Mendeses' mansion in Antwerp and were paid three thousand ducats of capital. ASF, *Not.*, matr. 504, Nicola Caprilli, b. 2, September 6, 1557; Andrea Cocapani, b. 9, November 2, 1557. Under the dates October 13 and October 24, 1555, and thus when they were already in Ferrara, the women granted two loans of two thousand scudi each to the duke's brother, Ippolito Cardinal of Este. Ibid., Nicola Caprilli, b. 2, September 6, 1557.

67. ASM, *Lettere particolari*, b. 885, Ferrara, November 19, 1555. In a letter of credentials for his banker Lamberti and her agent Odoardo Gomez, the duke requested that she trust them as she would trust him ("la istessa fede ch'ella farebbe

a me stesso se le parlassi, ché lo riceverò a molto grato piacere dalla S.V., alla quale mi offero di cuore, et prego Dio che da male la guardi").

68. ASF, *Not.*, Battista Saracco, b. 29, July 31, 1556. The sum that Gratia had deposited in the Vincenzi brothers' bank on July 18 was remitted to the duke, who in his own writing stated that it was in his hands ("se retrovano presso nui et nostra podestà").

69. ASM, *Lettere particolari,* b. 885, October 15, 1556. The letter, all in the duke's handwriting, is remarkable also for the corrections that he introduced, since they shed light on Hercules' attitude toward his addressee, and perhaps toward the Portuguese generally. The final sentence—the part added on the line in italics—is the following: "Rimettendomi al mio arrivo costì, *qual serà fra tre o quatro giorni piacendo a Dio,* di far quella resolutione *sopra ciò ch'ella mi ricerca* che mi parerà conveniente per tutti li rispetti che ben si può imaginare V. S., et con questo fine le prego ogni contentezza [et felicità" deleted].

70. Her death may be assigned to some time (*superioribus diebus*) before the end of July 1556, when Beatriz was declared the universal heir of her mother. ASF, *Not.*, Battista Saracco, b. 29, July 31, 1556; matr. 609, Domenico Zaffarini, b. 3, August 13, 1556.

71. Ibid., Battista Saracco, b. 29, petition (bearing the autograph signature of "Gracia Benvenisti") followed by the letter-patents issued in the ducal palace in Ferrara, January 14, 1557.

72. Ibid. ("donatio pro ill.mo d. Hercule secundo Estense duce Ferrarie a mag.cis d. Ariete de Luna et d. Augustino Enriches ambobus nationis portughensis sibi hoc specialiter comisum fuisse a d.na Beatrice de Luna"); b. 31 (Italian text of the agreement), January 18–19, 1557.

73. ASM, *Lettere particolari,* b. 979. The conclusion of the letter is as follows: "I will add no more expecting that Your Excellency will be pleased to favor us and regard us as her very obliged servants. May God extol the life of Your Excellency by increasing her states" ("et però io non dirò altro aspettando in questo che l'Exc.a V.ra sia contenta farci favore et haverci per suoi oblighatissimi servitori. Iddio la vita di V.ra Exc.a feliciti con augmento di maggiori stati").

74. Gracia declares that "inherendo eius carte dotali facte more hebreorum . . . et in hebraicha scripte . . . consignavit omnes eius pecunias et bona in dotem dicto eius marito." ASF, *Not.*, Giacomo Conti, b. 7, November 20, 1557. Actually she entrusted her dowry to Samuel with the understanding that her husband should merely trade it and that all dealings would be under the supervision of her uncle and guardian, Aries De Luna. When Enrico Nunes replaced the latter, he had to give security on one hand to the duke that Gratia would continue to dwell in Ferrara, and on the other to Gratia that she would be returned her estate ("pecunias bona et dotem") in due time and that Samuel would negotiate her dowry as a reliable merchant ("bene et diligenter et quemadmodum

quilibet alius vir prudens mercator peritus et legalis") with the assistance of Agostino Anriques. Ibid., Battista Saracco, b. 29; b. 31, August 31, September 2, 1557. It should not go unnoticed that recorded among Gratia's possessions were two loans she granted the duke in the very days of her wedding: twenty-seven thousand scudi on May 30, and twenty-five thousand on June 29, 1557. Ibid., Nicola Caprilli, b. 2.

75. The medal bears the inscription "A[nno] AE[tatis] XVIII": since she was born in June 1540, she had entered her eighteenth year.

76. ASM, *Lettere particolari*, b. 747, December 6 (to Beatriz De Luna), December 7 (to "s.r Gio. Miches"), 1557: "Mag.co s.r amico car.mo. Io scrivo alla s.ra Beatrice, mosso dalle promesse altre volte fattemi da lei, pregandola a prestarmi bona somma de denari in caso di mio bisogno, et perché hora son gravato di molta spesa per la guerra che m'è stata rotta, la priego a accommodarmene lei o mandar ordine a chi le pare in Vinegia che mi faccia credito, che l'assicurarò sopra qualsivoglia delle mie intradi *a sua eletione*, acciò sia certa di non dover sentir danno alcuno della commoditate che mi sarà fatta da lei, presso la qual, sapendo io quanto voi siate buono *et di autorità*, ho voluto farvi sapere che riceverò a molto grato piacere ogni ufficio che vi contentarete far perch'io sii compiaciuto da S. S.ria di ciò et ne tenirò viva memoria *con desiderio di rendervene il cambio in una qualche occasione*, et con questo offero et priegovi contento" (italics indicate the phrases added over the line). The tone of familiarity pervading the autograph letter, from its heading to its greetings, is remarkable. On January 8, 1558, Agostino Enriques and Odoardo Gomes lent Duke Hercules eight thousand scudi to be repaid them in one year with 480 scudi each of interest (*per cessato guadagno*): was this money too from their masters in Constantinople?

77. ASF, *Not.*, Battista Saracco, b. 29; b. 31, August 12, 1557. Actually, the assurance that Samuel would not move elsewhere without the duke's license ("habitabit in hac civitate Ferrarie et inde non discedet et non conducet alio habitatum d. Gratiam Benvenistam . . . nisi precesserit licentia ill.mi d. ducis"), on pain of twenty-five thousand scudi, was given by Enrico Nunes on behalf of Aries De Luna (see above n. 74).

78. ASV, *Consiglio dei Dieci*. Comuni, reg. 7, fol. 148r. The possibility that Samuel may depart "extra Italiam" is mentioned for the first time in a loan he granted to the "Portuguese nation" of Ferrara on December 14, 1557. ASF, *Not.*, Giacomo Conti, b. 7.

79. Ibid., Battista Saracco, b. 29; b. 31, May 16, 1558. The couple left the city in July-August 1559, months after appointing the Levantine Jew Salomon Dorderio their general agent in Italy. Ibid., Giacomo Conti, b. 8, January 9, 1559.

80. Ibid, Maurelio Taurino, b. 8, January 15, 1549.

81. Ibid., Giacomo Conti, b. 7, August 18, 1557, September 3, 1557; Cesare Sacrati, b. 1, August 29, 1543.

82. Ibid., Andrea Cocapani, b. 4, November 4, 1549.

83. Ibid., Cesare Sacrati, b. 2, December 4, 1549, September 27, 1552. Their names are Moise Franco, Rafael, son of the late Zadoch alias Conforto, Richa, wife of Samuel de Levi Tolosa. The Tolosa are listed among the Spanish Jews already in Ferrara in 1534. Aron di Leone Leoni, "Documents inédits sur la "nation portugaise" de Ferrare," *Revue des études juives*, 152 (1993), 158.

84. ASV, *Capi del Consiglio dei Dieci*. Comuni, fz. 48, n. 600, December 30, 1545.

85. ASF, *Not.*, Giacomo Conti, b. 4, August 30, December 1, 1549; Maurelio Taurino, b. 8, October 14, 1551.

86. Just before embarking for the Levant, Beatriz De Luna and her daughter ratified all that had been negotiated in Lisbon, Spain, Flanders, the duchy of Brabant, France, and Italy by their two agents (Guglielmo since 1525 and Odoardo since 1545) and confirmed that they had been paid their due (*sallario suo et stipendio et factoria*). ASV, *Not.*, Paolo Leoncini, b. 7818, August 4, 1552 fols. 191r–92v, 193v–94v.

87. ASM, *Lettere particolari*, b. 747.

88. ASV, *Consiglio dei Dieci*. Criminali, reg. 8. Benjamin Ravid, "Money, Love, and Power Politics in Sixteenth-Century Venice: The Perpetual Banishment and Subsequent Pardon of Joseph Nasi," in *Italia Judaica* I (Rome 1983), esp. 169–73.

89. Antonii Musae Brasavoli, *Medici ferrariensis De Medicamentis tam simplicibus quam compositis cathasticis, quae unicuique humori sunt propria*, Venetiis, apud Juntas, 1552, fol. 12v.

90. *Consiliorum sive Responsorum illustris ac praestantissimi iureconsulti d.* Marcabruni ab Anguillis *ferrariensis . . . Volumen . . . primum*, Venetiis, ex officina Damiani Zenari, 1583, cons. 93, fols. 361r–62r. It is noteworthy that the author (and jurist) terms Beatriz "illustris domina" and Brianda "domina."

91. *Oratio* Bartho. Ricci *pro Isacho Abravanelio haebreo ad Herc. II Atestium . . . ,* Ferrarae, per Franciscum Rubeum Valentianum, 1566.

92. ASF, *Not.*, Andrea Cocapani, b. 9, March 17, 1553.

93. Ibid., matr. 446, Bartolomeo Franchi, b. 8, undated, but inserted among deeds dated 1551; Andrea Cocapani, b. 4, July 24, 1551.

94. Ibid., b. 5, May 10, 1552.

95. Ibid., Gian Battista Codegori, b. 25, February 17, 1553.

96. Ibid., Andrea Cocapani, b. 9, March 26, June 15, 1557.

97. Ibid., Battista Saracco, b. 29, June 8, August 3, 1558.

11. Encounters Between Spanish and Italian Kabbalists

1. In addition to the following remarks, see also Moshe Idel, "Religion, Thought, and Attitudes: The Impact of the Expulsion on the Jews" in Elie Kedurie, ed., *Spain and the Jews: The Sephardic Experience, 1492 and After*

(London, 1992), 123–39. I elaborated there upon some other processes that were formative for the direction of the kabbalistic literary activity during this period. In the following I accept the view of Mary Douglas who believes that ideas do not "float free in an autonomous vacuum, developing according to their own internal logic bumping into other ideas by the chance of historical contact and being modified by new insight." See Mary Douglas, *Natural Symbols Explorations in Cosmology* (New York, 1982), 141. As we shall see below, the expulsion is the chance of historical contact, which enabled the encounter between mystical paradigms, each of them conditioned by the special circumstances of the two countries mentioned in this context.

2. See Hayyim Hillel Ben Sasson, "Exile and Redemption through the Eyes of the Spanish Exiles" (in Hebrew), in Salo Baron, Benzion Dinur, Samuel Ettinger, Israel Halpern, eds., *Yitzhak F. Baer Jubilee Volume* (Jerusalem, 1960), 220–21.

3. I hope to be able to show the problems with the hypothesis—accepted by many scholars as established fact—that the concept of Ẓimẓum, namely, the divine precosmogonic withdrawal, reflects the historical crisis of the expulsion or the exile it caused. The concept of Ẓimẓum was well-known from a series of kabbalistic texts composed in Spain, from the very beginning of Kabbalah up to kabbalists in the fifteenth century. See Moshe Idel, "On the Concept of Ẓimẓum in Kabbalah and Its Research" in Rachel Elior and Yehuda Liebes, eds., *Lurianic Kabbalah* (in Hebrew) (Jerusalem, 1992), 59–112. See also note 19 below.

4. For the time being, see Moshe Idel, "Rabbi Yehudah Halewah and His Book, Ẓaphnat Pa'aneaḥ" (in Hebrew), *Shalem* 4 (1984), 119–21; idem, "Spanish Kabbalah After the Expulsion," in Haim Beinart, ed., *The Sephardi Legacy* (Jerusalem, 1992), 2:166–78. There I attempted to map in a preliminary fashion the centers and the trajectories of the Spanish postexpulsion Kabbalah.

5. For Kabbalah in Spain before the expulsion see Gershom Scholem, "To the Knowledge of Kabbalah on the Eve of the Expulsion" (in Hebrew), *Tarbiz* 24 (1955), 167–206; idem, "The Maggid of Rabbi Joseph Taitatchek and the Revelations Attributed to Him" (in Hebrew), *Sefunot*, 11 (1971–1978), 69–11; Moshe Idel, "Inquiries in the Doctrine of *Sefer ha-Meshiv*" (in Hebrew), *Sefunot*, n.s., 17 (1983), 185–266; Joseph Hacker, "On the Intellectual Character and Self-Perception of Spanish Jewry in the Late Fifteenth Century" (in Hebrew), *Sefunot*, n.s., 17 (1983), 21–95, 52–56. See also the studies referred to in notes 6, 9, 10 below.

6. See his discussion in *Sefer Masoret ha-Ḥokhmah*, printed by Gershom Scholem, "The Kabbalist Rabbi Abraham ben Eliezer ha-Levi" (in Hebrew), *Kiryat Sefer*, 2 (1925–26), 125–26.

7. On these literary layers see Isaiah Tishby, *The Wisdom of the Zohar* (Oxford, 1989), 1:1–7.

8. See Gershom Scholem, *Major Trends in Jewish Mysticism* (New York, 1967), 203–4.

9. On the kabbalistic thought of this thinker, see Ephraim Gottlieb, *Meḥkarim be-Sifrut ha-Kabbalah*, ed. Joseph Hacker (in Hebrew) (Tel Aviv, 1976), 347–56.

10. On this issue, see Meir Benayahu, "A Source About the Exiles from Spain in Portugal and Their Departure to Saloniki After the Decree of 1506" (in Hebrew), *Sefunot*, o.s., 11 (1971–1978), 236–44.

11. See Scholem, *Major Trends*, 207–43; Tishby, *The Wisdom of the Zohar*, 1:230–67.

12. This, interestingly enough, became in the fifteenth century more open toward kabbalistic concepts; see, e.g., Zeev Harvey, "Kabbalistic Elements in Crescas's Light of the Lord" (in Hebrew), *Jerusalem Studies in Jewish Thought*, 2 (1982–83), 78–88.

13. See Moshe Idel, "Nahmanides: Kabbalah, Halakhah, and Mystical Leadership" (forthcoming). Cf. Gershom Scholem, *Origins of the Kabbalah*, trans. A. Arkush, ed. R. J. Zwi Werblowsky (Princeton and Philadelphia, l987), 394–96, who assumes that Isaac Sagi Nahor's students came to Provence in order to study Kabbalah with him. Scholem was followed by the scholars who wrote on this issue.

14. On this issue see Moshe Idel, *Maimonide et la mystique juive*, (Paris, 1991), 40–42, now in English, "Maimonides and Kabbalah," in Isadore Twersky, ed., *Studies in Maimonides* (Cambridge, Mass., 1990), 59–61.

15. See Gottlieb, *Meḥkarim*, 117–21; Joseph Hacker, "The Connections of Spanish Jewry with Erez-Israel between 1391 and 1492" (in Hebrew), *Shalem* 1 (1974), 133–37; Steven Bowman, "Who Has Composed the Books of Qannah and Peliyah?" (in Hebrew), *Tarbiẓ* 54 (1985), 150–52.

16. Cf. Bernard McGinn, *Apocalyptic Spirituality* (New York, 1979), 8–9.

17. See, e.g., Scholem, *Major Trends*, 246–49; Rachel Elior, "Messianic Expectations and Spiritualization of Religious Life in the Sixteenth Century," *Revue des études juives*, 145 (1986), 35–49. As in other cases, there is no good reason to attribute all the messianic discussions and beliefs to one factor, the expulsion. See the interesting and more open approach to this question in David B. Ruderman, "Hope Against Hope: Jewish and Christian Messianic Expectations in the Late Middle Ages," in Aharon Mirsky, Avraham Grossman, Yosef Kaplan, eds., *Exile and Diaspora Studies in the History of the Jewish People Presented to Prof. Haim Beinart* (Jerusalem, 1991), 185–202.

18. Gershom Scholem, *Explications and Implications*, (in Hebrew) (Tel Aviv, 1976), 205; also Elior, *Messianic Expectations*, 37, where it is argued that the linkage between the study of the *Zohar* and the coming of the Messiah "was not only discussed in every kabbalistic book of the sixteenth century but also pondered on its actual implication on the coming redemption." I am afraid that the above descriptions are true only if we consider a very small percentage of the kabbalistic oeuvre. Compare, for example, the important and neglected kabbalistic material described and analyzed in Elior, "The Kabbalists of Dra'" (in Hebrew), *Pe'amim* 24 (1985),

36–73. How many of these writings actually include significant messianic elements?

19. See Gershom Scholem, *Kabbalah* (Jerusalem, 1974), 69. How these two statements of Scholem relate to each other I dare not speculate. However, it seems that his more messianic interpretation of Kabbalah fascinated other scholars. See, e.g., note 17 above; and Isaiah Tishby, *Messianism in the Time of the Expulsion from Spain and Portugal* (in Hebrew) (Jerusalem, 1985), 52–53. See also Tishby's exposition of Scholem's views in his review of Moshe Idel, *Kabbalah: New Perspectives* (in Hebrew), *Zion* 54 (1989), 216. One possible interpretation of Scholem's stand is that what he considered to be new kabbalistic views, namely, the Lurianic concepts, were not innovated during the first generation of the expellee kabbalists, although, as Tishby correctly summarizes him (ibid.), a messianic turn among kabbalists and Kabbalah took place after the expulsion. See, however, note 3 above.

20. See also the similar assumption that Sabbateanism emerged as the result of the dissemination of the Lurianic messianism. Cf. Moshe Idel, "One in a Town, Two in a Clan: A Critical Appraisal of the Question of the Dissemination of the Lurianic Kabbalah and Sabbatianism" (in Hebrew), *Pe'amim* 44 (1990), 5–30.

21. See, e.g., Cecil Roth, "The Spanish Exiles of 1492 in Italy," in *Homenaje a Millas-Vallicrosa* (Barcelona, 1956), 2:293–302; Renata Segre, "Sephardic Settlements in Sixteenth-Century Italy: A Historical and Geographical Survey," *Mediterranean Historical Review* 6 (1992), 11–127. On the cultural situation on the Italian scene in this period, see David B. Ruderman, "The Italian Renaissance and Jewish Thought," in Albert Rabil, ed., *Renaissance Humanism, Foundation, Forms, and Legacy* (Philadelphia, 1988), 1:382–433; Robert Bonfil's important study, *Rabbis and the Jewish Communities in Renaissance Italy* (Oxford, 1990); and Sarah Heller-Wilensky, *The Philosophy of Isaac Aramah* (in Hebrew) (Jerusalem, 1956).

22. The single piece of evidence as to the presence of this kabbalist in Italy is a hint of R. Isaac ben Ḥayyim ha-Kohen, MS Oxford, Heb. f. 16, Neubauer, no. 2770, fol. 48b.

23. See Gershom Scholem and Malachi Beit-Arie, *Sefer Meshare' Kitrin* (in Hebrew) (Jerusalem, New York, 1938), where the most important bibliography on this kabbalist was collected in the introduction.

24. Several indications in the manuscript mentioned above show that he visited Italy, specifically, Ferrara. See note 22 above, fol. 25a.

25. See the section below entitled "The Silence About the Christian Kabbalah."

26. Cf. Gottlieb, *Meḥkarim*, 422–25. On this figure see Michal Oron, "Autobiographical Elements in the Writings of Kabbalists from the Generation of the Expulsion," *Mediterranean Historical Review* 6 (1991), 102–6.

27. Gotllieb, *Meḥkarim*, 404–22.

28. These reactions are more evident in the Ferrara edition, where the introduction is a little bit longer, revealing details that were not included in the Mantuan

edition. Both were printed in 1558. On the various commentaries on *Ma'arekhet ha-'Elohut*, see Gershom Scholem, "On the Questions Related to *Sefer Ma'arekhet ha-'Elohut* and Its Commentators" (in Hebrew), *Kiryat Sefer*, 21 (1944), 284–95.

29. Though not a full-fledged kabbalist, Yaaveẓ was sympathetic to this lore but very critical of Jewish philosophy; this certainly created an affinity between the two expellees. Although I assume that Ḥayyat and Yaaveẓ did not meet before their encounter in Mantua, their trajectory after the expulsion is similar. On Yaaveẓ, see Isaac E. Barzilay, *Between Reason and Faith: Anti-Rationalism in Jewish Italian Thought, 1250–1650* (The Hague and Paris, 1967), 133–149; Gedaliah Nigal, "The Opinions of R. Joseph Yawetz on Philosophy and Philosophers, Torah and Commandments" (in Hebrew), *Eshel Beer-Sheva* 1 (1976), 258–87; Ira Robinson, "Halakha, Kabbala, and Philosophy in the Thought of Joseph Jabez," *Sciences religieuses/Studies in Religion*, 11,4 (1982), 389–402.

30. Cf. Psalm 27:4. See also note 146, below, concerning the preoccupation with Kabbalah. Barzilai is right in noting Yaaveẓ's basically positive attitude toward Kabbalah; see *Between Reason and Faith*, 143. Scholem's assessement that Yaaveẓ's attitude to Kabbalah, "like that toward the philosophy of Maimonides, is one of extreme reserve," is unfounded. See Scholem, *Sabbatai Ṣevi: The Mystical Messiah*, trans. R. J. Zwi Werblowsky (Princeton, 1973), 21. In his *'Or ha-Ḥayyim*, quoted by Scholem, ibid., Yaaveẓ criticizes the study of Kabbalah by people that are not prepared for this esoteric lore. However, even the reserve of Yaaveẓ may be understood in the context of the development of the study of Kabbalah in Italy, where relatively young persons, like Alemanno and David Messer Leon, studied Kabbalah as youngsters.

31. As Gottlieb has shown, the author was an Italian kabbalist named Reuven Ẓarfati. See Gottlieb, *Meḥkarim*, 357–69. On the thought of this kabbalist, see Abraham Elkayam, "Issue, in the Commentary of R. Reuben Ẓarfati on the Book *Ma'arekhet ha-'Elohut*" (in Hebrew), M.A. thesis, Hebrew University, 1987.

32. Despite Ḥayyat's criticisms of the nature of this commentary, many parts of it were printed in the Mantuan edition of *Ma'arekhet ha-'Elohut*, beside those that were copied by Ḥayyat himself in his *Minḥat Yehudah*. As the printer of this edition, Rabbi Immanuel of Benivento, has acknowledged, he was not ready to leave out the views of the anonymous kabbalist, although he had some reservations about some of them.

33. Compare also the description of R. Isaac Mor Ḥayyim regarding the dispersion and fragmentation of the *Zohar*. This issue merits a detailed discussion that cannot be done here. I would like to point out that other kabbalists also testify to having been well acquainted with the *Zohar* (and I assume that this included also *Tikkunei Zohar*) already in Spain.

34. To be sure, Ḥayyat cited numerous long quotes from the later layer of the Zoharic literature, *Tikkunei Zohar*; nevertheless, for our purposes this does not

matter, so I shall simply refer to all his quotations from the Zoharic literature by the general term *Zohar*. The assumption that the preoccupation with the later layers of the *Zohar* saved the lives of the kabbalists recurs in another contemporary document. See Benayahu, "A Source," 261. Therefore, the assumption that the *Zohar* was canonized "consequent upon the expulsion" is premature or perhaps even wrong, at least insofar as the Spanish kabbalists are concerned; see Tishby, *The Wisdom of the Zohar*, 1:25.

35. See the unnumbered introduction to his *Minhat Yehudah* and also ibidem, fol. 165b.

36. On the basis of detecting Yohanan Alemanno's extensive quotes from Hayyat's work, in his *Collectanaea* and in his untitled book extant in MS Paris, Bibliothèque Nationale, 849, which was written in 1498, I proposed to date the composition of *Minhat Yehudah* between 1495 and 1498; see Moshe Idel, "The Study Program of Rabbi Yohanan Alemanno" (in Hebrew), *Tarbiz* 48 (1979), 330. Scholem dated the commentary between 1494 and 1500; see "On the Questions," 292. However, the earlier date is impossible because Hayyat was in Naples in 1494 and he mentions the conquest of the city by the French during this year. The later date is improbable, because Alemanno quoted the book already in 1498.

37. I hope to expand on this issue elsewhere.

38. This is also the case when we inspect the kabbalistic writing of Rabbi Joseph ibn Shraga, as we shall see below.

39. See, e.g., Elior, "Messianic Expectations," 36 and n. 4, where she refers to Hayyat in the context of her claim that he is the representative of those who expressed "various degrees of detachment from mundane life while striving to attain cultural segregation and a comprehensive spiritualization of all Jewish life." Since no specific page of a pertinent disussion was mentioned in the above article, my perusal of the two editions of *Minhat Yehudah* was not helpful in detecting these discussions or new formulations or particular emphasis. Perhaps someone will be able to detect such a shift in manuscripts of Hayyat.

40. Joshua 1:8.

41. Proverbs 6:21.

42. Deuteronomy 6:7

43. *Minhat Yehudah*, fol. 3b–4a. It is significant that the list of recommended kabbalistic books faithfully reflects the kabbalistic sources that informed most of the discussions in both the questions of Rabbi Yehudah Hayyat and in Rabbi Joseph Alqastiel's responsa to them. See the books quoted in the various pages of text edited by Scholem, "To the Knowledge of Kabbalah." Likewise, see the mention of three commentaries on Nahmanides' kabbalistic secrets and some folios from the book of the *Zohar* in an epistle addressed by R. Isaac Mor Hayyim, a Sephardic kabbalist, to R. Isaac of Pisa. We learn from the context that the Italian kabbalist did not possess these writings. See Yael Nadav, "An Epistle of the

Qabbalist R. Isaac Mar Ḥayyim Concerning the Doctrine of Supernal Lights" (in Hebrew), *Tarbiẓ* 26 (1957), 458.

44. This is particularely true in the first half of the thirteenth century; theosophical interpretations of this book are rare in the second half of the century.

45. *Minḥat Yehudah,* fol. 3a.

46. Ibid. The kabbalist is using the verse from 2 Kings 6:19.

47. Ibid., fol. 3b. It seems that Ḥayyat, like Yaaveẓ, was concerned about the dissemination of Kabbalah in wider circles. See note 30 above.

48. The word *Sha'ar* does not occur in the two editions of *Minḥat Yehudah,* but I have no doubt that it is a mistake of Ḥayyat.

49. The word *ve-ha-'Olam* stands, in my opinion, for another book of Isaac ibn Latif, which is not mentioned in the Mantuan edition of *Minḥat Yehudah.* On ibn Latif's books and positions, see Sarah O. Heller-Willensky, "Isaac ibn Latif: Philosopher or Kabbalist?" in Alexander Altmann, ed., *Jewish Medieval and Renaissance Studies* (Cambridge, Mass., 1967), 185–223.

50. The word *rabbim,* "many," occurs only in the Ferrara edition, but there is no reason to doubt that it is authentic since it also occurs in MS Oxford 1639, fol. 3b.

51. Ibid.

52. This epithet occurs only in the Ferrara edition.

53. There were kabbalists in this generation who, despite their general opposition to philosophy, were very positive toward Maimonides' thought, which they understood as an attempt to answer the spiritual needs of his generation by offering a Jewish response to alien philosophy. See, e.g., Rabbi Abraham ben Eliezer ha-Levi's position; cf. Idel, *Maimonides et la mystique juive,* 55–56; "Maimonides and Kabbalah," 75–76.

54. *Mateh Resha* (wicked rod), is a pun upon the name of ibn Motot (Matut). On his thought, see Georges Vajda, "Recherches sur la synthèse philosophico-Kabbalistique de Samuel ibn Motot," *Archives d'histoire doctrinale et litteraire de Moyen Ages* 27 (1960), 35 ff.

55. See Moshe Idel, "The Magical and the Neoplatonic Interpretations of the Kabbalah in the Renaissance," in Bernard Dov Cooperman, ed., *Jewish Thought in the Sixteenth Century* (Cambridge, Mass., 1983), 215–29.

56. See Idel, "The Study Program," 309.

57. An examination of Alemanno's *Collectanaea,* MS Oxford 2234, which contain the notes copied by Alemanno from different sources, shows that the *Zohar* was not mentioned in most of the manuscript. It occurs several times, but only at the end, between fols. 135a and 165a, influenced by Ḥayyat's *Minḥat Yehudah.* Thus we may conclude that he did not have a copy of the *Zohar* but simply collected some quotations from the writings of the Sephardic kabbalist. In Alemanno's earlier composition, *Sefer Ḥeshek Shelomo,* he refers to the *Zohar* only

twice, and in both cases it is very reasonable to assume that Alemanno took the concepts of the *Zohar* from Recanati's *Commentary on the Pentateuch*. In his later books, quotes from the *Zohar* recur several times, mostly in Hebrew versions. There can be no doubt as to the significant shift between the earlier ignorance of the *Zohar* and the much greater acquaintance with it in his last and incomplete commentary on Genesis, *'Einei ha-'Edah*.

58. Compare the relatively numerous quotations from the *Zohar* in the writings of Rabbi Joseph Yaavez, who was instrumental in inviting Hayyat to write *Minhat Yehudah*. Nevertheless, the messianic theme is very rare in Yaavez's thought.

59. *Minhat Yehudah*, fol. 155b.

60. See ibid., fol. 94a–94b: "If the view of the Rabbi is that the 'Atarah [namely, the last Sefirah] is not recipient of a damage because of the sins of Israel, let this view stand alone [kevodo bi-mekomo munah], since it is a philosophical speculation ['iyyun filosofi] but not a true view, (representative of) the wisdom of Kabbalah." Thus, perceptively detecting the philosophical background of some passages in *Ma'arekhet ha-'Elohut*, Hayyat does not hesitate to refute them in the name of what he considered to be the true, namely, mythical, stand of theosophical Kabbalah.

61. See *Minhat Yehudah*, fol. 177b, where he uses the phrase: "as I have compelled, according to the [view of] the *Zohar*" ("kefi she-hekhrahti mi-Sefer ha-Zohar").

62. On the antimythical attitude of this book, see Gottlieb, *Mehkarim*, 317–43.

63. See *Minhat Yehudah*, fols. 41a–41b, 42b, 44b.

64. See Gottlieb, *Mehkarim*, 399, 430, n. 25.

65. On the kabbalistic views of Genazzano, see Alexander Altmann, "Beyond the Realm of Philosophy: R. Elijah ben Benjamin of Gennazano" (in Hebrew), in Moshe Idel, W. Z. Harvey, Eliezer Schweid, eds., *Shlomo Pines Jubilee Volume* (Jerusalem, 1988), part 1, 61–101. See especially p. 99 for Altmann's view of Hayyat's critique of the Italian kabbalist. On the Renaissance background of some passages in Gennazano's book, see Moshe Idel, "Differing Conceptions of Kabbalah in the Early Seventeenth Century," in Isadore Twersky and Bernard Septimus, eds., *Jewish Thought in the Seventeenth Century* (Cambridge, Mass., 1987), 158–62.

66. See Idel, "The Magical and Neoplatonic Interpretations of Kabbalah"; idem, "Jewish Magic from the Renaissance Period to Early Hasidism," in Jacob Neusner, Ernest S. Frerichs, Paul V. McCracken Flesher, eds., *Religion, Science, and Magic: In Concert and in Conflict* (New York and Oxford, 1989), 82–117; idem, *Kabbalah: New Perspectives* (New Haven, London, 1989), 256.

67. See Idel, "Inquiries in the Doctrine of *Sefer ha-Meshiv*," 232–42.

68. For details on the whereabouts of this kabbalist, see Joseph Hacker, "Collection of Epistles on the Expulsion of the Jews from Spain and Sicily and on

the Fate of the Exiles" (in Hebrew), in *Studies in the History of Jewish Society in the Middle Ages and in the Modern Period Presented to Professor Jacob Katz* (Jerusalem, 1980), 64–70.

69. Moshe Idel, "Between the Conceptions of the Sefirot as Essence and Instruments in the Renaissance Period" (in Hebrew), *Italia* 3, 1–2 (1982), 89–90.

70. Nadav, "An Epistle," 448–49.

71. Ibid., 458.

72. Namely, the alleged author of the book of the *Zohar*.

73. Cf. A. W. Greenup, "A Kabbalistic Epistle by R. Isaac ben Samuel b. Ḥayyim Sephardi," *Jewish Quarterly Review*, n.s., 21 (1931), 370. Later on (374), he describes the kabbalistic theosophy as dealing with profound matters, concerning which "the absence of inquiry is better than its existence." See also Nadav, "An Epistle," 448, 455, 456.

74. De Balmes's apparently single kabbalistic treatise, an Aristotelian *Commentary on Ten Sefirot*, is extant in a unique manuscript, and I hope to publish it and analyze it elsewhere. See for the time being Esther Goldenberg, "Medieval Linguistics and Good Hebrew" (in Hebrew), *Leshonenu* 54 (1990), 203–5.

75. See Moshe Idel, "The Epistle of Rabbi Isaac of Pisa (?) in Its Three Versions" (in Hebrew), *Kovets Al Yad*, n.s., 10(20) (1982), 172–73, 181–84.

76. See Hava Tirosh-Rothschild, *Between Worlds: The Life and Thought of David ben Yehudah Messer Leon* (Albany, 1991), 211–18, 231–36; idem, "Sefirot as the Essence of God in the Writings of David Messer Leon," *AJS Review* 7–8 (1982), 409–25. It should be mentioned that despite his openness to general philosophical views in his more speculative thought David Messer Leon was deeply influenced by an Ashkenazic, "particularistic" approach to halakhah. Though I should like not to generate another simplistic dichotomy between Sephardic particularism and Italian universalism, at least insofar as Kabbalah is concerned, such an opposition seems to me significant. Compare Robert Bonfil, "The Historical Perception of the Jews in the Italian Renaissance: Toward a Reappraisal," *Revue des études juives* 143 (1984), 75–79. However, in other fields, such as philosophy, Sephardic authors like Yehudah Abravanel, better known as Leone Ebreo, were much more open and thus different from contemporary kabbalists.

77. See Chaim Wirszubski, *Pico della Mirandola's Encounter with Jewish Mysticism* (Cambridge, Mass., 1989), 136–52; Idel, "The Epistle of R. Isaac of Pisa (?)" 182–83, n. 118.

78. See Johannes Reuchlin, *De Arte Cabalistica*, trans. M. Goodman and S. Goodman (New York, 1983), 39–40. Some discussions on Kabbalah and Pythagoreanism can nevertheless be found already in Pico; see Wirszubski, *Pico della Mirandola's Encounter*, 122, 187, 197–99; and G. Lloyd Jones, introduction to Reuchlin's book, *De Arte Cabalistica*, 19–20. On the nexus between Pico's view of mystical mathematics and that of Reuchlin, see Ernst Cassirer, "Giovanni Pico

della Mirandola: A Study in the History of Renaissance Ideas," *Journal of the History of Ideas* 3, 143.

79. Reuchlin, *De Arte Cabalistica*. Interestingly enough, some Jewish traditions relating to the transmission of ancient Jewish mysticism regarded Italy as a major station on the westward trajectory of this mystical lore. Moreover, these traditions are found in the literature of Ḥasidei Ashkenaz, which is replete with numerological speculations. See Joseph Dan, *The Esoteric Theology of Ashkenazic Hasidism* (in Hebrew) (Jerusalem, 1968), 14–17; Ivan Marcus, *Piety and Society* (Leiden, 1981), 67–68. Since some of the speculative writings of the Jewish German masters were translated by Flavius Mithridates (see Wirszubski, *Pico della Mirandola's Encounter*, 11–12, 16, 18), and since in general this type of lore was known in Italy, Reuchlin may have been influenced by these traditions. There is, however, no mention of Pythagoras in these Jewish Ashkenazic traditions, though this figure was related during the Renaissance to other aspects of Kabbalah, especially metempsychosis. See Idel, "Differing Conceptions," 158–60; David B. Ruderman, *Kabbalah, Magic, and Science: The Cultural Universe of a Sixteenth-Century Jewish Physician* (Cambridge, Mass., 1989), index, s.v. Pythagoras.

80. Reuchlin, *De Arte Cabalistica*, 39, also 43.

81. Ibid.

82. I hope to deal with Reuchlin's views in much greater detail in a study on *prisca theologia* in the Renaissance.

83. See also Idel, "Jewish Magic," 82–90.

84. See his statement in Nadav, "An Epistle," 456.

85. Cf. Nadav, "An Epistle," 456.

86. On Recanati's stand, see Gottlieb, *Meḥkarim*, 308–10; Idel, *Kabbalah: New Perspectives*, 143–44.

87. Nadav, "An Epistle," 458.

88. See Greenup, "A Kabbalistic Epistle," 375; Nadav, "An Epistle," 447–58.

89. In fact, Mor Ḥayyim intended to write a more comprehensive critique of Recanati's position, but we do not know whether he realized this plan; see Nadav, "An Epistle," 458.

90. For the text of Alemanno and its analysis, see Idel, "Between the Conceptions of the Sefirot," 90–95.

91. Idel, "The Study Program," 329–30.

92. Kupfer, "The Visions," 397.

93. Namely, Italy.

94. Namely, Aramaic.

95. Greenup, "A Kabbalistic Epistle," 370.

96. See Idel, "Between the Conceptions of the Sefirot," 91. Alemanno adopts the stand of Recanati, combined with some philosophical and astral-magical views,

but he rejects Rabbi Isaac Mor Ḥayyim's—in my opinion correct—understanding of the text as pointing to the Sefirot as the essence of the divine.

97. A meticulously prepared list of the translated kabbalistic books and a detailed analysis of these translations can be found in Wirszubski, *Pico della Mirandola's Encounter*. In general, for a better understanding of the history of the Jewish kabbalistic literature much research is still needed to determine the significance of Mithridates' selection of texts to translate.

98. The first to observe that the book of the *Zohar* was not known (despite the quotations known through the intermediacy of Menahem Recanati's writings) by the first two important Christian kabbalists active in Italy was François Secret, *Le Zohar chez les kabbalistes chrétiens de la renaissance* (Paris, 1958), 25. See also Wirszubski, *Pico della Mirandola's Encounter*, 55, 253. Cf. however, Tishby, *The Wisdom of the Zohar*, 1:33. See also, more recently, the important remarks of Jordan S. Penkower, "A New Inquiry in Rabbi Eliahu Levita's *Massoret ha-Massoret*: The Belatedness of the Vowel-Signs and the Critique of the *Zohar*" (in Hebrew), *Italia* 8 (1989), 7–73. Penkower pointed out that the "evidence" on the "ancient" existence of the vowel signs, found in the allegedly ancient *Zohar*, was not accepted by Levita.

99. See Secret, *Le Zohar*, 25–26. On the possibility that an Aramaic text, quoted by the Christian kabbalists in Spain and attributed to the Zoharic literature but fraught with Christian implications, may stem from a lost, though genuine, fragment of the *Zohar*, see Yehudah Liebes, *Studies in the Zohar* (Albany, 1993), 140–45.

100. See Idel, "Between the Conceptions of the Sefirot," 93 n. 37.

101. Idel, "The Study Program," 310.

102. Ibid., 310–11, n. 68.

103. See Kupfer, "The Visions," 412, 417, 422. I hope to expand elsewhere on Abulafia's profound influence on Lemlein.

104. See Idel, "The Throne and the Seven-Branched Candlestick: Pico della Mirandola's Hebrew Source," *Journal of the Warburg and Courtauld Institutes* 40 (1977), 290–92.

105. Bonfil, *Rabbis and the Jewish Communities in Renaissance Italy*, 278–80. On this classic of ecstatic Kabbalah, written in Sicily and dedicated to two of Abulafia's disciples, see Moshe Idel, "Abraham Abulafia's Works and Doctrine" (in Hebrew), Ph.D. thesis, Hebrew University, 1976, 24–25, and 54–55, n. 161, for a list of manuscripts, many of them stemming from Italy, of this book.

106. See note 31 above.

107. This commentary to the *Guide of the Perplexed* was also translated into Latin by Flavius Mithridates. See Wirszubski, *Pico della Mirandola's Encounter*, 194, n. 31.

108. Only a very short passage of his, actually a pseudo-Zoharic eschatological passage written in Spain before the expulsion and transmitted by ibn Shraga, was printed in *Likkutei Shikheḥah u-Feah* (Ferrara, 1556).

109. The bibliography on this kabbalist is very limited, the most important discussion being Tishby's printing and analysis of his short messianic treatise; see Tishby, *Messianism*, 87–97, 131–49, and notes 111–112 below. Despite the fact that the important text published by Tishby regarding the four states of redemption reflects an explicit messianism, in ibn Shraga's *Commentary on the Liturgy*, MS Jerusalem, 8–0 3921, fol. 80a–80b, he discusses the same topic without even hinting at any actual meaning of this theme. Just as in the case of Ḥayyat, his kabbalistic writings, which were also well-known, to judge by the number of extant manuscripts, do not betray a substantial interest in messianism. Compare note 18 above.

110. Scholars do not agree as to the identification of the place named Agrigento. See below, note 111.

111. See MS British Library, Add. 27034, fol. 374a. Cf. Gershom Scholem, "The Real Author of the Forged Text, in the Language of the *Zohar* in the Lifetime of Rabbi Abraham ha-Levi: Rabbi Joseph ibn Shraga or Rabbi David of Argiento" (in Hebrew), *Kiryat Sefer* 8 (1931), 262–65, where the question of the place named Agrigento is addressed. It is interesting that, as in the case of the two other kabbalists discussed above, here too the Sephardic kabbalist writes for an Italian audience.

112. See the adoption of a Zoharic passage from *Midrash ha-Ne'elam*, copied in a manuscript at the beginning of the fourteenth century, which occurs in his kabbalistic secrets: MS Oxford 1663, fols. 134a–136a, published by Moshe Idel, "An Unknown Text from *Midrash ha-Ne'elam*" (in Hebrew), in J. Dan, ed., *The Age of the Zohar* (Jerusalem, 1989), 73–87, esp. 78.

113. See Alexander Marx, "Le faux Messie Ascher Lemlein," *Revue des études juives* 61 (1911), 135–38; Kupfer, "The Visions," 390–92, 396–97, 407–23; Tishby, *Messianism*, 91, n. 285. Despite the fact that Marx's text is corrupted and that the topic dealt with may be relevant to some issues related to the atmosphere dominant in the generation of the expulsion, the scholars who dealt with these issues did not read the pertinent material extant in manuscripts.

114. Shortly before this controversy over metempsychosis, there was an even greater controversy over the same issue in Candia; see Gottlieb, *Meḥkarim*, 370–95. In Italy, in the 1480s, a Candian author, Rabbi Elijah del Medigo, criticized the idea of metempsychosis; see his Commentary on Averroes' *De substantia orbis,* MS Paris, Bibliothèque Nationale 96B, fol. 41b. For a different appreciation of del Medigo's attitude toward Kabbalah, see Kalman Bland, "Elijah del Medigo's Averroist Response to the Kabbalah of Fifteenth-Century Jewry and Pico della Mirandola," *The Journal of Jewish Thought and Philosophy* 1 (1991), 23–53.

115. See Kupfer, "The Visions," 407.

116. See Lemlein's list of sources, which does not include more than one book recommended by Ḥayyat, *Sefer Yeẓirah,* but offers high praise for Abulafia's *Ḥayyei ha-'Olam ha-Ba',* which was criticized by Ḥayyat. See Kupfer, "The Visions," 412.

117. On the tensions between the Ashkenazic and Sephardic Jews in general, see Ben Sasson, "Exile and Redemption," 221–22.

118. MS Oxford 1663, fol. 129b MS Cambridge, Add. 651,7 fol. 13a. Again, the text printed by Marx, "Le faux Messie," is corrupted.

119. *Baba Batra*, fol. 10b.

120. MS Oxford 1663. fol. 129b.

121. Ibid., fol. 130b.

122. Ibid., fol. 132b.

123. Marx, "Le faux Messie," 138.

124. See *Minḥat Yehudah*, fol. 97b0–98a; this quote from Ẓarfati's commentary was also copied by Alemanno in his untitled writing, MS Paris, Bibliothèque Nationale, 849, fol. 67a. See also *Minḥat Yehudah*, fol. 17a, 98b.

125. See, e.g., Moshe Idel, *Language, Torah, and Hermeneutics in Abraham Abulafia* (Albany, 1989), 10, 41.

126. See Nadav, "An Epistle," 455. Nadav's version has the name Plato as the author of *Sefer ha-Perakim*, but it is possible, as was proposed by Shoshana Gershenzon, that the reference may be to *Enneads*, 6:6–7. See Shoshana Gershenzon, "Tale of Two Midrashim: The Legacy of Abner of Burgos," in David R. Blumenthal, ed., *Approaches to Judaism in Medieval Times* (1988), 3:144, n. 18. Another version, preserved by Rabbi David Messer Leon's *Magen David*, mentions, however, Galenus; see Gottlieb, *Meḥkarim*, 433, n. 44.

127. According to Gershenzon's very interesting proposal, in "Tale of Two Midrashim," the quote of Mor Ḥayyim stems from no other source than a writing of the famous apostate Abner of Burgos, who was well acquainted with Kabbalah. The whole question merits a more detailed examination.

128. In contrast to the arrival of Greek mythology and pagan philosophies to Italy from the East.

129. See Moshe Idel, *Studies in Ecstatic Kabbalah* (Albany, 1989), 137–38, 167, n. 175. Abulafia's influence on Rabbi Joseph Hamitz, a mid seventeenth-century Italian kabbalist, awaits a comprehensive study.

130. See Moshe Idel, "Major Currents in Italian Kabbalah," *Italia Judaica* 2 (Rome, 1986), 243–62; idem, "Differing Conceptions of Kabbalah in the Early Seventeenth Century," in Isadore Twersky and Bernard Septimus, eds., *Jewish Thought in the Seventeenth Century* (Cambridge, Mass., 1987), 137–200.

131. See Gershom Scholem, "Considerations sur l'histoire des débuts de la Kabbale chrétienne," in A. Faivre and F. Tristan, eds., *Kabbalistes Chrétiens* (Paris, 1979), 31–36. On the latter, see François Secret, "*L'Ensis P'auli* de Paulus de Heredia," *Sefarad* 26 (1966), 79–102, 254–71.

132. Scholem, "Considerations sur l'histoire," 31–32; Secret, "*L'Ensis P'auli*," 86–89.

133. Scholem, "Considerations sur l'histoire," 36–38; David R. Ruderman, *The World of a Renaissance Jew: The Life and Thought of Abraham ben Mordecai Farissol* (Cincinnati, 1981), 47–51.

134. De Heredia visited Sicily for a while, and this visit accounts, in my opinion, for his acquaintance with Rabbi Abraham Abulafia's kabbalistic thought, which was almost entirely ignored in Spain; see Secret, "*L'Ensis P'auli*," 100. On Mithridates and Sicily, see Shlomo Simonsohn, "Some Well-Known Jewish Converts During the Renaissance," *Revue des études juives* 148 (1989), 17–26.

135. See Wirszubski, *Pico della Mirandola's Encounter.*

136. See Ruderman, *The World of a Renaissance Jew,* 43–47.

137. On this issue see Idel, "Particularism and Universalism in Kabbalah, 1480–1650," in David Ruderman, ed., *Essential Papers on Jewish Culture in Renaissance and Baroque Italy* (New York, 1992), 324–44.

138. See David Kaufmann, "Elia Menachem Chalfan on Jews Teaching Hebrew to Non-Jews," *Jewish Quarterly Review,* n.s., 9 (1896–97), 500–8.

139. For other positive reactions to the first stage of Luther's activity, which was positive in relation to Judaism, see Hayyim Hillel Ben-Sasson, "The Reformation in Contemporary Jewish Eyes," *Proceedings of the Israel Academy of Sciences and Humanities* 4 (1970), 239–326.

140. Namely, Kabbalah.

141. In Hebrew *galuyot,* meaning, literally, "exiles." However, it seems that there is no reason to doubt that he refers to the expulsions, including perhaps also the expulsion of the Jews from Sicily.

142. See Idel, "The Magical and Neoplatonic Interpretations of Kabbalah," 186–87.

143. See note 138 above.

144. In Hebrew, *nokhri.* But it means a Christian in Italy.

145. In the original *zulati* is a rather vague form, and the whole sentence is rather clumsy.

146. Cf. Psalm 27:4. See also above, note 30, as well as the occurence of this verse in Hayyat's introduction. Abraham ben Eliezer ha-Levi's *Commentary on the Prophecies of the Child,* MS Firenze-Laurentiana, Plut. 44, 7 fol. 2b, printed in Abraham David, "A Jerusalemite Epistle from the Beginning of the Ottoman Rule in the Land of Israel" (in Hebrew), in *Chapters in the History of Jerusalem at the Beginning of the Ottoman Period* (Jerusalem, 1979), 42.

147. David, "A Jerusalemite Epistle," 40–44.

148. An expression pointing to an esoteric topic.

149. Namely, "send."

150. The disclosure.

151. The version is not so clear here. David, "A Jerusalemite Epistle," 59, reads the manuscript text as *hita'akti*, which makes no sense, and he proposed to correct it for *hit'amazti*, "I made efforts to," but this reading and analysis of the context (see p. 43) contradicts the preceding sentence. I propose therefore to amend the version to *hit'appakti*, "I refrained."

152. On this text, see Scholem's introduction to *Meshare' Kitrin*, 36–37.

153. Psalms 25:14.

154. See David, "A Jerusalemite Epistle," 59. See also p. 42, where David pointed out to the affinities between this epistle and Rabbi Abraham ben Eliezer ha-Levi's *Commentary on the Prophecies of the Child.*

155. I will not analyze here the possible implications of such a statement for the proper understanding of the propagandistic activity of Rabbi Abraham ben Eliezer ha-Levi. As to the implicit reticence about disseminating the *Commentary on the Prophecy of the Child,* see another letter, written by Rabbi Israel of Perugia, in which he describes the agreement of Rabbi Abraham ha-Levi to send his commentary to Italy and be read and copied by a certain Rabbi Moshe of Poland as a special gesture of the author. See Abraham Yaari, *Iggerot Erez Israel* (Ramat Gan, 1971), 176–77.

156. See Cordovero, *Commentary on the Tikkunei Zohar* (in Hebrew) (Jerusalem, 1975), 3:204. Thanks are due to Dr. Brakha Sak, who kindly brought this instructive text to my attention.

157. For more on these issues, see Idel, "Particularism and Universalism." On the different functions of Kabbalah in Italy, though in a later period, see also Robert Bonfil, "Changes in the Cultural Patterns of a Jewish Society in Crisis: Italian Jewry at the Close of the Sixteenth Century," *Jewish History* 3,2 (1988), 11–30; Moshe Idel, "Judah Muscato: A Late Renaissance Jewish Preacher," in D. R. Ruderman, ed., *Preachers of the Italian Ghetto* (Berkeley and Los Angeles, 1992), 41–66.

158. For example, the Christian Kabbalah, whose emergence as an intellectual phenomenon and its appearance in print left, in my opinion, a certain impression on the politics of dissemination among the Jewish kabbalists.

159. For Alemanno's attenuation of the more dynamistic kabbalistic views as exposed by Ḥayyat, see Idel, "The Magical and Neoplatonic Interpretations of Kabbalah," 222–23; idem, "Jewish Kabbalah and Platonism in the Middle Ages and Renaissance," in Lenn E. Goodman, ed., *Neoplatonism and Jewish Thought* (Albany, N.Y., 1992), 341–47.

160. See the bibliograhy mentioned in notes 56 and 66 above. The printing of the book of the *Zohar* in the mid sixteenth century by Italian, and not Sephardic, kabbalists is the result of an exoteric approach to Kabbalah, characteristic of the Italian kabbalists but not so appreciated by some of the Sephardic ones. It was not so much a clash between a messianic orientation of the printers and an alleged

nonmessianic attitude of those opposed to the printing of the book of the *Zohar* as is assumed by Isaiah Tishby, *Studies in Kabbalah and Its Branches* (in Hebrew) (Jerusalem 1982), 79–129. I hope to elaborate on this issue in a future study. Meanwhile, see Idel, "Major Currents in Italian Kabbalah," 248–49 and n. 33.

161. See Edgar Wind, *Pagan Mysteries in the Renaissance* (Harmondworth, 1967); Don Cameron Allen, *The Legend of Noah* (Urbana, Ill., 1963); idem, *Mysteriously Meant* (Baltimore, 1970), 279–311; Marco Ariani, *Imago fabulosa, mito e allegoria nei "Dialoghi d'Amore" di Leone Ebreo* (Rome, 1984). On the hermeneutical grille in the Renaissance period, see Ioan P. Couliano, *Eros and Magic in the Renaissance* (Chicago, 1987), 11–12.

162. Jean Seznec, *The Survival of the Pagan Gods: The Mythological Tradition and Its Place in Renaissance Humanism* (Princeton, 1972), 287.

12. The Ultimate End of Human Life

1. The poem was first published in Judah Abravanel, *Sefer ha-Vikuah* (Lyck, 1871), 6–11. It was published again by Jefim Hayim Schirman in his *Mivhar ha-Shirah ha-'Ivrit be-'Italyah* (Berlin, 1934), 216–22. This translation is by Raymond P. Scheindlin. It appeared in his "Judah Abravanel to His Son," *Judaism* 41 (1992), 190–99.

2. Complaints about Time constitute a literary genre in medieval Hebrew secular poetry. The genre was modeled after classical Arabic poetry in which Time was conceived as an impersonal and indifferent process of change that rolls on despite mankind's hopes or fears. The genre includes standard themes, expressing the poet's sadness about dislocation, wandering, separation from loved ones, loneliness, aging, decline of physical power, helplessness, suffering, and betrayal by friends.

For a detailed discussion of this genre and analysis of select poems, see Israel Levin, *The Embroidered Coat: The Genres of Hebrew Secular Poetry in Spain* (in Hebrew) (Tel Aviv, 1980), 209–67; idem, *Shmuel Ha-Naggid: Hayyav ve-Shirato* (1953), 163–81; Dan Pagis, *Changes and Tradition in the Secular Poetry: Spain and Italy* (Jerusalem, 1974), Eddy M. Zemach and Tova Rosen-Moked, *A Sophisticated Work* (in Hebrew) (Jerusalem, 1983), 27–80; and Raymond P. Scheindlin, *Wine, Women, and Death: Medieval Hebrew Poems on the Good Life* (Philadelphia, 1986), 135–75.

3. Aristotle defined Time as the number of motions in respect to before and after (*Physics*, book 4, chap. 10). For Aristotle "Time is one movement measuring other movements by parceling out the number of times the one takes place while the others take place." Abraham Edel, *Aristotle and His Philosophy* (Chapel Hill, N.C., 1982), 105. In Aristotelian philosophy Time is a dimension of change (or things changing), and change is the primary feature of the corporeal world. Already in the eleventh century the Jewish poets in Muslim Spain fused the

personification of Time in Arabic poetry with Aristotelian cosmological principles. See Zemach and Rosen-Moked, *A Sophisticated Work*, 50–58. Thus in the Sephardic imagination Time personified both the ever-changing nature of corporeal existence as well as the constancy of the laws of nature.

4. The concept was repeatedly discussed by ancient Greek and Roman philosophers. In the moral thought of late antiquity chance was personified and worshiped as the goddess Fortune. In the Middle Ages Christian writers depicted Fortune as an instrument of divine will but also as the cause of human misfortune. The belief in Fortune was particularly strong in the Renaissance. Fortune represented the arbitrary power that whimsically rules over human affairs, causing the precariousness of political life. Renaissance scholars—humanists, scholastics, and mendicants—were keenly aware of the miseries of life and the ills of earthly existence, especially at the turn of the sixteenth century. Reflection on the power of Fortune grew especially intense at the turn of the sixteenth century, when Italy was ravaged by wars, famines, the syphilis epidemic, earthquakes, political intrigues, and general social disorder. The diversity of opinions among Renaissance scholars makes generalizations about the Renaissance conception of Fortune very difficult. The major intellectual trends—Augustinianism, Stoicism, Aristotelianism, and Platonism—greatly overlapped and were often eclectically combined in the writing of a given individual.

For an overview on the conception of Fortune in medieval Christianity, see Howard R. Patch, *The Goddess Fortuna in Medieval Literature* (Cambridge, Mass., 1927). For an overview of major themes in Renaissance moral philosophy, see Paul Oscar Kristeller, "The Moral Thought of Renaissance Humanism," in his *Renaissance Thought and the Arts: Collected Essays*, expanded ed. (Princeton, 1990), 20–68, esp. 57–60. For a nuanced analysis of the interplay between the notions of Fortune, Providence, and Virtue in Renaissance thought, see J. G. A. Pocock, *The Machiavellian Movement: Florentine Political Thought and the Atlantic Republican Tradition* (Princeton, 1975), 31–48. For a detailed analysis of the variegated positions among the humanists, see Charles Trances, *Adversity's Noblemen: The Italian Humanists on Happiness* (New York, 1949); idem, *The Scope of Renaissance Humanism* (Ann Arbor, 1983), 243–363. For a close analysis of the interplay between the Stoic and Augustinian trends in Renaissance thought see William J. Bouwsma, "The Two Faces of Humanism: Stoicism and Augustinianism in Renaissance Thought," in Heiko O. Oberman and Thomas A. Brady, Jr., eds., *Itinerarium Italicum: The Profile of the Italian Renaissance in the Mirror of Its European Transformations* (Leiden, 1975), 3–60.

5. For a recent reconstruction of the Abravanel family, biography, and a pertinent bibliography, see Menahem Dorman, ed. and trans., "Judah Abravanel, His Life and Work," introduction to the Hebrew edition of Judah Abravanel, *Siḥot 'al ha-'Ahavah (Dialoghi d'Amore)* (Jerusalem, 1983), 13–96.

6. For a recent documentation of the refugee experience, see Joseph Hacker, "Pride and Despair: Chapters in the Spiritual and Social Reality of Spanish Exiles in the Ottoman Empire" (in Hebrew), in Robert Bonfil, Menahem Ben-Sasson, and Joseph Hacker, eds., *Culture and Society in Medieval Jewish History: A Collection of Essays in Memory of Haim Hillel ben Sasson* (Jerusalem, 1989), 541–86; idem, "A Collection of Letters About the Expulsion of Jews from Spain and Sicily," in Emmanuel Etkes and Joseph Salmon, eds., *Studies in the History of Jewish Society in the Middle Ages and in the Modern Period Presented to Professor Jacob Katz* (Jerusalem, 1980), 64–97; idem, "New Chronicles About the Expulsion of the Jews from Spain, Its Causes and Consequences," *Zion* 44 (1979), 201–29.

7. On the events immediately prior to the expulsion and the conversion of Jewish leaders such as Abraham Senior, see Haim Beinart, " The Expulsion from Spain: Causes and Consequences" (in Hebrew), in Haim Beinart, ed., *Moreshet Sepharad: The Sephardi Legacy* (Jerusalem, 1992), 384–496. For a sophisticated interpretation of Senior's conversion as the result of conflicting loyalties, see Eleazar Gutwirth, "Abraham Senior: Social Tensions and the Court-Jew," *Michael* 11 (1989), 169–230.

8. For a thematic analysis of the conception of exile, see Shalom Rosenberg, "Exile and Redemption in Jewish Thought in the Sixteenth Century: Contending Conceptions," in Bernard Dov Cooperman, ed., *Jewish Thought in the Sixteenth Century* (Cambridge, Mass., 1983), 399–430. Rosenberg has shown that after the expulsion Jewish thinkers developed a new conception of exile: it was no longer seen as a punishment but as an end in and of itself. The alleged goal of Jewish exilic existence was to alter reality culminating in the final redemption. Thus Israel's mission was to serve as a guide to humanity or as an agent for the performance of a specific mystical task, i.e., the gathering of the scattered sparks.

Rosenberg's study focuses on exile as a symbol for the collective existence of Israel. He makes no reference to the individualistic interpretation of exile and redemption in philosophical literature both before and after the expulsion. Especially for philosophers who incorporated Neoplatonic psychology, exile symbolized the imprisonment of the soul in the human body and redemption for the salvation of the individual soul through wisdom. The psychologization of traditional Jewish symbols enabled the philosophers to uphold traditional Jewish theodicy while diminishing its historical dimension.

9. Modern Jewish historiography has focused on messianism as the dominant Jewish response to the trauma of the expulsion. Recently, however, Moshe Idel has argued that such focus reflects the historians' Zionist proclivities (Gershom Scholem's, in particular), rather than an accurate reconstruction of historical realities. See Moshe Idel, "Introduction" to the reprint of A. Z. Aescoly, *Ha-Tenu'ot ha-Meshihiyot be-Yisrael* (Jerusalem, 1988), 10. Idel has sought first to refine the notion of Jewish messianic movements (in the sociological sense of the term

movement) and messianic speculations, and, second, he differentiates between the traditional eschatological and apocalyptic messianism, on the one hand, and the individual, ahistorical, apolitical "redemptive activites," on the other hand. The latter type was developed during the Middle Ages under the impact of Greek philosophy, indicating the interiorization of Jewish religious life. Idel has viewed these redemptive activities as "moderate" forms of Jewish messianism because they lack the catastrophic character of traditional Jewish messianism and because they were not predicated upon ending Jewish diaspora existence. The concepts of exile and redemption did not signify political situations of the Jewish people but symbolized psychological or metaphysical events. See Moshe Idel, "Patterns of Redemptive Activity in the Middle Ages" (in Hebrew), in Zvi Baras, ed., *Messianism and Eschatology: A Collection of Essays* (Jerusalem, 1983), 253–79.

While I endorse Idel's nuanced typology of redemptive activities as well as his insistence that the expulsion did not signify a rupture in Jewish culture, it seems to me that his analysis expands (rather than limits) the scope of Jewish messianism. Idel himself notes that the pursuit of individual salvation was not unrelated to the desire for collective redemption. Often (especially in the Maimonidean tradition) the former was considered a necessary condition for the latter (ibid., 274). Idel also does not ignore those Jewish thinkers (philosophers and kabbalists) who interpreted the expulsion and the imminent coming of the Messiah. Hence, I suggest that the hopes for a collective historical redemption and the efforts to attain individual salvation are expressions of the same impulse: the desire to transcend Time.

Needless to say, the desire for transcendence of corporeality is universal; it is present in all cultures and in all times regardless of historical conditions. Yet, it is reasonable to argue that acute stress and traumatic historical events tend to sharpen human awareness of life's finitude. In turn, such awareness intensifies the quest for immortality. Thus, a historical event could be said to trigger certain intellectual developments: the event poses a certain problem and creates certain perceptions that call for interpretation. The interpretation itself is carried out by means of existing paradigms or interpretative schemes. Precisely because the interpretative scheme existed prior to the event, it appears as if there was little change after the event. To understand the impact of the event(s), we must look for shifts in perspective within the contours of existing paradigms or for nuances in the way the paradigm was employed to make sense of the new historical conditions.

No one understood this better than Scholem. See Gershom Scholem, "Opening Address" to the Study-Conference held in Jerusalem, July 14–19, 1968, printed in R. J. Z. Werblowsky and C. Joyce Bleeker, eds., *Types of Redemption* (Leiden, 1970), 1–12.

10. Abravanel's messianism is an excellent example of my above argument: individual salvation and collective redemption are not mutually exclusive. In the writings of Isaac Abravanel, the former is viewed as a means for the latter. Though

much has been written on Abravanel's messianic posture, there is no systematic attempt to reconcile its various aspects into a consistent theory. For a recent (not entirely successful) attempt see Rivkah Schatz, "Kavim li-Demutah shel he-Hit'ore-
rut ha-Politit-Meshiḥit le-'Aḥar Gerush Sefarad," *Daat* 11 (1983), 53–66, and the
secondary literature cited on p. 56. For a recent summary of Abravanel's messianism in the context of the anti-Christian polemics, see Daniel Lasker, "Jewish-
Christian Polemics in Light of the Expulsion from Spain," *Judaism* 41 (1992),
151–53. On the connection between Abravanel's messianism and his astrological beliefs, see Shaul Regev, "Messianism and Astrology in the Thought of R. Isaac
Abravanel," *Sefer ha-Shanah le-Mada'ei ha-Yahadut shel Yad ha-Rav Nissim*
(Jerusalem, 1987), 1:169–87. Astrology manifested the regularity and constancy of
Nature and Time. Israel, however, is not governed by astral forces but directly by
God, i.e., through Torah. In other words, Israel's history is sacred, not profane.
Abravanel's distinction between natural providence (in which astrology can play a
role) and supernatural providence (in which God governs Israel directly) was ac-
cepted by most Sephardic philosophers after the expulsion from Spain. It enabled
them to study the science of astrology that flowered in the Renaissance while limiting its application for the interpretation of Jewish history. On the prevalence of
astrology in the Renaissance, see Eugenio Garin, *Astrology in the Renaissance: The
Zodiac of Life*, rev. trans. by Clare Robertson (London, 1982).

11. Moshe Idel has shown that at least three of these authors were influenced by
the anonymous *Sefer ha-Meshiv* (The Book of the Answering Angel), written in
Spain prior to the expulsion. *Sefer ha-Meshiv* is the most explicitly messianic docu-
ment of Spanish Kabbalah. It discusses the nature of the Messiah, the date of his
arrival, and the precise means to hasten his coming. See Idel, "Introduction," *Ha-
Tenu'ot ha-Meshiḥiyot be-Yisrael*, 21–22; idem, "Studies in the Thought of the
Author of *Sefer ha-Meshiv*: A Chapter in the History of Spanish Kabbalah" (in
Hebrew), *Sefunot*, n.s., 2, no. 17 (1983), 185–265. Idel cites the influence of *Sefer ha-
Meshiv* as evidence that these was no causal connection between the expulsion and
either the rise of sixteenth-century messianism or the dissemination of Kabbalah.
Other factors, such as the impulse to preserve kabbalistic oral traditions and the
encounter between the Sephardic kabbalists and groups of kabbalists in Italy and
in Greece were no less important. In fact, in comparison to *Sefer ha-Meshiv* the
messianism of the sixteenth century was rather "moderate" and "conservative." See
Moshe Idel, "Spanish Kabbalah After the Expulsion" (in Hebrew), in Beinart,
Moreshet Sepharad: The Sephardi Legacy, 503–12.

The debate about the impact of the expulsion on kabbalistic activity appears to
conflate two separate questions. (1) Was sixteenth-century Kabbalah messianic in
the traditional sense of that term? (2) Did the expulsion cause the proliferation in
Kabbalah in the sixteenth century? In note 10 I attempt to clarify (1) in partial
agreement with Idel. As for (2) let me say that the factors that Idel adduces to

explain the rise of Kabbalah are themselves outcomes of the expulsion from Iberia. It was the expulsion that inspired the need for consolidation and systematization of kabbalistic traditions, and it was the expulsion that facilitated physical contact between Sephardic refugees and kabbalists in Italy and Greece. Thus, whether or not the expulsion was a traumatic event, it did create new demographic realities and new existential needs that gave rise to intellectual changes. One result of these changes, but by no means the exclusive one, was the growing interest in Kabbalah among Sephardic intellectuals.

12. On Molkho's messianic activism in the context of Spanish millenarianism, see Richard H. Popkin, "Jewish Christians and Christian Jews in Spain, 1492 and After," *Judaism* 41 (1992), 248–67. On the kabbalistic sources of Molkho's worldview see Moshe Idel, "Shelomo Molkho as a Magician" (in Hebrew), *Sefunot*, n.s., 3, no.18 (1985), 193–219.

13. The redemptive significance of Torah study has been highlighted by Elisheva Carlebach, "Rabbinic Circles as Messianic Pathways in the Postexpulsion Era," *Judaism* 41 (1992), 208–16. Her insights correctly diminish the dichotomy between messianism and rabbinism current in modern scholarship. Her work (as well as this article) builds on the insights of Isadore Twersky, "Talmudists, Philosophers, Kabbalists: The Quest for Spirituality in the Sixteenth Century," in Cooperman, *Jewish Thought in the Sixteenth Century*, 335–69.

14. For a phenomenological analysis of mysticism and theurgy as two different strands within Sephardic Kabbalah, see Moshe Idel, *Kabbalah: New Perspectives* (New Haven, 1989). For clarifications and qualifications of Idel's phenomenology, see my review essay, "Continuity and Change in the Study of Kabbalah, " *AJS Review* 16 (1990), 161–92.

15. The term *philosophers* in this paper in somewhat ambiguous. The individuals discussed herein were all rabbinic scholars who were trained in philosophy and its preparatory liberal arts. At the same time, they insisted on the inherent limitations of human reason and subordinated philosophy to the revealed tradition. Technically speaking, these scholars were "theologians." However, since the term *theologians* might give the false impression that these scholars were interested in nothing but the interpretation of sacred texts, I prefer to designate them as philosophers.

16. Several words are used interchangeably to render the notion of ultimate happiness, felicity, or beatitude: 'osher 'elyon, hazlaḥa 'aḥaronah, and shelemut 'elyonah. These terms are part of a complex discourse on the good life, the ultimate end of human life, and the road to human perfection. That postexpulsion thinkers still speculated about human happiness in terms of ultimate end indicates their allegiance to Aristotelian teleology in direct continuity with preexpulsion Jewish philosophy. The discourse was featured as prominently in the writings of medieval Jewish philosophers as in the works of medieval Muslim and Christian thinkers, as well as the humanists and scholastics of the Renaissance. I am now writing the his-

tory of discourse in Jewish philosophy from the twelfth to the seventeenth centuries. This article builds upon my observations in "Human Felicity: Fifteenth-Century Sephardic Perspectives on Happiness," in Adele Seeff and Bernard D. Cooperman, eds., *Iberia and Beyond: Hispanic Jews Between Two Cultures* (forthcoming).

17. The biblical commentaries consulted for this study include Meir Aramah, *Me'ir Tehillot* on Psalms (Venice 1590; repr., Warsaw, 1898); Joseph Taitazak, *Lehem Setarim* on the Five Scrolls (Venice, 1608); *Porat Yosef* on Ecclesiastes (Venice, 1563; Venice, 1599), and his commentary on Psalms, printed in Yedaiah Bedersi, *Leshon Zahav* (Venice, 1599); Isaac Arroyo, *Tanhumot 'El* on the Pentateuch (Salonika, 1578); Moses Almosnino, *Yedei Mosheh* on Ecclesiastes (Jerusalem, 1986).

It is no coincidence that the theme of happiness looms large in the commentaries on Proverbs, Psalms, and Ecclesiastes and is prominent in the formal moral training of Sephardic Jewry in the Ottoman Empire. The Sephardic exiles instituted the custom of reading from the Psalter during the winter months and from Proverbs and *'Avot* every Sabbath between Passover and Shavuot. It was believed that by so doing the individual would attain moral perfection, reaching the high degree of self-purification necessary for the reenactment of the Sinaitic theophany on Shavuot. See Moses Almosnino, *Pirkei Mosheh* (Jerusalem, 1970), 4; Solomon ben Isaac Halevi, *Lev 'Avot*, 11 a–b. An English translation of the relevant paragraph is excerpted in Joseph Hacker, "Intellectual Activity of the Jews of the Ottoman Empire During the Sixteenth and Seventeenth Centuries," in Isadore Twersky and Bernard Septimus, eds., *Jewish Thought in the Seventeenth Century* (Cambridge, Mass, 1987), 111–12, n. 34. The institutionalization of moral training reflects a community obsessed with the pursuit of moral perfection.

18. The Sephardim brought with them a long-standing tradition inaugurated by Maimonides that fused rabbinic moral values distilled in Tractate *'Avot* with Aristotelian ethics. This philosophic tradition evolved through philosophic commentaries on *'Avot* and commentaries on Maimonides' *Eight Chapters*, the introduction to his commentary on *'Avot*. For an overview of this strand in medieval Jewish ethical literature, see Joseph Dan, *Hebrew Ethical and Homiletical Literature: The Middle Ages and Early Modern Period* (Jerusalem, 1975), 105–20. A detailed analysis of medieval moral philosophy is still a desideratum. In this study I focus on Isaac Abravanel, *Nahalat 'Avot* (New York, 1953); Moses Almosnino, *Pirkei Mosheh* (first printing Salonika, 1563; Jerusalem, 1970); and Solomon ben Isaac Halevi, *Lev 'Avot* (Salonika, 1565).

19. The history of the absorption of the *Ethics* into Jewish thought is yet to be written. Important steps in this direction were taken by the late Lawrence Berman. See Berman, "Ibn Rushd's *Middle Commentary on the Nicomachean Ethics* in Medieval Hebrew Literature," in Jean Jolivet, ed., *Multiple Averröes* (Paris, 1978), 287–311, and the references to his own work cited there.

References to and citations from Aristotle's *Ethics* abound in the biblical commentaries and commentaries on Tractate *'Avot* written by postexpulsion philosophers. Yet the most important contribution to this intellectual discourse was the new commentary on the *Ethics* by Moses Almosnino. Entitled *Penei Mosheh*, the commentary is extant in a single manuscript, MS Oxford-Bodleian Michael 409 (= Neubauer 1435), consulted for this study. The extant manuscript is incomplete. It consists of Almosnino's commentary on books 1, 2, and 10 of the *Ethics*, but references therein and in other extant works by Almosnino indicate that the original commentary covered all ten books of the *Ethics*. While modern scholars have long known about this manuscript, no one (at least to my knowledge) has studied it in depth. The text is extremely interesting both philosophically and historically, and I will discuss it in a separate study.

20. Given the primacy of exegesis in the postexpulsion period, there are relatively few treatises of systematic theology. The relevant texts consulted for this study include Solomon Almoli, *Sha'ar 'Adonai he-Hadash* (Salonika, 1532); Moses Almosnino, *Tefillah le-Mosheh* (Salonika, 1563); and Abraham ibn Megash, *Kevod 'Elohim* (Salonika, 1585; repr., Jerusalem, 1987).

21. The sermon was a prominent way of forming Sephardic collective identity after the expulsion from Spain. See note 66 below. For this study I consulted the sermons of Joseph Garcon published by Meir Benyahu, "The Sermons of R. Yosef b. Meir Garson as a Source for the History of the Expulsion from Spain and Sephardi Diaspora" (in Hebrew), *Michael* 7 (1982), 42–205; Isaac ben Samuel Aderbi, *Divrei Shalom* (Salonika, 1580); and Moses Almosnino, *Ma'amez Koah* (Venice, 1582).

22. This is a very large category that includes the vast *musar* literature. I refer specifically to manuals that were inspired by moral philosophy such as Moses Almosnino's *Libro Intutilado Regimiento de la Vida* (Salonika, 1564). It is written in Ladino with a Hebrew summary of the chapters' contents. A Hebrew translation of a few pages from the introduction is available in Simha Assaf, ed., *Mekorot le-Toledot ha-Hinnukh be-Yisrael* (Tel Aviv, 1954), 3:11–14. Prof. John Zemke of the University of Missouri at Columbia is now preparing a critical edition of this text.

23. See Moshe Idel, "The Impact of Expulsion on Jewish Creativity" (in Hebrew), *Zemanim* 41 (1992), 11–12; and consult also his articles cited in notes 10 and 11 above.

24. To date there is no comprehensive study of all facets of Jewish culture in the Ottoman empire in the postexpulsion era, even though each of these subfields has been treated in some depth. For a recent overview of Sephardic society and culture in the postexpulsion period see Joseph Hacker, "The Sephardic Exiles in the Ottoman Empire during the Sixteenth Century: Community and Society" (in Hebrew), in Beinart, *Moreshet Sepharad: The Sephardi Legacy*, 460–78.

25. Yosef Yahalom, "A Hebrew Renaissance in the Sephardi Diaspora" (in Hebrew), *Pe'amim* 26 (1986), 9–28.

26. See Hacker, "Intellectual Activity," 101–9; and idem, "Pride and Despair," 569–70.

27. For a summary of Sephardic religious rationalism see Herbert Davidson, "The Study of Philosophy as a Religious Obligation," in S. D. Goitein, ed., *Religion in a Religious Age* (Cambridge, Mass., 1974), 53–68.

28. The antiphilosophic posture of Joseph Yaaveẓ and Isaac Aramah must be understood in its proper context. It was not outright opposition to the study of philosophy or a denunciation of a rationalist approach to Judaism but a critique of a certain interpretation of Maimonideanism. Both Yaaveẓ and Aramah were schooled in Aristotelianism and continued to reflect on Judaism in the framework of Maimonidean rationalism. What they opposed was a certain (possible) interpretation of Maimonides according to which philosophy alone is salvific and the Torah is but the sociopolitical context in which one could attain philosophical perfection. Instead, Yaaveẓ and Aramah highlighted the qualitative differences between discursive knowledge and prophetic knowledge and demanded the subordination of philosophy to the revealed tradition. So long as philosophy was properly employed to articulate the meaning of divinely revealed propositions, it was permissible for Jews to engage in philosophy. Aramah's position was adopted even by thinkers who expressly preferred the study of Kabbalah to philosophy, such as Solomon Alkabez and Moses Cordovero. On their attitudes toward the study of philosophy, see Brachah Sack, "The Attitude of R. Solomon Alkabez to Philosophical Investigation" (in Hebrew), *Eshel Beer Sheva* 1 (1976), 288–306; and Joseph Ben Sholomo, "The Attitude of R. Moses Cordovero to Philosophy and the Sciences" (in Hebrew), *Sefunot* 6 (1962).

29. See Daniel Boyarin, "Studies in the Talmudic Commentaries of the Spanish Exiles," *Sefunot*, n.s., 2,17 (1983), 165–84; idem, *Sephardi Speculation: A Study in Methods of Talmudic Interpretation* (in Hebrew) (Jerusalem, 1989); Bentov Hayim, "Methods of Study of Talmud in the Yeshivot of Salonica and Turkey After the Expulsion from Spain" (in Hebrew), *Sefunot* 13 (1979), 39–102; and Hayim Dimitrovsky, "The Academy of R. Jacob Berab in Safed" (in Hebrew), *Sefunot* 7 (1973), 41–102.

30. On the term ḥakham kolel, see Tirosh-Rothschild, *Between Worlds: The Life and Thought of R. David ben Judah Messer Leon* (Albany, 1991), 39. For a reconstruction of the theory that underscored the pursuit of rabbinic and secular studies, see 105–38.

In his *Regimiento de la Vida*, Moses Almosnino gives us a clue about the composition of the curriculum for students interested in philosophy. Almosnino recommends the study of the trivium (grammar, logic, and rhetoric) and the quadrivium (arithmetic, geometry, music, and optics) as a preparation for the study of physics and metaphysics. However, he expressly states that the Torah encompasses all these sciences in the most perfect way so that one should master the secular sciences only to the extent that one needs to understand "the words of our sages in the Talmud." We shall return to this point below. The relevant passage in a Hebrew translation was published by Assaf, *Mekorot le-Toledot ha-Ḥinnukh*, 3:11–14.

Benjamin Halevi Ashkenazi memorialized the ideal of *ḥakham kolel* in an elegy written after the fire of 1545 in Salonika. The poem praises the comprehensive program of study in Joseph Taitatzak's academy, a program that included the study of logic, algebra, geometry, astronomy, and metaphysics in addition to talmudic studies. The poet hyperbolically states that the academy's students were as erudite in medicine as were Galen and Avicenna! The poem was printed in *The Ashkenazi Maḥzor* (Salonika, 1548), 186b, and excerpted in Meir Benayahu, "Rabbi Joseph Taitatzak of Salonika: The Head of the Sephardi Diaspora" (in Hebrew), in Zvi Ankori, ed., *Me-'Az ve-'Ad 'Atah* (Tel Aviv, 1984), book 2, 21–22.

31. The sociocultural portrait of this group still awaits systematic analysis. For now, consult Mark A. Epstein, *The Ottoman Jewish Communities and Their Role in the Fifteenth and Sixteenth Centuries* (Freiburg, 1980), Islam Kundlische Unterschuungen, vol. 56; and idem, "The Leadership of the Ottoman Jews in the Fifteenth and Sixteenth Centuries," in Benjamin Braude and Bernard Lewis, eds., *Christians and Jews in the Ottoman Empire: The Functioning of Plural Society* (New York and London, 1982), 1:101–13. For biographical information about individual members of the Jewish aristocracy, see Uriel Heyd, "Moses Hamon, Chief Jewish Physician to Sultan Suleyman the Magnificent," *Oriens* 16 (1963), 152–69; Meir Benayahu, "Moshe Benvenest, Court Physician, and Rabbi Jehuda Zarko's Poem on his Exile to Rhodes" (in Hebrew), *Sefunot* 12 (Book of Greek Jewry 2; 1971–1978), 123–44; and idem, "Rabbi David Ben Ban Venest of Saloniki and his Letter to R. Abraham ibn Yaish in Brusa" (in Hebrew), *Sefunot* 11 (Book of Greek Jewry 1; 1971–1978), 267–97. For an overview of the social stratification in the Ottoman Jewish community, see Hacker, "The Sephardic Exiles," 472–75, and the bibliography cited there.

32. For a description of the philosophical interests in the social circle of Joseph Nasi, see Cecil Roth, *The House of Nasi: The Duke of Naxos* (Philadelphia, 1948), 168–82.

33. The impact of the returning conversos on Sephardic scholarship in the Ottoman Empire during the sixteenth century has not been studied in full. For now consult Charles Singer, "Science and Judaism," in Louis Finkelstein, ed., *The Jews: Their Role in Civilization* (New York, 1978), 242–50. On Amatus Lusitanus, the most celebrated of the ex-converso scientists in Constantinople, see Harry Friedenwald, *The Jews and Medicine: Essays* (Baltimore, 1944; repr., New York, 1967), 332–80.

34. On the scientific erudition of Jewish scholars in sixteenth-century Italy and their response to the European discoveries, see David Ruderman, *The World of a Renaissance Jew: The Life and Thought of Abraham ben Mordecai Farissol*

(Cincinnati, 1982), 131–43; idem, "The Impact of Science on Jewish Culture and Society in Venice," in Gaetano Cozzi, ed., *Gli ebrei e Venezia: secoli XIV–XVIII* (Milan, 1987), 417–48; idem, *Kabbalah, Magic and Science: The Cultural Universe of a Sixteenth-Century Jewish Physician* (Cambridge, Mass., 1988).

35. Moses Almosnino's commentary is entitled *Bet 'Elohim*. It was composed in 1552 and is extant in several manuscripts. I consulted MS Oxford-Bodleian 2038 (no. 19323 in the Institute of Microfilmed Hebrew Manuscripts in Jerusalem).

John Sacrobosco taught at the University of Paris from 1230 to 1255. A collection of three of his works—*Tractatus de Sphaera, Alegorism vulgaris*, and *Compotus*—constituted the scope of astronomical knowledge for university students in the late Middle Ages. See Olaf Pedersen, "Astronomy," in David C. Lindberg, ed., *Science in the Middle Ages* (Chicago, 1978), 315. For an English translation of *De Sphaera* and its role in late medieval astronomy, see Lynn Thorndike, *The Sphere of Sacrobosco and Its Commentators* (Chicago, 1949).

36. Almosnino's commentary is entitled *Sha'ar ha-Shamayim*. It is extant in Oxford-Bodleian 2036/2 (no. 19321 in the Institute of Microfilmed Hebrew Manuscripts in Jerusalem), consulted for this research. Georg Peurbach (1423–1461) was the last medieval astronomer to attempt to improve medieval astronomy on the basis of traditional sources and presuppositions. See Pedersen, "Astronomy," 330.

37. See Naphtali ben Menahem, "Kitvei Rabbi Mosheh Almosnino," *Sinai* 10 (1946–47), 280, for the reference to the discovery of America in *Sha'ar ha-Shamayim*, and consult *Bet 'Elohim*, fol. 35a.

38. See Yahalom, "Hebrew Renaissance," 10–11; Yosef Tobi, "Hebrew Poetry in the East After the Spanish Expulsion" (in Hebrew), *Pe'amim* 26 (1986), 29–45, and the bibliography cited there.

39. See Yahalom, "Hebrew Renaissance"; Yosef H. Yerushalmi, "Castilian, Portuguese, Ladino: The Foreign-Language Literature of Sephardic Jewry" (in Hebrew), in Zvi Ankori, ed., *Me-'Az ve-'Ad 'Atah* (Tel Aviv, 1984), 2:35–53, esp. 48–50.

40. Solomon ben Jacob Almoli, *Sefer Me'asef le-Khol ha-Maḥanot* (Constantinople, 1530). The printed edition includes only the introduction; the bulk of the text is extant in manuscript. Selections from the introduction were published by Hanoch Yalon, "Chapters from R. Solomon Almoli's *Me'asef le-Khol ha-Maḥanoth*" (in Hebrew), *Aresheth: An Annual of Hebrew Book Lore* 2 (1960), 96–108. I understand that Shaul Regev is now writing a monograph on Solomon Almoli, but so far I have not seen anything in print.

41. See Yalon, "Chapters," 101. Almoli's condition reflects both the glut of Sephardic scholars in Constantinople and the fact that Almoli arrived in Constantinople without a family and had no family lineage of which to boast. To make ends meet, Almoli worked as a private tutor. However, according to his own testimony, he failed to gather a significant following. Even his private students

were not loyal to him; they did not appreciate his vast knowledge and forsook him for more famous scholars. Almoli, therefore, resorted to writing with the hope of being appreciated in the remote future.

42. Yalon, "Chapters," 102. This comprehensive list resulted from the fusion of two Jewish scientific curricula: one developed in Muslim lands, the other in Christendom. To situate Almoli's scientific encyclopedia in the context of Jewish scientific education, consult Harry A. Wolfson, "The Classification of Sciences in Medieval Jewish Philosophy," in Isadore Twersky and George H. Williams, eds., *Studies in the History of Philosophy and Religion* (Cambridge, Mass., 1973), 1:493–545.

43. The messianic import of the study of philosophy is spelled out in his introduction to *Sha'ar 'Adonai he-Ḥadash*, 13a–17a. Almoli continued in the footsteps of Isaac Abravanel, who also saw a causal connection between intellectual perfection of individuals and collective redemption. See Isaac Abravanel, *Yeshu'ot Meshiḥo* (1828), part 2, chap. 2.

44. On the obsessive preoccupation of Sephardic exiles with survival of death through children, see Hacker, "Pride and Despair," 547–55.

45. In the introduction to *Me'asef le-Khol ha-Maḥanot*, Almoli states: "Indeed, I know that this compilation [*kibbuẓ*] will be a blessing after I pass away, and that it will ensure my immortality more than having sons and daughters. Since they will surely die and perish, they cannot secure my personal survival. Yet the words of this book will remain for future generations so that I will be known forever after."

On the link between the quest for personal immortality and the desire for fame through the written medium in Renaissance humanism, see Paul Oscar Kristeller, "The Immortality of the Soul," in Michael Mooney, ed., *Renaissance Thought and Its Sources* (New York, 1979), 181–96, esp. 182.

46. In recent years Jewish historians have begun to study Jewish printing from a sociocultural perspective rather than a merely bibliographical one. Greater attention has been paid to the social status of Jewish publishers and printers, the contacts between Jewish and European publishing houses, and the significance of printing as an agent of change in Jewish culture. See Zeev Gries, "Printing as a Means of Communication Among Jewish Communities in the Period of the Expulsion from Spain: A Preface for Reflections and Discussion" (in Hebrew), *Daat* 28 (1982), 5–17, and the bibliography cited there; idem, "Toward a Portrait of the Jewish Publisher in the End of the Middle Ages" (in Hebrew) *Iggeret* (newsletter of the National Israeli Academy of Sciences) 11 (1992), 7–11; and Hacker, "Intellectual Activity," 113–16.

47. Undoubtedly, the number of philosophic texts printed in the Ottoman Empire during the sixteenth century was relatively small in comparison with works of Halakhah, biblical exegesis, and homiletics. See the survey of Abraham Yaari, *Hebrew Printing at Constantinople: Its History and Bibliography* (Jerusalem, 1967),

11–38; and the corrections and additions of Joseph Hacker, "Constantinople Prints in the Sixteenth Century," *Aresheth* 5 (1972), 457–93; and Abraham Habermann, *Chapters for the History of Jewish Printers and Booklore* (Jerusalem, 1978).

It is also true that technical philosophical works by medieval Jewish authors (e.g., the commentaries on the Aristotelian-Averröean corpora) remained in manuscript. This could not have been a coincidence. It reflects the general preference for theological works that argued for the superiority of revealed Judaism over philosophy and/or other religions. Accordingly, it was fitting that Abraham Bibago's *Derekh 'Emunah* was printed in 1522 in Constantinople, whereas his numerous commentaries on Averröes were not.

This article, however, argues that to understand the status of philosophy in the Ottoman Empire during the sixteenth century we need to consider not only works of philosophy proper but also the philosophical biblical commentaries, sermons, secular belles lettres, and interest in the natural sciences.

48. On the first editions of these texts, see Israel Mehlman, "The First Hebrew Prints (1475–1500)," *Aresheth* 5 (1972), 448–56.

49. On that controversy, see Isaiah Tishby, "The Controversy About Sefer ha-Zohar in Sixteenth-Century Italy," reprinted in Tishby, *Studies in Kabbalah and Its Branches: Researches and Sources* (Jerusalem, 1982), 1:79–130.

50. *Sha'ar 'Adonai he-Ḥadash,* 2a–b.

51. The commentary is extant in several manuscripts. I have consulted MS Parma 1218 (no. 28013 in the Institute of Microfilmed Hebrew Manuscripts in Jerusalem). An excerpt from the introduction of *Migdal 'Oz* was published by Francisco Cantera-Burgos, "Nueva serie de manuscritos hebreos de Madrid," *Sefarad* 19 (1959), 5–8; and idem, "A Hebrew Manuscript Rediscovered" (in Hebrew), in *Yitzhak F. Baer Jubilee Volume* (Jerusalem, 1960), 287–90. In his introduction Almosnino explicitly links the knowledge of philosophy (culled from al-Ghazzali's work) and the attainment of perfect happiness, i.e., personal immortality.

52. Almosnino states that he composed *Migdal 'Oz* at the request of Jewish students who were interested in the study of theology (*lemidat ḥemdat ha-dat*) and who were already accomplished in the study of the Talmud. Indeed, we learn from Isaac Arroyo (*Tanḥumot 'El* p. 1b), that al-Ghazzali's *Maqasid al-Falasifah* (The Intentions of the Philosophers) was widespread among the Jewish scholars of Salonika. For an English translation of the relevant passage, see Hacker, "Intellectual Activity," 105, n. 20. Arroyo's comment, however, is somewhat puzzling. Arroyo states that he would cite from al-Ghazzali's work because other works by "ancient philosophers"(*ha-filosofim he-kedumim*) were not available in Salonika at the time. It is unclear whom Arroyo had in mind. I conjecture that he refers to ancient Greek and Roman philosophers rather than to medieval Muslim and Jewish philosophers.

The renewed interest in al-Ghazzali must be viewed in light of the perception of al-Ghazzali in the sixteenth century and the fact that his views became widely known in Europe with the publication of Averröes's *Incoherence of the Incoherence* in Italy in 1497. In that work Averröes defended Aristotelian philosophy against al-Ghazzali's attacks in *Tahafut al-Falasifa* (The Incoherence of the Philosophers). While postexpulsion Jewish thinkers continued to study Aristotelian philosophy through the commentaries of Averröes, they were more sympathetic to al-Ghazzali's delicate balance between philosophy and prophetic religion. Like them, al-Ghazzali spoke with respect of science and philosophy so long as they stayed within their own areas. Whereas philosophy could and should be used to interpret natural phenomena, only a revelation from God could lead man to the afterlife. On the relationship between the knowledge culled from the efforts of human reason and the suprarational wisdom of divine revelation in al-Ghazzali's thought, see Richard Joseph McCarthy, *Freedom and Fulfillment: An Annotated Translation of Al-Ghazali's al-Munqidh min al-Dalal and Other Relevant Works* (Boston, 1980), esp. introduction and ix–lx. I thank my colleague Scott Alexander for directing me to that work.

Furthermore, al-Ghazzali's *Maqasid al-Falasifah* was written early in his academic career as a summary of Avicenna's Neoplatonized Aristotelianism prevalent among Muslim intellectuals during the eleventh century. On the key issue of personal immortality, Avicenna's philosophy was easier to reconcile with traditional religious beliefs than Averröes's philosophy. By the same token, the Neoplatonic tendencies of Avicenna's philosophy made it more compatible with the Platonic themes in kabbalistic ontology and cosmology and with the rising popularity of Platonism in Renaissance culture. As we shall see below, postexpulsion Sephardic thinkers incorporated both Kabbalah and Renaissance Platonism into the Aristotelian framework of their inherited philosophic tradition.

53. On *Penei Mosheh* see note 19 above. Almosnino's commentary on Aristotle has to be viewed in the broader context of Renaissance interest in the *Ethics*. During the 1540s and 1550s Italian and French humanists composed new commentaries on the *Ethics*. Thus the Benedictine scholar Joachim Perion—an avowed Ciceronian—translated the *Ethics* in 1540. His translation provoked much criticism from other humanists and led to a new translation by the French humanist Denys Lambin. That translation was published in Venice in 1558 and later in Paris. See John O'Brien, "Translation, Philology and Polemics in Denys Lambin's Nicomachean Ethics of 1558," *Renaissance Studies* 3, no. 3 (1989), 267–89. For an overview of translations and commentaries on the *Ethics* in the late Middle Ages and the Renaissance, see George Wieland, "The Reception and Interpretation of Aristotle's Ethics," in Norman Kretzmann et al., eds., *The Cambridge History of Later Medieval Philosophy* (Cambridge, 1982), 657–72.

54. On this lost text, see Naphtali ben Menahem, "The Writings of Rabbi Moses Almosnino" (in Hebrew), *Sinai* 10 (1946–47), 283–84.

55. See Assaf, ed., *Mekorot le-Toledot ha-Ḥinnukh*, 3:13.

56. Joseph ibn Shem Tov's commentary on the *Ethics* was written in 1455. It is extant in several manuscripts. I consulted MS Oxford-Bodleian Michael 404 (= Neubauer 1431). Ibn Shem Tov's *Kevod 'Elohim* (Ferrara, 1556) was in effect a short commentary on the *Ethics*, whose major purpose was to show Jews how Aristotle's *Ethics* could be compatible with the teachings of the Torah. For an analysis of Joseph ibn Shem Tov's contribution to the interpretation of the *Ethics*, see "Human Felicity," cited in note 19 above.

Ibn Shem Tov's commentary is cited on almost every other page of *Penei Mosheh*. However, Almosnino often debates with ibn Shem Tov's rendering of Aristotle's original text or his understanding of Aristotle's original intent because Almosnino consulted other translations and commentaries on the *Ethics*. The translation of the *Ethics* by Alguades with the commentary of Joseph ibn Shem Tov were also cited by Solomon Almoli (*Sha'ar 'Adonai he-Ḥadash*, 20a–b). I believe, though I cannot yet prove, that ibn Shem Tov's commentary was the major source for the knowledge of the *Ethics* among Sephardic scholars in Salonika during the sixteenth century.

57. Meir ben Solomon Alguades, the chief rabbi of Castile and court physician of several Castilian monarchs, translated the *Ethics* in 1405 at the request of another Jewish courtier, Don Samuel Lavi of Aragon. The translation is extant in several manuscripts. I consulted Oxford Bodleian Pocock 17 (= Neubauer 1427). Alguades's introduction to the translation was published by Lawrence Berman in *Jerusalem Studies in Jewish Thought* 8 (*Shlomo Pines Jubilee Volume*, vol. 1; 1990), 147–68. Alguades's translation was based on the Latin translation of Averröes's *Middle Commentary on the Ethics* by Hermann the German, a supercommentary on that text ascribed to Thomas Aquinas, and the standard Latin translation of the *Ethics* by Robert Grosseteste.

58. About 1485 Baruch ibn Ya'ish composed a new translation and commentary on the *Ethics* that relied on both Bruni's and Argyropoulos's translations. The translation is extant in three manuscripts, MS Paris Heb. 1001, 1002, 1003, that have not been studied so far. It is very possible that the translation was occasioned by the first printed edition of Aristotle's *Organon* with the *Ethics* in 1483, edited by Nicoletto Vernia.

One intriguing question about this text concerns its place of composition. In the colophon of MS Paris Heb. 1001 we read as follows: "I, Samuel bar Solomon of Tortosa, translated this text [*he'etaktiv*] and wrote down what I heard from my master, R. Baruch ibn Ya'ish, may God bless and sustain him. And I completed it [*ve-hishlamtiv*] in the town of Benevento in the year [5]285." The statement is somewhat ambiguous. It is not clear if both master and student were together in Benevento, Italy (where both the translation and commentary on the *Ethics* were done), or whether Samuel bar Solomon studied with Baruch ibn Ya'ish in Spain (perhaps in Tortosa) and only completed the writing of the commentary in

Benevento, Italy. Given the spread of Italian humanism in Spain during the 1480s, it is not inconceivable that ibn Ya'ish had access to the translations of Bruni and Agryropoulos already in Spain. If so, more attention should be given to the impact of humanism on Sephardic Jewish thought prior to the expulsion from Spain, especially given the role of conversos in the dissemination of humanist scholarship in Spain. And if ibn Ya'ish's translation and commentary were produced entirely in Italy it would support the claim (expressed by Arthur Lesley and other scholars, myself included) that there were Jewish humanists in Italy already in the 1480s. See Tirosh-Rothschild, "In Defense of Jewish Humanism," *Jewish History* 3 (1988), 31–57.

Almosnino considered ibn Ya'ish's translation superior to the one produced by Meir Alguades. He therefore referred to it quite often and debated with Joseph ibn Shem Tov on the basis of ibn Yaish's rendering of the text. For example, fols. 14b, 31b, 33b–34a, 41b, 71a, 103b.

59. Leonardo Bruni (1374–1444), the famous humanist and chancellor of Florence, composed a new translation of the *Ethics* in 1416–1417. The translation was no more than a revision of Grosetteste's translation, but it became a great success. Bruni's translation reflected the role of moral philosophy in the *studia humanitatis*, the humanist ideal of eloquence, and the Renaissance rereading of Aristotle on the basis of textual analysis. Bruni also wrote a short introduction to the *Ethics* entitled *Isagogicon moralis philosphiae*.

Moses Almosnino refers to Bruni's translation in *Penei Mosheh*, fol. 14b. It is not clear to me whether he also knew of the *Isagogicon.*

60. In 1457 John Argyropoulos translated the *Ethics* from Greek into Latin. In *Penei Mosheh*, fol. 31b, Almosnino states that Argyropoulos's translation is considered to be the best translation of the *Ethics* in Latin. For a detailed reconstruction of Argyropoulos's academic activities and influence in Florence, see Arthur Field, *The Origins of the Platonic Academy of Florence* (Princeton, 1988), 107–26.

61. Eustratius was a twelfth-century Byzantine commentator whose commentary on Aristotle's *Ethics* was suffused with Platonic and Neoplatonic themes. Almosnino refers to this commentary in *Penei Mosheh*, fol. 105v, but it is not clear whether he had access to the original or whether he knew it through commentaries of the late Christian scholastics, especially Walter Burley and John Buridan.

62. *Penei Mosheh*, fol. 40b. The Latin translation of the *Ethics* by Robert Grosseteste (1246–47) was the standard version of the *Ethics* throughout the late Middle Ages. Albert the Great wrote the first complete Latin commentary on the *Ethics* in Cologne during the years 1248–1252 and a second commentary in the form of a paraphrase sometime between 1263 and 1267. Thomas Aquinas, Albert's student, became acquainted with the *Ethics* while studying in Cologne. In 1271–1272 Aquinas wrote his own commentary on the *Ethics*. On these commentaries to the *Ethics*, see Wieland, "Reception and Interpretation of Aristotle's *Ethics*," 660–61.

63. Gerald Odo (or Geraldus Ododins) was the minister general of the Dominican Order in the first decades of the fourteenth century. Almosnino refers to him as "*Odo ha-komer*" in *Penei Mosheh*, fol. 24r, where he states that he consulted his commentary on the *Ethics*. The commentary is entitled *Expositio in Aristotelis Ethicam* and was published in 1500 in Venice. On the manuscripts of this text, see Charles H. Lohr, "Medieval Latin Aristotle's Commentaries: Authors G-I, *Traditio* 24 (1968), 149–245, esp. 163–64. Odo's views were incorporated into John Buridan's commentary on the *Ethics*, from which Almosnino copied extensively. On Buridan's indebtedness to Odo, see James J. Walsh, "Some Relationships Between Gerald Odo's and John Buridan's Commentaries on Aristotle's *Ethics*," *Franciscan Studies* 35 (1975), 237–75.

64. John Buridan (c. 1295–1356), the French philosopher and scientist, studied philosophy at Paris with William Ockham, remained there as a member of the arts faculty and was twice its rector. His *Questions super decem libros Ethicorum* (Commentary on the Ethics) was published in Paris in 1489 and again in 1513. Buridan viewed the science of ethics as practical science, namely, ethics is the productive science of goodness. Identifying the knowledge of ethics with prudence, Buridan regarded ethics as closely related to rhetoric, which he called the *logica moralis*. In accordance with the Ockhamist demarcation between reason and faith, Buridan sharply distinguished between theology and ethics. Theology is the only science that directs human action toward its eternal goal; through revelation theology grasps this goal "in detail." Ethics, on the other hand, concerns goodness in this world alone. The science of ethics pertains to the free man, a theme Buridan culled from his consultation of Seneca's moral philosophy whose *Letters to Lucilius* were frequently cited in Buridan's commentary on the *Ethics*.

Buridan's approach to ethics inspired several fifteenth-century Italian humanists as much as it recommended itself to Moses Almosnino. In *Penei Mosheh* Almosnino cites Buridan's work in fols. 32v, 105v–6v, 146r–51v and follows Buridan's position on the interplay between the will and the intellect on the road to happiness. Buridan's influence accounts in part for the frequent references to Seneca as well as for the nexus between rationality, virtue, and freedom in the writings of Almosnino and his younger contemporary Solomon ben Isaac Halevi.

65. Almosnino refers to "Burleo" in his commentary in *Penei Mosheh*, fol. 105v. Walter Burley, professor of liberal arts at Merton College, Oxford, composed his *Expositio Gualteri Burley super Decem Libros Ethicorum Aristotelis* between 1333 and 1345. For a discussion of Burley's moral philosophy, see G. Gomes, "Foundations of Ethics in Walter Burleigh's *Commentary on Aristotle's Nicomachean Ethics*," Ph.D. diss., Columbia University, 1973.

66. In *Penei Mosheh*, fol. 40v, Almosnino refers to commentary on the *Ethics* by "*Fabro he-hacham*." This is the famous French humanist, Faber Stapulensis Jacobus (1460–1536), whose commentary on the *Ethics* illustrates the so-called

humanist Aristotlelianism in which humanist philological methods were used to reinterpret the Aristotelian text in order to show that it is compatible with the teachings of the early church, especially St. Paul. Lefevre edited Patristic texts and launched a major research program on the Bible. He wrote commentaries on the Psalms, the Epistles of Paul, and the Gospels, along with commentaries on Aristotle and works on mathematics. For a general overview of Lefevre d'Etaples's intellectual and literary activities, see Eugene F. Rice, ed., *The Prefatory Epistles of Jacques Lefevre d'Etaples and Related Texts* (New York, 1972), xi–xxv and 548 for bibliographical references about his commentary on Aristotle.

67. Moses Almosnino mentions specifically Nifo's commentary on *Aristotle's Physics*, in *Penei Mosheh*, fol. 144a.

Agostino Nifo (1469/70–1538) was a student of Nicoletto Vernia at the University of Padua during the 1490s. Nifo succeeded to Vernia's chair after his death in 1499 and became involved in the famous controversy on the immortality of the soul occasioned by the publication of Pietro Pomponazzi's *De immortalitate animae* (1516). Although Nifo began his career as a convinced Averröist who supported the doctrine of the unity of the intellect, he changed his views in his *De intellectu* (1497), in which he attacked Averröes and Alexander for denying personal immortality. Nifo did not write a commentary on the *Ethics* but discussed the problem of human happiness in his *De immortalite animae*, written to refute Pompanazzi's *Tractatus de immortalite animae*. For an excellent study of the academic controversy on the nature of the human soul and the end of human life, see Martin L. Pine, *Pietro Pomponazzi: Radical Philosopher of the Renaissance* (Padua, 1986), and the bibliography cited there.

The academic debates in Italian academe were well known to Jewish scholars in Italy such as Obadia Sforno, Abraham de Balmes, and Jacob Mantino. Jewish scholars were intimately involved with the translation and publication of Aristotelian-Averröean corpora during the early decades of the sixteenth century. See Edward Kranz, "Editions of the Latin Aristotle Accompanied with the Commentaries of Averröes," in Edward P. Mahoney, ed., *Philosophy and Humanism: Renaissance Essays in Honor of Paul Oscar Kristeller* (New York, 1976), 116–28. On Nifo's direct influence on Obadia Sforno, see Reuben Bonfil, "The Doctrine of the Soul and Holiness in the Teachings of Obadia Sforno" (in Hebrew), *Eshel Beer Sheva* 1 (1976), 200–57.

The academic controversy on the nature of the soul and the immortality of the personal soul reverberates in the writings of Jewish philosophers in Salonika during the second half of the sixteenth century. See, for example, Isaac Aderbi, *Divrei Shalom*, 35b–41b; Abraham ibn Megash, *Kevod 'Elohim*, chaps. 23, 29, 30 31, 32. Interestingly, Isaac Arroyo echoed Pompanazzi's position when he said that "human reason is unable to decide" whether the soul is a divine substance or merely an intellectual substance, separated from matter. See Isaac Arroyo, *Tanḥumot 'El*, 13b.

68. See Joseph Sermoneta, "Scholastic Philosophic Literature in Rabbi Yosef Taitatzak's *Porat Yosef*" (in Hebrew), *Sefunot* 11 (Book of Greek Jewry 1; 1971–1978), 135–85.

69. In *Lev 'Avot*, for example, Solomon ben Isaac Halevi cites Plato, Aristotle, Seneca, Cicero, and the Stoics, and in *Kevod 'Elohim* Abraham ibn Megash often refers to Plato, Aristotle, Alexander Aphrodisias, Themistius, Avicenna, al-Ghazzali, and Averröes on a variety of philosophical questions.

70. This fusion of philosophy, Kabbalah, and homiletics existed already prior to the expulsion, for example, in the works of Isaac Aramah and Joel ibn Shuaib. The two scholars differed in regard to the relationship between their preaching activity and their written homilies. Whereas the former separated his oral preaching from his written work, the latter saw his oral and written activity to be closely intertwined. See Carmi Horowitz, "Preachers, Sermons, and the Homiletical Literature in Spain," in Beinart, *Moreshet Sepharad: The Sephardi Legacy*, 309–20. On the fusion of exegesis and homilies among postexpulsion authors, see Joseph Hacker, "The Sephardi Sermon in the Sixteenth Century: Between Literature and Historical Source," *Pe'amim* 26 (1986), 108–27. For an overview of Jewish preaching in the Ottoman Empire in the context of Jewish preaching in the Middle Ages and early modern period and an analysis of individual sermons by Joseph Garson, Moses Almosnino, and Solomon ben Isaac Halevi, see Marc Saperstein, *Jewish Preaching, 1200–1800: An Anthology* (New Haven, 1989).

71. For an overview of the commingling of philosophy, Kabbalah, and aggadah in these philosophical biblical commentaries, see Kalman P. Bland, "Issues in Sixteenth-Century Jewish Exegesis," in *The Bible in the Sixteenth Century* (Durham, N.C., 1990), 50–67, 210–15. I thank Professor Alan Cooper for directing me to that article. Bland focuses on Isaac Caro's commentary to the Pentateuch and shows how the study of Scripture itself was considered a "process of live intellectual inquiry. . . . Revelation and religious experience . . . are taken to be opportunities for instruction in the metaphysical and religious sciences" (56). Bland's work supports the observations of this article.

Modern biblical scholarship has tended to denigrate the importance of these biblical commentaries, viewing them as derivative, lacking originality, and uninspiring. Recently, however, Alan Cooper has argued to the contrary that these philosophical commentaries "add richness and depth to biblical commentary, illustrating the continuing vitality and relevance of biblical scholarship, as well as its contiguity with the full range of Jewish (and non-Jewish) discourse." Cooper, "An Extraordinary Sixteenth-Century Biblical Commentary: Eliezer Ashkenazi on the Song of Moses," in Barry Walfish, ed., *Frank Talmage Memorial Volume* (Haifa, 1993), 129–50.

72. See, for example, Isaac Caro, *Sefer Toledot Yizḥak*, 3a; Joseph Taitatzak, *Porat Yosef*, 28b; and Almosnino, *Tefillah le-Mosheh*, 41a.

73. See Tirosh-Rothschild, "Maimonides and Aquinas: The Interplay of Two Masters in Medieval Jewish Philosophy," *Conservative Judaism* 39 (1986), 54–66; and idem, *Between Worlds*, chap. 5, esp. 105–33 passim.

74. The commentary of Abraham Rimoch on Psalms is an excellent example of the nexus between the Jewish philosophic reflections on happiness and the Jewish-Christian polemics in fifteenth-century Spain. Rimoch was one of the participants in the Tortosa debate of 1413–1414 that ended in a defeat for the Jewish delegation. Not coincidentally, the central theme of Rimoch's biblical commentary is the desire for the contemplative life, culminating in the soul's cleaving to God. For Rimoch, the true intellectual exemplifies the ideal of the righteous man in the Psalms. The perfect man (*ha-shalem*) eschews material success, devotes his life to study, and secludes himself for long stretches of time in order to contemplate intellectual substances. The ultimate achievement of the perfect individual is a mystical intuitive grasp of philosophical truths, reflecting the soul's cleaving to God and the bestowal of suprarational knowledge. See Frank Talmage, "Trauma in Tortosa: The Testimony of Abraham Rimoch," *Medieval Studies* 47 (1985), 379–411, esp. 389–91. Throughout the fifteenth and sixteenth centuries Sephardic intellectuals read the Psalter as a book on human felicity. A typical example of this approach written prior to the expulsion is Joel ibn Shuaib's *Nora' Tehillot* (Salonika, 1568); Meir Aramah's *Me'ir Tehillot* exemplifies the continuation of this approach after the expulsion.

75. It seems to me that fifteenth-century Jewish scholars in Spain were familiar with Aquinas's view on human happiness not so much from his commentary on the *Ethics* as from his more popular *Summa Contra Gentiles* (especially book 3, chaps. 16–40) and his *Summa Theologiae* (1–2, q. 1–21). For an overview of Aquinas's position, see Harry V. Jaffa, *Thomism and Aristotelianism: A Study of the Commentary by Thomas Aquinas on the Nicomachean Ethics* (Chicago, 1952; repr., Westport, Conn., 1979). For a different position that highlights the opposition of Jewish scholars to scholastic achievements see Moshe Idel, "Jewish Thought in Spain," in Beinart, *Moreshet Sepharad: The Sephardi Legacy*, 215.

76. As heirs of the Maimonidean tradition the Sephardic exiles were deeply immersed in the dogmatic formulation of Judaism. Though most regarded the Thirteen Principles of Maimonides as the authoritative rendering of Jewish dogmas—see, for example, Isaac Arroyo, *Tanḥumot 'El*, 71a–b—some followed other formulations of Jewish dogmatism, primarily Joseph Albo's. See, for example, Isaac Aderbi, *Divrei Shalom*, 67a. In general, the precise enumeration of Jewish dogmas became less important after the expulsion because the dogmas of Judaism as a whole constituted "the path of faith" (*derekh 'emunah*) that led to salvation. Isaac Arroyo appropriately summarized this view when he stated that "happiness is predicated on faith" ("ha-haẓlaḥah teluyyah ba-'emunah"), *Tanḥumot 'El*, 62b.

For a history of Jewish dogmatism, see Menachem Kellner, *Dogma in Medieval Jewish Thought: From Maimonides to Abravanel* (Oxford, 1986). For a detailed analysis of dogmatism in the work of a sixteenth-century Italian scholar in the Ottoman Empire, R. David ben Judah Messer Leon, see Hava Tirosh-Rothschild, *Between Worlds*, 139–83.

77. A typical example of such creative misreading of Maimonides is Almosnino's analysis of the primacy of the human will and practical wisdom in *Penei Mosheh*, fols. 105–6. Contrary to Maimonides, Almosnino predicates the ultimate union with God on the will rather than the intellect. The primacy of the will reflects not only the growing impact of humanist psychological theories but also the awareness of the exiles that their own fate resulted from their choice to remain loyal to Judaism. In the period after the expulsion, therefore, loyalty to Judaism was viewed as the result of one's free will rather than the necessary outcome of the philosophic demonstration that Judaism is rationally superior to Christianity. The new emphasis on human will on the one hand and the recognition of the limitations of human reason on the other hand led Sephardic thinkers to state that even women could attain ultimate happiness and enjoy personal immortality. Women were expressly excluded from the ultimate bliss in rationalist literature prior to the expulsion. See Isaac Aderbi, *Divrei Shalom*, 105b; Isaac Arroyo, *Tanḥumot 'El*, 57a–58a; Moses Almosnino, *Ma'ameẓ Koaḥ*, 216a. The inclusion of women in the community of the perfect ones who enjoy personal immortality did not reflect egalitarianism on the part of these thinkers, however. They still continued to uphold that women were intellectually inferior to men. The new assessment of the will in relations to the intellect and the inclusion of women in the pursuit of happiness are discussed below.

78. On one manifestation of the Maimonidean controversy during the 1520s in Salonika between David ben Judah Messer Leon and Meir ibn Verga see Tirosh-Rothschild, *Between Worlds*, 85–98. On the renewal of the debate in Constantinople during the second half of the century, see Joseph Hacker, "Agitation Against Philosophy in Istanbul in the Sixteenth Century: Studies in Menachem de Lonsano's *Derekh Ḥayyim*," in *Studies in Jewish Mysticism, Philosophy, and Ethical Literature Presented to Isaiah Tishby on His Seventy-Fifth Birthday* (Jerusalem, 1986), 507–36.

79. In *Lev 'Avot*, 59b, Solomon ben Isaac Halevi states that "*Sefer ha-Zohar* was composed one thousand and two hundred years ago." The emphasis on the antiquity of the *Zohar* reflects both Halevi's attempt to refute charges that the *Zohar* was but a medieval innovation (expressed, for example, by Judah Messer Leon) as well as the impact of humanist historiography.

80. On the principles of kabbalistic psychology, see Isaiah Tishby, *The Wisdom of the Zohar* (in Hebrew) (Jerusalem, 1961), 2:3–82.

81. The emphasis of theosophic Kabbalah on the infinity of Torah reflects the kabbalistic conception of God as the Infinite (*Ein Sof*). See Moshe Idel, "Infinities of Torah in Kabbalah," in Geoffrey H. Hartman and Sanford Budick, eds., *Midrash and Literature* (New Haven, 1986), 141–57. In postexpulsion philosophic literature the infinity of Torah was interpreted to mean that the Torah is the only immutable eternal Law that addresses the infinite variety of ever-changing particulars. The application of Torah to particular conditions manifested divine providence over particulars, extended to Israel alone. See, for example, Moses Almosnino, *Penei Mosheh*, fol. 169a.

82. See, for example, Joseph Taitatzak, *Porat Yosef*, 28b; Isaac Arroyo, *Tanḥumot 'El*, 4a; Almosnino, *Pirkei Mosheh*, 6. On the evolution of this view in Spanish Kabbalah, see Gershom Scholem, *On the Kabbalah and Its Symbolism* (New York, 1965), 37–44.

83. Solomon le-Bet Halevi, *Lev 'Avot*, Introduction, 2a: "And I know that invariably many things in my commentary are hinted [*nirmazim*] and anticipated [*neḥezim*] in other precious, priceless books because human nature is such that it is impossible for one to escape the commonality of wisdom especially in regard to matters about which numerous books have been written. Therefore I labored, took my time, and made a special effort to seek many interpretations, minimally three for each Mishna, so that my loyal readers will find some innovation in it and will have no qualm against me."

84. Abraham ibn Megash, *Kevod 'Elohim*, 17a.

85. Isaac Arroyo, *Tanḥumot 'El*, 92a.

86. *Divrei Shalom*, 25b.

87. *Tefillah le-Mosheh*, 64a, and consult also 10b, 34b, 48a, 51b, 55a. The same position is reiterated in his *Yedei Mosheh*, 79–109; *Bet 'Elohim*, 17a.

88. The literature on the renaissance cult of rhetoric is too vast to be cited here. The following two paragraphs are indebted to William Bouwsma, "Changing Assumptions in Later Renaissance Culture," *Viator* 7 (1976), 422–40.

89. On the dissemination of Italian humanism in Spain, see Royston Oscar Jones, *The Golden Age of Prose and Poetry: The Sixteenth and Seventeenth Centuries* (London, 1971), 6–9. One of the most important contributors to the dissemination of Italian humanism in Spain was Alonso de Cartagena, the son of the famous converso Pablo de Santa María. On his translations of Leonardo Bruni's *De Militia* and several compositions by Seneca into Castilian, see Fernando Díaz Esteban, "The Literary Activity of Jews in Spanish" (in Hebrew), in Beinart, *Moreshet Sepharad: The Sephardi Legacy*, 338–39.

90. See Popkin, "Jewish Christians and Christian Jews," 252.

91. The point was already made by Moshe Idel, "Kabbalah and Ancient Philosophy in R. Isaac and Yehudah Abravanel" (in Hebrew) in Menahem Dorman and Zeev Levy, eds., *The Philosophy of Love of Leone Ebreo* (Haifa, 1985), 73–111.

92. *Bet 'Elohim* and *Penei Mosheh* provide ample evidence for Almosnino's knowledge of Greek. Romaniote scholars introduced the Sephardic newcomers not only to the Greek language but also to philosophic and scientific texts not known in Spain. On the interest in science and philosophy among Ottoman Jews see Ephraim Wust, "Elisha the Greek: A Physician and Philosopher at the Beginning of the Ottoman Period" (in Hebrew), *Pe'amim* 41 (1990), 49–57; Steven B. Bowman, *The Jews in Byzantium, 1204–1453* (University, Ala., 1985), 147–70.

93. Moses Almosnino *Bet 'Elohim*, fols. 35a–42b, is replete with contemporary geographic knowledge. Almosnino employs his knowledge of geography to situate famous ancient and medieval individuals (e.g., Alexander the Great, Galen, Pliny, Virgil, Cicero, Ptolemy, Alfasi, Maimonides, and Agostino Nifo) with their respective cities. Similarly, he situates names of famous places in biblical, rabbinic, and Greek literature in their precise geographic location.

94. Judah Messer Leon in *Nofet Zufim* (printed in 1476), was the first Jewish scholar to attempt to prove that the Bible consists of classical figures of speech and that it instructs the reader in the art of rhetoric in a manner that corresponds to the teachings of the ancient orators. Scholars (including myself) have demonstrated the humanist rereading of the Bible among Italian Jewish scholars. See Arthur Lesley, "Jewish Adaptation of Humanist Concepts in Fifteenth-and Sixteenth-Century Italy," in Maryanne Cline Horowitz et al. eds., *Renaissance Rereadings: Intertext and Context* (Urbana and Chicago, 1988), 51–66; idem, "Proverbs, Figures, and Riddles: *The Dialogues of Love* as a Hebrew Humanist Composition," in Michael Fishbane, ed., *The Midrashic Imagination: Jewish Exegesis, Thought, and History* (Albany, 1993). This article suggests, however, that the humanist perspective was not limited to Italy and infiltrated Sephardic scholarship in the Ottoman Empire during the second and third quarters of the sixteenth century.

95. See, for example, Moses Almosnino, *Yedei Mosheh*, 248. This image of King Solomon emerged in the writing of Yohanan Alemanno, especially his *Heshek Shelomo* and its introduction, "Shir ha-Ma'alot 'Asher li-Shelomo." King Solomon was portrayed as an exemplary figure who combined scientific learning, royal magnificence, just government, and mystical speculation. For a detailed analysis of this view, see Arthur Lesley, "*The Song of Solomon's Ascents*, by Yohanan Alemanno: Love and Human Perfection According to a Jewish Associate of Giovanni Pico della Mirandola," Ph.D. diss. University of California, Berkeley, 1976, esp. 102–92. On the reading of Bible as a biography of virtuous men, see idem, "Hebrew Humanism in Italy: The Case of Biography," *Prooftexts* 2 (1982), 163–77.

96. Beginning with Petrarch, Renaissance thinkers exalted the poetic excellence of King David as matching that of the Greek and Roman poets. See James L. Kugel, *The Idea of Biblical Poetry: Parallelism and Its History* (New Haven, 1981), 212–18. Thus while the Jewish preoccupation with the Psalms was primarily for

their ethical content, they indirectly also insisted on the Jewishness of the greatest poet.

97. Moses Almosnino refers to "*kat ha-istoicos*" (i.e., the Stoics) in *Penei Mosheh*, fol. 144a, but he mentions Cicero and Seneca by name a good number of times. See Almosnino, *Tefillah le-Mosheh*, 5b, 23b–24a; idem, *Pirkei Mosheh*, 235; and *Penei Mosheh*, fol. 14v, 16v, 32v, 129v. Solomon ben Isaac Halevi was equally familiar with Stoic writings, as is evident from the introduction to *Lev 'Avot*, 2a–10b.

It was the impact of Stoicism that accounts for the thematic novelty in the philosophic discourse on happiness in the postexpulsion period. Two elements in particular—the association of happiness with freedom (*ḥerut*) and the central role of suffering in the acquisition of moral virtue—reflect the indebtedness of Jewish scholars to Stoicism. These themes will be discussed in greater detail below.

So far scholars of Jewish ethics in the sixteenth-century have tended to focus on the ethical literature of Safed, Italy, and Eastern Europe, leaving unexplored the moral philosophy discussed in this paper. See Dan, *Hebrew Ethical and Homiletical Literature*, 175–229; Mordecai Pachter, "The Homiletical and Ethical Literature of Safed's Scholars in the Sixteenth Century and Its Major Ideas," Ph.D. diss., Hebrew University, 1976.

98. See Almosnino, *Penei Mosheh*, fol. 172b; *Yedei Mosheh*, 85.

99. To date the most systematic discussion of Maimonides' conception of human happiness is Menachem Kellner, *Maimonides on Human Perfection* (Brown Judaic Studies, no. 202; Atlanta, 1990). Needless to say, Kellner's interpretation is but one possible reading of Maimonides' ambiguous teachings. The methodological problems involved in the interpretation of Maimonides have recently been explored by Alfred L. Ivry, "Strategies of Interpretation in Maimonides' Guide of the Perplexed," *Jewish History* 6,1–2 (1992), 113–30; and Menachem Kellner, "Reading Rambam: Approaches to the Interpretation of Maimonides," *Jewish History* 5,2 (1991), 73–93. My own reading of Maimonides' conception of happiness cannot be developed here, but suffice it to say that the key to the understanding of Maimonides, in my view, lies in the connection between ontology, ethics, and hermeneutics.

100. Kenneth Seeskin, *Maimonides: A Guide for Today's Perplexed* (West Orange, N.J., 1991), 74.

101. In accordance with the Aristotelian tradition, postexpulsion thinkers understood the duality of matter and form in genderized categories: form (*ẓurah*) relates to matter (*ḥomer*) as the male relates to the female, respectively. See, for example, Moses Almosnino, *Tefillah le-Mosheh*, 26a, 35a; Isaac Arroyo, *Tanḥumot 'El*, 7a. I concur with recent feminist scholars who argued that this was by no means an innocent metaphorization but rather a value judgment on the relative worth of women and the proper relations between the sexes. According to Aristotle

the human female was an incomplete male because her rational faculty was by nature deficient; she lacks the capacity to think abstractly. Hence, the male should complete and perfect the female. In social terms that meant that the man must rule over the female. Postexpulsion thinkers took this notion for granted but departed from the rationalist tradition by placing more emphasis on the human will. In turn, this led them to include women in the community of those who could attain personal immortality even though their intellect could never reach perfection. For a feminist critique of Aristotle, see, for example, Genevieve Lloyd, *The Man of Reason: "Male" and "Female" in Western Philosophy* (Minneapolis, Minn., 1984), esp. 1–9.

102. For an overview of rabbinic psychological theories and their ramifications for religious doctrines and rituals, see Nissan Rubin, "From Monism to Dualism: Relations Between the Body and Soul in Talmudic Thought," *Daat* 23 (1989), 33–64.

103. Isaac Arroyo, *Tanḥumot 'El*, 42b, 92a.

104. See Joseph Taitatzak, *Porat Yosef*, 33a; Meir Aramah, *Me'ir Tehillot*, 110a; Isaac Aderbi, *Divrei Shalom*, 36b; Moses Almosnino, *Tefillah le-Mosheh*, 10b; *Pirkei Mosheh*, 70; *Penei Mosheh*, fols. 47r, 96r. The notion that the soul is "carved" from under the Seat of Glory is *Tikkunei Zohar*, Tikkun 22, 65b. Isaac Arroyo was more loyal to the dominant view of the *Zohar* that located the origin of the soul in Sefirah Malkhut. See Isaac Arroyo, *Tanḥumot 'El*, 7a.

105. See Joseph Taitatzak, *Porat Joseph*, 7a; Isaac Arroyo, *Tanḥumot 'El*, 6b; Moses Almosnino, *Tefillah le-Mosheh*, 23b, 34b. All three scholars insist that the descent of the soul into the body serves a moral purpose: by performing good deeds and acquiring the knowledge of truths, the soul spiritualizes the body and cleanses herself from the negative impact of the body. The reward for perfection is commensurate with the degree of perfection.

106. Isaac Arroyo, *Tanḥumot 'El*, 3a, 6b, 8b; Moses Almosnino, *Pirkei Mosheh*, 4; *Penei Mosheh*, fol. 47r. Arroyo (who apparently had rather strong kabbalistic inclinations) went further to claim that the souls of non-Jews are associated with the realm of evil and the forces of impurity (*sitra aḥra, sitra mesava*). As such, non-Jews are not only ontologically inferior to Jews but are also fundamentally evil.

107. This was Crescas's definition of the soul in *'Or 'Adonai*, 3:2, 1, which preexpulsion Sephardic scholars accepted at large. That the soul is an incorporeal substance was held by both Avicenna and Judah Halevi, Crescas's most obvious sources. For a recent analysis of Avicenna's psychology, see Lenn E. Goodman, *Avicenna* (London, 1992), 149–83 and the bibliography cited there. For Halevi's conception of the human soul, see Herbert Davidson, "The Active Intellect in the *Kuzari* and Halevi's Theory of Causality," *Revue des études juives* 131 (1972), 363–65. Crescas's definition of the soul was commonly accepted by fifteenth-century scholars in Iberia.

108. Almosnino, *Ma'amez Koah,* 5lb.

109. Isaac Arroyo, *Tanḥumot 'El,* 62b, 120b; Solomon ben Isaac Halevi, *Lev 'Avot,* 57b. Abraham Bibago's *Derekh 'Emunah,* which was printed in Salonica in 1522, was the immediate source of these discussions.

110. Isaac Arroyo elaborates the Platonic doctrine of recollection (*anamnesis*) in *Tanḥumot 'El,* 8b. The literature on this famous doctrine of Plato is extensive and cannot be cited here. Some of the pertinent studies include R. E. I. Allen, "*Anamnesis* in Plato's *Meno* and *Phaedo,*" *Review of Metaphysics* 13 (1959), 165–74; N. I. Gulley, "Plato's Theory of Recollection," *Classical Quarterly,* n.s., 4 (1954), 194–213; Terrence Irwin, "Recollection and Plato's Moral Theory," *Review of Metaphysics* 27 (1974), 752–79; and Gregory Vlastos, "*Anamnesis* in the *Meno,* " *Dialogue* 4 (1965), 143–67.

111. Moses Almosnino, *Tefillah le-Mosheh,* 41b.

112. Moses Almosnino, *Tefillah le-Mosheh,* 12a; Isaac Arroyo, *Tanḥumot 'El,* 8b. Almosnino and Arroyo perpetuated the Maimonidean notion that the acquisition of moral and intellectual virtues removes the barriers that separate the human and the divine. But if Maimonides viewed the body as a barrier to intellection of abstract truths, Almosnino and Arroyo viewed the body as a barrier that prevents the mystical union with God.

113. Moses Almosnino, *Tefillah le-Mosheh,* 26b; *Pirkei Mosheh,* 22.

114. Almosnino, *Pirkei Mosheh,* 70.

115. Already Aristotle (*Ethics,* 1138b 30) posited ethics as a science for the healing of the soul as much as medicine is the knowledge necessary for the healing of the body. Maimonides Judaized this view when he attempted to show that the Torah provides the best cure for physical as well as mental illnesses; his view was shared by all subsequent Jewish philosophers who understood the interdependence of physical and mental health.

116. See Moses Almosnino, *Pirkei Mosheh,* 4, 98.

117. Moses Almosnino, *Tefillah le-Mosheh,* 9b. According to Arroyo, since the soul is a particle of God, God Himself experiences the misery of Israel directly. Since God is Himself in exile, the liberation of Israel (collectively and individually) is God's own liberation. See *Tanḥumot 'El,* 42b.

118. Almosnino's interpretation of Psalm 42 in *Tefillah le-Mosheh,* 11a–b, is a typical example of this psychological reading of the Psalms that recaptured the personal mood of these hymns. In contrast to earlier political interpretations of this psalm, Almosnino interprets its central verse ("As a hind longs for the running streams, so I long for you, my God") as a metaphor for the yearning of the soul to free itself from exile in the body.

119. Almosnino, *Pirkei Mosheh,* 114; *Tefilah le-Mosheh,* 7b; Solomon ben Isaac Halevi, *Lev 'Avot,* 22b.

120. See Almosnino, *Tefillah le-Mosheh,* 33a–b; 34a.

121. For an overview of kabbalistic asceticism in Safed and a translation of seminal texts, see Lawrence Fine, *Safed Spirituality* (New York, 1984).

122. Almosnino, *Penei Mosheh*, fol. 20v; Solomon ben Isaac Halevi, *Lev 'Avot*, 6a.

123. See, for example, *Tefillah le-Mosheh*, 23b, 24a–b, 33a–b; *Pirkei Mosheh*, 235; *Penei Mosheh*, fol. 172v. Solomon ben Isaac Halevi, *Lev 'Avot*, 17b.

124. See note 97 above.

125. In *Tefillah le-Mosheh*, 23b, Almosnino adopts the notion that the virtue of patience (*savlanut*) is one of the prerequisites for happiness, an idea that is not found in the teaching of Aristotle and is quite close to Stoic teachings on equanimity. The doctrine of equanimity, of course, was not the monopoly of the Stoics. It was commonly taught by the Sufis and entered Jewish philosophy and Kabbalah through the influential teachings of al-Ghazzali. See Moshe Idel, "Hitbodedut as Concentration in Ecstatic Kabbalah," in Moshe Idel, *Studies in Ecstatic Kabbalah* (Albany, 1988), 103–69.

126. Arroyo, *Tanhumot 'El*, 19a; Almosnino, *Tefillah le-Mosheh*, p 51b.

127. On Abulafia's psychologistic interpretation of the messianic idea, see Idel, "Patterns of Redemptive Activity," 275–78.

128. See Solomon ben Isaac Halevi, *Lev 'Avot*, 5a–10b. The notion that rationality is the source of human freedom was of course the hallmark of Greek philosophy, especially in Stoic philosophy. See Shlomo Pines," The Historical Evolution of a Certain Concept of Freedom," in Yirmiyahu Yovel and Paul Mendes-Flohr, eds., *Between Theory and Practice: Essays in Honour of Nathan Rotenstreich* (Jerusalem, 1984), 254–55.

129. See, for example, Isaac Aderbi, *Divrei Shalom*, 49a.

Following Abraham ibn Ezra and the Jewish Neoplatonists of the late fourteenth century and in contrast to Maimonides, postexpulsion thinkers took the science of astrology very seriously as a scientific tool for the understanding of natural causality. However, the gist of the discourse on happiness was to show that Israel can transcend nature because it is endowed with a divine soul and has received the grace of divine revelation. Jews who live by the Torah do not fall under natural determinism because they are governed directly by God. See, for example, Almosnino, *Tefillah le-Mosheh*, 54b; Abraham ibn Megash, *Kevod 'Elohim*, 31 a–b, 40 a–b.

On the cultivation of astrology by Jewish philosophers in Iberia and their indebtedness to Abraham ibn Ezra, see Dov Schwartz, "The Theology of Shem Tov ibn Shaprut," in Norman E. Frimer and Dov Schwartz, *The Life and Thought of Shem Tov ibn Shaprut* (Jerusalem, 1992), 139–48. Ibn Shaprut's *Even Bohan* was among the most popular texts among the Sephardic intellectuals in Salonika.

130. Almosnino, *Tefillah le-Mosheh*, 48a, 51b.

131. Isaac Arroyo, *Tanhumot 'El*, 73b.

132. Moses Almosnino, *Tefillah le-Mosheh*, 36a.

133. For a recent analysis of Maimonidean ethics and bibliography, consult Raymond L. Weiss, *Maimonides' Ethics: The Encounter of Philosophic and Religious Morality* (Chicago, 1992).

134. Recently scholars of Aristotle have devoted considerable attention to his notions of rational wish (*boulesis*) and choice (*prohairesis*). For a summary of this scholarship, see Nancy Sherman, *The Fabric of Character: Aristotle's Theory of Virtue* (Oxford, 1989), 57–117 and the bibliography cited there.

135. The impact of Scholasticism on Jewish philosophy in the fifteenth and sixteenth centuries is yet to be explored in full, notwithstanding the recent studies of S. Pines, A. Ravitzky, W. Harvey, S. Feldman, J. Sermoneta, and myself. In general, I think it is safe to say that during the fifteenth century Maimonidean philosophers were open to the intellectualism of Thomas Aquinas for the same reason that they defended Maimonides against Crescas. In the sixteenth century, however, when Jewish scholars were more ready to incorporate Crescas's critique of Maimonides, they turned to Duns Scotus and the Franciscan theologians who highlighted the centrality of the will in the pursuit of perfection. The scholarship on Aquinas's intellectualism and Scotus's voluntarism is voluminous. For a short summary, consult Patrick Lee, "The Relation Between Intellect and Will in Free Choice According to Aquinas and Scotus," *Thomist* 49 (1985), 321–42.

136. The most extensive analysis of the interplay between the intellect and the will is in *Penei Mosheh*, book 10, chap. 8. He presented a short popular summary of that philosophical discourse in his *Tefillah le-Mosheh*, 57b.

137. Almosnino, *Pirkei Mosheh*, 37. For the scholastic background of this viewpoint, consult Bonnie Kent, "The Good Will According to Geraldus Odonis, Duns Scotus, and William of Ockham," *Franciscan Studies* 46 (1986), 119–39.

138. Almosnino, *Tefillah le-Mosheh*, 21b; *Penei Mosheh*, fol. 4v. Though Almosnino presents this view as the correct reading of Maimonides, in fact, it is a marked departure from the teachings of the "master."

139. Aristotle (*Ethics*, VIII.2, 3) distinguished three types of love: love of the pleasant, love of the useful, and love of the honorable (or noble). The gist of his analysis was to show that human happiness requires life in a community of morally perfect individuals who are united by the love of the honorable, the good that is desired for its own sake. Maimonides took over this distinction in his *Eight Chapters* and stated that the love of God is the love of the noble and that it is commensurate with the knowledge of God.

Maimonides' reduction of love to knowledge yielded little discussion of the meaning of love in Jewish philosophy of the thirteenth and fourteenth centuries. But Crescas's critique of Maimonides in *'Or 'Adonai* changed that by making the love of God the highest religious value. During the fifteenth century Sephardic scholars such as Joseph Albo, Joel ibn Shuaib, and Joseph Ḥayyun, followed in

Crescas's footsteps to focus on the meaning of love within the framework of Aristotelian philosophy. That tradition reached its culmination in the most systematic analysis of love—Judah Abravanel's *Dialoghi d'Amore.* For an excellent summary of Abravanel's views, see T. A. Perry, *Erotic Spirituality: The Integrative Tradition from Leone Ebreo to John Donne* (University, Ala., 1980).

Following Joel ibn Shuaib, Almosnino suggests that Aristotle's analysis of love can be subsumed into two categories already known to the rabbis in Tractate *'Avot.* Love of the pleasant and the useful are "conditional love" (*'ahavah teluyah ba-davar*) and only love of the good is "unconditional love." To love God is to love Him unconditionally for the sake of the good.

140. *Penei Mosheh,* fol. 47r. Almosnino's portrayal of Man as an intermediary being between angels and beasts bears very close resemblance to Pico Della Mirandola's famous oration "On the Dignity of Man" in Ernest Cassirer et al., eds., *The Renaissance Philosophy of Man,* 223–54.

141. Almosnino, *Penei Mosheh,* fols. 146v–49v. Almosnino's argumentation is by no means original but relies heavily on John Buridan's commentary on the *Ethics.* See note 63 above.

142. See Almosnino, *Penei Mosheh,* fol. 148r. This distinction is derived from Buridan. See James J. Walsh, "Teleology in the Ethics of Buridan," *Journal of the History of Philosophy* 18 (1980), 265–86.

143. Medieval Jewish thinkers—philosophers and kabbalists—used the term *hitbodedut* to mean either solitude and seclusion or mental concentration and meditation on God. The two meanings were often intertwined, since for most Jewish thinkers the latter depended on the former. That fusion reflects the influence of Sufism on Judaism and entered Jewish philosophy through the writings of ibn Bajja and ibn Tufayl. See Moshe Idel, "Hitbodedut as Concentration in Ecstatic Kabbalah," in Moshe Idel, *Studies in Ecstatic Kabbalah* (Albany, 1988), 103–40. The thinkers discussed in this article employed the terms *hitbodedut* to denote mental concentration that can be attained within the social order through contemplation of Torah and performance of good deeds toward others.

144. Almosnino, *Penei Mosheh,* fol. 148r.

145. Almosnino, *Tefillah le-Mosheh,* 57b. Not surprisingly, Almosnino continues to think about the psychological makeup of human beings in genderized categories. Yet instead of talking about the intellect and the body as male and female, respectively, Almosnino here discusses the intellect and the will as male and female. The "feminization" of the will is understandable given the association of the will with the body and with the practical, moral life.

146. *Penei Mosheh,* fol. 149r.

147. *Ethics,* VI.7, 1141b 15; VI.8, 1142a 14; 20–22; VI.11, 1143a 29; 32–34. For an excellent analysis of practical reason in Aristotle's *Ethics,* see Richard Sorabji,

"Aristotle on the Role of the Intellect in Virtue," in Amelie Oksenberg Rorty, ed., *Essays on Aristotle's "Ethics"* (Berkeley, 1980), 201–19, esp. 206.

148. Almosnino, *Tefilah le-Mosheh*, 56a; *Penei Mosheh*, fol. 149v; *Ma'amez Koah*, 17b.

149. The idea that the man of prudence is the ideal man originated with Seneca, one of John Buridan's major sources of moral philosophy. Almosnino thus "Judaizes" moral ideals that were very common among the late Christian Scholastics. On Buridan's dependence on Seneca, see James J. Walsh, "Buridan and Seneca," *Journal of the History of Ideas*, 27 (1966), 23–40.

150. *Penei Mosheh*, fol. 120v. In his commentary to book 6 of the *Ethics*, which is not extant in the single manuscript, Almosnino apparently provided a full-fledged philosophical analysis of the virtue of prudence. His position can be reconstructed from the numerous (though not entirely philosophical) references to prudence in his biblical commentaries.

151. Almosnino, *Pirkei Mosheh*, 154; cf. *Penei Mosheh*, fols. 149r–51r, where Almosnino offers a subtle analysis of love as perfection of the will and prudence.

152. Almosnino, *Yedei Mosheh*, 8b, 20b.

153. See Moses Almosnino, *Tefillah le-Mosheh*, 24a, 57a; *Penei Mosheh*, fol. 20v; Isaac Aderbi, *Divrei Shalom*, 46a–48b.

154. Almosnino, *Penei Mosheh*, fol. 149r; *Pirkei Mosheh*, 45.

155. Almosnino, *Pirkei Mosheh*, 67, 154.

156. Arroyo, *Tanhumot 'El*, 103a; Isaac Aderbi, *Divrei Shalom*, 118a; Almosnino, *Ma'amez Koah*, 6b.

157. See Almosnino *Ma'amez Koah*, 216a; Isaac Aderbi, *Divrei Shalom*, 105a; Isaac Arroyo, *Tanhumot 'El*, 57a.

158. I suspect that the fact that women such as Doña Gracia Nasi were patronesses of Jewish learning had more to do with this new appreciation of their religious merits than anything else. Almosnino's eulogies for Doña Gracia Nasi and for the wife of Meir Aramah printed in *Ma'amez Koah* bear witness to the new public respect accorded to women.

13. Hebrew Manuscripts and Printed Books

1. There are no monographs, to the best of my knowledge, that deal with Hebrew manuscript making in Sepharad in the second half of the fifteenth century. There are, however, a number of relatively recent publications that offer valuable information on Hebrew paleography and codicology in general, including many aspects of the subject under discussion here. See Malachi Beit-Arié, *Hebrew Codicology*, 2d ed. (Paris 1981); and idem, *The Makings of the Medieval Hebrew Book* (Jerusalem, 1993); Binyamin Richler, *Hebrew Manuscripts: A Treasured Legacy* (Cleveland, 1990); Colette Sirat, *Min ha-Ketav 'el ha-Sefer* (Jerusalem, 1992); and Michael Riegler, "Colophons of Medieval Hebrew Manuscripts as

Historical Sources" (in Hebrew), Ph.D. diss., Hebrew University, Jerusalem, 1995. Of course, the most important source for the study of medieval Hebrew manuscripts is the multivolume, still unfinished work by Colette Sirat and Malachi Beit-Arié, eds., *Manuscrits médiévaux en caractères hébraïques* (Jerusalem-Paris, 1972). For illuminated manuscripts, see Bezalel Narkiss, *Hebrew Illuminated Manuscripts in the British Isles*, vol. 1: *The Spanish and Portuguese Manuscripts*, 2 parts (Jerusalem and London, 1982).

2. On Hebrew printing in Spain and Portugal in general, see the old survey by Joshua Bloch, "Early Hebrew Printing in Spain and Portugal," in Charles Berlin, ed., *Hebrew Printing and Bibliography* (1938; repr., New York, 1976), 7–56. On Hebrew printing in Portugal, see Arthur Alselmo, *Les origines de l'imprimerie au Portugal* (Paris, 1983). For thorough and detailed treatments of some aspects of Hebrew printing on the Iberian Peninsula, see H. Z. Dimitrovsky, *S'ridei Bavli: Fragments from Spanish and Portuguese Incunabula and Bibliographical Century Printing of the Babylonian Talmud and Alfasi: An Historical and Bibliographical Introduction* (in Hebrew), (New York, 1979); Eleazer Hurvitz, *Mishneh Torah of Maimonides* (in Hebrew), (New York 1985), introduction, esp. 39–44; and Peretz Tishby, "Hebrew Incunabula: Spain and Portugal (Guadalajara)" (in Hebrew), *Kiryat Sefer* 61 (1986–87), 521–46.

3. Eleazar Gutwirth's forthcoming article, "Jewish Readers and Their Libraries in Late-Medieval Spain" is expected to shed light on the subject. See Elazar Gutwirth and Miguel Ángel Motis Dolader, "Twenty-Six Jewish Libraries from Fifteenth-Century Spain," *Library* 18 (1996), 27–53, esp. note 4.

4. Beit-Arié, *The Makings of the Medieval Hebrew Book*, 78.

5. See Gabrielle Sed-Rajna, *Manuscrits hébreux de Lisbonne: Un atelier de copistes et d'enlumineurs au XVe* (Paris, 1970); and Thérèse Metzger, *Les manuscrits hébreux copiés et décorés à Lisbonne dans les dernières décennies du XVe siècle* (Paris, 1977). The fact that some famous scribes worked with apprentices (Richler, *Hebrew Manuscripts*, 41) and that many manuscripts were written by more than one scribe in stereotype scripts (Beit-Arié, *The Making of the Medieval Hebrew Book*, 78–79), does not necessarily mean that these were institutional efforts. As Beit-Arié points out: "Hebrew manuscripts in the Lisbon workshop and in the various Rabbinic academies (see below), may have been the exception and may have been initiated by the workshop or the academy." See also Riegler, "Colophons," 107.

6. See Sed-Rajna, *Manuscrits hébreux*, 51, 107; but see Metzger, *Les manuscrits hébreux*, 14–17, according to whom the influence was not as pronounced as it was proposed by Sed-Rajna. On the affinity between Hebrew manuscripts and the first products of the Hebrew press in general, see Beit-Arié, *The Making of the Medieval Hebrew Book*, 251–77.

7. On manuscripts copied in study houses and yeshivot, see Riegler, "Colophons," 162–72.

8. Sirat and Beit-Arié, *Manuscrits médiévaux*, 3:3 and nn. 2,4.

9. Ibid., 3:5.

10. British Library, Harley 5779 (Catalogue Margoliouth, no. 901).

11. Manuscript R 1351 in the Library of the Jewish Theological Seminary.

12. See Tishby, "Hebrew Incunabula"; A. K. Offenberg, *Hebrew Incunabula in Public Collections* (Nieuwkoop, 1990), 187.

13. Sirat and Beit-Arié, *Manuscrits médiévaux*, 3:62 and n. 1; Riegler, "Colophons," 169.

14. Dimitrovsky, *S'ridei Bavli*, 61–70.

15. Ibid., 25 ff., 58 ff.

16. Published by Hayyim Hillel Ben-Sasson, in *Tarbiz* 31 (1961), 68 (line 53).

17. Both books contain Rashi's commentary to the Pentateuch, testimony to the popularity of this work among Jews. The Italian edition was printed in Reggio di Calabria (Offenberg, *Hebrew Incunabula*, no. 112), the Spanish one in Guadalajara (Offenberg, *Hebrew Incunabula*, no. 113).

18. See the literature listed in note 2.

19. A list of places, dates, and printers is found in Offenberg's *Hebrew Incunabula*, 186–94.

20. Jacob ben Asher, *Tur Yoreh De'ah* (Hijar, 1486–1487), colophon: *le-nes hi' be-khol peh* (see A. Freimann, *Thesaurus typographie hebraicae saeculi XV* [Berlin, 1924–31; repr. Jerusalem, c. 1967], B 9,2; Offenberg, *Hebrew Incunabula*, no. 72); Pentateuch (Hijar, 1490), colophon: *re'u sefer ve-'ein kofer le-mofetav, mattan 'elokim* (Freimann, B 11,4; Offenberg, *Hebrew Incunabula*, no. 16); Rashi on Pentateuch (Zamora, 1492 [?]), colophon: *'ale deyo neyyar she-lo ke-derekh* (Freimann, B 13,3; Offenberg, *Hebrew Incunabula*, no. 114 bis); Former Prophets (Leiria, 1494), colophon: *mel'ekhet shamayim* (Freimann, B 27,5; Offenberg, *Hebrew Incunabula*, no. 28); Pentateuch, colophon, from the Genizah, quoted by Hurvitz, *Mishneh Torah of Maimonides*, 30, end of n. 101: *me-'et h[a-shem] hayeta zot*.

21. In the colophon of Former Prophets (Leiria, 1494) (Friemann, *Thesaurus*, B 27,5; Offenberg, *Hebrew Incunabula*, no. 28). The relevant passages from the colophon are quoted and discussed by Isaiah Tishby, *Messianism in the Time of the Expulsion from Spain and Portugal* (in Hebrew) (Jerusalem, 1985), 25, n. 41.

22. Dimitrovsky, *S'ridei Bavli*; Hurvitz, *Mishneh Torah of Maimonides*.

23. Bloch, "Early Hebrew Printing," 9–16; Hurvitz, *Mishneh Torah of Maimonides*, 39–44.

24. Yosef Hayim Yerushalmi, *Leaves from the Oldest Illustrated Printed Haggadah* (Philadelphia, 1974), 7–18, supplement to Yosef Hayim Yerushalmi, *Haggadah and History* (Philadelphia, 1974).

25. Joseph Hacker, "Patterns of Intellectual Activity of Ottoman Jewry in the Sixteenth and Seventeenth Centuries" (in Hebrew), *Tarbiz* 53 (1984), 569–606, esp. 579 and n. 25.

26. In the colophon to the 1505–1506 Constantinople edition of the Bible, see Abraham Yaari, *Hebrew Printing at Constantinople* (in Hebrew) (Jerusalem 1967), 60. He says that the books were lost on "dryland and on the sea." Similarly, in a report by Joseph ibn Shraga, it is mentioned that books were lost at sea. Hacker, "Patterns of Intellectual Activity," 579.

27. Dan Manor, "Abraham Sabba: His Life and Work" (in Hebrew), *Jerusalem Studies in Jewish Thought* 2 (1982–83), 227. He refers to his books as his writing instruments.

28. Hacker, "Patterns of Intellectual Activity," 579.

29. Isaac Abravanel, *She'elot le-Rabbi Sha'ul ha-Kohen* (Venice, 1574), 18a.

30. See the interesting statistics in Beit-Arié, *The Makings of the Medieval Hebrew Book*, 49. About Italy as the "homeland" of Hebrew manuscripts, see Abraham Berliner, *Ketavim Nivharim* 2 (Jerusalem, 1949), 83.

31. *The Cantos of Immanuel of Rome*, ed. Dov Jarden (Jerusalem, 1957), 1:161–66.

32. On King Manuel's decree to seize Hebrew books, see report of Abraham Saba, William Popper, *The Censorship of Hebrew Books,* introduction by Moshe Carmilly-Weinberger (New York, 1969), 20; Manor, "Abraham Sabba," 212–13; Meir Benayahu, "A New Source Concerning the Spanish Refugees in Portugal and Their Move to Salonika" (in Hebrew), *Sefunot* 11 (1971–77), 244–45.

33. See note 23.

34. JTS Manuscript, Bible collection, L 6. See *Illuminated Hebrew Manuscripts from the Library of the Jewish Theological Seminary* (New York, 1965), no. 6.

35. JTS Manuscript no. 1969. See Benayahu, "A New Source," 236 ff., esp. 262, where the marginal inscription is quoted. On King Manuel's decree, see note 30 above.

36. Sirat and Beit-Arié, *Manuscrits médiévaux*, 3:51.

37. Ibid., 3:49, also 55. Cf. Joseph Hacker, "New Chronicle on the Expulsion of the Jews from Spain: Its Causes and Results," *Zion* 44 (1979), 202, n. 6.

38. On the influence of Hebrew printing in the Ottoman Empire and the literature about it, see Hacker, "Patterns of Intellectual Activity," 576–77, and n. 13. On the Constantinople *'Arba'ah Turim*, see A. K. Offenberg, "The First Printed Book Produced at Constantinople," *Studia Rosenthaliana*, 3 (1969), 96–112, where the literature on the subject is reviewed.

39. Yaari, *Hebrew Printing*, no. 2; Nigel Allan, "A Typographical Odyssey: The 1505 Constantinople Pentateuch," *Journal of the Royal Asiatic Society*, ser. 3, 1,3 (1991), 343–51.

40. Yaari, *Hebrew Printing*, no. 5.

41. Ibid., no. 6.

42. Ibid., no. 2, p. 60; Allan, "A Typographical Odyssey," 350.

43. Yaari, *Hebrew Printing*, no. 6, p. 63.

44. Hacker, "Patterns of Intellectual Activity," 585, n. 39.

45. Ibid., 583–93.

46. Ibid., 578, n. 20.

47. On this method, see Daniel Boyarin, *Ha-'Iyyun ha-Sefaradi: Le-Farshanut ha-Talmud Shel Megorashe Sefarad* (Jerusalem, 1989).

48. Hacker, "Patterns of Intellectual Activity," 577–79.

49. Ibid.

50. *Maḥzor*, Ashkenazi rite. Salonika c. 1555–1556 (no pagination), in the *kinah*, "Le-Mi 'Oy le-Mi Hoy" (Israel Davidson, *Thesaurus of Mediaeval Hebrew Poetry* [New York, 1970], *lamed*, 1085).

51. See A. Friemann, "Die hebraischen Pergamentdrucke," *Zeitschrift für hebräische Bibliographie* 15 (1911), 46–57, nos. 31, 32, 34, 35, 37, 40, 41, 42, 45, etc.

52. Hacker, "Patterns of Intellectual Activity," 578, n. 20; Yaari, *Hebrew Printing*, 122–23.

14. A Converso Best-Seller

1. Some of these transformations are discussed by Peter N. Dunn, *Fernando de Rojas* (Boston, 1975), 19–23. On the social-religious climate of late medieval Spain, see Stephen Gilman, *The Spain of Fernando de Rojas: The Intellectual and Social Landscape of "La Celestina"* (Princeton, 1972), 157–204; and José Antonio Maravall, *El mundo social de "La Celestina,"* 3d ed. (Madrid, 1972).

2. Observed by Maravall, *El mundo social de "La Celestina,"* 32–78.

3. Dunn, *Fernando de Rojas*, 50.

4. Unless otherwise indicated, the edition of *Celestina* from which I cite is that of Peter E. Russell, ed., *Comedia o Tragicomedia de Calisto y Melibea* (Madrid, 1991). The work known as *Celestina* was initially known by the title *Comedia de Calisto y Melibea* and later expanded as the *Tragicomedia de Calisto y Melibea*.

5. The question of authorship has been treated at length; see, e.g., Manuel Criado de Val, "Índice verbal de *La Celestina*," *Revista de Filología Española*, 64 (1955); Martín de Riquer, "Fernando de Rojas y el primer acto de *La Celestina*," *Revista de Filología Española*, 41 (1957), 373–95; Peter E. Russell, "Literature in the Time of the Catholic Monarchs (1474–1516)," in *Spain: A Companion to Spanish Studies* (London, 1973), 273–76; idem, *Comedia o Tragicomedia*, 24–31; Miguel Marciales, ed., *Celestina. Tragicomedia de Calistro y Melibea*, prepared by Brian Dutton and Joseph T. Snow, 2 vols. (Urbana, 1985), 1:30–39, 274–79; Fernando Cantalapiedra Erostrarbe, *Lectura semiótico-formal de "La Celestina"* (Kassel, 1986). See also the curious claims put forth by Antonio Sánchez Sánchez Serrano and María Remedios Prieto de la Yglesia, *Fernando de Rojas y "La Celestina:" el escritor y la literatura* (Barcelona, 1991).

Another difficulty surrounding *Celestina* is its genre classification. Stephen Gilman early on stressed *Celestina*'s "ageneric" quality; see Gilman, *The Art of "La Celestina"* (Madison, 1956), 194–206; Charles F. Fraker takes issue with Gilman on several crucial points. See Fraker, *"Celestina": Genre and Rhetoric* (London, 1991).

On novelistic aspects of *Celestina*, see Alan D. Deyermond, *La Edad Media*, Spanish version by Luis Alonso López of *A Literary History of Spain: The Middle Ages* (Barcelona, 1973), 301–13; see also Dorothy Sherman Severin, *Memory in "La Celestina"* (London, 1970), 57–66; idem, "Is *Celestina* the First Modern Novel?" *Revista de Estudios Hispanicos*, 9 (1982), 205–09; idem, *Tragicomedy and Novelistic Discourse in "Celestina"* (Cambridge, 1989).

For an appreciation of *Celestina*'s dramatic qualities, see Maria Rosa Lida de Malkiel, *La originalidad artística de "La Celestina,"* 2d ed. (Buenos Aires, 1970 [1962]), 27–78; idem, "La técnica dramática de *La Celestina,"* in L.Schwartz Lerner and I. Lerner, eds., *Homenaje a Ana María Barrenechea* (Madrid, 1984), 281–92; Juan Villegas, "La estructura dramática de *La Celestina,"* *Boletín de la Real Academia Española*, 54 (1974), 439–78; Pierre Heugas, "*¿La Celestina*, novela dialogada?" in Pedro M. Piñero Ramírez and Rogelio Reyes Cano, eds., *Seis lecciones sobre la España de los Siglos de Oro. Homenaje a Marcel Bataillon* (Seville, 1981), 161–77; Cándido Ayllón, *La perspectiva irónica de Fernando de Rojas* (Madrid, 1984); and Ivy A. Corfis, "*Celestina* as Drama: Commentary by a Sixteenth-Century Reader," *Romance Philology* (forthcoming).

6. For biographical details, see Gilman, *The Spain of Fernando de Rojas*.

7. Fernando del. Valle Lersundi, "Documentos referentes a Fernando de Rojas." *Revista de Filología Española* 12 (1925), 385–96; idem, "Testamento de Fernando de Rojas, autor de *La Celestina,"* *Revista de Filología Española*, 16 (1929), 366–88; idem, "Testamento de Fernando de Rojas, autor de *La Celestina* (La biblioteca de Fernando de Rojas)," *Revista de Filología Española*, 17 (1930), 183; see also Gilman, *The Spain of Fernando de Rojas*, 530–36.

8. Manuel Serrano y Sanz, "Noticias biográficas de Fernando de Rojas, autor de *La Celestina*, y del impresor Juan de Lucena," *Revista de Archivos, Bibliotecas y Museos*, 6 (1902), 245–99; Gilman, *The Spain of Fernando de Rojas*, 65–109, 505–29.

9. The earlier (1956) of Gilman's two main studies on *Celestina*, namely, *The Art of "La Celestina,"* occasioned a vigorous exchange between the venerable Leo Spitzer and the youthful Gilman. See Gilman, *The Art of "La Celestina"*; Cf. Spitzer's response, Leo Spitzer, "A New Book on the Art of *The Celestina,"* *Hispanic Review*, 25 (1957), 1–25; Gilman, "A Rejoinder to Leo Spitzer," *Hispanic Review*, 25 (1957), 112–21.

Gilman's later *The Spain of Fernando de Rojas* (1972) produced a similarly polemical response by a number of scholars. See Marciales, *Carta al Profesor Stephen Gilman*, multigraph ed. (Mérida, Venezuela, 1975): New printing, *Sobre problemas rojanos y celestinescos (Carta al Dr. Stephen Gilman a propósito del libro "The Spain of Fernando de Rojas")* (Merida, Venezuela, 1983); Nicholas G. Round, *The Spain of Fernando de Rojas* (review), *Modern Language Review*, 70 (1975), 659–61; Keith Whinnom, *The Spain of Fernando de Rojas* (review), *Bulletin of Hispanic Studies* 52 (1975), 158–61; and Peter E. Russell, *Temas de "La Celestina" y otros estudios* (Barcelona, 1978), 343–75.

For contrary perspectives, see Américo Castro, *"La Celestina" como contienda literaria (castas y casticismos)* (Madrid, 1965); Juan Goytisolo, "La España de Fernando de Rojas," *Triunfo* (Aug. 30, 1975), repr., *Disidencias* (Barcelona, 1977), 13–35; and Yirmiyahu Yovel, *Spinoza and Other Heretics*, 2 vols. (Princeton, 1989), 1:85–127.

Finally, note the perceptive analysis by Nicasio Salvador Miguel of the "Jewishness" of *Celestina*. See Salvador Miguel, "El presunto judaísmo de *La Celestina*," in Alan Deyermond and Ian Macpherson, eds., *The Age of the Catholic Monarchs, 1474–1516: Literary Studies in Memory of Keith Whinnom, Bulletin of Hispanic Sudies* (special issue) (Liverpool, 1989), 162–77.

10. "Así mismo pensarían que no quinze días de unas vacaciones, mientra mis socios en sus tierras, en acabarlo me detoviesse, como es lo cierto." See Russell, *Comedia o Tragicomedia de Calisto y Melibea*, 186.

11. Clara Louisa Penney, *The Book Called "Celestina" in the Library of the Hispanic Society of America* (New York, 1954), 8.

12. On early editions of *Celestina*, see Penney, *The Book Called "Celestina"*; J. Homer Herriott, *Toward a Critical Edition of the "Celestina": A Filiation of Early Editions* (Madison, 1964); F. J. Norton, *Printing in Spain: 1501–1520, with a Note on the Early Editions of the "Celestina"* (Cambridge, 1966), 141–56; Keith Whinnom, "The Relationship of the Early Editions of the *Celestina*," *Zeitschrift für Romanische Philologie*, 82 (1966), 22–40; Erna Berndt-Kelley, "Algunas observaciones sobre la edición de Zaragoza de 1507 de la *Tragicomedia de Calisto y Melibea*," in Manuel Criado de Val, ed., *"La Celestina" y su contorno social. Actas del I Congreso Internacional sobre "La Celestina"* (Barcelona, 1977), 7–28; idem, "Elenco de ejemplares de ediciones tempranas del texto original y de traducciones de la obra de Fernando de Rojas en Canadá, Estados Unidos, y Puerto Rico," *Celestinesca*, 12 (1988), 9–34; Marciales, *Celestina*; Charles B. Faulhaber, "The Heredia-Zabálburu Copy of the *Tragicomedia de Calisto y Melibea* 'Sevilla 1502' [i.e., Rome: Marcellus Silber, ca. 1516]," *Celestinesca*, 16 (1992), 25–34.

13. Marciales, *Celestina*, 1:1.

14. This is the so-called *Auto de Traso*. See David Hook, "The Genesis of the *Auto de Traso*," *Journal of Hispanic Philology*, 3 (1978–79), 107–20; and Marciales, *Celestina*, 1:xii–xiii, xv, 139–40, 162–75.

15. Joseph T. Snow notes that Marciales edited Sedeño's verse translation of *Celestina*, first printed in Salamanca in 1540. See Snow, "La *Tragicomedia de Calisto y Melibea* de Juan de Sedeño. Algunas observaciones a su primera escena comparada con la original," *Celestinesca* 2 (1978), 13–27; idem, *"Celestina" by Fernando de Rojas: An Annotated Bibliography of World Interest, 1930–1985* (Madison, 1985), no. 1084. Only a few copies of Marciales's edition appeared.

16. This work, the *Celestina comentada*, is currently being edited by a team of scholars under the direction of Louise Fothergill-Payne. Note, as well, M. J. Ruggerio, *"La Celestina*: Didacticism Once More," *Romanische Forschungen*, 82

(1970), 56–64; and Peter E. Russell, "The *Celestina comentada,*" in Alan D. Deyermond, ed., *Medieval Hispanic Studies Presented to Rita Hamilton* (London, 1976), 175–93; reprinted as "El primer comentario crítico de *La Celestina*: Cómo un legista del siglo XVI interpretaba la *Tragicomedia,*" in *Temas de "La Celestina" y otros estudios* (Barcelona, 1978), 295–321.

17. On the rich and varied *Celestina* tradition, see the fundamental study by Pierre Heugas, *"La Celestine" et sa descendance directe* (Bordeaux, 1973).

18. Keith Whinnom argues persuasively for eliminating the definite article "La" from the title. See Whinnom, " 'La Celestina,' 'The Celestina,' and L2 Interference in L1," *Celestinesca,* 4 (1980), 19–21; Cf. Steven D. Kirby, "¿Cuándo empezó a conocerse la obra de Fernando de Rojas como *Celestina?*" *Celestinesca,* 13 (1989), 59–62.

19. Kathleen V. Kish, ed., *An Edition of the First Italian Translation of the "Celestina"* (Chapel Hill, 1973). See also Emma Scoles, "Note sulla prima traduzione italiana della *Celestina,*" *Studi Romanzi,* 33 (1961), 155–217; idem, "La prima traduzione italiana della *Celestina*: repertorio bibliographico," in Carmelo Samona, ed., *Studi de Letteratura Spagnola* (Rome, 1964), 209–30.

Marciales advances the rather curious notion that only native Italians "de la Toscana o del Lacio" are capable of producing a reliable edition of Ordóñez's text. Marciales, *Celestina,* 1:222. Of greater value is his observation that this translation is based on the non-extant Toledo 1504 edition; Marciales, *Celestina,* 1:195.

20. Both texts appear in a facsimile edition, preceded by a useful introduction by the editors; Kathleen Kish and Ursula Ritzenhoff, eds., *Die Celestina-Übersetzungen von Christof Wirsung: "Ain hipsche Tragedia" (Augsburg, 1520); "Ainn recht liepliches Buechlein" (Augsburg, 1534)* (Hildesheim, 1984).

21. Albert J. Geritz, "*Calisto and Melebea*: A Bibliography," *Celestinesca,* 3 (1979), 45–50; idem, "*Calisto and Melebea* (ca. 1530)," *Celestinesca,* 4 (1980), 17–29.

22. Penney, *The Book Called "Celestina,"* 19.

23. On English translations and adaptations, see Gustav Ungerer, "*La Celestina* in England," in *Anglo-Spanish Relations in Tudor Literature* (Bern, 1956), 9–41; repr. (New York, 1972); Gerard J. Brault, "English Translations of the *Celestina* in the Sixteenth Century," *Hispanic Review* 28 (1960), 301–12; and Guadalupe Martinez Lacalle, ed., *Celestine or the Tragick-Comedie of Calisto and Melibea,* trans. James Mabbe (London, 1972).

Special notice should be taken of the recent bilingual edition containing Mabbe's 1631 translation, edited by Dorothy Sherman Severin; see Dorothy Sherman Severin, ed., *"Celestina," with the Translation of James Mabbe (1631)* (Warminster, 1987). In her review of Severin's edition, Ivy A. Corfis discusses several versions of Mabbe's *Celestine.* Ivy A. Corfis, review of *"Celestina," with the Translation of James Mabbe (1631), Romance Philology,* 46 (1992), 221–23.

24. On the 1527 translation, see Gerard J. Brault, *"Celestine: A Critical Edition of the First French Translation (1527) of the Spanish Classic "La Celestina"* (Detroit,

1963); idem, "Textual Filiation of the Early Editions of the *Celestina* and the First French Translation (1527)," *Hispanic Review*, 36 (1968), 95–109. On the 1578 translation, see Denis L. Drysdall, *"La Célestine" in the French Translation of 1578 by Jacques de Lavardin* (London, 1974). Also of interest is Joseph T. Snow "The Iconography of the Early *Celestinas*, I: The First French Translation (1527)," *Celestinesca* 8 (1984), 25–39.

25. For a history of Flemish translations, see Kathleen V. Kish, "Celestina Speaks Dutch—in the Sixteenth-Century Spanish Netherlands," in John S. Miletich, ed., *Hispanic Studies in Honor of Alan D. Deyermond: A North American Tribute* (Madison, 1986), 171–82.

26. Theodore S. Beardsley, Jr., "Kaspar von Barth's Neo-Latin Translation of *Celestina* (1624)," in Ivy A. Corfis and Joseph T. Snow, eds., *Fernando de Rojas and "Celestina": Approaching the Fifth Centenary* (Madison, 1993), 237.

On Barth, see Marcel Bataillon, *"La Célestine" selon Fernando de Rojas* (Paris, 1961), 250–68: Bärbel Becker-Cantarino, *"La Celestina* en Alemania: El *Pornoboscodidascalus* (1624) de Kaspar Barth," in Criado de Val, ed., *"La Celestina" y su contorno social*, 377–82; Marciales, *Celestina*, 1:254–58.

27. Marciales, *Celestina*, 1:1.

28. A compendium of *Celestina* translations and adaptations, ranging from the bizarre to the inspiring, is found in Snow, *"Celestina" by Fernando de Rojas: An Annotated Bibliography of World Interest, 1930–1985*, 71–87.

29. Biographical information is derived from a number of scholars. Moshe David Cassuto, "Me-Shirei Yosef ben Shmuel Zarfati: Ha-Komediah ha-Rishonah be-'Ivrit" ["The Poetry of Joseph ben Samuel Zarfati: The First Comedy in Hebrew"], in Salo W. Baron and Alexander Marx, eds., *Jewish Studies in Memory of George A. Kohut, 1874–1933* (New York, 1935), 121–28; D. W. McPheeters, "Una traducción hebrea de *La Celestina* en el siglo XVI," in *Homenaje a Rodríguez-Moñino Estudios de erudición que le ofrecen sus amigos o discípulos hispanistas norteamericanos*, 2 vols. (Madrid, 1966), 1:399–411; Renato Spiegel, *Encyclopaedia Judaica* (1972), s.v. "Sarfati"; Dwayne E. Carpenter, "The Sacred in the Profane: Jewish Scriptures and the First Comedy in Hebrew," in Corfis and Snow, *Fernando de Rojas and "Celestina": Approaching the Fifth Centenary*, 229–36.

30. In this regard, see Hava Tirosh-Rothschild, *Between Worlds: The Life and Thought of Rabbi David ben Judah Messer Leon* (Albany, 1991).

31. McPheeters, "Una traducción hebrea de *La Celestina*," 403.

32. See also Carpenter, "The Sacred in the Profane."

33. I would like to register a special debt of gratitude to Ivy A. Corfis, Ann Kahn, and Bernard Septimus for their unstinting editorial and linguistic assistance. Any errors of fact or infelicities of style are my responsibility alone.

34. The Hebrew text is that of Cassuto, "Me-Shirei Yosef ben Shmuel Zarfati," 124–28. Note that the poem refers to a treatise of Melibea and Calisto, with

Melibea's name appearing first. McPheeters's study and Spanish translation, "Una traducción hebrea de *La Celestina*," while useful in many respects, contains a number of serious errors, My rendition of Zarfati's poem is an attempt to provide an accurate and pleasing verse translation. The difficulty of this task, compounded by obscure allusions and tortured syntax in the original, will be obvious to anyone who has endeavored to render Renaissance Hebrew poetry into English. I am fortunate, however, to have as a model Raymond Scheindlin's exquisite translations of medieval Hebrew verse. Finally, I have occasionally provided in the notes a more literal rendering of a given passage.

35. "And their wiles, which are arms of violence, to sow ruin and calamity in the hearts of men."

36. "And there," i.e., in "The Treatise of Melibea and Calisto." Cf. the introduction to Judah ben Solomon Al-Harizi's *Taḥkhemoni*.

37. Cf. Isaiah 13:8: "And they shall be affrighted; pangs and throes shall take hold of them, they shall be in pain as a woman in travail." All citations are from the Soncino edition.

38. Calcol (also Chalcol) appears fleetingly in I Chronicles 2:6 and I Kings 5:11.

39. Observe the wordplay in the original.

40. "In love there is no shelter or cover, and no one who shows pity or performs acts of kindness."

41. "I shall compare her deeds to an absence of rain, though the heavens be full of winds and clouds."

42. "And it is emptiness to moan like mothers over their only sons."

43. "Newborn," lit. "youth."

44. I.e., "according to his desires."

45. "Food," lit. "pottage." The allusion is to Jacob and Esau (Gen. 25:29).

46. "Each day these [women] with their sorcery carry off the sons of men, and they destroy all living creatures."

47. "Abhor their looks, for indeed in the end you will be pierced by sharp thorns and have skewers through your heart."

48. I believe that the sense of verses 45–47 justifies the use of the imperative.

49. This seems to me to be the sense of the phrase, although it remains obscure.

50. "I am Joseph, son of Rabbi Samuel, prince of the monotheists, who maintain the true faith."

51. "A wellspring of wisdom and source of counsel; a stakelike support of Jacob's tent."

52. "To sweeten [the life of] the poor and troubled, and to soothe the heart of the discountenanced."

53. "I translate only the substance, and I place the beauty of my discourse before my fellow Jews." Zarfati's aim is to translate the essence of the material, the themes, rather than to produce a slavish, literal rendition. Cf. the case of

Maimonides' *Guide of the Perplexed*, which was twice rendered into Hebrew in the early thirteenth century, first by Samuel Ibn Tibbon, who produced a highly regarded literal version, and then by Judah Al-Harizi, the author of a much less rigorous translation.

15. Sephardic Ceremonial Art

I would like to thank Sharon Wolfe for all of her technical assistance, offered, as usual, with grace.

1. Gabrielle Sed-Rajna emphasizes the many manuscripts that were saved, carried into exile; Gabrielle Sed-Rajna, "Hebrew Illuminated Manuscripts from the Iberian Peninsula," in Vivian B. Mann, Thomas F. Glick, and Jerrilyn D. Dodds, eds., *Convivencia: Jews, Muslims, and Christian in Medieval Spain,* Jewish Museum exhibition catalog (New York, l992), 133. In contrast, Haim Beinart draws attention to the many losses due to confiscation and forced sale; Beinart, "Books from Sefarad, An Exhibition Commemorating the Five-Hundredth Anniversary of the Expulsion from Spain," in Rafael Weiser, ed., *Books from Sefarad,* Israel Museum, exhibition catalog (Jerusalem, l992), x, also xi.

2. The excavated examples are discussed in the following literature: Bezalel Narkiss, "Un objet de culte: la lampe de Hanuka," in Bernhard Blumenkranz, *Art et archéologie des Juifs en France médiévale* (Toulouse, 1980), 191 and fig. 5; P. Atrian Jordan, "Lamparas de Hanukkah en ceramica popular turolense," *Revista Teruel* 65 (1981), 175–84; Ana María López-Álvarez, *Catalogo del Museo Sefardi de Toledo* (Madrid, 1986), no. 5.

In this census of ceremonial objects, illuminated marriage contracts, long the focus of Judaica study in other lands, have been counted as a single object, since all are variations on a single type with no discernible development: a central text surrounded by bands of decoration, either floral, abstract, or calligraphic. Francisco Cantera Burgos was the first to draw attention to a Navarrese group including Teruel, 1300; Milagro, 1309; Tudela, 1324; and Tudela, 1356 (Gobierno de Navarra, Departamento de Educación, Cultura y Deporte, Archivo Real y General, Pamplona, Cámara de Comptos, Caja 192, nos. 2, 54, 1 and 64). He also noted two fragments in the same collection and three *ketubbot* discovered by Millas: Barcelona, 1277; Mallorca, 1380 (a fragment); and Barcelona 1386, (in the royal Aragonese archives, perg. 191 bis caja 1 de documents hebreus). Another contract, now lost, came from Trijeuque (province of Guadalajara) and is known from three copies; Francisco Cantera Burgos, "La 'Ketuba' de D. Davidovitch y las Ketubbot espagnolas," *Sefarad* 33 (1973), 375–86. Shalom Sabar added to this list Mallorca, c. 1428 (Barcelona, Biblioteca de Catalunya, manuscript no. 254; *Ketubbah* [Philadelphia and New York, 1990], 9.) Another was published in Elena Romero, ed., *La Vida Judía en Sefarad,* Museo Sefardi, exhibition catalog (Toledo,

1991–1992), no. 102: Torrelobaton, 1479 (Valladolid, Archivo de la Real Chancilleria, Pergaminos, Carp. 13, num. 11). Two examples of undecorated contracts are illustrated in the same catalog, nos. 100 and 101. A fragmentary example is in *Books from Sefarad*, no. 90, p. 155: Segura, 1480–1489 (Jerusalem, Jewish National Library 80 901/36), and another fragment is in a private collection, Connecticut.

3. Rachel Wischnitzer, "Illuminated Haggadahs," *Jewish Quarterly Review*, n.s. 13 (1922–23), 193–218; Joseph Gutmann, "The Illuminated Passover Haggadah: Investigations and Research Problems," *Studies in Bibliography and Booklore*, 8 (1965), 3–25. See also below, n. 11.

4. In addition to the responsa cited below (nn. 21, 32), the following are a sampling of other Spanish responsa pertaining to ceremonial art:

R. Asher ben Yehiel (1250–1327), *She'elot u-Teshuvot Rabbenu Asher* (New York, 1954), 2:8, on the materials to be used for a *tallit* and *ẓiẓit*.

R. Judah ben Asher (1270–1349), *Zikhron Yehudah* (Jerusalem, 1972), no. 21, on the issue of using decorated rugs in the synagogue.

R. Yomtov ben Abraham Ishbili (1250–1330), *She'elot u-Teshuvot ha-Ritba'* (Jerusalem, 1958), no. 34, on the making of a Torah and crown according to a bequest; no. 159, discussing the case of two men who attempted to steal silver Torah finials (*tapuḥim*) and a silver crown from the Ark; no. 161 mentions a *tik*, a binder, and a silver crown for the Torah.

R. Solomon ben Abraham ibn Adret (1235–1310), *She'elot u-Teshuvot ha-Rashba': First Printing Rome, ca.* 1470 (Jerusalem, 1976), no. 73, on the use of Torah crowns; no. 93, concerning the reuse of a gravestone; no. 128, the description of a Torah scroll; no. 416, on the use of wax candles for the Sabbath lights.

R. Simon ben Ẓemaḥ Duran, *Sefer Tashbeẓ*, 3 vols. (Lemberg, 1891), 1, no. 6, on illuminated ketubbot; 2, no. 135, on using Torah ornaments to raise money; 3, no. 301, on illuminated ketubbot.

5. *Catálogo del Museo Sefardi de Toledo*, no. 5; Ma. J. Sánchez Beltran, "Restauracion de una pileta trilingue de marmol del Museo Sefardi de Toledo," *Noticias* 5(1991), 2; Romero, *La vida judía*, no. 6, suggests the unlikely interpretation of a serpent. For a large corpus of similar symbols, see Erwin Goodenough, *Jewish Symbols of the Greco-Roman Period*, vol. 3 (New York, 1953).

6. Narkiss, "Un objet de culte: la lampe de Hanuka," 190–91.

7. Mann, Glick, and Dodds, *Convivencia*, no. 96, there the older literature; M. Keen, *Jewish Ritual Art in the Victoria and Albert Museum* (London, 1991), 38.

8. P. Atrian Jordan, "Lámparas de Hanukkah en cerámica popular turolense," *Revista Teruel* 65 (1981), 175–84; P. A[trian Jordan], "Informe sobre las excavaciones realizadas en la Plaza de la Judería," *Boletín informativo de Teruel* 53 (1979), 46; Romero, *La vida judía*, no. 37; Mann, Glick, and Dodds, *Convivencia*, no. 79.

9. The Museo Sefardi in Toledo recently acquired replicas of a silver service discovered in the *judería* of Burgos. "Nuevas adquisiciones," *Noticias* 7 (1992), 4. Its mudejar decoration, however, gives no hint of a specific function.

10. Iris Fishof, "Lusterware Passover Plate," in Jay A. Levinson, ed., *Circa* 1492, Washington National Gallery of Art, exhibition catalog (Washington D. C., 1991), no. 54 (there the older literature); Weiser, *Books from Sefarad*, nos. 39, 78.

11. For comparable Christian and Muslim examples, see Mann, Glick, and Dodds, *Convivencia*, nos. 78, 86, also p. 169 and fig. 66.

12. Leila Avrin drew attention to the similarity between the form of the Israel Museum plate and that depicted in a scene of the so-called Sister Haggadah, which shows the distribution of matzot prior to the seder (London, British Library, Or. 2884, fol. 17r). She also notes that Christian examples of the same ceramic form inscribed *Exsurge Domine* were used for the distribution of candles; Avrin, "The Spanish Passover Plate in the Israel Museum," *Sefarad* 39 (1979), 44.

The same shape appears in Spanish Bible illustrations of the implements of the Temple for the same generic purpose, to hold bread, i.e., the twelve shewbread. For examples, see Bezalel Narkiss, *Hebrew Illuminated Manuscripts in the British Isles* (Jerusalem and London, 1982), figs. 310, 327.

13. Mann, Glick, and Dodds, *Convivencia*, no. 85.

14. Michael E. Keen, *Jewish Ritual Art in the Victoria and Albert Museum*, no. 48, there the older literature.

15. There are two such illustrations in the extant Spanish Haggadot, both in the same manuscript: on fols. 24v and 26r of the Barcelona Haggadah; Narkiss *Manuscripts in the British Isles*, figs. 215, 217. In contrast, illustrated Ashkenazic Haggadot contain depictions of tower-form containers or aspects of havdalah set within the frame of a tower form. (For example, the Yahuda Haggadah, Jerusalem, Israel Museum, MS 180/50, fol 5r; and the Second Nuremberg Haggadah, Jerusalem, Schocken Institute, MS. 2407, fol. 5v.)

16. According to several sources, Rabbi Ephraim of Regensburg (d. 1175) kept spices for havdalah in a glass container; R. Isaac ben Moshe of Vienna, *'Or Zaru'a* (Zhitomer, 1862), 2:92.

17. The lack of Sephardic custom to support Narkiss and Keen's interpretation of the object in the Victoria and Albert Museum as a spice container was recently noted by Braha Yaniv, "Nisayon le-Shiḥzur Izuvam Shel Rimonei Migdal mi-Morocco 'Al-Pi Degamim mi-Sefarad," *Pe'amim* 50 (1992), 75, n. 24. She concludes, however, that the container must represent a localized usage not followed elsewhere.

18. Mann, Glick, and Dodds, *Convivencia*, no. 107, there the older literature.

19. Lee I. Levine, ed., *The Galilee in Late Antiquity* (New York and Jerusalem, 1992), fig. 6.

20. The comparison was first made by Friedrich Sarre in 1930, "A Fourteenth-Century Spanish Synagogue Carpet," *Burlington Magazine* 56 (1930), 89–90.

21. See, for example, Kurt Erdmann, *Seven Hundred Years of Oriental Carpets* (Berkeley and Los Angeles, 1970), 143, fig. 181, where the rug is described as the "so-called Synagogue Carpet."

22. R. Asher ben Yehiel, *She'elot u-Teshuvot Rabbenu 'Asher* (New York, 1954), 5:2; The translation is my own. This text confirms Friedrich Sarre's supposition, made by analogy with the Beit Alpha mosaic, that the carpet was spread on the pavement of a synagogue.

23. Donald King and David Sylvester, *The Eastern Carpet in the Western World*, Hayward Gallery, exhibition catalog (London, 1983), fig. 30.

24. For example, a twelfth-century mortar in the Museo Nacional de Arte Hispanomusulman, Granada, no. reg. 380. Mann, Glick, and Dodds, *Convivencia*, no. 94.

25. For the inscription, see Mann, Glick, and Dodds, *Convivencia*, no. 104, there the older literature.

26. Francisco Cantera Burgos and José María Millás Vallicrosa, *Las inscripciones hebraicas de España* (Madrid, 1956), 389–93.

27. Braha Yaniv recently published a detailed comparison of the rimmonim and the verges or stave ends, and concludes that Jewish ceremonial objects like the finials could easily have been modeled on Christian forms, given the close professional relationships between Jewish and Christian silversmiths who worked for each other's houses of worship. Yaniv, "Nisayon le-Shiḥzur," 73–76.

28. See, for example, E. Arnáez, *Orfebería religiosa en la provincia de Segovia hasta 1700* (Madrid, 1983), 1:49, fig. 1; 79, fig. 32. Similar forms continued to be made in the seventeenth century. See M. Seguí Gonzales, *La platería en las catedrales de Salamanca (siglos xv–xx)* (Salamanca, 1986), nos. 31–32.

29. See note 2 above for a list of surviving ketubbot and fragments.

30. Mann, Glick, and Dodds, *Convivencia*, no. 44, there the older literature.

31. Isadore Epstein, *The Responsa of Rabbi Simon b. Zemaḥ Duran* (London, 1930), 83–84.

32. F. Fita, "Edicto de los Reyes Católicos (31 Marzo, 1492) desterrando de sus estados a todos los judíos," *Boletín de la Real Academia de la Historia* 2 (1887), 518; and Henry Kamen, "The Expulsion: Purpose and Consequence," in Elie Kedourie, ed., *Spain and the Jews*, (London, 1992), 89.

33. For example, on Rabbi Abraham of Lunel's discussion of silver Torah crowns, see Franz Landsberger, "The Origin of European Torah Decorations," in Joseph Gutmann, ed., *Beauty in Holiness: Studies in Jewish Customs and Ceremonial Art* (New York, 1970), 94–96.

34. Eleazar Gutwirth, "Toward Expulsion, 1391–1492," in Kedourie, *Spain and the Jews*, 72.

35. Babylonian Talmud, *Pesaḥim* 108b; *Berakhot* 51a. For a discussion of the relationship between Jewish law and Jewish ceremonial art, see Vivian Mann,

"Introduction," in *A Tale of Two Cities: Jewish Life in Frankfurt and Istanbul 1750–1870*, Jewish Museum exhibition catalog (New York, 1983), 17–23.

36. Narkiss, *Manuscripts in the British Isles*, figs. 188, 209, 210, 222, 295, 296, 304; Mann, Glick, and Dodds, *Convivencia*, fig. 52. For color plates of some of these scenes, see Romero, *La vida judía*, 194 and 260, no. 34; Thérèse and Mendel Metzger, *Jewish Life in the Middle Ages* (Fribourg, 1982), figs. 101, 165, 378; R. Loewe, *The Rylands Haggadah* (London, 1988), fol. 19b.

37. Ibn Adret, *She'elot u-Teshuvot ha-RashBa'*, no. 371.

38. From the 153 prewar Jewish communities of Bohemia and Moravia, the Jewish Museum in Prague has only thirty-odd pairs of Sabbath candlesticks in its collection.

39. Mann, "Introduction," 23, n. 4.

40. A refectory scene dated c. 1300 in the old cathedral of Lérida shows the following objects on the table: circular bread (identical in shape to the matzot of seder scenes), knives, a small ewer and two bowls holding long, narrow forms. See, Montserrat Blanchi, *Gothic Art in Spain* (Barcelona, 1972), 204–5. The closest parallel in a seder scene is that in the Rylands Haggadah, fol. 19b, dated to the 1330s, which also features goblets, an essential feature of the seder service. Metzger, *Jewish Life in the Middle Ages*, fig. 165.

41. Suzanne Landau, ed., *Architecture in the Hanukkah Lamp*, Israel Museum, exhibition catalog, 1978. It is important to note that lamps with architectural backplates are not limited to lands of the Sephardic diaspora; they also appear in Germany, Italy, and Poland.

42. Yaniv, "Nisayon le-Shiḥzur"; V. B. Mann, ed., *Gardens and Ghettos: The Art of Jewish Life in Italy*, The Jewish Museum, exhibition catalog (New York, 1989), figs. 97, 107, 112.

43. V. B. Mann, "Jewish-Muslim Acculturation in the Ottoman Empire: The Evidence of Ceremonial Art," in Avigdor Levy, ed., *The Jews of the Ottoman Empire* (Princeton, 1994), 559–71; Esther Juhasz, ed., *Jews of the Ottoman Empire*, Israel Museum, exhibition catalog (Jerusalem, 1990) 97–113.

44. Sabar, *Ketubbah*, 9.

45. Dora Liscia Bemporad, "Jewish Ceremonial Art in the Era of the Ghettos," in Mann, *Gardens and Ghettos*, 120–21.

46. Mann, "Jewish-Muslim Acculturation," 559–71.

47. Mann, *Gardens and Ghettos*, no. 141, there the older literature.

48. J. Mills, *Carpets in Paintings* (London, 1983); D. King and D. Sylvester, *The Eastern Carpet.*

49. Richard Ettinghausen, *Prayer Rugs*, Textile Museum exhibition catalog (Washington, 1974–75), no. v, there the older literature; Mann, "Jewish-Muslim Acculturation."

50. Mann, "Jewish-Muslim Acculturation," 566–67, fig. 8.

51. Shalom Sabar, "The Beginnings of *Ketubbah* Decoration in Italy: Venice in the Late Sixteenth to the Early Seventeenth Centuries, " *Jewish Art* 12–13 (1986–1987), 96–110.

52. Mann, *Gardens and Ghettos*, no. 103.

53. See Sabar, *Ketubbah*: *Ketubbot Italiane* (1984); Sabar, "Decorated Ketubbot," in Juhasz, *Ottoman Empire*, 218–37.

54. For example, Mann, *Gardens and Ghettos*, no. 53.

55. Mann, *Gardens and Ghettos*, figs. 92, 111; *A Tale of Two Cities*, no. 200 (colorplate); *Sephardic Journey*, Yeshiva University, exhibition catalog (New York, 1992), figs. 40, 51.

56. Cecil Roth, *The Sarajevo Haggadah* (London, 1963), fol. 34r.

57. Mann, *Gardens and Ghettos*, nos. 197, 205; Juhasz, *Ottoman Empire*, figs. 23, 33; *Sephardic Journey*, fig. 45.

58. Yaniv, "Nisayon le-Shiḥzur," 72, and n. 12.

59. Alexander Scheiber, *Jewish Inscriptions in Hungary* (Budapest and Leiden, 1983), no. 153.

60. Mann, *A Tale of Two Cities*, colorplate p. 14; Juhasz, *Ottoman Empire*, fig. 35.

61. Jerrilyn Dodds, ed., *Al-Andalus: The Art of Islamic Spain*, Metropolitan Museum of Art exhibition catalog (New York, 1992), no. 115.

62. For other examples, see Juhasz, *Ottoman Empire*, fig. 13, 19, and pl. 5a.

63. Roger G. Calkins, *Illuminated Books of the Middle Ages* (Ithaca, 1983), 57–60.

64. Stephen S. Kayser and Guido Schoenberger, *Jewish Ceremonial Art* (Philadelphia, 1955), no. 4.

65. *The Anatolian Civilisations* vol. 3: *Seljuk/Ottoman*, Topkapi Palace Museum exhibition catalog (Istanbul, 1983), nos. E147, E149, E151.

66. Kamen, "The Expulsion: Purpose and Consequence," 91.

67. Gutwirth, "Toward Expulsion: 1391–1492," 72.

Index